CAESAR IN ABYSSINIA

CAESAR IN ABYSSINIA

G. L. STEER

With an introduction by
Nicholas Rankin

faber and faber

This edition first published in 2009
by Faber and Faber Ltd
Bloomsbury House, 74–77 Great Russell Street
London WC1B 3DA

All rights reserved
© G. L. Steer, 1936
Introduction © Nicholas Rankin, 2009

The right of G. L. Steer to be identified as author of this work
has been asserted in accordance with Section 77 of the
Copyright, Designs and Patents Act 1988

This book is sold subject to the condition that it shall not, by way of
trade or otherwise, be lent, resold, hired out or otherwise circulated
without the publisher's prior consent in any form of binding or cover other than
that in which it is published and without a similar condition including this
condition being imposed on the subsequent purchaser

A CIP record for this book is available from the British Library

ISBN 978–0–571–25515–3

INTRODUCTION

Nicholas Rankin

George Lowther Steer was a top foreign correspondent of the 1930s, best remembered today for drawing the attention of the world (and Pablo Picasso) to the bombing of Guernica during the Spanish Civil War. Yet that adventure, together with his superb book on the Basque campaign, *The Tree of Gernika*, was outside his usual area of interest.

Steer called himself 'a South African Englishman' and the other five books he published in his brief lifetime – he died in a jeep crash a month after his thirty-fifth birthday – were long reports on events in Africa. All of them were interested in African aspiration; none of them celebrated European dominion. The first of these five was *Caesar in Abyssinia*, his remarkable, and partisan, account of the last great episode of armed colonial conquest in Africa, the Italo-Ethiopian war of 1935–6, which he had reported from Addis Ababa for *The Times*.

When Hodder & Stoughton first published *Caesar in Abyssinia* in London in late 1936, it came out at the same time as another book on the same subject with a similar title which was written by the fashionable novelist Evelyn Waugh. But *Waugh in Abyssinia* is very different from *Caesar in Abyssinia*. It takes the opposite side of the conflict: Evelyn Waugh champions the Italian, and G. L. Steer the Ethiopian, cause.

Why should we bother with their historical scribblings of over seven decades ago? First, because both men were, in their different ways, very good writers. Steer, in this fresh and youthful first book, depicts character with wit and describes with a painterly eye sometimes reminiscent of T. E. Lawrence. Second, because that now forgotten war – 'an unimportant series of massacres' says Steer – ignited the powder-chain that burned out the old League of Nations and eventually exploded in the Second World War, which killed 50 million people. 'Thus,' as the British diplomatist Robert Vansittart noted in his 1958 autobiography, 'because a few askaris had died by brackish water-holes in an African waste, was taken the first step to the second German Holocaust.'

History has passed judgement on this ancient controversy too. Evelyn Waugh later suppressed the embarrassing last two chapters of *Waugh in Abyssinia*, which one contemporary denounced as 'a Fascist tract'. In the final chapters of Steer's *Caesar in Abyssinia*, by contrast, a good reporter rises to the dangerous occasion and finds his true voice.

George Lowther Steer was born one hundred years ago, on 22 November 1909, in the Cambridge district of East London, Cape Colony, South Africa, a British enclave in the Xhosa heartland that later became a crucible of the African National Congress. He was the only child of British-born parents who were active pillars of their local Anglican church, St Saviour, and the mild Christianity that he inherited from them seems to have given him sympathy for the underdog as well as inoculation against totalitarianism. His mother, Emma, was a busybody for charitable causes and his father, Bernard, was the managing editor and later chairman of the East London *Daily Dispatch*, a newspaper of liberal principles edited decades later by Donald Woods, whose friendship with the Black Consciousness activist Steve Biko was depicted in the Attenborough film *Cry Freedom*.

Young George Steer was a ferociously bright but initially frail lad (he suffered from osteomyelitis in boyhood) who liked to talk to the black servants. Having learned early to read from newspapers spread out on the floor, he devoured books and won classical scholarships to both Winchester College (where he edited *The Wykehamist*) and to Christ Church, Oxford from where he graduated with a double first. Taught by Gilbert Ryle and Maurice Bowra and steeped in ancient civilisations, he began thinking like a historian. (He also founded Oxford University's Africa Society, dedicated to studying 'the native peoples of Africa, their present condition and future development.')

Steer then trained as a reporter on the *Cape Argus* in South Africa and was editing the 'London Notes and Comment' of the *Yorkshire Post* in Fleet Street in the spring of 1935 when he hooked the assignment to Ethiopia from *The Times*. He stepped up to a world-famous newspaper and became a foreign correspondent just as the world was toppling towards a second great war. Steer was to cover three of its violent precursors, in Abyssinia, Spain and Finland, watching small nations go under bigger battalions. When the 'phoney war' ended in 1940, he stopped reporting and joined the British Army. 'This is my generation's fight,' he said. When he died in Bengal on Christmas Day 1944, Steer was a lieutenant colonel in the Intelligence Corps, commanding the front-line Indian Field Broadcasting Units that he had founded for the Special Operations Executive.

As a child of the British Empire, whose sea voyages between England and the Cape of Good Hope took him up and down the west coast of a continent divided up by Dutch, British, German, Portuguese, Belgian, French and Spanish imperialists, Steer had an early grasp of the European scramble for Africa. The opening of the Suez Canal in 1869 had set Mediterranean Italy looking for its 'place in the sun' too, first acquiring Eritrea on the Red Sea and then negotiating for part of Somaliland facing the Indian Ocean.

Italy first attempted to join its two colonies into one *Africa Orientale Italiana* in 1895 by trying to annex the mountainous country in between them. This was Ethiopia, the ancient and semi-mythic country of the Queen of Sheba, Prester John and Rasselas, a ramshackle but still independent land also known as Abyssinia. The massive defeat of the Italian expeditionary force by Emperor Menelik II's barefoot soldiers at the battle of Adowa (also spelled Adwa and Adua) on 1 March 1896 resounded in the world's capitals. Like the retreat from Kabul in Afghanistan, the Little Big Horn in North America, or Isandlwana in South Africa, it was an iconic victory by non-white warriors over a modern imperial armed force.

Italy had to recognise Ethiopia's independence in the Treaty of Addis Ababa, but the humiliation of that defeat lingered for decades. Italy's fortieth prime minister, Benito Mussolini, who came to power by coup d'etat in 1922, was keen to wipe away the stain on Italy's national honour before the fortieth anniversary. He nursed the resentment that Italy, which had fought with the Entente Allies against the Central Powers in the First World War and helped found the League of Nations, had not been rewarded with colonial mandates at the Treaty of Versailles in 1919. As *Duce* or Leader of the Italian Fascist Party,

Mussolini built a totalitarian state at home and planned a new Roman Empire abroad.

By 1935, Ethiopia was the larger of the two unconquered countries remaining in Africa. The other, Liberia, was a colony on the Atlantic coast, founded by former slaves from the United States. The crowning of Ras Tafari Makonnen as Emperor (*Negusa Nagast*) Haile Selassie I of Ethiopia on 2 November 1930 had drawn the world's press and newsreel cameras to the little-known country in search of barbaric splendour. The coronation was also an exercise in international public relations. Like King Amanullah of Afghanistan, King Faisal of Iraq or Emperor Hirohito of Japan, Haile Selassie could present himself as the modernising monarch of a backward country, being helped to progress by foreign advisers who, in his case, came from Sweden, Belgium, Great Britain, the United States, Russia and Turkey. In 1923, Ethiopia had pledged to abolish slavery within its borders, and signed the Covenant of the League of Nations, the intergovernmental organisation founded in the aftermath of the First World War to prevent aggression through 'collective security'.

As Steer relates in *Caesar in Abyssinia*, in early January 1935 he was in the Saar – a coal- and iron-rich province disputed between France and Germany – 'freelancing the plebiscite' in which 90 per cent of Saarlanders voted for reunion with the swelling Nazi Germany, when the news came of the protocol signed in Rome by Pierre Laval and Benito Mussolini. This Franco-Italian deal adjusted some of their disputed colonial borders, but there was also ominous talk of Italy now being given 'a free hand' by France in eastern Africa. Once again, it was a matter of lines on maps. A month earlier, there had been a serious frontier fire-fight between Ethiopian and Italian Somali armed forces at Wal Wal in the contested Ogaden region, which seemed to signal the ratcheting up of Mussolini's aggressive designs on Ethiopia. Steer could see the geo-politics and was ambitious enough to realise that getting to the trouble-spot early would give him an edge over the journalistic competition.

Steer had been a brilliant student; as conflict in Ethiopia beckoned, he embarked on a campaign to get aboard *The Times*, making use of his boyhood talent for absorbing arcane information and re-transmitting it clearly in examination essays. He had good credentials for 'The Thunderer': a first-class establishment education, journalistic training and a prosperous father who was prepared to bankroll a foray to East Africa (in those days it took a fortnight, voyaging by train and ship, just to get to Addis Ababa). But Steer also mugged up on Ethiopia's history, culture and Semitic language. With the help of a doctor friend, the use of a hospital room and a throat bandage to limit his speaking, he bluffed his way through an oral in Amharic by a professor from SOAS, before being hired by Ralph Deakin, the Imperial and Foreign News editor of *The Times*, at a salary of £60 a month. Steer was twenty-five and a half years old when he set off for Africa with his *sola topi*, khaki shorts, Mauser rifle, typewriter and copy of *Notes for Correspondents*.

When he arrived in Addis Ababa in the second week of July 1935, the trickle of journalists had not yet turned into the great flood of those expecting the Italian invasion at the end of the rainy season in early October. The US diplomat John H. Spencer described Steer as 'boyish, small-bodied, fox-faced with a mischievous glint in his eyes' (in *Ethiopia at Bay: A Personal Account of the Haile Sellassie Years*, Reference, 1984) and the Emperor's financial adviser, Everett Colson, another American, confessed himself 'amazed' that an august journal like *The Times* could send such a youth as its special correspondent. He revised his first impression as the young reporter set to work. Steer's salary from *The Times* soon increased to £80 when the *New York Times* started taking (and bylining) his stories.

Steer quickly befriended the British and American advisers, but his great coup was getting closer to the 'noble and intelligent' Haile Selassie. (One cannot really be 'friends' with emperors, or walk easily with kings of kings, but this relationship endured for years, through difficult times and in other lands, as shown most fully in Steer's last African book, *Sealed and Delivered*, which Faber Finds are also republishing.) Their acquaintance began with an hour and a half's personal interview at the Little Gibbi palace, granted because the Emperor needed *The Times* to communicate certain diplomatic and strategic points to the world, and it developed into a mutual warmth. Steer became trusted.

Of Emperor Haile Selassie in 1935 you could truly say: '*L'état, c'est moi.*' Although little, he was the 'big man' at the apogee of an imperfectly modern autocracy welded on to the traditional

African polity based on fealty to chieftainship. Steer benefited from this command structure. It was under the Emperor's aegis that Steer made the unique tour of the Ogaden front in August 1935 that features in chapters VI and VII of *Caesar in Abyssinia*, and it was to the Emperor as well as *The Times* that he reported back his findings of the woeful Ethiopian preparations against Italian tank and air attack. It was the Emperor who summoned Steer to be flown alone by aeroplane north from Addis Ababa to Dessie before Christmas 1935, as described in Chapter XIII. And it was the broken Emperor who Steer witnessed returning to Addis Ababa in Chapter XX at the end of April 1936, his armies defeated, his rases refusing orders, and his soldiery becoming mutinous looters.

As Marshal Badoglio's victorious forces advanced on the capital, law and order disappeared and the bonds of society broke apart. Steer captures this chaos superbly in the final chapters of *Caesar in Abyssinia*. He relishes the adrenalin, knowing he has the story to himself at last, an exclusive scoop. Amidst scenes of death, he celebrates life by getting married to a fellow journalist, Margarita de Herrero y Hassett; champagne corks pop amid the gunfire.

Haile Selassie's going into exile has the feel of a tragedy, in the modern sense of a grievous catastrophe, but also in the older classical meaning of a great man brought low. In *Caesar in Abyssinia* it is not just the modern terrors of war being visited on a medieval society that evoke pity. There is also the betrayal of an idealistic African leader by the 'international community', represented by the League of Nations. The Haile Selassie so deftly sketched by Steer is a neat, precise, rational man who believes in the verbiage of diplomacy with its notes, points, and protocols. We come to see that in a world of *realpolitik* the Emperor's trust in the decency of a papier-mâché system is utterly misplaced.

Steer frankly admires those Africans who do not try to ingratiate themselves, like the two bloody-minded Ethiopian warriors who despise every interfering foreigner and give their lives for their land. The first is grim old Ras Mulugeta, the sword-wielding Minister of War who is the last relict from Menelik's age, incredibly brave and utterly wrong-headed, dying, raging, on his feet in the awful retreat from Amba Aradam. The second is one of the dedicatees of Steer's book,

Dedjazmatch Afewerk of the Ogaden, fatally wounded at his Oerlikon gun while contemptuously fighting off swarms of Italian fighter-planes and bombers.

Steer saw in Afewerk something of the new Ethiopia that Haile Selassie was trying to create, by encouraging the alert and the capable of all tribes and classes, not just the corrupt old gang who squatted at the top of every hopeful ladder. And Steer admired Afewerk as a black hero: 'I thank God that made me and Africa, and bound us together in such a bitter union, that once in my life I met this man.' Part of the tragedy of the Italian invasion and occupation of Ethiopia was its destruction of such people's possibility of helping their nation develop in freedom.

'We think it a very promising little war,' declares the media magnate Lord Copper in Evelyn Waugh's immortal satire *Scoop* (1938), 'A microcosm, as you might say, of world drama.' Lord Copper's newspaper, the *Daily Beast*, proposes to give it the fullest publicity, but incompetently sends out to 'Ishmaelia' the wrong man, the hapless nature-writer William Boot, instead of the heroic explorer John Boot, and quite by accident, he triumphs. *Scoop* is still the comic lens through which many British readers see the second Italo-Ethiopian war.

Evelyn Waugh of the *Daily Mail* and George Steer of *The Times* first met briefly on the platform of an Ethiopian railway station on 21 August 1935. Their separate trains were going in different directions, up and down the line between Jibuti and Addis Ababa, just as their views on Ethiopia were opposed. In *Evelyn Waugh in Ethiopia: The Story Behind 'Scoop'* (Edwin Mellen Press, 2001) Michael B. Salwen writes: 'Waugh and Steer met in Ethiopia. They did not have cordial or inimical relations, or relations of any kind. They were professional colleagues.' Nonetheless, the two writers were wary rivals, enmeshed in the futile hysterias of the Foreign Press Association at the Imperial Hotel, and the drunken practical jokes of the squabbling media-scrum.

Evelyn Waugh had been to Africa in 1930 and sent dispatches about Emperor Haile Selassie's coronation to *The Times*, the *Daily Express* and the *Graphic*. He also got two books out of the trip: a non-fiction travelogue, *Remote People*, and a comic novel, *Black Mischief*. In 1935, Waugh wanted to represent *The Times* again but had been pipped to the post by Steer, 'a zealous colonial reporter' who was six years younger. 'The heaviest fighting is among the journalists,' Waugh wrote waspishly to Diana Cooper. 'The Times correspondent [–] a very gay South African dwarf – is never without a black eye.' (*Mr Wu and Mrs Stitch: The Letters of Evelyn Waugh and Diana Cooper*, edited by Artemis Cooper, Hodder and Stoughton, 1991.)

When he reviewed *Caesar in Abyssinia* in the Catholic weekly *The Tablet* in 1937, Waugh wrote with exquisite malice that Steer 'had great sympathy, I think it not unfair to say affinity, for those nimble-witted upstarts who formed the Negus's entourage, like himself African born, who had memorized so many of the facts of European education without ever participating in European culture. He genuinely liked them and it is to his credit that he now defends their memory.' This last, more generous, sentence marks the difference between the two men, I think: it is hard to imagine Waugh making African friends.

Matters were also awkward at the British Legation in Addis Ababa, a place where Steer was at home and regularly briefed. Waugh had turned Abyssinia into barbaric 'Azania' for *Black Mischief*, his 1932 novel in which he ridiculed the modern pretensions of 'Emperor Seth' and parodied the British Minister Plenipotentiary and his family as nincompoops. On returning in 1935, Waugh discovered that Sir Sidney and Lady Barton, who had offered him hospitality in 1930, were still in post in the Ethiopian capital. Their fiery daughter Esmé, whose fictional avatar in *Black Mischief*, the promiscuous Prudence Courteney, had ended up in a cannibal hot-pot devoured by her fiancé, reviewed Waugh's novel decisively by emptying a glass of champagne over its author in an Addis Ababa nightclub. 'Most amusing,' repeated Waugh, dabbing at his face with a napkin. (Four years later, Esmé Barton was to become George Steer's second wife, and bear his two children.)

The feverish atmosphere of intrigue and rumour created by 120 foreign journalists looking for non-existent news in Addis Ababa is the absurd background to *Scoop*. Evelyn Waugh spent so much time at the Italian Legation in Addis Ababa that he was assumed to be an Italian spy. Never politically correct and often rude, Waugh expressed distaste for Ethiopians and dislike of their country, which he left in order to spend Christmas at Bethlehem in the Holy Land. Waugh got out of Dessie just before it was bombed on 6 December, and had abandoned Ethiopia altogether by the time the real war started. On 22 December 1935 the Italian Air Force began dropping yperite or mustard-gas bombs on Ras Imru's warriors in the north of Ethiopia. Two days later, in the south, General Graziani began spraying on people and livestock the first of hundreds of tons of phosgene and mustard gas shipped through the British-controlled Suez Canal. The use of toxic gas in warfare was an inhumane practice then outlawed under the Anti-Gas Treaty that Italy had ratified in 1928, but *Waugh in Abyssinia* called it 'sterilising the bush along the line of advance.'

G. L. Steer's *Caesar in Abyssinia*, on the other hand, treats Italy's use of poison gas against Ethiopians seriously, and also tracks the Italian tactic of deliberately bombing and machine-gunning Red Cross ambulance units from the air, in order 'to clear foreign witnesses out of the way while illegal methods of war were being used by the Italians.' Steer's colleague, Walter Holmes of *The Times*, was the first to report first-hand the use of poison gas in the north in March and April 1936, and Steer also talked to the British Red Cross doctors John Melly and J. W. S. Macfie who treated its effects. This was a story on which *The Times* led, and it embarrassed those appeasing elements in the British government anxious not to drive Italy towards the embrace of Nazi Germany.

In his review of *Caesar in Abyssinia*, Waugh also said that it was 'not Mr Steer's fault that the most valuable and exciting section has been contributed by another hand.' Michael B. Salwen wrongly considers this to be a boastful reference by Waugh to his own book, but in fact Waugh was pointing to Chapter XVIII of *Caesar in Abyssinia*. This is an account of the Emperor's last battle, as witnessed by the only European on the Ethiopian side, the White Russian Colonel Fedor Evgenievich Konovalov (whom Steer spells Konovaloff). Steer probably got a copy of Konovalov's story in French just before the Italians expelled him on 16 May 1936. As Konovalov was intending to stay on in Addis Ababa, he does not mention poison gas; the Russian was trimming carefully in order to survive the Italian occupation.

Caesar in Abyssinia ends with the Italians marching into Addis Ababa on 5 May 1936, and with George Steer and his first wife, Margarita de Herrero y Hassett, being expelled from Italian Ethiopia. But history never ends like a book. The great mudslide towards world war had begun. In early June, Steer welcomed the exiled Haile Selassie to London, and at the end of the month, the Ethiopian emperor addressed the League of Nations at Geneva. Were small nations all to be subject to powerful ones? Haile Selassie enquired of the delegates. Leaving the podium, the Lion of Judah prophesied: 'It is us today. It will be you tomorrow.' Within weeks, the Spanish Civil War had broken out, and soon Steer was off to Spain, reporting how German and Italian forces were helping the military rebels. Meanwhile in Berlin, the Nazis smilingly hosted the 1936 Olympic Games, while plotting to rule the world. Evelyn Waugh returned to Addis Ababa to hymn a paean to Roman Civilisation à la Hilaire Belloc, but found the Italian occupiers armed and tense, fearful about the continuing Ethiopian insurgency.

George Steer left *The Times* in September 1936 to complete his own Ethiopia book: he wrote the introduction to *Caesar in Abyssinia* in Nationalist-held Burgos as murderous repression stalked Spain, neighbour turned on neighbour, and refugees clogged the French frontier. 'War against the civilian population breaks it up into its warring parts', Steer concluded. The military take-over of free Ethiopia had shaken one Oxford dreamer out of his 'undogmatic slumbers'. International fascism was on the march, and through the text of *Caesar in Abyssinia*, Steer wanted 'our leaders' to get the urgent message: 'Ethiopia is nearer to Europe than they think.'

TO THE DEAD

TO ALAN BLAKEWAY, MY TUTOR AT WINCHESTER AND FRIEND AT OXFORD, WHO GROUNDED ME IN ANCIENT HISTORY, THIS ESSAY IN THE INGLORIOUS PRESENT.

TO AFEWERK THE DEDJAZ-MATCH OF THE OGADEN, WHO FACED DEATH IN BATTLE WITH THE SAME CARELESSNESS, THIS TRIBUTE TO HIS COURAGE IN A SPINELESS WORLD.

INTRODUCTION

THIS BOOK, which casts a narrow sidelight on an unimportant series of massacres known as the Italo-Ethiopian War, bears, I am sorry to say, a title which will disappoint many. Cæsar in Abyssinia conjures up a picture of cohorts, horse-hair-crests and Commentaries, all centring round the great Julius himself ungasmasked in the field. But look where I might in Abyssinia, with the assistance of Holmes, Collins, Harrison, Lowenthal and the British Red Cross, I could never find the fellow. Afterwards the Military Correspondent of *The Times* explained to me that he was playing the part of a dynamo in Rome.

He compares ill with his rival, who handled an anti-aircraft gun and a machine-gun against Europeans fitted with far superior weapons.

I have no desire, however, to belittle the military achievement of Italy in Ethiopia. I believe that an absurd excess of force was used; that considering the condition of the Italian Treasury the war might have been waged more cheaply, and that the war provides no index whatsoever of the behaviour of an Italian Army, even of the organisation of an Italian Army, fighting against an equal enemy.

The Italians, nevertheless, did reach their objective, Addis Ababa, within seven months of the outbreak of aggression.

My task is rather in this book to show what was the strength and spirit of the Ethiopian armies sent against a European Great Power. My conclusions are that they had no artillery, no aviation, a pathetic proportion of automatic weapons and modern rifles, and ammunition sufficient for two days' modern battle. I have seen a child nation, ruled by a man who was both noble and intelligent, done brutally to death almost before it had begun to breathe.

The Italians do not figure much in these pages, which are more the study of the Ethiopian people under fire than of the mechanical means and processes used to destroy their resistance. The primary cause of their defeat was that they had no arms, and were allowed none. The secondary cause of their defeat was Italian air supremacy, exploited eventually by the spraying of mustard gas.* The great Ras said that they could not fight the heavens or the burning rain.

The Danakil expedition and the Gondar mechanised column had no effect upon the war or contact with the Ethiopians, therefore they are not mentioned here.

The bombardment of Harrar, registered as a hospitalisation centre in December, had no effect upon the war. All the Red Crosses in the town were hit and the material damage was great, but it was a purposeless operation and is therefore not mentioned here.

There is one thing which I must describe in this introduction, not in the text.

Addis Ababa was during the last two months of the war frequently reconnoitred by Italian aeroplanes, who also machine-gunned the aerodrome. The population became more and more nervous with each new raid. The object, of course, was to create popular tension.

On April 27 pamphlets were dropped on Addis Ababa which read:

"People of Shoa, listen!

"I am the head of the victorious Italian Army, and will enter Addis Ababa with the help of God. The Emperor and his First Army are useless and defeated. Gondar Sokota and Dessye are taken by us. We are masters of the Ogaden, and will enter Harrar within a few days. These leaflets should be a greeting to

---

* It will be noticed that Konovaloff does not mention gas. He is still in Addis.

the Ethiopian people. I do not want the Christian Ethiopian people to be destroyed. We bring peace and civilisation.

"Do not shed any blood among you. You who were at the front, go home to your land and possessions and continue your farming as before. Do not turn yourself against the police and those charged with the maintenance of order. Do not destroy the roads or oppose the advance of my Army, because we do not want your lives, your possessions, or your money. But if you destroy our roads or try to oppose the advance of my Army, then the Italian Army will destroy and kill without pity, the aeroplanes will massacre from the air and destroy everything that exists."

It was after the scattering of this pamphlet that the movement for individual security began which was to end in the sack of Addis Ababa. It was neither the breakdown of the central authority—which has broken down often in Ethiopian history—nor the barbarian's love of theft nor the black man's hatred of the white that caused the sack of Addis. It was the threat of gas from the air that demoralised its people. The crowds that gathered round Lady Barton's committee rooms for masks were evidence of that.

Precisely the same thing will happen in the capital of any European state that is defeated. War against the civilian population breaks it up into its warring parts.

It seems to me important that our leaders should understand this. Ethiopia is nearer to Europe than they think.

I owe a great debt of gratitude to *The Times*, who allowed me complete freedom and even free publicity in Ethiopia. Particularly, I am grateful that they woke me from my undogmatic slumbers, and showed me a path from which I shall not deviate.

In the unexpurgated phrase of General Queipo de Llano: "All honour to such a grand paper."

Burgos, 1936.

MAPS

		FACING PAGE
1.	THE OGADEN DESERT	88
2.	ADDIS ABABA	152
3.	DESSYE	264

The Maps reproduced by kind permission of "The Times."

Mrs. Colson, wife of Everett Colson, the Emperor's financial adviser, liked to offer tea to the Addis journalists who visited the house for news at six o'clock every evening. She made marvellous cakes, was nice and rather stout and slow, had white hogged hair and a way of drawling stories which put a vital fact in a comic setting. The humour was there, but Mrs. Colson did not care to press it.

"It was 1933," Mrs. Colson dawdled forth. "Mrs. Moosa, the Egyptian Consul-General's wife, was taking little Michel to Victoria College in Cairo to school. Michel was a bright little boy. His mother was American, and he looked American too.

"There was a nice Italian merchant on board from Mogadiscio. He made friends with Mrs. Moosa—as Italians like to do—and he told her that all the merchants in Mogadiscio had been ordered from Italy to buy nothing but stuff that was useful for war—food and lorries and such. He thought that she was going back to America.

"He made friends with little Michel too, and the day before they arrived in Port Said Michel did something that the merchant did not like. 'That's not the way a little American boy should behave,' said the Italian. 'I'm naat a little American boy,' twanged Michel. 'I guess I'm an Eegyptian.'

"'Ow!' said the Italian merchant, and his face fell.

"Then they got off at Port Said. He didn't know they were going to Egypt and would send the story back to us.

"That was the first time we knew the war was coming."

Mrs. Colson paused a moment to ruminate and to consider all sides of the question, her eyes lost in the wallpaper.

"Or perhaps the Italian was a born actor and did it just to frighten people—anyway it looks like true," she finished, dawdling back again.

It was August last year, and Colson came in to tell us of another note sent to the Secretary-General.

I

IN AUGUST, 1931, Dedjazmatch Gabre Mariam, formerly chief of Ras Tafari's bodyguard and a man of trust, left Harrar, his governorship, with twelve thousand men. Fitorari Shefara left his Gibbi (government house) at Jijiga with three thousand men. The two armies marched south to clear the *bandas* out of the Ogaden.

For two years now the Italians had been deliberately arming certain of the more restless elements among the Somali nomads in the north of their territory with old-patterned Italian rifles. The armed men, called Dubats, were organised into *bandas*. Their uniform was a turban, the white to dirty Somali skirt, and the bandolier. None of your extravagant Somali tartans: these men were on service, they had work to do. The only symbol which marked them off from their fellows was the colour of a sash round their waists, green, red or blue according to the banda: that was the beginning of regimental colours for the Somalis—by now they must be playing football.

It would be unfair to the Italian of 1931 to allege that the *bandas* were encouraged to create frontier incidents. No frontier had been demarcated on the ground, and there were no Ethiopian troops near the one hundred mile line from the coast where it should have run, according to treaty: these conditions were enough to prevent incidents, which abhor a vacuum. The *bandas* were instructed simply to encroach in obedience to the policy then reigning in Rome; that of expansion into waste places in order to satisfy the elementary needs of the Italian people. Recasting Tacitus, the new Cæsar made a few more deserts and called them an Empire.

Great Britain enjoyed the same experience in the Sudan

at much the same time, when an Italian column occupied the Oases of Kufra, far outside their frontier and within ours. The Somalis, too, were told to make for water-points, which control the thorn waste of the Ogaden.

Starting from Mustahil, where the perpetual river of the Webbe Shebeli and the dry depression of the Fafan nearly join, and from Galkayu to the East, the *bandas* were told to occupy the waterline of wells stretching east and west from Wardair, through Walwal, Ubertaleh, Afdub, Gerlogubi, Gorahai and Gabridihari on the Fafan. Of these Gabridihari was the northernmost point. Simultaneously parts of the Shaveli tribe, under their sultan Olol Dinle, were paid to declare themselves for Italy, and the habitable places of the Webbe Shebeli were occupied up to Imi, where the Ethiopian province of Bale begins.

The wells were only loosely held. The Dubats built their ball-like Somali huts round them and shot off their game in the dense thorn thickets. No forts were built. Only a road was made from Ferfer, an admitted Italian post, to Gabridihari, via Shellabo and Gorahai. The usual sequel, the white officer beginning to negotiate with the tribes who frequented the waterholes, had scarcely taken its place in the chain of Imperial encroachment when the Emperor Haile Selassie, fresh from his coronation and his assumption of full powers, ordered the intruder to be driven forthwith from Ethiopian territory.

That was why the war-drums were beaten in Harrar and Jijiga, and the levy of fifteen thousand men was led south with rations for three months into a new land. Till then the deepest penetration into the Ogaden bush had been to Daggahbur, on the Tug Jerrer, one hundred and four miles south of Jijiga.

Shefara took his three thousand down to Daggahbur. Gabre Mariam marched east along the Harrar mountains to Babilli, halfway to Jijiga, where a few huts in rocky ground mark the point from which the caravan track leads to Daggahmodo. At Daggahmodo a few lone wells prick the dry region between the Webbe Shebeli and the Tug Fafan, level west of Daggahbur. Here he was joined by Shefara, who had stored food in huts at Daggahbur. The whole force trailed away south, through Jigo, to the junction of the two river beds, the wet and the dry. It was a clever move.

Olol Dinle to the west ran away down river. The *bandas* to the east, at Gorahai and Gabridihari, melted into the bush. The Somali is quick, spiritually lithe. But as a fighting man he cannot stand against the terrible, organised Habash. Fifteen thousand of them on his lean flank were more than he could wait to face. So Gabre Mariam proceeded from well to well until he came to Mustahil.

There were Italians at Mustahil, and they did not budge. The army sat down for a week while the big men negotiated with the whites. Either an agreement was reached or the Ethiopian rations ran out and the buck ran away before the crackle of Ethiopian rifles. Gabre Mariam left a small garrison at Tafere Katama, "The Fighting Village," on a rocky prow in the bush above the Webbe, a few miles across level land from Mustahil. Here the green-yellow-red of Ethiopian independence was unfurled against the green-white-red of Savoy. Gabre Mariam withdrew by Gorahai and Gabridihari along the Fafan's sandy corridor between two thick rows of camel-thorn. At the hill of Gabridihari he established another garrison, who built the neat square houses that they had learnt to build at Jijiga and Daggahbur; for in Ras Tafari's old province of the Ogaden and Harrar they had developed beyond the round tukuls of mud of their fatherland the plateau, or the huts entwined out of skin grass and sacking that the Somalis feel cool in.

Gabre Mariam either forgot or had no time to visit the system of wells which stretches between Ubertaleh and Wardair, including the great wells of Walwal. He therefore left in Italian hands the whole waterline running east of Gerlogubi; while the other water system which it crosses at right angles at Gorahai and which runs north and south along the Fafan was again in Ethiopian hands, which had a right to it by treaty. The Italian road between Ferfer and Gabridihari also fell into Ethiopian hands, and encouraged them to continue the lorry-track from Gabridihari northwards through Daggahbur to Jijiga—through waterpoints made famous in the subsequent war, Borkut Sasabaneh and Anale. And so it happened that the Emperor of Ethiopia, Haile Selassie, was the first African ruler to organise a mechanised force.

The whole area was placed under the Governor of Jijiga, but its real ruler was Gerazmatch Afewerk, Director of

Jijiga. Under the Imperial reforms, a director was appointed to certain provinces or municipalities to put more energy into the local governor.

Afewerk was an administrative genius. He organised military camps throughout the Ogaden and showed the Ethiopian for the first time that, given modern communications and measures of hygiene, it was an attractive place for the simple lifer. Descended himself from one of the subject races of Ethiopia, he ruled his Somalis firmly but humanely. He killed twelve of them with his sword in open battle, but it was only in full battle-heat that he ever shed blood. Spies and treacherous chiefs, whom the other side would have shot out of hand, were spared for hard labour.

In August, 1934, the month when the Emperor of Ethiopia protested against the increase of Italian military forces in Eritrea, the Italians sent a white *commendatore* to Walwal. Under his orders a fort was built out of material left by the Mad Mullah, ruins of whose rough pillboxes crumbling beside almost every water-hole reminded the Ogaden Somalis of their old religious solidarity, and of the time when the Ethiopian borderlands saw white men only ambushed.

Afewerk, who had a quick tactical mind, rapidly occupied Gerlogubi, barring access to the Fafan water system from the east. Tenure of the water-holes, as he knew, meant control of the Somali tribes who used them.

A small Ethiopian force now held the Ogaden for the first time. Fear of the unknown had kept them out before. Fear of the heat, to which the Ethiopian highlander takes time to inure himself, fear of fever and dysentery and of Somali treachery. The Ethiopians long believed that the water-holes were poisoned against Christians. Gabre Mariam's expedition put an end to many traveller's tales; they soon found that the heat was endurable, fever rare and dysentery limited to certain areas. They grew used, almost attached, to the scant grass, whirl-twisted thorn and long level hills under a sandy sky. Game was common, and the Ethiop loves to chase the antelope.

The vacuum had disappeared. The stage was manned for the incident.

On December 5th the clash occurred at Walwal, within Ethiopian territory as fixed by treaty between Ethiopia and Italy; between Italian Somalis, a white officer, aeroplanes and an armoured car on one side, and the Ethiopian bodyguard of the Anglo-Ethiopian Grazing and Boundary Commission on the other. Each side says that the other fired the first shot; certainly the Ethiopian command were entirely unprepared. Their chief, Fitorari Alemayu, was shot down leaving his tent in the first five minutes. His second in command, Shefara, a mild type with no liking for war, sold off his stock of cartridges to his troops and hustled off to Jijiga "to bury the dead in consecrated ground." It devolved on a former interpreter of the British Consulate in Maji, who had found military service under the Emperor, to fight on. The Mohammedan Ato Ali Nur was brave, did as well as he could, at last retired on Afewerk at Gerlogubi when the armoured car which his men tried to heave over had killed more than one hundred of them and broken the swords of the rest.

For the aeroplane, which dropped bombs at a considerable distance from the battle, they had a great contempt. Later it bombed Ado, where the Commission's baggage lay, and Gerlogubi, an acknowledged Ethiopian post in Ethiopian territory. The Italians at the time denied that they had bombed Gerlogubi, but I have seen the bomb-holes and the splinters there, remote I must admit from the circular camp which was their target. Afewerk, to strengthen the morale of his troops, made a knife out of one bomb and ate his daily meals with it.

Ato Ali Nur was promoted to be Balambaras, which means captain of the hill-fort.

Signor Mussolini demanded a salute to the Italian flag and £15,000 indemnity. The Emperor refused, recalling the terms of the Italo-Ethiopian Treaty of Friendship of 1928 and the Covenant of the League.

I was in the Saar, free-lancing the plebiscite, when the terms of the Laval-Mussolini agreement were announced in the Press. There was vague talk of Italy being given a free hand in Ethiopia. I remembered that only a month before the Walwal incident, when I was editing the London Letter of a great provincial paper, an innocent individual had offered me a note—based on Italian information. The Italians, it read, were alarmed for the safety of their African colonies . . . the Emperor of Ethiopia had organised a huge army in his central province of Shoa . . . its weapons were modern, and it was feared that the Emperor might proclaim a holy war. . . .

Sir John Simon was still our Foreign Secretary. It seemed certain that Italy would attempt to conquer Ethiopia. Down to the unwillingness of every European nation to stand by its commitments under the Covenant, all the circumstances were set for aggression.

I wanted a holiday in Africa. It was snowing and dirty on the cobbled tramlines at Saarbrucken: sun on yellow grass seemed better—I had to go.

Sir John Simon resigned, after Italian chances of a straight walk-over had lengthened on the silences of Stresa. On that blue, unreal lake Ethiopia was a subject for experts only. The statesmen proceeded blandly with their policy of Franco-Italian conciliation. While Italy poured material into East Africa, the statesmen could not bother themselves with an affair which was to jeopardise the whole existence of the League.

Simon's successor showed some disposition to resist Mussolini. The dispute took upon itself the grander dimensions which the British Legation at Addis had always prophesied, which followed directly from the attitude of the Ethiopian Emperor, determined to take his stand upon the Covenant and to resist aggression.

The Italian press attack opened on Great Britain. Mr. Eden's Zeyla offer was rejected by Signor Mussolini. I had my teeth stopped and my tonsils hauled out bodily. Leonard Barnes gave me a box of English peppermints against digestive troubles in foreign parts, and the *Yorkshire Post* staff bought a special solar topee draped in the Old Wykehamist colours. I was off in late June.

It was dark in Addis when we arrived. Pasteau, French diplomatic chief of the Djibouti railway, took his guns off the rack and showed me the hotel proprietor down the sights. George Mendrakos was fighting with the porters: a blow to the right, a blow to the left cleared their meagre red-turbaned heads out of the way. The Arab porters jumped croaking aside. He forced his aggressive chest to the side of the railway train, peered through horn-rimmed spectacles to sort the first from the second-class passengers, chose me because I looked weak-minded as well, and drove me off to the Imperial Hotel. A long barracks of a place, two storeys, one bathroom and one billiard table. Two melancholy men, journalists, looked up from a dusty chess-board as I passed in to dinner, to grease and artichokes and Greek sweetmeats. They were Barber, an American, later awarded the Pulitzer Prize for dying on his job, and Angelopoulos, a young Greek advocate with a goatee holding up the flag of Hearst in Addis Ababa.

After ten more months of journalism, during which he restlessly shaved off his moustache, shaved off his beard, grew a moustache and finally shaved it all off, Angelopoulos was ordered by the Italians to leave Addis in the same train as myself. A lawyer to the last, he argued that under the Klobukowski Treaty signed between France and Ethiopia after the first Adowa, such an order was improper. He would however have to yield to superior force, which he hoped they would not use. And so we had Angelopoulos at the beginning and Angelopoulos at the end.

My first sight of Addis was in the dark; and in the dark as I went to sleep I dreamed, not of Addis, which I had not seen, but of the railway and the three days that it took to get there. The young Ethiopian who said that he would eat the Italians like macaroni (and he did, until the macaroni poisoned him); the French railway employees who hoped and knew that the Italians would win. At Diredawa, where you eat at night in the open, between the rustling orange-trees and the heavy bougainvilleas' scent hanging over your coffee, an Italian spy (they were common as mud) sat at my table. I did not know it then. As the wind took the lanterns in that dim garden I noticed shadows passing over an Ethiopian face, fine-eyed and thinly bearded, at a table beside our own. It was watching to see if I would speak to my companion; I did not, and Lij Andarge Masai, the Ethiopian consul of Djibouti, trusted me afterwards. The Sandford children sat up and clamoured for more fruit at a table farther away;

Sandford was taking them and his wife to the coast and I wondered whether they would meet again.

Then a confused impression of Joseph, the Roman Catholic interpreter who afterwards turned bandit, teaching me the Amharic for grass, tree, antelope, sky, sun, wind and mountain as they all struggled past the lazy carriage window. Tall grass, mimosa trees in green parasol, the buck leg-high amid grass and trees, twitching their tails against white rumps, and studying with young liquid eyes our little white tramway as it prattled on. The sky and sun brilliant and clear, the clouds occasional, for rains do not disturb the railway zone. At evening the wind blew zephyr-cool, and all the time to the south of us were the mountains, immobile on the splendid horizon, false bastions on which the Ethiopians relied too much.

Last night had been spent at the Hawash, another Greek hotel and bougainvillea garden in the middle of Danakil. Desert stretched from the front step, and the back step fell into the crumbling Hawash gorge, whose sides drop sheer shale into that crooked stream. Looking down, one could see the bottom of Africa, the Rift Valley at its lowest, the final boring result of immense geological effort. The world can be very dull when it is in an expansive mood, and all the Rift Valley could offer at the Hawash was its yellow rocks, ugly and irregular as a lion's yawn. Nothing alive but lizards who lay on rocks looking ever skyward, the earth being too revolting to regard. I had turned back to the hotel, stumbled over the dead whisky bottles which border the garden path, and wakened up the countless lean cats which linger there to catch the lizards, and now and then a sleepy snake. Inside the bare hotel, from under the bottles of Zibib and Ouzo and other Greek intoxicants, proceeded a hideous angular miaow, wrenched from a cat whose small windpipe alone seemed capable of reaction to the immense weight of whisky-cases which had fallen upon it. I moved forward to release the cat. "No matter," said the Greek barman, "he is thin enough to get out of anything," and with this futile remark still fooling in my head I turned over in my Addis sheets, prayed briefly that I might be the same, and went to sleep in supreme discomfort.

II

I WOKE UP EARLY, jumped out of bed, and waited for the dust to settle. Then I moved on to my wooden balcony and looked at Addis—superb. The chill of the previous day, which had descended upon our shivering khaki shorts as the train clambered past the lava at Hawash up the plateau edge, scattered before a hardy sun. Over the tin roofs and plaster lineaments of Armenian Piccadilly towered to the north Entoto, the mountain a thousand feet above Addis which Menelik chose for his first capital. Conquerors love mountain seats, from which, with a wave of the fist, one can explain, "I made it mine!" Menelik climbed down after Adowa, and planted the rambling palace on the hill to my right, in mid-Addis. To the left, behind a tattered triumphal arch, marked "Vive l'Empereur" for the coronation of Haile Selassie, stood the dim circle of St. Giorghis, Coptic cathedral built by Italian prisoners' hands, and beyond it more mountains, dressed in grey-green eucalyptus like Entoto. Eucalyptus dangled its flat, finger-like leaves and dropped its sweet bark all over Addis.

I took a run round the hotel, under whose rustling red roof the servants in their tunic shirts and jodhpurs were now busily moving. They don't clean your room in the Imperial Hotel; you have to bring along your own house-boy. Those who were not yet working, since their masters were still enjoying the rich, dry sleep of the plateau, huddled close to the doors on their haunches, legs wide open and knees jutting sideways, confusedly counting and recounting their cartridges until they were decided that nobody had pilfered their belts during the night. Then, in full sense of their security they began to polish their masters' boots

—very slowly. But they differed from other Africans, I thought, in the look of their faces when they were at work: quicker, more intelligent, finer features, more cunning eyes. I heard two quarrelling. They struck attitudes, held out the palms of their hands in protest, flung their *shammas** over their shoulders, then brandished their right arms violently, as if throwing stones at each other. Ethiopians employ this gesture always to emphasise an assertion in a court of law. They shrieked and shouted at each other, "Ba Haile Selassie ymut." "Haile Selassie amlak." "May Haile Selassie die if I'm false." "By the guardian angel of Haile Selassie."†

On the other side of the hotel, the station in grand stucco and stone arrested and explained the longest asphalt road in Addis. From its distant balcony flew the two flags of France and Ethiopia in friendly juxtaposition, signifying the everlasting faithfulness of the more civilised to the smaller power. Beyond it and the neat long rows of customs sheds eucalyptus smothered the levels of the Shoan plain which, broken by flooded rivers bearing in general the name Akaki, settled very gently towards the Hawash. But mountains again barred the view of that far junction as the plain cleared itself of trees. Sequala, a holy mountain of the Ethiopians, sat like a giant burr near the skyline. On Sequala is a leper colony, where the most sacred and supposedly most infectious lepers live without fear of corrupting the unleprous and sacrilegious world. This side of Sequala there were frequent little hills, covered with brown huts whose thatch roofs glistened only dully in the magnificent morning sun. More mountains and a green sugar-loaf hill that ends the Wochochu range closed the scene to the south-west. A glaring speck of white, its masts

* "Shamma" is derived from the Greek word "himation" and represents the same garment. The shamma has been worn in Ethiopia since the period of the Hellenistic kingdom of Axum.

† These oaths had only been current for about two years, during the time that the Emperor had been strengthening his hold on the country in fear of the Italian attack, which he saw dimly approaching as far back as 1933. Before that they swore by Menelik. Italian propaganda in the Gojjam, Tigre and Wollo played up the dead Menelik and his supposed will, by which Lij Yasu succeeded to the throne. The Emperor, Haile Selassie, therefore abolished the old oaths through his new provincial governors—as he abolished the local oaths in their names, and recalled through the Bank of Ethiopia the thaler issues which bore the Menelik head.

as high as pins beyond the eucalyptus, stood a modern building, separated from Addis by about five miles—the Italian-built radio-station which was going to send our messages to the world, "urgent" like the others, or at pedestrian rates like mine.

I spent a week settling in to the town. The Legations had to be visited, the French almost as soon as my own, for on July 14th they were taking the Bastille, and I was invited to participate. You could dance with an Armenian, or a Syrian, or a White Russian, as your fancy led you on, for they were all French protégées, all in at the death of the Bastille. When the Minister's back was turned there was a row near the champagne counter between a Syrian and an Armenian. The French Minister carefully kept his back turned until they had been thrown through the glass doors by a high official of the Franco-Ethiopian railway. Then there was a lottery, which the French always run so well and so enthusiastically, the Bastille cake was cut by the prettiest White Russian who still found life in Addis profitable, and we, all shades of creed and colour, toasted the principles of the Republic—the Republic of 1935. Liberty to interpret the Covenant, Equality with Germany, and Fraternity with the man who organises the lottery.

There was not much shade in Addis, but the British Legation was full of it. I sat down in Barton's study for the first time. I already knew something of his China career: Barton, as our Consul-General in Shanghai, was chiefly responsible for the breach between the Kuo-min-tang and the Communist Party.

A brisk manner indicated a power to get things done quickly. He spoke of the Emperor in short terms of admiration: with something of a snap in his voice as if one should dismiss expressions of feeling as rapidly as possible. When he spoke of things which he disliked, such as Italian policy in Ethiopia, he simply twitched the long nose which jutted a little bonily from his thin intelligent face. He showed rather sharp teeth when he talked.

Barton knew everything about Italian aims and activities in Ethiopia. He sent back a full report before the Stresa Conference.

He was a first-class executive. In dealing with the Ethiopian he put everything down on paper first, then hammered the document sharply home. There was no loose discussion on matters of no moment. The paper lay on the table, and Barton sat in the chair at the table-side until the paper was agreed to.

He would have made an extremely good soldier. He was Ulster but he knew how to make and how to stand fast upon a concession. I think, too, that he rather enjoyed tripping people up.

There were two things that he would not tolerate. One was mention of the measures which he was taking for the defence of the Legation in case of need; the other was white alarmism, which saw in the Ethiopian an unnatural readiness for rape, loot and massacre.

He knew that the Ethiopian, at the bottom of his heart, suspected the European, but he was sure that only in the extreme case of the breakdown of civil institutions would he attempt a small revenge for his suspicion. Events were to justify him.

At the time of the Walwal incident Barton had advised the Emperor not to carry the dispute before the League. But Haile Selassie—it was his own choice—believed that the words of Treaties, that the pledges of one nation to another meant something. He did not deviate from his League policy.

Barton admired thoroughness. Japanese methods particularly attracted him. The Japanese had sent a trade mission to Ethiopia which spent years examining the Ethiopian market, prices, the ways things were sold in Ethiopia, the Ethiopians' needs. The little Japanese had travelled all over the country before going back to Japan: they had left behind their chief investigator, who learnt Amharic and made friends with the Foreign Minister. Thick reports were continually crossing the Indian Ocean from west to east. "Why don't we do that?" asked Barton, rather testily. I asked him if he had suggested to the Foreign Office that we should; and Barton gave me his views on frontiers.

Unorthodox views before the Italo-Ethiopian war, when Ethiopia was universally regarded as the specimen bad neighbour. Barton was the first Englishman to show me that frontier fighting started on both sides of the Ethiopian boundaries. Great Britain, France and Italy as well as the Emperor of Ethiopia, did not maintain the police necessary to prevent nomads from being nomads; it could be proved from official reports.

But Sir Sidney Barton was not yet happy. His Sikhs whom he was conducting with great secrecy from India had not yet arrived. It was not because he had no protection, it was because he liked the look of the British Army that he wanted to see them.

He gave me a cigarette and sent me away. It was long before I realised that he was preparing plans for the parking of British missionaries in safe places. Unlike the other Legations, Barton acted in fairness to the Emperor and did not seek publicity for the measures that he was taking for the protection of British subjects. He was determined not to suggest that there were any grounds for panic: keeping, all the time, his powder dry.

Barton's weakness was low blood pressure. He worked very hard and often got tired and cross.

Colson suffered from high blood pressure, which limited the use of his temper as an instrument of policy.

Where Barton was sharp and penetrating, Colson was heavy, brutally cool and steady. Besides the Emperor these were the two leading personalities in Ethiopia. They admired but did not love each other. In career as well as character they stood out in clear contrast.

Both began in the Far East, where Colson had twice been an administrative officer in the Philippines,[*] and later, for the space of six months, an official in the American-China Consular Service. He was of an opposite tradition to Barton; the tradition not of thrust but of peaceful digestion of the enemy. Trade for this tradition did not follow the flag but more circuitously the Bible.

Colson later was attached to the State Department for special financial work. As Deputy Receiver-General in Hayti, he helped to restore the money and the economic system of that island, and at the same time, learnt to deal with people of a violently different colour. He was always an idealist: now he became a Wilsonian of Wall Street.

[*] 1904–11 and 1916–17.

To his natural conservatism (he came from Scots-Irish stock in Maine) he gave the economic rein. To the idealism which had become part of him in the East he added an inherited stock of hard-headedness.

He was the sort of Wilsonian that you could not catch bending.

When the Emperor applied to Washington for a financial adviser at the time of his coronation, the State Department immediately asked gold-standard Colson if he would like the job. He would.

By the beginning of the crisis with Italy Colson was already the Emperor's chief all-purpose man. In strength of purpose and steadiness of aim, he stood head and shoulders above Virgin, the Swede, and Auberson, the Swiss.

He was combatively anti-Imperialist. He distrusted the three limitrophe powers in the following order: Italy, France, Great Britain. But in his personal dealings with their representatives he behaved perfectly; he made friends of many.

Colson saw the weaknesses of Ethiopian national character quite clearly. He knew that there was a lot of graft; that much time was wasted on discussion; that they were oversuspicious and made unnecessary enemies; that they could not say no; that their conceit was phenomenal.

He thought and said that Mulugeta, the old War Minister, was incompetent. "Here they tell you So-and-so's a very intelligent man," said Colson, "and that means he can speak French."

Colson served the Ethiopians loyally, but frankly. That was why they liked and depended on him. He regularly told them, with that sarcastic twist of his under the grey moustache, and looking at them steadily between the eyes, when he thought them asses—"unwise" he would say.

He and the Emperor co-operated easily. The two would discuss the lines of a note.* Colson would express the

* Colson writes me: "This paragraph gives an altogether incorrect idea of procedure in drafting notes up to the time that the 'Trinity.' disbanded as a result of the departure of two of its members. You ignore Virgin and relegate Auberson to the task of a French scribe. You also ignore Tasfai. The first step was usually an oral discussion between the four of us; if any important political move was involved we went in a body to see the Emperor and ascertain his views. Sometimes we took with us a written draft to serve as basis for discussion: sometimes we delayed the making of a draft until after such discussion. More frequently

argument on which they had agreed in French, in his typical blend of diplomacy and common sense. Auberson would improve the French. The Emperor would approve the draft, or ask for alterations of emphasis.

As diplomatic documents, the Ethiopian notes struck me as perfectly drawn. It would have been easy for a small African country to make a mistake in its dealings with the League; so many of the Powers fatigued with the poverty and remoteness of Ethiopia would gratefully have struck out of their diaries all their engagements with her, had she given them the chance. The delicate reminders which were addressed to them and left them no escape were written by an American financial expert; and expressed the feelings of a pure African who had spent less than a year outside his country.

The first time that I saw Colson he looked at me steadily, then walked away.[†] The second time, he was lying on his sofa at home, reading the *Wall Street Journal*, and smoking a pipe. In this position he was more accessible, and slowly measuring his words he told me that he thought all anti-gold standard men were cranks.

I entirely disagreed with him; on this basis we became great friends. I guess that if I had said that I thought the gold standard was wonderful he would not have liked me.

He lived in a small house on the road to the station. Later it became a sort of Press bureau, more useful than the draft was made by Auberson, less frequently by myself, and not at all by Virgil, whose French was not so good; but it always represented the views upon which all of us had previously agreed. I do not think that I was more fertile in ideas than my colleagues: Auberson's excellent knowledge of French gave the notes their style and served to present the ideas which all had advanced; and if these are to be described as 'perfectly drawn' no one of us is entitled to any more credit than the others. Not infrequently a draft note was written by the Emperor himself, and on his own initiative, and communicated to us for criticism and discussion. Generally these notes required little alteration.

"The impression should not be given that discussions were usually limited to the Emperor and myself. We all went together, except during the periods that Auberson or Virgil, or both, were out of the picture because of illness, and we all expressed our views, in which there was never any important divergence." (I would on no account belittle the work of Auberson and Virgin. But a longer run of good health and, I feel, a rare force of character, made Colson the greatest of the Trinity.—G.L.S.)

† Now, as I write this book, he tells me:—"I was amazed that such a journal as *The Times* should send to Ethiopia . . . such a person as you appeared at first blush to be. It was probably to hide my amazement that I turned away. This first impression, however, was very quickly revised."

the official one. Colson added to his functions that of the quiet diffusion of news. Not only did he keep the League awake: he kept the light of publicity on Abyssinia. There were six rooms and an enclosed veranda in the house of this remarkable man. The cooking of delicacies was done by Mrs. Colson, a staunch Presbyterian. The drawing-room was decorated by "When did you last see your Father?" and small prints of D. G. Rossetti. A fox-terrier, Tuffy, was allowed great liberties. All that was unusual in this pleasant house was the owner's stamp collection and his mind.

III

I SENT NO MESSAGE to *The Times* for my first week in Addis Ababa. Half my days were spent riding round the town to look it up and down. Filthy though it was, Addis Ababa exhilarated me. Nine thousand feet up, a sparkle in the air, clear sunlight between leaves and storms of rain. And after rain, the smell of dripping eucalyptus, which made me feel careless and fresh as a child: for it brought back memories of young years in the Cape.

Addis is a large African town plastered here and there with modern improvements. Basically it is Africa and completely shapeless; but the Armenians, the Greek hotel-keepers, the German architect Hertl, the French railway, and finally the Emperor Haile Selassie, have all contributed their styles, the two first in the cheapest materials possible, the last according to his means.

When Menelik built Addis his principal chiefs staked out their claims to this or that plot of rising ground. Here they built their local Gibbis, which means a Palace on a Hill. Roads led from Gibbi to Gibbi, and the two main hills were crowned by the Great Gibbi of Menelik and the Cathedral of Saint Giorghis, patron of Adowa, on whose day the victory was won and on whose plinth the Italian prisoners afterwards laboured.

Menelik was far more African than Haile Selassie. Where Menelik was big and impulsive, and even in his most astutely diplomatic moments sprawled, the son of Menelik's Ras Makonnen was elegant, reflective, a lover of neatness, order, tenue.

Addis Ababa was only later the town of the Emperor Haile Selassie. Its Great Gibbi is Menelik, a huge thing scattered pell-mell. The streets are Menelik, lumbering about anywhere. Its size is Menelik, immense.

Under Haile Selassie a certain polish was added to forty year old Addis Ababa, and in some parts a mask. The central roads of the town were smoothed with tarmac. The open spaces were adorned with gilt statues, illuminated Masonic triangles, a clock tower copy of the famous obelisk at Axum, a Parliament House in the modern featureless style. Two new churches, with glittering domes, two capacious schools, well and strongly built, flanked a correction of the alignment of roads that had twisted. Patchment arches, emblems of the poverty and hurried improvisation of the Emperor's Coronation, flapped their giant framework across the hill road to the Gibbi and the hill road to Giorghis.

The Italians contributed the powerful radio station at Akaki. This was the period of peaceful penetration. Cora, whom Haile Selassie loved, was minister, not Vinci. When they had received their pay for building it they expected to run it.

An aerodrome with a workshop was established at Janmeda, alongside the racecourse of the diplomatic corps, within the town boundary. A bigger aerodrome was at Akaki, a few kilometres west. Near it, when I arrived in Addis, a model prison was building.

There were traffic police in the streets wearing white knee-breeches, blue tunics, khaki puttees and white topees with a red band. They had fixed ideas about traffic discipline, knocked into their heads by the men at the top. Cars were allowed to park only on the side of the road on which they travelled. There were one-way streets. When I was in a hurry and cantered my pony, a policeman would blow his whistle fit to pierce the skies and yell in a voice as penetrative, "Kas-bil, Kas-bil"—GO SLOW. Cantering was not allowed.

But the police were Africans. In the early days the man in charge of the one-way traffic in the centre of the town used to relieve himself at his post. The white topees and breeches were never spotless and often torn. Arrests were not carried out with the dignity of the London force: it was common to see a traffic policeman darting barefoot through the crowd to catch the culprit. Whistle, post, traffic-duties, often the precious topee were forgotten in the traditional hue and cry after crime.

The currency too was composite. Thalers and piastres were the old style. Under Colson the silver piastres were replaced gradually by a nickel centesimal system, bearing the fine profile of Haile Selassie. The Bank of Ethiopia issued Haile Selassie notes from two dollars upward. All these systems lived comfortably together; but the silver Maria Theresa thaler, the old Abyssinia, was the rock bottom of the currency.

A little off the centre of Addis lay the market; in the rains a vast mud-bath covered by rusty corrugated iron sheets, under each of which four sticks lifted to disclose a stall. Under the iron sheeting was the real Addis Ababa, selling mules and tins, coffee and cotton stuffs and cathartics, and all the leather oddments that the Ethiopians hang around them. An indescribable mess of cartridge belts, sword sheaths, slippers and amulets. At separate stalls the Gurages, an enfranchised tribe of South-western Ethiopia who never wash their clothes, practised their monopoly of the meat trade and of porterage. (The Gurages are miserly. They say that washing not only costs money, but that it wears the clothes out before their time.)

Real Addis Ababa was a disorganised town proletariat, acknowledging no chiefs, but obedient to the orders of the municipality: created by the railway and the influx of cheap iron and cotton goods, and by the draw which Addis exercised on the imagination of the young Ethiopian countryman who wanted to move. It was always full of great men, the "tillik sauoch" that the Ethiopian system throws up with every generation. Addis was crowded not so much with their retainers as with the young Ethiopians who wanted a job with them, were they Amhara or Galla, poor peasants but freemen, serfs or runaway slaves.

The streets were full of loungers. A youth would hang round the rich man's gate for weeks, waiting to be noticed and addressed. He would make friends with the servants: do work for them if they were lazy (and to devolve in Ethiopia is always a function of the Ethiopian's desire for repose): invisibly he would become a member of the master's household and reflect new glory upon him as he travelled with his retinue in the street.

The greater the household, the more refined its functions. A man to put the master's hat on: a man to support him into the saddle: a third to hold the left side of the mule's rump in the street, and a fourth to control the right.

It made many of the Amhara or mixed Amhara-Galla great men of Addis, selfish. It is some tribute to the Ethiopian race that it did not deprive them either of the physical strength or of their battle spirit.

But even so, the loungers were only part absorbed. The rest did odd jobs, based on the market. A proletariat, disorganised but living in freedom and far greater health than the native proletariat of European towns in Africa. The smell in the poorest part of Addis Ababa was never so resonant as the smell at Djibouti. The only overcrowding was among the prostitutes.

When it rained, the other half of my days, I stayed indoors. My first visitors were Blatta Kidane Mariam Aberra and Ato David, in European dress and topees.

Blatta Kidane and Ato David were both young, and like many of the bright young men in the Emperor's Civil Service, they were Eritreans or Tigreans. Kidane, who liked jazz and dancing and had a frank laugh and friendly manner at the bar, was educated at the Emperor's cost in France. He spoke French and Italian perfectly. He had been made Director of Public Instruction and Fine Arts: one of his jokes was that the latter function enabled him to drink in the afternoon as well as the evening. "Let the Fine Arts flourish" was a favourite toast of his.

In spite of his gaiety Blatta Kidane was a patriot. He organised the Young Ethiopia Society, and later a parallel organisation among the Ethiopian women, the results of which sometimes made him laugh aloud.[*] The Emperor had put him temporarily in charge of the European Press.

Ato David, more covert in manner and far more difficult to deal with, had been educated at the Emperor's charge in Beirut. He spoke English and French and was a master at one of the Emperor's schools in Addis. This was closing now and he was to assist at the new Press Bureau. Blatta

---

[*] At one meeting the wife of the Emperor's chauffeur told them they must not be shy.

Kidane, if he had anything to say, always told me the truth; Ato David as regularly the reverse.

They arranged an interview for me with the Emperor. Kidane, I found at once, was thoroughly sociable. After a few drinks I noticed that he was taking *sirop*.

He explained that he never drank anything else, with a sad but confiding gesture, because his stomach was so weak. Perhaps it was. Though he stayed in the cinema-bars of Addis until midnight, chatting amiably to all the Europeans, I never saw him drink anything stronger. He had, besides Public Instruction, the Fine Arts and the Press Bureau, two other functions which called for a clear head. One was to maintain friendly contacts with all Europeans, which fitted him down to the ground; the other was to report on their activities, their friends and their attitude towards Ethiopia, on which I am less qualified to judge.

The more whisky Ato David swallowed the more close and crablike did he become.

On Tuesday I was commanded to the Little Gibbi, where the Emperor would receive me. Ato David was rather obscure about dress; his only hopeful comment was "the blacker the better." I found all the necessary parts of morning dress at the British Legation.

The Little Gibbi, at the northern end of Addis towards Mount Entoto, was the latest of the Emperor's demonstrations of order and neatness to his people. It was planned, I believe, on the model of a country house which he had visited in England, and it was furnished by Messrs. Waring & Gillow. The Emperor disliked the systemless meanders of the Old Gibbi, built and chaotically extended by Menelik: he used the old buildings of the Gibbi Hill only for meetings of his State Council, and for the offices of the Imperial Secretary.

Two sentry boxes, striped diagonally in the colours of Ethiopia, green, yellow and red, held the front gate of the Little Gibbi. Inside was the nearest approach to Europe in the Empire. A long elliptical gravel drive; well-kept gardens; a working fountain. At the bottom, quarters of the Imperial Guard. At the top, the portico of the Imperial Palace.

The Little Gibbi, large and neat enough, but completely unpretentious, was typical of the Emperor whom I was going to see. Of the rooms below the largest were two high, airy salons for dancing and receptions, and a long corridor room, with a recess for the Emperor's seat, where he gave dinners. Other rooms were the Emperor's study, his library and his documents room, and several drawing-rooms; the Empress and the Princesses had a special pavilion of their own.

All these rooms were connected more by wide-curtained openings than by doors. In cold weather the Gibbi was rather draughty and fires were lit in the apartments on the ground floor. The decorations were in good taste.

There had been a development of the Emperor's taste since his Coronation. Then was the period when he had small means and grandiose ideas. The ex-Kaiser's coach was imported to stun the populace. He bought the biggest Hungarian horses in the world. A cup was presented for the races at the Imperial Club, on the pretty tree-girt course at Janmeda: this enormous catafalque of silver with a tap at its broad bottom was meant to hold champagne; twelve silver cups sprouted from top to base, like candles on a Christmas tree, resting on brackets of the same material.

Frau Hertl, the ex-midwife who had become the Empress's Lady-in-Waiting, had influenced this phase in Ethiopian art. But the Emperor, who had only made one journey to Europe, was quick to note where his judgment had failed. After Hertl's days as arbiter were over General Erik Virgin, who had long frequented the Swedish Court, took over the direction of elegance and based it more firmly on the Scandinavian concept of simplicity. He also introduced into the Court a highly formal etiquette.

The Emperor of Ethiopia, Haile Selassie the First, as he was styled in state documents, was devoted entirely to Western forms. His own instincts were Western; his ruling instinct was for order and applied reason. He believed implicitly in the diplomatic method of settling disputes, civil or external. The vulgarities of the West, which came to him jumbled up with its refinements, as they come to every African or Asiatic who deals with the West, did not long confuse him. Early in his reign Europe came to him through the worst Europeans, those who had followed the Adowa tradition out to Africa: but he was quick to sift them away.

He was not immensely rich, and Ethiopia was a poor country. He therefore restricted his private outlay and spent a huge proportion of his fortune on public amenities.

People who have met him have called him, on the one hand, a sham who put up a lot of pretences to catch the eye of England and France; on the other, a grasping merchant monarch, worth millions and unwilling to part with them.

The schools and Parliament House and prisons that he built, the small force of planes and landing grounds that he organised, the wireless stations, the roads to Dessye and Jimma, the establishment of missions abroad and of an army capable of maintaining internal unity, the price of foreign advisers, civil and military, and of the organisation of police—all these were costs upon his private purse. To call them a *façade*, as they have been called, is futile. The reforms of Ethiopia cost the Emperor all but the whole of his income. Who ever was so keen on building a *façade* that he had nothing left to lavish on the house? And if he was grasping, which of these items of expenditure could give him the return that it cost him?

A servant of the Court, his white shamma tied respectfully across his chest, his sword-arm covered and his trim beard pointed, greeted us and led us into the Emperor's study. Ato David was there to do the interpreting. The Emperor does not speak English, but Ato David was four times corrected on points of interpretation during the interview that followed.

Directly facing the door by which I entered his study, and with his back to a window, the Emperor of Ethiopia sat behind his heavy gilt table dispatching business. Two little dogs lay at his feet and a big fire of eucalyptus crackled in a grate at his side.

He bowed gravely and waited for me to open the conversation, which lasted for an hour and a half.

Other people have remarked the Assyrian perfection of

his features, the delicacy and length of his hands, the serenity of his eyes and the great dignity of his bearing. The first thing that I noticed was the extreme rapidity of his mind.

If he had been a European, it would have been comprehensible; but I was somebody whom he had never met before. He had only been to England once, years ago, and he did not know many Englishmen besides Barton, his old administrative adviser De Halpert, and Collier, his banker. He answered every question as freely as if he had known me all his life: there was none that he refused to meet.

He spoke without hesitation and without any correction: quickly, with the authoritative voice of a logician. He had an immensely able mind, and he knew his own views to the last detail.

July was the month after Mr. Eden had visited Rome and made the Zeyla offer. The parties to the dispute, England, France and Italy (Ethiopia did not count), were being asked by England to discuss the "Ethiopian question" on the basis of the 1906 Treaty relative to Ethiopia, to which they were the signatories. Under this treaty Ethiopia was divided into three economic spheres under the three powers.

The object of this manœuvre was to save the face of the League before the League had been given a chance to expose it.

If England particularly, and France after her, could prevail upon Italy to accept a big slice of Ethiopia instead of the whole, then they could together put pressure upon the Emperor not to lay the dispute before the League. The Emperor was determined to resist such pressure, and that was the significance of the interview which he gave to *The Times*,

He bore himself, then as ever, as the perfect diplomat, ready on occasion with a thrusting phrase. Unwilling to offend a nation which might one day be his ally, he chose not to denounce the 1906 Treaty as a means. On the other hand, he showed clearly that its machinery could not work by definining the limited concessions that he was prepared to make.

My shorthand notes of the dialogue perished in the sack of Addis Ababa in May, 1936. I have only the more formal report in *The Times*.

When Addis Ababa filled up with the world's Press and the Ethiopian radio was handling over 30,000 words of journalistic matter daily, interviews with the Emperor were often devolved to Colson. Questions were put in writing, Colson typed out the answers, the Emperor approved the draft and saw the interviewer for a few minutes' friendly talk. But my questions came from the blue and were as directly answered.

Throughout, the Emperor economised gesture and sat perfectly straight in his seat. Only the jewelled hand moved a little from under his black cloak. A man of great intelligence, completely controlled by himself. The dogs lay by his feet for an hour and a half with the same motionless obedience.

"Ethiopia (said the Emperor) *acknowledges the value of the 1906 Treaty as an instrument of pacification, but Signor Mussolini is still sending troops and munitions, and threatens to put in a personal appearance; action under the Treaty seems valueless now, especially as Britain is the only one of the three signatories to pay it any respect. As regards methods of negotiation, Great Britain has not made proposals to Ethiopia, but the Emperor is delighted with the attitude of Sir Samuel Hoare and Mr. Eden, and there is no criticism of the method of a free hand for Britain in a constructive effort for peace. So far neither Italy nor any other country has put a proposition directly to Ethiopia regarding an Italian railway joining Eritrea and Somaliland. Even if an offer were made the details would not easily be settled, but Ethiopia is still willing to discuss the question."*

In the matter of territorial concessions, the attitude of the Emperor was particularly definite.

"I have in view only an exchange of territory. If the Zeyla offer is maintained I am willing to surrender to Italy an equivalent. The precise extent of the territory that might be ceded cannot now be decided, but the district in which it will be found is definite. Ethiopia utterly refuses to concede any of the northern provinces and the districts of Arussi. Bale, Liban, and Borana are equally out of the question. Only part of Ogaden is cedable, anywhere from Walwal to Dolo, including therefore the possible concession of the Webbe Shebeli.

"But the Zeyla offer must stand. During my journey in Europe I emphasised to the British and French Governments

Ethiopia's need of a seaport on the Red Sea. I still regard that as much more important than loans or other financial assistance. I insist that the main factor barring Ethiopia from civilisation is the lack of a seaport, and if Italy's motive for the conquest of Ethiopia is to civilise the country, I find in her resistance to the Zeyla offer reason for some sarcasm." But he pointed out that no proposals of a territorial nature had yet been received by the Ethiopian Government from any source.

In reply to the Italian threat to raise the question of slavery at Geneva, the Emperor was gratified that Italy used Geneva for any question whatsoever, but he objected that slavery was not confined to Ethiopia, since it flourished too in Tripoli and Eritrea, a fact not denied by the Italians themselves and one of which the League was well aware. It was an insufficient argument for the transfer of the so-called colonial provinces which were member States of Ethiopia by treaty and in historical fact.

The Emperor expressed surprise that the export of arms caused any hesitation, seeing that the Treaty of 1931 allowed arms to maintain Ethiopian independence and integrity, and he felt that all the world knew that Ethiopia stood for peace at that moment. *"If Italy is still allowed to send munitions and export licences for arms for Ethiopia are withheld, Ethiopia will be unable to maintain her independence. I am particularly injured at the attitude of Czechoslovakia and Belgium, where Ethiopian agreements with private firms had previously received official consent.*

"The Italian threat to peace appears to me to be flagrant. If Italy declares war, or her troops dare to cross the frontiers, Ethiopia will fight immediately and simultaneously appeal to the League."

The Emperor preferred one to walk out of his presence backwards. Later a carpet was laid to indicate, to the geometrically minded, the precise course on which they should direct that blind part of their body which they carried behind them. I passed the door without this ingenious aid. An American colleague was not so accurate, and bruised his bumper bars.

The Emperor, who had been waiting for this moment, relaxed into a charming smile.

IV

PART OF THE Addis Ababa proletariat were independent of the search for Ethiopian masters; they ministered to the needs of foreigners. They sold curiosities, silver ornaments, spears and shields, skins and Ethiopian paintings. At their head, because they were the richest of those in contact with the West, were the taxidrivers, a race of insolents apart.

These made touch with the West through its material needs alone. They knew the prices of its objects, the way that its iron wheels went round. They learnt, too, its material tastes: Greek liquor, the tinned food of the Armenian stores, cigarettes, shoes and solar topees.

They picked up foreign languages as they went along, foul words first. Then the parts of motor-cars.

The West came to Addis Ababa as well through the schools of the Emperor and the Missions. These were the moral agents of the West. They were the centre of propaganda for the humanitarian concepts of the nineteenth century—self-control, sobriety, patriotism, self-enlightenment, truthfulness, and the perfectability of human nature.

The products of this education, who developed European material tastes besides, mingled with a strange ease with the taxidriver class: they formed a layer between the Emperor, his chiefs and civil service, and the still Ethiopian town proletariat.

It was this layer, for one reason or the other receptive of Western ideas, that the Emperor chose as mouthpiece of his schemes for war-preparedness.

Khaki was one of the mass preparations which Ethiopia, under his guidance, was making for the war. The other was *marching in step*.

Under my hotel balcony stood five Ethiopians, each with something to sell. Two of them wore the white high-collared shirt and jodhpurs traditional to Shoa, with the ancient white shamma thrown idly over one shoulder. On the other three were the type of khaki tunic and jodhpurs which I had noticed on my interpreter Joseph in the train. The Shoans, he told me, had been buying khaki for camouflage against planes throughout 1935. Importers of "abujidid" or cotton sheeting, Japan's leading export to Ethiopia, were advised by the Emperor to buy all the Khaki Abujidid that they could.

"Light and Peace," the Emperor's paper, advised khaki in innumerable issues. Such priests as were capable of exegesis quoted biblical texts in support of khaki to their parishioners—"Hide thee in the earth. . . ."

From the street beyond the hotel wall, with a startling rasp, came an African voice, followed by the soft but unusually rhythmical pad of many bare feet, with the flat-soled echo of a slipper bringing up the rear. "Gra-Ken," it said; "Gra—Gra—Gra-Ken-Gra!" Over the wall black heads bobbed sympathetically, for "Gra" means left and "Ken" means right.

A swart corporal of the Imperial Guard, in almost British uniform save that his cap carried for badge the top-heavy Solomonion crown and his buttons the Lion of Judah, and that his feet were nude, instructed the employees of the General Post Office and the Radio in the art of marching straight, the mystery of fours.

The Ethiopians have never marched to battle in anything like order, though they both fight and camp under a certain discipline. Their favourite formation in movement is the bee-line, and though they march at great speed their moments of progress from one point to another are those when they are least amenable to military control. The Emperor was determined to reduce Shoa, at least, to discipline. It was his misfortune that he had neither the time nor the expert European advice available to carry their instruction further—or, indeed, as far.

And so it happened that the corporal used the narrow tarmac street in front of my hotel to teach the G.P.O. employees how to meet the Italians. Not to bemuse them too much over the difference between a turn and a wheel, he shouted right turn in Amharic and right wheel in French. Much difficulty was encountered in the swinging of arms. The Abyssinian of Addis Ababa, who had long admired the ceremonial parades of the Belgian military mission, was obsessed with the combative value of stiffness.

When the recruits had been thoroughly grounded in "Gra-Ken" (which they loved) they were taught to emphasise the beat on the "Gra" by a sharp blast of the whistle, made in Japan. I tried to use my camera: but the corporal, who dreaded the publication of military secrets, only allowed me to photograph his squad when I had taken a flattering close-up of him whistling.

Idle infants watched the recruits at labour. Some joined the ranks; so far as I could see, anybody was welcome. Up the street a tyrannical child with a little whip was trying to discipline his friends in the universal Belgian manner. Two dotards, long ejected from the squad for slobbering on parade, followed the movements of their juniors in feeble dumb-show. The preparations of Addis Ababa for her mobilisation were truly general.

A parade in the grounds of the Little Gibbi next Thursday gave me my first view of the Imperial Guard. Four battalions, in khaki uniform, occupied three sides of a square. There were now three battalions in the Emperor's province of Harrar. That was the total of the Imperial Guard, except for a ceremonial company of lancers who appeared at this Addis review.

Training to increase the force had been going on in Addis. Thirty-two new Ethiopian officers were sworn in to-day, their hand on the colours. The Emperor, in European uniform, rode round the ranks. The parade work was excellent, and my friends told me that they hoped to have ten thousand more ready on this model by the time that the war began. I wondered whether they would know much more than Gra-Ken.

For the first and last time when I was in Ethiopia, the Emperor addressed the notables of the Empire in the Parliament House on the plain below the Great Gibbi. He travelled from the parade-ground in his Rolls-Royce.

The building was crowded with old counsellors, their

heads swathed in bandages. Concealment of the features from the vulgar is believed by the conservatives in Abyssinia to be essential to the dignity of rank; sometimes only an ancient nose takes the air. There were many younger men, as well as Mohammedans from Jimma, Harrar and the Ogaden. The whole swarmed on to the floor of the Parliament, and the Ministers occupied their high seats in mantles of brown, mauve, grey, blue and black. They looked up to three boxes where on the left sat Ras Mulugeta, the Minister of War, the Abuna, head of the Ethiopian Coptic Church (fast asleep), and the Echegi, chief Abbot of the monasteries of Ethiopia. On the right were Court officials.

At midday a pink silk veil dropped from the centre box. It disclosed the Emperor standing in his field uniform in front of his throne. (The Emperor must not be seen by the people in the common motions of rising or sitting.) The Court Chamberlain took his place in the middle of the assembly, carrying his silver-topped staff, and without further formality the Emperor read his speech.

The Ethiopian Constitution is a young growth, and as usual in Abyssinia the general brown public penetrated the place of assembly as well as those more qualified to attend as deputies. Their proportion in this case was about three to one, but the Chamberlain, a tall and martial aristocrat, kept them with their backs to the wall throughout. The Parliament at Sparta must, I think, have been somewhat similar.

It must be remembered that at this time those who wished to save the face of the League had other plans in reserve in case the 1906 Treaty broke down. They proposed to concentrate on the so-called lawlessness and backwardness of Ethiopia, which had nothing to do either with Italian designs upon her or with the more local dispute at Walwal. But it could be used to press upon the Emperor a League mandate and to recommend such a scheme to an ignorant public opinion in Great Britain: in fact, the "lion's share" under a mandate would go to Italy, as the Press later explained. Ingenuously it was added that this procedure would not only be bound to satisfy Italy, but would be easiest to follow because neither of the other two great Powers were interested to impose themselves upon Ethiopia. In other words, they only interested themselves in the lawlessness and backwardness of Ethiopia so far as these factors allowed Italy to get what she wanted under a show of legality.

In his speech on this particular day the Emperor showed that he was not the fool they thought him. He rejected a mandate or protectorate of any kind under any country whatsoever. He left the details to be filled in by diplomatic correspondence with his representatives in Europe.

Already he had made up his mind to reap what advantages he could from the situation. If Europe was so worried about Ethiopian lawlessness and backwardness, why not take Europe at her face value and ask for financial assistance? Europe had never given him the means to civilise and unify his country. He had no money of his own to spend on a large system of *gendarmerie* and public works outside his capital. He would accept the principle of League assistance, reserving to himself the right to approve *personnel*.

But on this public occasion he wished to kill the rumours that he sought an accommodation with the enemy. It was the favourite sport in the European Press at this time to pretend that the Emperor of Ethiopia was not only feeble but weakening.

He attacked Italian policy from beginning to end. Signor Mussolini, he said, wished to pay out the old Adowa account in bloody fashion. The Italian aggressor, pretending by cruel modern and scientific means of aggression to civilise them, would find a united people. All would stand together, Christians and Moslems, in face of the invader. Women would play their part in the war, going to the front to encourage and feed the soldiers and to tend the wounded. God, the one God of both creeds, was their shield and buckler against the modern equipment of their enemies of to-morrow.

"And I, your Emperor, who address you," he said, "will be in your midst, not hesitating to pour out my lifeblood for the independence of Ethiopia." He carried out his word behind the Oerlikon at Koram and the machine-gun in the plain of Maichow.

Yet *"Je ne suis pas un soldat,"* he had told the British Legation at Addis. Strange contrast with his Italian conqueror; but Europe is full of old front-line fighters who struggle now with the microphone.

That day I heard a phrase which I could not understand.

"Soldiers, when you have heard that in the battle-fire a loved chieftain has fallen, do not weep or despair. The man who dies for his country is happy. Blind death destroys in peace as well as in war. Better die free than live as slaves. Remember your fathers who fell at Adowa!"

Only the war taught me what the Emperor meant, when I met the fugitives of the dead Afewerk at Jijiga and the broken armies of Bidwoded Makonnen at Dessye. Ethiopians cannot fight after the chief has gone: the unit has lost its unifying principle, and the loud crying of the soldiers is symptom of the extreme pain of the whole in dissolution. In Europe there are various political systems which talk of a mystical leadership principle. In Ethiopia, where manliness is not bolstered by an abounding military material, this principle finds a physical existence. The chief, who is perhaps the only man with a machine-gun, leads his men into battle carrying it. His name is sometimes engraved on the barrel and enables the body to be identified.

At the end of the Emperor's speech, as he stood motionless, the pink curtain was raised over the Imperial box. He had spoken for half an hour with scarcely a movement of his body, no gesture at all. His voice had been even and hard throughout: he never raised or lowered it. No trace of feeling was allowed to break through his impassive mask. He thought public emotions vulgar, and he disliked public poses.

While his Ministers maintained dignity when the assembly had to be cleared, the Addis Ababa public rushed hither and yon. None of them knew which door was the exit, and their confusion was increased by Likaba Tasso, the Court Chamberlain, who hit them about with his wand of office and with resounding ferocity. They issued from the Parliament House in a battered condition, but still clung in dumb curiosity to the steps, whence they had to be swept by men with lithe willow wands and others with scabbarded swords.

One would have thought them by now insensible, but

when the Emperor descended the steps to his car, they broke out into the vibrant Li-li-li-li of Ethiopian applause. It spread along the thousands in the mud at the roadside as he drove back to the Little Gibbi. Officers of the Guard, their flat uniform caps and their epaulettes topped with lion's hair, ran beside the car all the way, some barefoot and others wearing silver-buckled sandals.

The Italian Minister, Count Vinci, took grave offence at the Emperor's speech. To suggest that Italy was preparing an act of aggression was incorrect: she was preparing an act of civilisation, to improve Ethiopian manners. To give an example of his own, he refused to attend the Emperor's birthday levee on July 23rd. It made no difference to the scene, whose draw was purely exotic.

In the early hours explosions of varying intensity and irregular punctuation hurtled from the Palace hill. Ethiopian artillery men are enthusiastic but uncertain of their weapons. The ragged salvo of twenty-one shots from one cannon ushered in a sulphurous dawn.

The streets were packed with footmen carrying rifles, who surrounded chiefs entering the capital on their mules. Velvet rifle-cases flapped behind their saddles like russet flags as they made for the Palace. Houses in Armenia were sprinkled with the green, yellow and red of Ethiopia, and the French and Greek colony hung out their national ensigns to show how pleased they were that the Emperor was forty-five. (They forgot when he was forty-six.)

The Imperial Guard marched from their barracks uphill to the Gibbi gates. The Emperor entered the immense throne-room of Menelik, with his priests and councillors, at nine o'clock. The Alga, the Oriental bed-throne with four posts and a canopy, was freshly arrayed in scarlet velvet to receive Haile Selassie. He was dressed in a black cape embroidered in scarlet and gold, and wore the Golden Collar of Solomon. Under the aura of dark hair and in that dim chamber there was something of royal mystery in his face as he sat there immobile, looking straight in front of him, his regular features fronting the wide door.

One forgot the fact that Addis Ababa was a sordid town.

Lining the long, steep slopes to the Palace were the

modernised Imperial Guard. The steps of the throne-room, high above the melee, bristled with lion's manes and spears, and were rich with the gold-encrusted targets of rhino-skin, striped silk jodhpurs, and showy leather capes of the great men come to do the Emperor obeisance. Europe: had begun to wake up to the notion that a picturesque Ethiopia existed, a fact which European statesmen had long tried to conceal. In front of nearly every gorgeous Dedjazmatch there crouched a sordid Press photographer flashing magnesium.

Obeisance was made to the Alga. The great Shums went in one by one and, laying their shields on the ground, bowed deeply to the monarch. The Diplomatic Corps kissed his hand. The young officers of the Imperial Guard saluted him: behind stood the Likamaquas, the Court official whom Imperial tradition orders to dress up as the reigning monarch in battle and wave the red umbrella to deceive the enemy.

Distinguished local foreigners, Greek hotelkeepers, Armenian photographers, Syrian school teachers, lined up in an outlandish row to congratulate the monarch who had made the foreigners' life easy in Addis. They made money that their wits, let alone their talents, could not have made elsewhere: they had their own special court for litigation with Ethiopians, and their Consulates for processes against other Europeans. They thrived on State contracts. Most were already secretly in the service of Italy, and had begun the whispering campaign which demoralised Addis long before the Italian planes were seen in Shoa. With their greasy caps or grey homburgs in their hands, the pallid, squat Levant pretended fealty.

The Emperor knew what most of them were up to. He regarded them more as problems than as enemies. They were protected by their Legations, and the Legations were representative of League members. Nothing to be gained by severity or suspicion. He bowed gravely.

Forty Moslem envoys prostrated themselves in a body before the throne. Children of the Imperial schools presented nosegays, of which the Ethiopians are fond: soldiers of the Imperial Guard itself were often to be seen returning from parade with rose-petals protruding from their noses. The Emperor dwelt over the flowers for some time. Then, when all strangers had left the throne-room he left, escorted by some of his airmen, for the banqueting hall, where a great meat feast, or *gebir*, had been prepared for five thousand soldiers, high and low.

The object of all *gebirs* is to keep the monarch in touch with his fighting-men. Foreigners are excluded, because the Press had described these occasions as uncivilised, and the Emperor was particularly sensitive when the word civilisation was used. The Emperor on this day discarded the veil which usually covered his high table. His guards and he were exposed, poised above the feast. The rest of the soldiers kept their spears and rifles by their sides and their swords fast by the right hip. All ate a huge meal and drank copious draughts of *tej* (mead), served at the high table in European decanters, at the lower benches in more generous if cruder receptacles.

The Homeric atmosphere thickened with the entry of whole oxen and sheep which were conveyed round the table raw, on poles. Choice slivers were hacked off by the warriors, and while one end was put into the mouth, the rest was released by an upward cut of the knife, missing the nose by a margin whose width varied with the henchman's fuddlement. Tej was drunk until the warrior felt in a fit state to boast of his warlike achievements, which was done standing up if possible.

Boasting was curtailed at the Emperor's last birthday in Addis. Haile Selassie had recognised that the superiority complex of the Ethiopian was the most serious military problem that he had to face.

Behind him in the darkness gleamed the gold and silver threads of a portrait of Menelik, sprawling moodily in his chair, holding in his fist the thick stick that he always carried. There was a tradition to be broken; a tradition which bound Ethiopia together.

We saw him once again in the throne-room, in the middle of August. The Three-Power negotiations on the 1906 Treaty were about to open in Paris: the Emperor and his advisers, determined to keep the dispute before the League, had prepared a statement of his policy showing the Three Powers how far they could conspire together to save the League's face. His advisers wrote:

"Ethiopia desires, with the collaboration of the other nations, to progress and achieve a higher degree of civilisation, and therefore she needs peace.

"She will continue to advance as means allow, and to further that advance we, the Emperor of Ethiopia, are convinced of the necessity of friendly collaboration with the nations who, without prejudice of race or religion, are disposed to lend their support freely and loyally."

And the Emperor added, with the Biblical directness which was his nature:

"It is impossible here below to do anything lasting or useful without the help of others."

His advisers wrote:

"Ethiopia, careful of her internal tranquillity, will never accept proposals capable of injuring her liberty, diminishing her sovereignty, or affecting the prestige of the Emperor, his people and his army. We renew our faith . . . etc. We put particular trust in England . . . and in . . . France . . . etcetera."

Haile Selassie said that he would write the peroration himself. His was a production inspired by the Joshua from whom the Ethiopians claim descent:

"But if the efforts of other nations and our own fail, and devilish violence takes the opportunity to open war, sowing misfortune, shame and misery with the world as its field, Ethiopia will rise up, the Emperor at her head, and follow him in her hundred-thousands with the valour and staunchness famous for a thousand years. Leaning on the Divine arm, she will resist the invader to her last drop of blood, fighting from the natural fortresses of mountain and desert that the Lord has given her."

Last drop of blood was picturesque phraseology. They fought to the last round of modern ammunition that ever reached the war zone.

How far *could* the Ethiopians wage a modern war?

V

DISAPPOINTED MILITARY CRITICS sitting in England before inadequate maps of Ethiopia, whose sheer precipices, non-existent diseases, and procrastinating rains they hoped would do the work of the League of Nations, have set down the defeat of the Ethiopian as an organisation in the field to his incapacity as a guerilla fighter. They have found, largely by the law of contraries, that the Italian has become a first-rate soldier, well led, ardent and accurate: and that the Italian Air Force is the finest in the world—as it is, undoubtedly, the most experienced.

I believe that these are fallacies. Italian military prowess in my view is as wildly exaggerated after the Italo-Ethiopian war as were the material means of Ethiopia before it.

Modern war is not won by courage: it goes to the man with the most powerful material. Cæsars do not trick the enemy, as they did in the Gallic wars, by stratagem or speed. They are heavier creatures: they roll over him and crush him. They are students of physics, who burn him up.

How, in terms of rolling and burning, were the Italian and Ethiopian armies compared?

The Italian Air Force in the north was calculated in Addis to be over three hundred machines: in Italian Somaliland, about one hundred. Their bombers were first-class; the pursuit planes which had nothing to pursue were less fast and powerful.

The Ethiopians had eleven planes, eight of which could leave the ground: of these eight the Emperor had given one to the Red Cross. None were armed or of a speed equal to the Italian machines. They were set apart to carry the Emperor's dispatches at safe times—at dawn or dusk—to safe places far from the Italian lines.

The Ethiopians had three hundred and seventy-one bombs and, of course, imported no gas. If they had, assuredly their position as the victims of aggression would have been reconsidered by the Council. The whole problem facing Geneva could have been solved without a stain on the Covenant.

To meet the Italian gas, if they were going to use it, the Ethiopians had no masks that I could discover, though it was reported that they had bought a limited number for the Imperial Guard in August. To add to Ethiopia's long list of crimes against civilisation, these were said to have been made in Japan.

The "intense anti-aircraft reaction" described later in Italian communiques after heavy bombing raids was put up by eight anti-aircraft guns in the north and five in the Ogaden, all inadequately supplied with ammunition. Only the longest ears could ever have heard them barking in unison.

One would have imagined the Ethiopians capable of a good showing in point of armament upon the ground—if one had not been in Ethiopia. There, the material weakness of Ethiopia was exposed to one immediately in the publicity guaranteed under the 1930 Arms Treaty between Italy, France, Great Britain and Ethiopia.

They would have put up a longer fight if it had not been for the embargo on the import of guns imposed by Great Britain and France, the two limitrophe powers, until the Italian act of aggression had been perpetrated.

The arms embargo, which thus became the European fashion, spreads its dark shadow over the history of the Italo-Ethiopian war. For a mountain guerrilla war, large numbers of small arms, light automatics, and, above all, ammunition are needed. The effect of the embargo was to cut these off, almost entirely, from the Northern Front.

In Ethiopia there are no fine roads or railways to supply the soldiers at the front. To a limited degree, and under powerful escort, they could be sent by mule transport. But in this war a man took his rifle and ammunition for the campaign with him.

The army of the Centre, under Ras Mulugeta, the Minister of War, and the Imperial Guard had to leave Addis Ababa between October 17 and 21, 1935. Military necessities of the moment, the threat of the Italians to Makalle and perhaps beyond, revolt of the population in Gojjam, rendered it impossible for them to remain longer in Addis.

A few small driblets of arms arrived in Addis before they left. The other northern Rases, Imru Kassa and Seyyum, and Dedjazmatch Ayelu were even more wretchedly supplied.

All through the war the arms embargo was going to show itself: in the weakness of the North, which could never be supplied: in the strength of the Ogaden army, despite its small numbers, because it lay across the route by which munitions made their tardy appearance.

In July of last year I wrote that Ethiopian supplies of arms and munitions of war were in quantity hopelessly inadequate for a campaign of moderate length, and in quality incapable of carrying a campaign to a speedy victory.

It was in July that the embargo was imposed.

For the purposes of the northern war, therefore, the arms that Ethiopia possessed in July, 1935, were almost all that need to be considered. The Italians chose to fightthe issue in the north.

From January to July, 1935, the Emperor imported sixteen thousand rifles, six hundred machine-gun rifles and five and a half million rounds of small arms ammunition. In a normal year like 1934 he had imported three thousand rifles, fifty-nine machine-gun rifles and forty-eight thousand rounds.

I wrote at that time that Ethiopia could have, at the very most, only fifteen million rounds and thirty thousand modern rifles. With greater knowledge now, I should say fifty thousand to sixty thousand modern rifles, half of which were in the hands of the local chiefs.

Carefulness with his piece was not a quality of the Ethiopian. Unless he was an old hunter with experience, or was kept under the eye of a martinet officer he did not clean his rifle. The sights were sometimes used as tin-openers and the muzzle was frequently pushed into the mud. A rifle in Ethiopia could only call itself modern for about four years, at most.

My estimate of small arms ammunition was roughly correct: about twice what the Italians were to expend in the three days of the battle of the Shire. Ammunition, above all, was what the Ethiopians needed. Stores were so low that only the Imperial Guard was able to do a little practice, although marksmanship, which many Ethiopians lacked, is a vital necessity of the guerrilla fighter.

In the arsenal of Koramach, sixty kilometres north-east of Addis, and in the hands of the Ethiopians, there were in July about five hundred thousand rifles of all sorts, of which the commonest dated from the period just before 1880. Bound with decorative brass the celebrated Fusil Gras, called Wujigra by the Abyssinians, fired a lead bullet of fearful destructive power in an unpredictable parabola. Among the unknown quantities which governed its flight were perversity of tube, craziness or total absence of sights, and the immense range of ammunition which could be stuffed into the breech.

Governors of great provinces would generally surround themselves with a bodyguard of men armed with modern rifles and machine-guns, who passed as professional soldiers and were paid for their continuous military service. The rest of the male Amhara, mixed Amhara-Galla, or Amharacised-Galla population owed military service of two months a year in return for freedom to work their land. These carried the Fusil Gras.

Quite a third of these guns would be useless. Internal order would have to be maintained, as well as precautions taken against the possibility of revolt in Gojjam. In the pure Amhara provinces, where every man was supposed to answer the call, a fair population would have to stay behind to work the fields. In the so-called "colonial" provinces, part of the garrison, soldier-settlers of Menelik's conquest, would be able to fight.

Making allowance for these facts, the Emperor was able to call up about two hundred and fifty thousand men for war, one-fifth of whom had modern weapons. By the beginning of the war there were over three hundred thousand metropolitan and native troops in the Italian colonies. In numbers as well as in armaments the Italians were superior.

In machine-guns the disproportion of Ethiopian armament was even more marked. In the two years 1934–35, the Emperor had imported six hundred and fifty-nine machine-guns, nearly all of them light machine-gun rifles. Seven heavy machine-gun companies had been organised in the Imperial Guard.

Mulugeta had five machine-guns, fired and cleaned by a Cuban revolutionary. His chiefs had others. In the Ogaden the most they could collect was ten. They were all of different systems. So were the one hundred and fifty which the Emperor was supposed to be holding in reserve.

One thousand light automatics entered Ethiopia during the war. Most found their way into the hands of the Ogaden army. The rest got no farther than Addis to the front.

The fiercer resistance which the Italians were to experience in the Ogaden was due to the proportionately stronger armament which Nasibu's army enjoyed, lying as she did across the munitions route at Jijiga. Even here, as the Turkish military advisers of Nasibu reported halfway through the war, in the ordinary proportion of machine-guns to rifles, the Ethiopians were lacking by ninety per cent.

Rifles and machine-guns were needed by the Ethiopians to fight a guerrilla war: they lacked both. Where guerrilla war was essential—in the north—the odds were even more brutally against them.

The heavier arms were almost non-existent in Ethiopia. Her most powerful gun was a French .75 given to the Emperor by the Marechal Franchet D'Esperey; she had two or three batteries of light mountain artillery and a few trench-mortars. The rest of her cannon were those captured from the Italians at Adowa or toy pieces bought second-hand from France and Greece. There were no trained artillery men in the Ethiopian army. These facts were all known to the British Government which imposed the arms embargo.

Lacking the material means to fight a guerrilla war, the Ethiopians were also handicapped in at least three other ways. First was their nature, or, rather, the tradition of their renaissance as a fighting race under the Emperor Theodore, and under the three other great Ethiopian Emperors who succeeded him.

Defeated only by the Magdala expeditionary force of Napier, the Ethiopians were until the end of this war one of the most overwhelmingly conceited races that it has been my pleasure to behold. Their conceit did not usually take an offensive outward form: it was simply their spiritual bottom, the bedrock principle which informed invisibly their military theory. The sons of Solomon thought themselves unconquerable: they only had to swoop down like a troop of roaring lions and the macaroni melted.

This view was never shared by the Emperor or by any of his high Ras, but it was the source of the ordinary Amhara's readiness for war.

Adowa impressed the ordinary Amhara as a natural conclusion to twenty years of military success, the culminating proof of his invulnerability in his own mountain land. He did not bother to analyse the issue of Adowa; the numerical disproportion of the forces engaged, which could not be repeated in this war; the glaring strategical errors of the Italian command. The similarity of the material and equipment of both sides were considerations which did not interest the Ethiopian. He did not know that in 1896 Adowa was almost unknown country to the Italian, but that 1935 found the whole Tigre better mapped and spied upon by Italy than by Addis Ababa. The revolution in armament caused by automatic weapons was only beginning to dawn upon him: he had an idea of machine-guns, but none of massed machine-guns. Tanks, armoured cars—above all aeroplanes and thousands of lorries that distributed troops in rapid mass behind the enemy lines—were new factors of which, before the Italo-Ethiopian war, he had no comprehension.

At Walwal some of the Ethiopians under Ali-Nur tried to sabre the Italian armoured car, and others proposed to turn it over. Nor were they ever clear when an aeroplane came down voluntarily and when it was brought down. There was a firm and unshakable tradition, established even among the formal artists who sold their brightly coloured works in the capital, that an Abyssinian with his country's incredible skill in marksmanship shot down an Italian plane on the battlefield, though the real reason of its descent was that it had run out of bombs.

Infused with Adowa the same artists always depicted Ethiopians fighting full face "because they are brave," and Italians or subject races in profile "because they are looking with the other eye where to run away."

A booklet was compiled by the Emperor and circulated to all army leaders describing measures to be taken against aeroplanes, armoured fighting vehicles, massed artillery and machine-guns and poison gas: though no provision was made against the spraying of corrosive poison from the air. Advice was also given as to the folly of attack on strongly entrenched positions and the necessity to abandon the mass manœuvre, in view of the danger to marching columns from the air and to groups in battle from the machine-gun.

Their victories over the Italians, Egyptians, Mahdists, the Mad Mullah, and the peoples of the "colonial provinces" had all been won by the mass manœuvre. Presented by its intelligent old chiefs with the rifle, the Ethiopian force was the most orderly and the best-armed mass force in Africa.

The traditional titles of its high officers are significant of that.

The Fitorari or Front of the Rhinoceros who leads the vanguard and establishes touch with the enemy, the Kenyazmatch or leader of the Right Wing, and the Gerazmatch or leader of the Left Wing who envelop him, and the reserve under the Dedjazmatch or Commander of the Threshold who are thrown in where he proves to be weakest to annihilate or rout him by penetration of his front. All these units are under higher officers, leading Dedjazmatches, Fitoraris, Ras or heads, and finally the Emperor himself.

Battles on this model ranged from bloody affairs like Adowa and the battles against the Egyptians and the Sudanese to a mere mass discharge of firearms without serious injury, exemplified by the wars which, under Menelik, re-established the Ethiopian Empire of mystic tradition in Harrar, in the south and in the south-west.

In the little red books, *Infantry Training*, Vols. I and II, that one used to read for examinations in the Officers' Training Corps at school, the British War Office laid great emphasis upon the virtues of the bayonet. In heavy type it was written: "OFTEN THE MERE THREAT OF THE BAYONET, IN THE HANDS OF TROOPS KNOWN TO BE WELL SKILLED IN ITS USE, HAS PROVED THE BREAKING-POINT IN THE ENEMY'S MORALE."

The Ethiopian had similar views, but no bayonet. His main objective, if he could not frighten the enemy off by noise, was to close with him and use the Ethiopian longsword, of which he was a master. Poverty gave him more excuse than the British soldier, for his rifle was seldom a weapon of precision. Regarded as an honourable ornament, it was often discarded in the stern realities of battle, which called the heavy blade from the Ethiopian's right hip, under the thick white tie of his folded shamma.

Observers of the wars of Menelik noted that, in spite of their tendency to mass, the Ethiopians showed great sensitiveness in their use of cover and exploitation of natural features. They were also—the older soldiers— careful of their ammunition until the great clash came. In battle, however, they showed an almost insane élan, hurling themselves into the assault, completely careless of death.

In fighting for the first time against the highly developed mechanised array of the West they had to change their tactics. The Emperor's whole war energy was devoted to this task. He had the Ethiopian tradition to fight against, and in the end it combined with other factors to defeat him. But at the beginning of the Italo-Ethiopian war he had this tradition completely under control: the first Ethiopian manœuvres were cleverly executed. They presented no mass front, they penetrated suddenly, and they concealed their movements and their numbers from the air.

The second handicap under which they suffered was a lack of leaders trained in war outside their own frontiers, or against foreigners. The whole period since the first battle of Adowa had been one of material modernisation in the capital, the slight disturbance of the social system which resulted growing in intensity as the power of the central authority, personified in Menelik, gradually decayed: followed by a period of acute civil wars, which spilled blood over all the mountains of Ethiopia. From 1916 to 1930, undisturbed by any foreign menace, the struggle between the centre and the Ras, between modernisation and suspicion of anything foreign continued to be crowned in the end by the triumph of Power of the Trinity the First.

During this period the last Emperor of Ethiopia had been the sole channel of modern influence in his country: apart from the automatic modernisation caused without plan by the ordinary commercial contacts. Eventually it was fatigue with war and disorder that turned the Ethiopian population at the centre to Haile Selassie. He personified for them diplomatic wisdom, peacefulness, order and neatness.

From 1916 to 1930 the vague Ethiopian "feudal" system, which is really a tough man system, liable at any moment, as it has been throughout the centuries, to sudden collapse and regeneration round a dominant type, was interested only in itself. It was Ethiopia's private tragedy that this was the period of the World War. Fighting in the far-away clouds of the plateau and the unexplored provinces, she could learn nothing of the fearful military progress made in the world outside.

Compare the attitude of Menelik who imported the most modern rifles of his day and that of Zauditu, the Empress, his daughter, who refused to allow her heir, Ras Tafari, to assemble an aeroplane in Addis because it was an accursed modern invention.

In the event, the Italo-Ethiopian war produced distinguished soldiers on the Ethiopian side, some of whom, dead or alive, remained in Ethiopia after the great defeat:

Imru, Ayelu, Afewerk, Malion. But was it to be expected in the summer of 1935 that any of them would know much about modern war? Particularly would they realise how enormously the disparity between Italian and Ethiopian armaments had spread since Adowa?

Apart from the essential introversion of Ethiopian leadership during the civil wars, the Ethiopian chief was not only a man of arms. Under the Emperor he was the general administrator of his province, with little leisure between tax-gathering and the hearing of legal cases to read the profounder works of modern military science, even if the mission bookshops had stocked them. There was no military college for chiefs in Addis Ababa and what, for the sake of abbreviation, was called in articles the General Staff consisted of widely disparate bodies, scattered abroad over the face of Ethiopia. A White Russian with a sense of humour in the Tigre . . . an Assyrian instructor of infantry in the Far West . . . Belgians in Dessye . . . Belgians being cut by Turks in Jijiga . . . a Belgian trying to turn three hundred camels into a Camel Corps at Ginir in the south . . . Tecla Hewariat and Professor Jeze sending advice from Geneva . . . Swedes being snubbed by Belgians in Addis Ababa . . . a few nice Ethiopian boys, beautifully attired, back from St. Cyr . . . old Ras Mulugeta, the Minister of War, sitting in hawk-eyed solitary state at the Gibbi or in his wood-and-iron War Ministry, ordering now a flogging and now a chaining.

It was only in January, 1935, that the first Ethiopian Cadets' School with a little over a hundred pupils, was inaugurated at Gunnet, some fifty kilometres west of Addis Ababa. The scheme was General Virgin's; he brought out five Swedish officers to organise a military course in infantry, artillery, signalling and engineering. As sixteen months was required for the course, the cadets were fully trained by the time the last Ethiopian War was over. During the last four months of the war they were instructed in the use of the new German anti-tank guns, which never saw battle. The only war-like activity of these boys—they were all between seventeen and twenty-one—was an O.T.C. camp, set up for a few days on Mount Tarmaber, to meet ten thousand Italians advancing from Dessye to Addis

Ababa. Many of them were murdered in the Addis riots; two helped to rescue the ex-*Reichswehrman* who had taught them anti-tank artillery, and sheltered in the German Legation.

Cognate with the lack of leadership was the lack of liaison and strategic control. The Emperor, when war came, was able to give Ras Desta in the south, and Ras Kassa in the north, each a radio set. He had already a fixed station and spare set at Harrar, and two portables in the Ogaden: he kept two portables for himself, ready for his Imperial progress to the northern front. By relayed telephone the Emperor could address Debra Markos, in Gojjam; Gondar and Amba Bircutan in the far north-west; Dessye and the whole eastern edge of the plateau up to Makalle; Erga Alem, the capital of Sidamo in the south; the railway zone, Harrar and the Ogaden. But the Ethiopian telephone is an erratic and slovenly instrument; it sometimes takes days to work. The Ethiopian radio was used on a code changed so rarely that the Italians found no difficulty in breaking it.

In the field organisation and liaison between the various army groups followed its two thousand-year-old model. The great Ras, though not necessarily jealous of each other, were often too proud to ask each other for help. They fought apart. Or they sent friendly messages by foot.

As scouts, except in the poaching districts of the Borana south of Sidamo, where Ras Desta was to attempt his invasion of Italian Somaliland, the Ethiopians were singularly deficient. Scouting is a nomad virtue, but the Ethiopian has been an agriculturist for two thousand years. He never learnt how to make a thorough reconnaissance, and though in civilian life capable of collecting complete information on every foreigner in Ethiopia, Military Intelligence in time of war was beyond him.

Something else disturbed the Emperor more.

Guerrilla warfare, which he preached, depends in the first place on freedom of movement between the points of contact with the enemy. Movement of such a kind was impossible in day time, because of the Italian Air Force. He gave orders that during the day time the men should keep in caves and under the scant bushes of the plateau, or dirty their shammas and lie on the ground when the aeroplanes were overhead. Even if bombs were dropped they were not to break cover.

He did not, I think, at first realise that the great majority of the Italian planes would concentrate, as they did, on the reconnaissance and dispersal of armies in the field. Nor did anybody else in Addis Ababa. They all foresaw mass air raids on the few towns and the single railway of Ethiopia, or on marching columns.

As it was, the vast number of first-class machines, of which the Italian Air Force disposed, literally tied to the ground the guerrilla forces of Ethiopia. From dawn to nightfall they kept up their droning survey; and when they had forced the guerrilla fighters under cover, they exploited their supremacy by means which will later be described.

Marching could only be done at night, as the Emperor knew. Considering that most of his troops were strangers to the province of Tigre, where the war was fought, control over these scrambling columns was going to be a serious business.

Guerrilla warfare depends in the second place on the readiness of the civilian population to support, feed, hide, encourage the guerrilla fighters. In its true form, in Spain, it was originally the war of the whole population.

The Tigre population were ready at first to support the fighting men; they followed Ras Seyyum rather than Dedjazmatch Haile Selassie Gucsa.

Aerial retribution, as intensive as it was rapid, was loosed upon the civil population of the Tigre villages. Areas where Ethiopian forces were believed to lurk were smashed up, and punitive expeditions followed to burn churches and search for arms.

It was the Emperor's plan to abandon part of the Tigre to the invader. The population here, ceded to the Italians by the exigencies of the Emperor's League policy and his guerrilla tactics, were made to understand clearly that so long as they supported the war they would be decimated, and that when they ceased to support it they would be left in their huts in peace.

Warfare against the civilian population magnifies the differences which already exist between its component parts. In Ethiopia, as the Emperor was to find, it led to strife between the races. In Europe it will lead to war between the classes.

Like all of us, the Emperor was waiting to see what the air could do.

In the north the Emperor's strategic plan (which was to be destroyed by the defection of Dedjazmatch Haile Selassie Gucsa) was as follows:

1. Cession of the Adowa-Entiscio-Adigrat line along the Shire-Adigrat range of mountains, on a line running parallel to the Eritrean frontier of the Mareb and fifteen to twenty miles south. This cession of territory was necessary for two reasons. In the north the Italians disposed of an overwhelming superiority of numbers in the front line; the Emperor knew that they would move three Army Corps from their three roads facing Adowa, Entiscio, Adigrat and radiating from Asmara. Against these he had only thirty thousand men of Seyyum and Haile Selassie Gucsa.

Italy, too, had to establish herself as the aggressor by invasion.

2. Tenure of Wolkait, the difficult region of north-western Ethiopia facing the Eritrean frontier, here much less strongly held by the Italians, between Om Ager on the Sudan border and the Shire uplands to the east. If possible, Dedjazmatch Ayelu was to cross the Takkaze river and create a diversion by invading Eritrea.

3. Withdrawal of Seyyum and Dedjazmatch Kassa Sebhat of Agame (Adigrat province) to a line half-way between the Adowa Adigrat line and Makalle. Of this line, Haile Selassie Gucsa was to form the centre. Defence of Makalle as long as possible, without risk of encirclement or open battle.

4. Meanwhile Kassa of Gondar and Mulugeta, the Ministers of War, to march their armies up in reserve, with the levy of Wollo, the province of the Crown Prince.

5. Ras Imru of Gojjam to move northwards to Gondar with his forces and take over the revictualment of the western part of the northern armies, also standing in reserve.

6. Ras Getatchu of Kafa, the far province in the south-west, to establish himself south-east of Dessye and await

a possible advance across Danakil from Assab. This threat was long taken seriously.

In the south the problem facing the Emperor was of an entirely different character. The Italian forces were, according to Ethiopian information, only fifty thousand compared with the two hundred thousand of Eritrea. Owing to the waterlessness, fever and intense heat of Somaliland, the proportion of native to European troops was abnormal, and this ill-balanced army had nearly one thousand kilometres of frontier to protect.

There was no question of Italian invasion on a broad front. The enemy could only follow the great Somaliland rivers in columns, the confluents of the Juba from Dolo in the west, or the Webbe Shebeli in the centre. Or they could pursue the wells of Gorahai, Sasabaneh, Daggahbur along the dry Tug beds of the Fafan and the Jerrer, wet-weather rivers.

The Juba confluents led to no objectives worth the risk. The other two routes led to Harrar, the second city of the empire, and the Emperor's own estate. Forces were therefore fixed on both of these, at Imi on the upper reaches of the Webbe Shebeli under the command of Dedjazmatch Bayenna Mared, Governor of Bale, and at several of the waterposts in the broad thorn waste of the Ogaden, under Dedjazmatch Nasibu, Governor of Harrar.

Ras Desta of Sidamo, the Emperor's son-in-law, and considered by him to be an able soldier, was to raise as large as force a possible and march it down the rivers Dawa Parma, Ganale Dorya and Web Gestro, under cover of their gigantic palms. There he would threaten the Italians at Dolo. If he could he was to infiltrate western Italian Somaliland on the flank of Dolo.

The armies at Imi and in the Ogaden were to hold their positions until a suitable moment arrived.

Never at any moment did the Emperor of Ethiopia believe that he could win by himself alone. He placed his hope entirely in the efficacy of League assistance: he decided to be the first to appeal to Article XVI of the Covenant as an aid in war. Barton, always the true friend, advised him not to settle the Walwal dispute by recourse to the League; but the claims of Italy were so enormous, the pretensions of her ruler so total and Haile Selassie's principles of honour so deeply rooted, that he could not settle the difference by surrender.

The League Policy was of his own choosing. He had always been an enthusiast for the League, partly because he believed that it promised him security to develop his country, partly because membership of the League seemed to him a proof that Ethiopia was advancing to equality with other nations.

This was mainly because the peaceful settlement of disputes was engrained in him. His whole career was evidence of it. He was demanded in 1916 as Regent, by a collective and uniform demarche of the British, French and Italian Ministers, because he would not, like Lij Yasu, meddle in the East African war, and because he wished to restore internal order. He never took the initiative of force against his enemies in Ethiopia: he left to them the privilege of revolt. By his peculiar methods of compromise and discussion, which his European critics called palaver and payment, peace and a growing prosperity were restored to the torn Ethiopia of his youth.

His fault was an unusual one in Africa: lack of suspicion. He believed in trusting people, hating to remove friends who had let him down. It was a long time before he admitted to himself, though he had all the proofs before him, that Dedjazmatch Haile Selassie Gucsa was going to betray him. Corrupt governors who had once served him well were not replaced . . . "their faults must be proved" . . . "the vice of my nation is intrigue and suspicion one against the other, I will believe nothing ill of him unless it is proved."

He also believed that the signatories of the Covenant would stand by their signatures. If they did, his military dispositions might well delay Italy until the Covenant began to squeeze her.

Haile Selassie never thought of his army as anything but a delaying force.

Lacking all arms, but perfectly satisfied with their prospects of victory, how were the Ethiopians prepared to meet the shock of disillusion?

In Addis patriotic societies were founded and for a short

time flourished. Except for a few of the older generation of Ethiopians brought up by the Roman Catholic Church, patriotism probably meant something more to the educated Ethiopian than it does nowadays to the emancipated Anglo-Saxon. Education in Africa is always a few decades behind the times; the French school text-books abounded in the spirit of Fashoda and even the Armenian schoolmasters professed a love of home.

Ethiopian patriotism, however, was not showy. They did not knock white men's hats off when the Imperial Guard band played the Tafari March. When a prominent English journalist clapped loudly at a film showing Italian army manœuvres at the outbreak of war, Lij Andarge Masai and Kidane Mariam, though bitterly offended, did not stir or say anything in their seats behind him. Italian subjects were not molested, even after the bombardment of Adowa. Two months of war passed before the young Ethiopians found that the enamelled plaque of the Casa Italiana was still in its old position; in one unparalleled organised effort they pulled it from its place, threw it into the street, jumped on it and kicked it. Afterwards they were rather ashamed of themselves.

The wealthy people of Shoa gave generously to Red Cross funds and war funds. But outside Addis Ababa and the province of Shoa, with its modern notions, patriotism did not mean much. It was another principle that prepared them for war. To understand what it was, one must draw back and take a long view at the Ethiopian plateau.

Ethiopia is a country which for centuries has lived quite statically and contentedly on the border-line between savagery and civilisation.

The Amharic centre has two main languages. Gheez for religion and the derived Amharic with provincial patois for everyday life. They correspond exactly to Latin and Italian in Italy.

In the far north the province of Tigre speaks Tigrina, an explosive tongue, distantly related to Amharic. It looks over the Eritrean frontier to its brothers in Eritrea, who are colingual. Just as the Italian-ruled Tyrolese, themselves on an edge of the mountains, look over a frontier on other fair people who share their speech and ways.

All these Ethiopian languages are written. Ethiopia is the only African country inhabited by a non-Mediterranean stock which has a written language.

At the same time it is mechanically backward. It has never made a wheel. Between the loaded mules and ponies of the plateau and the Chevrolet trucks of Mohammedally and Nasibu's Ogaden army, there are no gradations.

The earth, rich with millet, maize, wheat, guinea corn, is scratched by two pieces of a tree lashed together and shod with iron. That is their plough, older than Virgil's, in its parts far less neatly contrived than Odysseus' boat hammered in the isle of Calypso.

Small oxen—animals are small but sturdy in Ethiopia—drag the wood over large Ethiopian fields, whose soil is rich and heavy. In most parts they sow twice, in some even three times a year.

Particularly their barley is good, growing fat green heads in the damp mountain valleys, cosseted by the runnels cut down the hill-sides where the stone houses of the Amharas stand immune from the deluge each behind its lych gate. The grain grows up to the edge and into the fissures of the rock. The Gallas, wearing only the dirty loose jodhpurs that long Amharic rule or immixture has given them, bend their brown bodies over the barley to strip it with the hand.

On the plain, reaping is done with the short knife. When the Italians entered Addis Ababa they shot many peasants who owned these instruments, which they chose to consider weapons.

The crop is dried in neat little stooks and then divided into granary huts and small tufted haystacks. A beer called tella is made out of the barley and passed into big pottery jars. For feasts wild honey is taken from the trees and fermented to make tej, an African mead which gave me heartburn after every celebration.

At feasts, which follow regularly the vigorous fasts of the Coptic church, the Ethiopians eat raw meat. They believe that it makes them strong and honourably ferocious. An after-effect, for the meat is not always new, is often worms. This common Ethiopian affliction, excuse for much indolence and release from many dull engagements, is swept away in a devastating purge by a brew from the Kosso-tree.

Staple tree of the Ethiopian system, the kosso grows to

great size and greenery in every Ethiopian village. Its long red sprays, symbol of complete evacuation, dangle over nearly every Ethiopian landowner's hut.

So extensive and continuous is it in its operation that the happy patient can lie abed for days, refusing to go to the front, and at the same time evading unwelcome visitors with the simple statement, uttered sonorously through the soundboard of a servant: "His honour has taken medicine."

Refuge of the shirker, sure bastion from the bore, kosso eased many social contacts and lubricated the Ethiopian engine in more ways than one.

I allowed my servants kosso only once a month.

Living in this atmosphere of primitive calm, disturbed but occasionally by the fruit of the national tree, the Ethiopian was nevertheless the most advanced of the African race. His manners were, to the full degree of the words, spontaneous and perfect: the most formal acts of courtesy seemed to be done with enthusiasm. It may have been the tenth time in the day that he dismounted from his mule to kiss a friend four times consecutively in the street, but he still did it with a look of acute pleasure in his eye. Chiefs in the country, wives of my friends, even chance acquaintances were invariably hospitable to me. I was immediately seated in the most comfortable chair, which would be ulphostered in Armenian plush, and presented with coffee, whatever the hour. If coffee was rejected, something else was offered; in the end I had to open my mouth and let it pass.

For sign that I was really welcome and would be considered a friend until I proved myself the contrary, food was put into my mouth by the hand of my host. This amicable form of forcible feeding was often accompanied by a hearty slap between the shoulders, inviting me to drink as its owner had drunken.

All Ethiopians eat, and the rich very delicately, with the hands. They wash them between courses with water poured out of a ewer. Ewer seems an artistic word to use for a country not so poor as to depend upon its own pottery, nor rich enough to import the plate of a city company. In short, they poured the water out of a glorified coffee pot.

A deadweight upon Ethiopian development, yet somehow the mean of her advance, lay the Ethiopian Coptic Church. Its monasteries, translation of the celebrated "Debra" which prefixes so many Ethiopian place-names, were scattered all over the plateau, teaching the Ethiopian to write, yet at the same time restricting his economic growth. For the Church is a great landowner and maintains the principle of serfdom with a rigidity founded, like everything arguable in Ethiopia, upon the Old Testament and the tradition of Solomon and Sheba.

The church schools, since they taught a common caligraphy, spread a common culture over Ethiopia. But this unifying force was discounted by their extreme laziness as a class. They loved nothing more than political intrigue, provided that they could sit down to it. They were used by the Emperor for his espionage service, but they were easily intimidated by any display of force.

At the centre of this quiet country life, and framework of the peasantry and the Church, both of whom paid it vast respect, lay the peculiar Ethiopian system of chieftainship.

It has been described, and I shall describe it in shorthand, as a feudal system. But it has little kinship with the feudal systems of Europe. It was, above all, the element in Ethiopian life which *changed*. The peasantry remained the same, the Church and language remained the same. But the chiefs and the King of Kings at its head, changed continually.

The Ethiopian system was not a feudal system: it was a tough-man system. Its type was Ras Mulugeta, the Minister of War when I was in Ethiopia; or Fitorari Hapta Giorghis, the Galla who was Minister of War before him.

These men rose through their warlike abilities in the time of Menelik. They began with the rank of simple Ato — the Ethiopian esquire; they went through all the grades that were open to them. Hapta Giorghis was not a Ras, because he was pure Galla: but as the Fitorari and ruler of rich provinces he was the equal if not the superior of the Ras of the plateau.

With new Emperors, new men sprang to the front and, according to the strength of the central power, were given provinces on the periphery. Families which, because of their connection with an older dynasty, considered themselves the equal of its successor were either eliminated or absorbed.

In peaceful times absorption was the more usual method. It led to the establishment of a Blood Royal. Direct rules of succession did not exist in Ethiopia: the strongest man of the blood succeeded, supported by his retainers and his wisdom.

Equally vague was the marriage system in Ethiopia. Church marriage, which was very rare, was indissoluble. The Emperor Haile Selassie, who wished to stabilise Ethiopian conduct, encouraged Church marriage among his young nobility.

But the prevailing marriage was purely civil. Divorce could be obtained by either party at will and upon an even division of the common property. In Ethiopia women had equal rights. Women owned land, were notoriously fickle, had much power in the home. There was no attempt to hide them. The veil was an attribute of the upper class of both sexes, and served to protect the face from the sight of the vulgar and the ravages of the sun.

The same elastic dualism existed in the law. There were the judges of the Emperor, either his experts in Addis Ababa or his governors in the provinces, who judged according to the rigid laws assembled in Gheez since time immemorial.

But the commonest way to settle a dispute was that of neighbourly justice. Cases were tried in the streets or in the country-side by any stranger by whose decision both parties agreed to abide. This system of rough equity corresponded closely to the matrimonial system outlined above. In their way they were more rational than any other system of law or of marriage that I have met or read of in Africa. But they shared the Ethiopian vice of being vague, slipshod, remiss.

Political systems which are based upon such ill-defined and generous standards as the Ethiopian find compensation in some unifying principle of startling severity. The Ethiopian principle was that of chieftainship.

There was one order to which all Ethiopians responded at once; that of the *tillik sau*, the great man, He inflicted often the most terrible punishments: he commanded his followers to face the most fearful risks: he fed them on the most astounding amount of bullocks and mead. His word, his whips, his generosity, the unquestioned objects of his intrigue were the sole law for them. He entered into counsel with his equals or with his sub-chiefs, but he admitted no popular assembly.

The people obeyed him. That was the basis of Ethiopian defence. As long as their chiefs seemed capable to meet the aggressor they would follow them.

VI

SOME PEOPLE IN AUGUST, when England relaxes, thought that there would be no war. Committees were sitting in Europe: it was hoped that, at any rate, the Walwal dispute would be settled. It was!

Italy agreed to a formula. One could distinguish the international relief far away on the African plateau. Anything to put off the terrible day when the League powers would have to carry out their pledges. Almost any formula would do.

Barton had to sound the Emperor on the farthest he would go in the way of concession. To the old offer of territorial exchange—the Ogaden for Zeila—the Emperor added the Sultanate of Aussa, magnificent ranching country behind Italian Assab, for a sum of money, the amount and the uses of which were to be discussed.

The Emperor and Colson, however, had decided that war was inevitable. Money was needed for arms, and more publicity for the Ethiopian cause. The embargo still obtained, although England and France had relaxed the embargo on transit through Djibouti and Berbera. A meaningless concession! As long as Britain maintained the pressure which she called a policy, the states who sold arms to Ethiopia continued to refuse licences for export. She still led the world.

Colson had to get the money. He wanted two million pounds at least; he knew a good deal about the mineral possibilities of Ethiopia, and Rickett knew enough. The famous Rickett concession was drawn up. Only a small part of the purchase could have gone towards the buying of arms, but it was believed in Europe that the whole would. Ethiopia was selling all that she could sell—her own mineral resources, belonging to her Emperor and alienable only by him.

Britain was hurt at the suggestion that she had her interests in Ethiopia to defend, and, believing that there was English capital in the concession, made speed to kill it.

I missed Rickett. He was going up to Addis with Evelyn Waugh and Emeny, of the *News Chronicle*, when I was on my way down the line to Diredawa. We met halfway: a few words were exchanged with his group at a midday halt. I took him for another journalist.

When his story broke I was deep in the Ogaden.

Earlier in August the Emperor had smartened up his Press bureau by the addition of Lorenzo Taezaz. Lorenzo came from Harrar, where he had kept touch with the British, French and Italian consuls as the Governor's "political director," and where he had created an Imperial Ogpu, mild but omniscient.

Lorenzo was born in Eritrea and received his first education in the Italian schools. He rose to be secretary to the Governor in Asmara when he was still very young, for Lorenzo is quick as lightning. It was the highest position that he could reach: Lorenzo is not a white man. Embittered by his servile condition, he could bear it no longer after a scene in a small cinema to which Italian friends had invited him. Other Italians hissed them for bringing in a coloured man. Lorenzo was already miserable enough. With his savings he fled to Aden, and waited there in poverty until the Emperor picked him up.

The Emperor's main weapon of reform was his civil service, formed of men, some now middle-aged, some passed over already to the Italians, who owed their foreign education and their position in Ethiopia to him. The older men of rank, who still wore baggy white jodhpurs, with bandages round their heads and straggly beards round their chins, and like as not the patent-leather shoes that Menelik affected—these did not like the civil service. The young men entered their so-called Ministries as "Directors." The Directors, the old men felt sure, were certain to displace them one day. So to keep them in their places they made these young men with moustaches and European clothes bow down to the ground in the presence of age; and if the young whipper-snappers still wore shammas, they had to tie them across their chests out of respect for the old men's blood and rank. Meanwhile the old men would sit heavily in their chairs exchanging words of primeval wisdom, supporting their policy by proverbs, and pretending not to notice the callow youth around them. These, whether the old men were talking or silent, had to keep their tongues still.

They let off steam at the Young Ethiopians' Society. Not only did the educated returned from Europe belong to this institution: there was room for those who had only a primary education in the Emperor's schools in Addis, and who were then drafted off to do technical or clerical work at the radio, the post office, the customs or the railway. The second class, as it were, of the Emperor's civil service.

All these young men—they must run into thousands—owed everything to the Emperor. Some of them were spoilt, as are many who come suddenly into contact with the West. But not the majority. Most did their work painstakingly, rather ploddingly and dully—like civil servants the world over.

Above and beyond them were a chosen few who were close to the Emperor's person. Wolde Giorghis, the boy of no birth but profound capacity for quiet calculation, who, from a dispenser in a mission hospital, became the Emperor's Imperial Secretary. His enemies—he had a ruthless manner—say that he learnt his French off the labels, but that seems to give him too great a power of self-improvement.

Ato Belatchu, director of the railway company, the frankest and most helpful Ethiopian that I ever met. Much younger, Sirak Herrouy, who was his father's secretary at the Ministry of Foreign Affairs: Sirak had been at B.N.C. when I was at the House, a good slow bowler. Ato Tasfai Tegan, the stout Director of Foreign Affairs. Tasfai enjoyed his comforts, his wine, his girl-friends. He did not like to be hurried. He had travelled a lot in Europe. He dressed European, with perfect good taste. His French was also perfect. He had a great sense of lazy humour. There was a border-line between his insouciance and his intelligence that was difficult to fix. Suddenly he could be serious and work hard and well. At other times he curled up in the Emperor's throne in the Council Chamber, and fell into a light sleep.

And Lorenzo, to whom the Emperor now gave the Press bureau.

Lorenzo had been sent by the Emperor to the University of Montpelier, where he studied law. He came back Maitre Lorenzo Taezaz. He served as a judge on the Mixed Anglo-Ethiopian Boundary Commission, and followed the Walwal incident on the spot. As chief of the Ogpu, he expelled Monfreid, the French author of "Hashish," from Diredawa: and he opened out the tangle which was to lead to the arrest of the Comte de Rocquefeuille at Jijiga that very month of August. A bright, penetrating mind, with a love of the mysterious engendered by his new profession. The Ethiopian cloak that he always wore over his European suit gave rare romantic covering to the trait of character that engaged me most.

I had several secret meetings with Lorenzo, who braced up the Press bureau to higher standards of efficiency: even fixing hours when there would be someone in the office. Lorenzo could be sharply amusing. When I felt out of patience with a colleague he would restore me with an accomplished imitation of the faking brute. He moved nimbly from point to point in his car and in his mind as well. There were no languors in conversation with him. When he had finished, off he ran.

We used to talk, with maps, about the Ogaden and about what Desta was going to do. Lorenzo rapidly traced on my sheets the new Ogaden roads, cut by the Boundary Commission and after.

He arranged for me a journey to the Ogaden.

I left, all muffled up in secrecy, by the Diredawa train on August 20. Only an Armenian tailor saw me off, shrieking for payment, and panting along the permanent way.

A pink-faced French engineer sat in front of me. His charm, for he was young, was marred by a huge growth on one of his cheeks. He told me that he was *chef de section* of the area including the Hawash bridge. It would take a month to replace it by the corvee system if it were damaged by bombardment: the substitute would be to the south of the present bridge.

I sent this information off from Harrar two days later. The operator obligingly translated it into Amharic and the receiver in Addis translated it back into French. Anglicised by Rohrbaugh, the American missionary who was acting for *The Times*, it might have caused a war if it had been published. It would certainly have shaken the committees at Geneva. It began: "The tangled wreckage of the Hawash bridge, blow up and then down again by Italian aeroplanes..."

Rohrbaugh thought he had better confirm that.

Like nearly all the French, the engineer disliked the Ethiopians intensely. Hatred of Ethiopia was the obverse of that coin on whose other side were impressed the two heads of Laval and Mussolini, Rome *Janvier* 1935. For the engineer, the Ethiopians had *"très mauvaise mentalité."* They did not prevent the Danakil from cutting the company's telephone wire or putting stones on the rails for fun. The engineer attributed nearly every tropical check to the *mauvaise mentalité* of the Ethiopian governing class, who needed to be civilised and put in their place. He used the phrase four times.

It was because of the predatory habits of the Danakil that the railway company had to instal cheaper wire. The government telephone on the other side of the railway line lay for long unhappy stretches on the ground. "But," said the engineer, "it's better than ours because it's copper. If the Danakils cut the Government's wire the Government take all their cattle away. But they don't do that for us—never! They just delay for months on end. We present a huge bill for damages every year, but do you think they ever pay it?" he asked.

"No," said I, "their *mentalité* is too *mauvaise*."*

South of Miesso, in the Arussi country, are numerous

* Actually all damages of this kind were paid annually by the Government at the time of the annual settlement of accounts, that is, by way of deduction from the amount due from the company to the Government as dividends on the Government's shares and as the Government's contractual participation in the profits of the company.

coffee plantations run by white men. A thin, grey-haired French planter was lunching there—at the clean little Greek restaurant where the trains stopped at noon. He was going home, after thirty years in Africa. It was no good. Dedjaz Amde, the Governor, had mobilised all the men who worked for him and taken all the mules that he used to hire. Amde showed no consideration. There were only six planters left in Arussi. There used to be forty, but gradually Ethiopians learnt to be overseers and pushed the others out. Gloom descended steeply over the old man. After thirty years in Africa pioneers assume that they have given everything to the ungrateful continent.

Diredawa! The Greeks are reading their alarmist news sheet avidly. Everybody is on the border of panic. An Ethiopian station guard has just biffed an Italian courier over the head because he persisted, after remonstrances, in pushing baggage through the carriage window instead of through the carriage door, in contravention of the company's bye-laws.

Lij Worku, a friend of mine who was chief of the railway police at Diredawa, had seen the incident. "Yes," he said, with great satisfaction, "and even when he got down to Djibouti he had to be carried by four men."

For six dollars I got a seat next the driver in a lorry going up to Harrar—fifty-six kilometres. Lij Worku fixed everything up.

It was a funny lorry. Two Ethiopian boys sat on the front mudguards "for stones," said the driver. This cryptic remark was explained later at turnings in the mountain road to Harrar, when the boys jumped off and fixed stones behind the wheels until the engine cooled down.

The back was filled, really filled, with bundles, natives of Ethiopia, chickens and mules. They got on excellently from start to finish. Now and then one of the live stock rolled over another, while the natives were continually jumping off the lorry to buy or sell things at the roadside. Looking at them with an economist's eye, I was quite dazzled by the ease with which they exchanged the rôles of retailer and consumer. Sociologically too there was a lot to be said for the lorry: in motion, a perfectly peaceful relationship bound together man, beast of burden, and feathered fowl. They all looked with half-glazed eyes towards Harrar, their earthly goal.

I thought that I would be alone with the lorry driver, when Haji Asfar Omar turned up. The Haji was unknown to me then, but he greeted me as if that made no difference. In face and figure, even to the prosperous smile, he resembled exactly the Aga Khan leading in a winner. He was huge, his hair was white, his slippers slapped broadways on the Diredawa pavement. His long Somali coat, dazzlingly white, covered a powerful frame now running to fat, and over his arm hung, like a toy baton, a full-size black umbrella. The Haji was chuckling as he sat down beside me, leaving me the notoriously uncomfortable position between the gear-handle and the brake. I trembled to think that at any moment he might slap me on the back and render me unfit for war-service.

Instead, he turned his magnificent horn-rimmed spectacles upon me, and said, in blithe, broken English: "So you going to Ogaden? You want informations? You want bedding?"

From that day to this I have been unable to settle the question of Haji Asfar Omar: how he knew that I was going to the Ogaden and, above all how he knew that I had left all my kit in Addis.

He took out his card and handed it to me. He expressed himself with some freedom about the Ethiopians. "They won't win, they can't organise," he said. "And your Somalis?" I asked. "They'll talk a lot, and they'll follow the stronger." True enough!

Haji Asfar Omar did not like the English much. He was a British Somali, but he had fallen out with the Government of British Somaliland. "Don't you know my case?" he asked, and proudly pulled from his portmanteau a thick dossier of typewritten paper describing a claim laid by the Haji before the Secretary of State. He shook with pleasure when I assured him that, if my influence had any weight, his case (which was incomprehensible to me) would be ventilated in *The Times*. "The English," he said, "they are the best rulers in the world. It is all mercy, pity, peace—and they squeeze the blood out of you." A long chuckle followed this devastating witticism.

On my return I was shewn the papers of a man who had been arrested on a charge of espionage for Italy. A single entry took my attention. "An old Somali says that an Englishman, St. George, has gone down to the Ogaden."

Even now I had alarming premonitions. Since our conversation was always leading us back to the Ogaden, I pretended an overwhelming interest in the view of the country-side around us. The make-believe was a game well worth while.

Diredawa is a collection of bungalows built by the French when the town was their concession, in square blocks, with electricity laid on. There is a bank, a barber's shop, a series of Greek hotels and grocers, a French consulate, houses of the railway administration and its polyglot employees, tennis courts, and an Armenian soccer ground.

It was a matter of a minute to get out of dusty Diredawa, up a dry river bed carpeted in smooth mud. To the right we passed a tumbledown house of stone and corrugated iron; an enclosure spotted with aged cannon, unwieldy barrels on tiny wheels or rusted iron blocks. Some pointed to heaven, others to Diredawa or to earth. Many lay wearily on their sides, quite overcome with grass. Grass grew rank over the compound. The Ethiopians are vague about these guns; all they know for sure is that they should have been dragged all the way to Harrar, but the road was too tiring and the guns too heavy, so they stayed just a little outside, and a little above, Diredawa. They are said to be of Austrian manufacture, and one legend connects them with the Adowa campaign, another with the civil wars after the death of Menelik.

We started to climb. The road, a good earth-road only two years old, supplanted a more primordial track which wound fantastically among the thin-bushed mountains to the left. Spiny cactus and grey-green euphorbia, all knots and crazy candelabra, fringed the older path along which now and then protruded the gross heads of camels, swinging forward, far away, over the dry riverbed. The only noise above the frizzle of the radiator when the lorry stopped was the single-note creak of insects in the heat. Silently, troops of baboons paraded rump-high along the ledges across the river, scouts squatting before and behind. In small patches next the wide sandy channel natives kept dry fields of mealies. It was so dry and hot that one could almost hear the stalks crackle and break beneath their feet as they walked slowly through the fields. Nothing bent before the pressure of a light wind from Harrar—the mealie leaves flapped stiffly like thin wood on hinges, the mimosas which sprinkled the burnt grass over valley and mountainside maintained their shadeless rigidity. The earth was scored with fissures, dry and burning to the touch, where the sun had knifed the solid ground. The Ethiopians behind began to drink water. Haji told me a marvellous story about the guns which I found it too hot to remember.

Behind us was the Danakil plain, dry and serrated beyond Diredawa, stretching without end north, east and west. The sky looked yellow, transparent and cruel as a cat's-eye above it. Over the Danakil levels, broken sometimes by hard round hills of seeming rock, there were no clouds. It was the same harsh sight that I saw again from the Galla borderlands near Dessye—a tangled unromantic pattern of all the colours that give no relief, from dirty white through dull yellow and brown to dingy purple, exposed in pitiless detail and leaving no impression but an inward heat. Over these bones of the world wheeled a few lean-necked birds without eyelids.

There are sudden changes on the road to Harrar. In fifty-six kilometres you climb 2,500 feet. You rise to the fresh air of the Harrar upland—the broken plateau of the Harrar-Gue, rich in fruit, corn and cattle, where a city has existed, and ruled itself, on a trade with Arabia for hundreds of years. Harrar was once the greatest slave and coffee staple of the Red Sea world. You find a culture quite separate from that of the people round Diredawa, or that of any unit in Ethiopia.

The gate to this new world used to be made of two pieces of corrugated iron, supported by two wooden posts and kept rather unwillingly together with a rusty padlock. I believe the Italians have demonstratively knocked it down. The iron was marked "Wolverhampton."

At this gate, fixed roughly halfway upon the road and surrounded by *khat* groves, you used to show your pass to Harrar. I had none but slipped through by the simple process: *When in difficulties and in Africa, keep quiet.*

The air was fresher, the earth a deeper red. Instead of breaking like old cake it held in warm clods. Khat, the tall bare-stalked shrub whose glossy dark green leaves Harraris chew for dope, grew in neat rows around. As we passed, bare-breasted Galla women of the Harrar country side pressed themselves against the rock-face in fear of our swaying machine; on their backs were heavy loads of the smooth leaf.

We were through the gates. We passed the soft mountain lake of Harrarmaya, where the young Tafari once saved himself from drowning when the rest of his boat-load went under. In the maize, which pestilence had killed, heavy loll-humped Zebu oxen were munching the rotten stalks. It was a huge maizefield, inexplicably struck down.

On a short slope more women had set out baskets. This was a market where they sold injura, the Ethiopian bread made in flat porous pancakes, coffee beans and khat. As we drew level, two men got out of an old Ford and stopped us. First they talked with the driver, who shook in succession his head, his body and his arms, and uttered excitable noises of protest. Then with Haji Asfar Omar, who put on one of his most learned airs, as if he indeed were receiving secret "informations." The Haji came back and said: "You must get down and go with them. They are very suspicious about you. They say, where's your pass."

Fearful, but clutching my rifle still, I abandoned my baggage and stepped, as they grimly invited me, into the old Ford. One of the two Ethiopians was in khaki with a topee to match and a fluffy blue feather to the side of it; he looked sporting, I hoped he would give me a chance. He talked with a stutter, had an athletic rawbone face. The other, who drove, was much smaller and more delicately made, an obvious clerk.

We drove rapidly towards Harrar, leaping over obstructions

in a way that would have given Henry, the father of all Fords, more pleasure than an old-age pension. I was terrified. Who were these bandits?

When the lorry was well behind, their features relaxed into a friendly grin and they introduced themselves. The soldier, Balambaras Ali Nur: "I am to take you all over the Ogaden for the Emperor"; the civilian, Ato Haile: "I am the secretary of the Governor of Harrar, who is in the Ogaden, but in his place I will give you fruit, whisky and sodawater. You will sleep in Lorenzo's home at Harrar."

Harrar appeared over the hill. A few European buildings, then the new stucco-Imperial palace of the Duke of Harrar, the Emperor's second and favourite boy, for whom Nasibu was now ruling. The town-wall, of mud and stone; narrow gates under whose crumbling lintels a crowd of human beings jostled in and out. Harrar, immemorially, is the only fenced city in Ethiopia. Above the town, whose houses were a continuous brown-washed maze without gardens, almost without streets, rose two high pinnacles, dirty white, and the purer towers of a thick-set building whose blinding white square dominated the mound of Harrar. The pinnacles were the Mosque, the towers stood watch on the old palace of Ras Makonnen, Menelik's great governor and the Emperor's father, Ethiopia's first modernist. The half-eroded lions at their gate now guarded Ethiopia's second wireless station. The whitewashed French hospital, whose courtyard was shaded by the pink showers of the pepper trees and the pink oleander, stood across the road at the town-centre, Feres Magallo. Below and to the south, a brown and ancient honeycomb, lay Harrar old town, built with sand, dark wall jammed against dark wall, packed with people and smelling to high heaven.

The Harrar women were beautifully dressed and all in the same range of colours: a multiple design of black, crimson and bright yellow. Bangles held arms and ankles, the head was covered with a sari, the soft legs were veiled in muslin trousers which tightened above the foot. They walked about freely; their features were small and elegant.

Lepers stood to right and left of the narrow road, exposing

their choicest parts and invoking in one monotonous breath the divine pity and the financial backing of the foreigner.

Dark bearded soldiers swaggered round barefoot in khaki. Officers in foppish high-heeled sandals talked indolently in the Greek liquor shops. This side of the town was a small undulating plain on which soldiers were drilling under a white instructor. It was once more the remorseless Left-Right, the Gra-Ken of the Imperial Guard recruits. N.C.O.'s were being trained to go back to the highland provinces of Chercher and the Arussi, where they would drill and command the household troops of Dedjas Amde and Lij Sefu. Three thousand men. Four Belgian instructors, well-paid and well-covered.

Soldiering's final phase lay along a gully to the right. In shady fat-leaved trees above Harrar's ancient burial ground sat black and white ravens cleaning their beaks upon the branches: for interment in Harrar was not necessarily deep. Mohammedan tombstones, bones and offal lay just beyond the parade ground dust.

To the right and left, but most into the deep valley to the south, stretched far away the garden-farms of Harrar, where the people live and work in the daytime, watering their fruit-trees, bananas and oranges, tending their coffee and lolling in the Eastern shade, distracted languidly by khat. The Harraris are a soft, complacent people who gave no difficulties to the Amhara conqueror. They professed a longing for independence something akin to the Croatian, for they were too cultured to fight for it. In Harrar city they were ruled under their own laws, which are Koranic, and for a long time they were not mobilised for the war against Italy.

I was taken to a house a mile outside the city. I only stole away once to see old Feron, the bearded Roman Catholic doctor who runs a leper hospital under the city walls. His is an uphill struggle; leprosy uncured and exhibitionist is profitable in Harrar.

Feron believes in catching them young and marrying them off early. He lent me a camera, and with an artist's enthusiasm showed me his best close-ups of the disease. His lepers are happy couples who dwell peacefully in their own huts and are given money to prepare their own food. They live to a ripe old leprosy and die in the odour of Feron's surgery, at just about the age you and I die.

Their philosophical attitude, supported by faith in the copper with which Feron injects them, encouraged me too to bear the mysteries of my present existence with contentment. Where Ali Nur was going to take me I knew not, but the balmy air of Harrar soon rolled me in a pleasant sleep.

VII

BEFORE I LEFT NEXT MORNING I spoke to Ato Ambai, an Eritrean like Lorenzo, whom he had succeeded as Political Director at Harrar.

Ato Ambai told me that he had left Eritrea like all who had reached a certain level of education and could not bear a racial tyranny. These were his own words. He was a sombre man who thought a lot and spoke very little; there was no optimism in him to encourage me.

"The Tigre will be our hardest war. It has always stopped small-scale invasions, but it cannot stop this one.

"The Eritrean soldiers of Italy despise their masters after what they saw of them in the Libyan campaign. We know that it was our men who won Libya for Italy. But they will be loyal to Italy: they are well armed and well clothed, and it is that that keeps them. I think that the Eritreans will beat our men.

"You have let us down like savages in the matter of arms. When you give up your pious embargo it will be too late."

I took down what he said in a note-book as we jostled away in a government lorry to Jijiga. Ato Ambai, like his Emperor, had very little hope of a military victory, but he behaved with perfect loyalty to his people until the end. As I look at the dusty page now, he seems to have spoken with a prophet's voice.

We were supposed to leave Harrar at eight that August morning, but punctuality is not an Ethiopian vice, and we were ready at 2.15. Ali Nur had to find me a cook and a bodyguard. The soldiers, who belonged to his own corps, appeared at once in their strange uniforms, khaki coats and shorts, stockings with the feet cut off to preserve the calf against the Ogaden thorn, dirks and forage caps with long flaps falling down the neck behind, and a single pointed piece of cloth sticking up defiantly in front. "That," said an interpreter, "is to make them look brave, like buffaloes." Ostrich feathers protruded from the muzzles of their rifles, against the Ogaden dust. They were good lads, well-disciplined and quick: Ali Nur had organised them since Wal Wal.

Moosa, the cook, took a deal more finding, said Ali Nur when he came back from Harrar town at two o'clock. Moosa was an unprepossessing creature, basically negroid in appearance, but superficially owing much of his peculiar style to the operations of smallpox. His smile might have been described as disarming if it had not exposed a row of yellow teeth. In figure Moosa was squat and slavish. By what process he was enlisted to be my cook I never knew. Moosa was both ignorant and contemptuous of the best methods of preparing food. There was nothing he liked better than to open a tin.

At first I treated him like a dog; it was only later in the Ogaden journey that I discovered in the downtrodden but careless Moosa seeds of good servile humour. Till then he had concealed from me the low opinion he had of everybody else his own colour. When the Ethiopians spoofed me at Gerlogubi, he could restrain himself no longer. His coarse laugh broke the desert silences, and from then until I said good-bye Moosa could not be stilled.

As we went away, Ali Nur took his seat at my side.

It was 8.30 when he reached Jijiga, over two flooded rivers, the Fafan and the Errer, and over sixty miles of mountain earth track, shapen by lorry wheels and the feet of mules into an execrable road.

Enjoyable discomfort for me: I found Ali Nur so engaging a companion.

Ali Nur, if he is still alive, has an unusual record. He is about thirty-five years old, and says that he was born in Wallamo. He is not Amhara. His Mohammedanism sits easily upon him, for he drinks whisky, gin, champagne, beer, tej, and when he can find it in the Ogaden, water. Aden Gold Flake is his favourite kind of cigarette. This African freelance was once in the King's African Rifles; later (though he pretended to me that he could not speak

English), he served Captain Pennefather-Holland in Maji as consular interpreter. He was obviously devoted to Holland, whose prowess with the revolver—"he killed crocodiles"—had graven itself indelibly on Ali Nur's martial mind. Captain Holland died "in my hands," said Ali Nur, describing in painful detail the last moments of blackwater fever. But not before Holland had taught Ali Nur that it was wrong to shoot a sitting bird—"kufu, kufu," said Captain Holland ("bad, bad"). "In England we flog people for doing that."

It was three months later, when I revisited Jijiga, that Ali Nur took me aside and said: "Why don't you English who tell people not to kill birds sitting, tell the Italians to stop using their aeroplanes on us as we lie on the ground. It was cruel at Gorahai. You must stop the Italians, or give us planes." Ali Nur's whole attitude to war was the sporting one.

After the Consul's death he had taken service with the Emperor, who liked to use Mohammedans. His experience as a soldier and his distinction as a shot got him a job which exactly fitted him. Ali Nur, the bow-legged and friendly sportsman, was sent to organise a special corps of Somali scouts in the Mohammedan Ogaden. The men in the peculiar uniforms who accompanied us were his products. A sort of Ethiopian Foreign Legion, they were composed of all sorts of bandits, Somali roughnecks, the furthest rolling stones of the highly nomadic Ogaden, elephant hunters and men thrown out of our own Camel Corps for drunkenness, theft, desertion, insubordination, not polishing their boots and all the other marks of a good soldier.

Under Ali Nur, who treated his men with the same surehanded familiarity as do the best English officers, this mobile thieves' kitchen became a real *corps d'élite*. They stood their ground against the armoured cars and the plane at Wal Wal, when the others ran away. They were the backbone of the Ogaden resistance in the months to come.

Ali Nur had two other functions. He was Game Warden and Chief Intelligence Officer of the Ogaden.

He liked animals; as we went along the Jijiga track through the mountains, ravines, massive mimosas and wide grain-fields of the Harrargue, ever uphill and down dale, he told me the Amharic names of all the birds that flew over the radiator. He added to his capacities that of mastery-over the automobile. We were three in front of the lorry; when the driver seemed to be tiring—the track was that of a switchback with alternate rocks and holes instead of rails— Ali Nur took the wheel and drove with an incredible care and smoothness. A slow puncture was noticed long before I detected anything odd, and the tyre repaired and replaced in twenty minutes. It had to be repaired: Ali Nur, who was also generous to a fault, had given our spare wheel to another lorry in difficulties ten kilometres back.

Asthma was a complaint of Ali Nur's. At a stop he said "azma" to me in his funny stutter, and took a small tin out of a kitbag at the back of the lorry. It contained a bottle and a hypodermic syringe. I wondered what this world was in which I travelled, as a regenerate Somali brigand in khaki delicately injected pituitary into a sporting Wallamo.

Nightfall in the Harrar mountains was a rich purple blush in the sky behind black walls of rock. Flying foxes sped across our headlights as we fetched up against another corrugated iron gate, where a sleepy porter rubbed white encrustrations out of his eyes to recognise the permit of Ali Nur. We rolled down the eastern side of the pass of Karramarra in deep night. Huge clouds of dust in the flat, no trees, half-hidden lights rimming the doors of houses scarcely outlined along a dark street, a wind steadily cooling from the south told me that we were in Jijiga, headquarters of the Ogaden.

Three or four Ethiopians flashed torches. We stopped. I was taken into a two-roomed house, behind the usual Ethiopian palisade. With grave courtesy I was shown the lavatory, which was altogether salubrious.

As they led me back to the dining-room, where a feast of sardines and various kinds of wot, the Ethiopian curry, was ready, they explained to me that these modest but cleanly quarters of mine were the town house of Gerazmatch Afewerk, Director of Jijiga and the Ogaden, now commanding the advanced posts on the Fafan and the Webbe Shebeli.

Ali Nur is a hero-worshipper. "He has been nine months solid in the Ogaden—there's a soldier for you."

Afewerk was half Amhara, half Kafa—a slave race. He had risen to military command from the Empress's household. Like Ali Nur, he commanded many soldiers; with Ali Nur he was the most important officer in the south. Neither of these men had birth to aid them, and the two had one Amhara parent between them. Yet Ethiopia will, I suppose, go down to history as a country with a decayed feudal system, whose subject races were cruelly oppressed.

In the Ethiopia of Haile Selassie, the young man of character or intelligence, whatever his race, had more opportunities that he will ever have under European rule. The tragedy of the Ethiopian war was that not enough of them had risen to squeeze out the old politicians and fixers of the civil wars who sat so heavily at the top. But in Harrar and the Ogaden, provinces under the Emperor's own hand, the keen men had their full liberty. It is to that, and to the ease with which arms were supplied to the Ogaden front, that I attribute its stubborn resistance at the finish.

As we settled down to the sardines there was a scuffle at the door. It was Ali Nur playing with a buck that he had caught in the Ogaden and brought up on the bottle. Round the corner the young Kudu stuck its head, already overgrown by one twist of the curling horns. It was called Afewerk "because it can butt." But at meal-times Afewerk behaved perfectly: he came up to be given bread and pressed his cold black nozzle into one's neck for more.

The photograph of Afewerk in court dress superintended our dinner-party from the wall. I raised the lamp to look at it. It was a head and shoulders, blurred at the edges by the uncertain art of the Armenian photographer, who was clearly unwilling to make any positive and final statement about anything for fear of a massacre. But even the vague mist which he threw about the chest-spread shamma and high, ferocious hair of Afewerk could not remove the impression of force in the features. Afewerk looked fiercely in front of him: there was none of that mildness and quietist poise which I had seen in photographs of the great northern Ras at Addis. His dark, large eyes were not those of peace or repose; they were full of fire. His lips, though wide, were set upon a firm, straight line. The chin, heavy and jutting, was that of an African or indeed any man courageous enough but without the means to defend his property. Afewerk hated Europeans.

Director of Jijiga before the preparations for the war, he had taken an interest in the Tafari Makonnen School, whose prize-givings he attended. A speech of his on one of these occasions praised "the scholars for their tenacity and the teachers for their civilisation." He saw to it that when the Anglo-Ethiopian Boundary Commission started off on its survey of the pastures, watering-places and confines of the Ogaden, almost half the Jijiga boys' school should follow the Ethiopian section to study the management of wireless, measures of health, camp commissariat, the care of lorries on a long trek. He liked cleanliness, order, technical ability, in addition to the normal African taste for book learning. But he wanted his country to fend for itself, and was ready to resist any foreign intrusion, whether the method were peace or war.

Other Ethiopians who resisted European influences did so on the basis of conservatism. They wished to preserve ancestral usages. To Afewerk these meant little: the Western accretions upon him were not superficial. A black man, he knew the value of thinking for himself outside the customary circle of the Ethiopian mind. The Italians he knew wanted to rob him of his country and basically, he felt, all these Europeans with their common tradition whatever their collective promises, would stick together. He felt sure that no European nation would take Ethiopia's side if Italy attacked her. Ethiopia was too remote for pledges to her to have any value. In all his dealings with Europeans he saw their clannishness sticking out a yard. He detested them all.

Like most Ethiopians, he had no taste for decoration, except that of dress. Around him on the wall hung the following masterpieces: Huntley and Palmer's almanac, with coloured portrait of Queen Mary. Faded photographs of the Emperor and the Empress in coronation robes. An advertisement of Johnnie Walker. A group of the Imperial family. A gorgeous Greek oleograph, featuring the Admiral Kountouriotes, President of the Greek Democracy, his eyes an honest china blue and his cheeks pink as a hunting coat, being crowned with victorious laurel by Themistocles and a fat girl called Public Opinion.

The Admiral's moustaches won both the prizes at the flower show. Their length and strength would have supported the Greek Navy's heaviest sails without a tremble.

Finally, a map of Ethiopia given by Major Dothée, chief of the Belgian Military Mission "*en souvenir d'un très beau voyage et avec tous mes remerciments. Jijiga, 15 Novembre 1934*" —the month before Wal Wal.

Fitorari Shefara, Governor of Jijiga, a dear little man with a mild Falstaffian face, entered with two servants carrying tej. That night I slept on a bed of iron, a military structure belonging to Afewerk. Curfew sounded at nine and soldiers in blankets went through the streets seeing that it was obeyed.

Jijiga is a new Ethiopian town which sprang, fully built, from the methodical little head of Tekla Hewariat, then chief Ethiopian delegate to the League of Nations. Tekla Hewariat was Governor here in 1916, during the Lu Yasu troubles. He first built the fort at the eastern end of the town on the Hargeisa road, then laid out low flat-roofed houses of simplified Arabian style, in square streets north and east of the regular shaped Jijiga market place. A wall, pierced by a wide gate, bounded the southern end of this open space. At this time of year a dust-laden wind blows up great clouds from the Ogaden into the market. It wraps in a dirty sheet the fine pasturelands and many waterholes south of the town where Somali cattle are grazing. I walked down to the wells of Jijiga next morning: the plain was pocked with them, new wells, old wells, and wells falling in. Deep holes in the ground, cradled with frames of wood which give a foothold to the Somali watercarriers. These fill their oval clay pots in the little runnel at the bottom and pass them from man to man to the top, singing a song addressed to the cattle, "come and drink sweet water." At the surface a Somali pans the water into the cattletrough, made of dried mud. An Ethiopian soldier knelt beside one of them washing his thick hair with lime to keep out the lice. All the Somalis do this: half the men that you see in the Ogaden saunter along on their slim easy walk, their hair copper with dried whitewash. For cleanliness, Afewerk had ordered his men to do likewise.

On the dead wells grew rank weeds with large white flowers like moonflowers. The Jijiga wells are cleaned by the population once a year in the main dry season.

At Jijiga Afewerk had organised a large garage and petrol depot. The Ogaden is almost perfectly flat. There are, of course, low hills along the rivers or the dry beds of the Tugs, which are rivers only for sudden swirling periods after rain. But over its vast extent, four hundred miles in length by a width of two hundred and fifty miles from the Webbe Shebeli to the Somaliland border, it is flat waterless country covered with low bush, mimosa soon giving way to more savage desert thorns.

In this country roads had been made by lorries butting through the undergrowth: men followed up the lorries to hack away the stumps and clear the fairway. The road was finished, and continual traffic kept it up.

None of the laborious and expensive surveys of alignment, excavation of mountain sides and cost of upkeep and repair after the rains that made permanent roads in the plateau. While there was only one motor road in Northern Ethiopia, the Ogaden was, in 1935, a little network of roads, over most of which I travelled between August 24 and September 1. From Jijiga to Daggahbur, From Daggahbur to Awareh eastward, from Daggahbur to Bulale, Harradigit and Ado southward, from Daggahbur to Sasabauch, Anale Gabridihari and Gorahai southward, from Daggahbur to Daggahmodo westward. From Gabridihari to Badu Danan westward, from nearby Gorahai to Gerlogubi eastward. From Gerlogubi an old route to Ado. From Gorahai, the road of the Italian bandas down to Moustahil on the Webbe Shebeli—built by Italian engineers when they attempted their first invasion in 1931. These roads through the bush gave promise of a new mobility. At Jijiga, their base, Afewerk organised the only mechanical transport ever run by an African state.

The Gibbi of Jijiga, a long white-washed building of two storeys, standing alone at the north of the town, used to hold the Governor and its courtyard the Governor's mules, camels and servants.

Afewerk had the courtyard roofed in and parts of the floor cemented. It became the lorry garage and repair shop of the Ogaden, under the supervision of a capable

Cypriot motor engineer, Elias Nasser. There were a hundred new lorries, and between thirty and forty old ones in the garage. In an exposed position on the hillside beyond Jijiga, to the east, stood a white building, the Ogaden petrol dump, containing five thousand cases of petrol.

The military objectives of Jijiga were clear enough.

They lay at either end of the saddle of treeless downland in the middle of which the town rested. To the west was the pass of Karramarra, with the Harrar mountains only breaking steeply into plain along a line south of it. To the east were low hills, also running south and parallel to the last outposts of the Harrar-Gue. Between them the cultivated plain of Jijiga, then farther north the wells and pasture, then the Jijiga ridge which closed and sealed the Ogaden waste from the rest of Ethiopia.

Isolated at either end of the ridge, west and east, were the two white buildings that the planes might at any time bomb. Only at the very end of August were the Ethiopians beginning to move their benzine out to holes in the hillside. Afewerk was away at the front: Shefara, except in retreat, was a somnolent Governor.

Afewerk had also developed the telegraphic communications of the Ogaden. Field wirelesses were installed by him at Tafere Katama, his southernmost post facing Moustahil on the Italian frontier, and at his field headquarters halfway down the Ogaden, which he moved from Gerlogubi in the deep bush to Gorahai on the Fafan, at the beginning of August. A third wireless was set up at Jijiga just after I left. All were based on the station at Harrar, which communicated direct with Addis Ababa.

Ceaseless vigilance, unified command, well-organised and rapid supply and thorough training for his troops were the watchwords of Gerazmatch Afewerk, whom I was going to see. Without exception, he was the most capable Ethiopian that I ever met. His reserves of energy were enormous. Until his death at the end of November he organised the whole of the southern war.

A few hundred soldiers of Fitorari Shefara lived in the huts around Jijiga. Every day some of them came into the Gibbi to report: their food for marching, they said, was ready.

Ali Nur took me over the road to his house, where his food too was being prepared. Under a pink oleander in his courtyard I saw three jiggra, blue-necked guinea-fowl, and a pair of Egyptian vulturine, phœnix-like birds with the same rich feathers of powder-blue. They scratched in the shade. He had collected them, like the Kudu, in the Ogaden.

War provisions were drying in the sun, scattered thin on a wide sheet which was pegged to the earth. The woman had made injura, Abyssinian bread, out of the millet grain, and the bread had first been dried and broken into crumbs. These were given their second cooking in the sun: after that they would be ready for the pouch. All that was needed to mix with them was pepper of the chilli and melted butter, which was sold in old whisky bottles. Jijiga was a great centre of this business, said the local representative of Mohammedally, the British Indian trading firm.

"The water here," he confided to me, "is frightfully constipating." Ruefully he explained that he had to take at least an hour's exercise, walking, every day to avoid this distressing complaint. Very bad for business.

At midday I noticed a sudden entry of drunks into the town and a great commotion in the market square.

It was the first time that I had ever seen a real mobilisation of Ethiopian troops for the front. It was an unforgettable sight. Five lorries had assembled to take down to Tafere Katama the frontier post, Nagadras Basha, the new commander, his personal troops (about sixty men), an old French five-pounder and twenty boxes of ammunition with rations and clothes.

All the soldiers were roaring drunk and fighting with the town police. Two of them, after posing for a photograph, were taken off to prison. Their driver, a stout and jolly British Somali, drove me out to the wells: it was thought best to assemble the men there as the fighting was disturbing the normal torpor of Jijiga market.

The women who sat behind shields of sacking and hide, against the Ogaden wind, selling purges and peppers and scents for women who would marry, shuffled off into the shelter of Mohammedally's arcade.

My Somali driver explained to me that he was chosen by the Ethiopian Government as a chauffeur because he was Islam and did not drink "else who work machine?"

A fearful volley resounded from the back of the lorry. Behind the driver's cab could be heard the exchange of loud blows and the thud of heavy falling bodies. In my extreme nervousness I reached for the door. "Don't worry," laughed the Somali, "they're only shooting into the air. That means 'Good-bye, I'm going to the war, may not come back Jijiga again, so here's how.'"

At the wells more ammunition was expended on the indifferent sky. In spite of the hand-to-hand fighting none of the expeditionary force was injured and all seemed very happy. A woman came running out of the town gate shrieking to be taken to the war: they shoved her into a lorry. Nagadras Basha paid some thalers over to the Jijiga police. The two soldiers who had carried intoxication too far were gently led out of the prison and unchained. By two o'clock our mobilisation was finished, and lorries rumbled off on the long three days' drive to Daggahbur, Gorahai, Tafere Katama, a billowing line of dust and brandished rifles and swords. Going to war is a big show in Ethiopia; sometimes you are drunk for days.

On the afternoon of the next day we left too, fairly sober. Fifty men and four lorries, one of which carried my fruit and another my whisky and soda water.

If you take the map of the Ogaden published by the War Office you will find that the road from Jijiga to Daggahbur is full of villages. None of these villages exist. The only population who stand still in the Ogaden are the dead. The road from Jijiga to Daggahbur is sown with the stones of Somali burial grounds, no more. Once past the cultivated land of Jijiga, ten kilometres down the valley, the hills fall away on either side and it is bush, thick bush, the whole of the way.

Undergrowth tangles the feet of the mimosas. Top-heavy hornbills stick their beaks out of the scraggy branches. At no point can one see more than fifty yards to right or left of the road: I climbed a tree and saw for miles a tortured grey sea of thorn, resistant to wind and sun.

Only seldom did we pass anything living. Three herds of cattle plunging in the bush, and a dark, small-featured horseman with a spear showed that somewhere nearby there was water and a Somali camp. A couple of donkey caravans—four donkeys apiece—passed us trotting slowly: a string of camels with hard flat layers of hides upon their backs. Two lorries, with more of the Ogaden skins aboard, for the lorry drivers of Jijiga engaged in commerce on the return journey. Somalis sat on top of the skins, grinning with pleasure, their slight bodies swaying to the turn of the wheel. "Somalis," said my interpreter, who stood throughout the journey on the running-board at my side, "like another place." It was his way of saying that the Ogaden tribes are the most restless nomads on earth.

Driving against the hot wind was a terrible experience. To my surprise, all the soldiers with me took out woollen Balaclava caps and pulled them over their luxuriant hair. They said it stopped earache: they did not seem to bother about their eyes.

So we drove for eight hours, in daylight raising slant pillars of dust from the reddish bush track, which our headlights converted at night into stormy clouds of reflected fire. We had done all except eight of the hundred and fifty-five kilometres between Jijiga and Daggahbur when Ali Nur suddenly ordered the lorries to stop.

He knew the difficulties of Ethiopian mobilisation. If we went into Daggahbur to-night the men would scatter among the houses and it would be impossible to collect them till nine in the morning. The two low Ethiopian tents were hauled out of the lorry for Ali Nur and me and we encamped at a rare clearing in the thorn. The sky, so bronze yellow in the day, sparkled crisply with a thousand stars, and the wind freshened.

I ate: Ali Nur took nothing except pituitary. The men separated quickly and made seven camp-fires with the abundant crackling thorn. Some ate injura and most ate nothing: they chattered long into the night. Before I turned in I looked a long time at them.

The fire leaped in the middle of one group next my tent. They stood talking with quick gestures seen in black silhouette against the flames, their shammas wound tightly round their heads in the Ogaden style. Their fierce features and jutting beards showed in flickering light and shade against the night sky: the cartridges blazed round their waists and the guns on their shoulders pointed aggressively towards the dark. To them this was a great adventure.

The rest lay down to sleep, some with a blanket or cotton shamma underneath them, but all without covering. They fell asleep at once, although the ground was full of broken thorns.

The dark twirls of the camel-thorn, man-high, cut us off from the rest of the world. We were deep in the Ogaden, impenetrable desert of bush that tears at everything that touches it. Above us, on crazy posts which sprouted greenery and sometimes on appropriate trees, ran the single telephone line to Daggahbur.

We entered Daggahbur just after dawn: the garrison were at their devotions.

For an African village Daggahbur was extremely neat and well-disciplined. It was the last of the old Ethiopian villages built before the march of Gabre Mariam in 1931. The thorn had been cleared well away from Daggahbur, which stands on rising ground facing the bush to the south. Its houses, with oblong walls of clay, roofed with turf and fenced with brushwood, stand far apart in gardens of cotton. The few streets of Daggahbur were beaten earth and like those of Jijiga cut to a rectangular plan.

In the middle of the village a disconsolate guard stood at attention in front of the brushwood Gibbi and garage, where a silk cloth separated four lorries from the judgment seat.

"All the others have gone to church," he said, "Kenyazmatch Malion too." At Daggahbur there were three hundred soldiers and four or five machine-gun rifles. At the sound of our lorries, most of this armament came pouring out of church, with the Kenyazmatch striding along in the middle, a fine-looking tall man, with a Wordsworthian stride but a more pleasant smile. Malion was the son of a bastard boy of Theodore: about forty-five, he had the same easy way with his men as Ali Nur. But he was more a gentleman: he lacked the flourish of the soldier of fortune.

After the two had kissed each other thoroughly, Malion was introduced to me, and in two minutes told me everything about his camp and soldiers. Three of the men who were supposed to be part of my guard now began to make complaint. Why were they forced to go to Gorahai? They would not serve under anyone but their own chief, and he was at Bulale. Malion tried to silence them by joking with them, but they were dead serious. The household tradition was engrained in them, and they would not be comforted. Twenty minutes' argument and they were allowed to go to Bulale: "What idiots," said Malion, pulling rather comically at his beard.

I looked in at the garrison church. In the centre of a courtyard, contained by a strong wooden fence, stood a square whitewashed building topped by a double cross, a St. Andrew's as it were astride a St. George's. The ends of the cross were executed somewhat bulbously with seven ostrich eggs. A soldier with me kissed the doorposts before entering to take his place at the end of an L-shaped line of men in khaki. Before them stood three priests holding an ikon, and a little boy singing solo under a black umbrella. The soldiers bowed forward again and again as they chanted in response, very slow and rather reminiscent of the gloomy opening notes to the Volga Boat Song "O Kristos, O—O Kristos."

A few women who had somehow got down to Daggahbur worshipped more silently in a corner of the compound.

Down the street was the telephone exchange: the southernmost in the Ogaden. The wire dropped, or rather sagged from a mimosa tree above a small square tukul. Inside an old man, very tired, was leaning against the frail wall of Daggahbur telephone exchange, grinding the handle of the Swedish apparatus, and occasionally piping "Jijiga, Jijiga." But no Jijiga answered. "It's no good," I said to him, "come out and be photographed."

"All right," said the old man, "but I'm only the servant of the telephonist of Daggahbur. He started trying to get Jijiga at six o'clock yesterday evening, but as there was no answer by six this morning, he left me to go on trying and went to church."

"I've only been at it an hour," he added, "my master is much stronger."

It was already hot when we left for the south at eight

o'clock. An Ethiopian tent is unbearable in this temperature, and the soldiers of Daggahbur were quartered in the lay houses of the village. They were moving in as we moved out.

Seven kilometres out of the town we found the telephone line lying severed upon the ground. Six old men and a thorn fence were the bulwark of Daggahbur to the south, but they were beginning to dig the long trenches which, in the event, saved it from heavy casualties in thirty air bombardments.

Hills rose to the left. "There is water there," said the soldiers, "that is the place of Sasabaneh, but there are no men there." Thirty-four kilometres south of Daggahbur. From now on hills, very low and level, flanked the route to right and left. But there was no relief to the thorns except where we crossed wide sandy stretches of riverbed at speed, not to sink axle-high. We stuck twice: Ali Nur, recovered from his asthma, took it philosophically and cleaned his teeth with a piece of wood. We were on the edge of the Tug Fafan; in this strange country the nearer you are to its spasmodic rivers the sparser is the bush. The thorn grows thickest where no water can be found at any time. Seventy-three kilometres: "The wells of Anale," said the soldiers, "we will drink and eat."

It was blistering hot.

In the sand I found four water-holes. Moosa went down and filled all our empty bottles. The men were hungry and thirsty, with reason.

Most of them had neither eaten nor drunk anything since we left Jijiga the day before. Ali Nur and the drivers had only drunk tea with water from the radiator.

His men hauled out their injura, burberi (chillies) and ghee. Squatting round a wide bowl, they quickly mixed their meal and took it in their hands to eat. One man kept watch in the sweltering sun. In their free hands, or in the crooks of their arms, they kept their rifles. They did not like to be looked at eating. "This food makes us strong," they said, coughing over the chillies but gulping them down.

All watering places of the Somali camels are infected with a small bug, colourless and difficult to see, called the Gordit. It is a kind of tick, minute, but in its crabbish, diagonal way, highly mobile. The soldiers advised me to put on riding boots: the bite of the Gordit develops into sores and a general fever.

It was where I sat, under the thorns on a ridge of the dry Tug, just above the wells, that the Ethiopians were to rout a mechanised Italian column in November, and postpone Graziani's Ogaden offensive until April. A young Somali came down to the wells, strolling in his long dust-coloured shirt and broad sandals, his head shining with butter. White calves of the herd followed him; but when he saw us with our rifles he turned hurriedly away.

Except for him and his calves, nothing lived at Anale but the Gordit. I noticed that here, where the bush was sparser, the surface soil was friable as sand on the sea coast. The soldiers offered me their food: gritty stuff with a sting in it.

We drove off at noon into thicker sand, the low hills of the Ogaden running level on either side, for we were in the depression of the Tug Fafan. Six kilometres onward was the water of Borkut, as the Italians called it in this war, though my soldiers called it Kurkut. The soil hardened again to a dry grass flat on which our two-ton lorries did fifty-five kilometres to the hour; but our average was always twenty.

Gabridihari was our objective that day—a hundred and seventeen more kilometres down south. We had passed three groups of waterholes since Daggahbur—shaded Sasabaneh, Anale and Borkut in the valley heat, victims of the sand and the sun. From now on there was no water at all.

Later in the war, after the battle of Anale, the Ethiopians under the Turk Tarik Bey, fortified these three posts, and Malion took over the command of the front at Borkut. But there was no one here at the end of August: no trenches were dug until the war was two months old.

And as we left the water, driving became easier on the flat. A wide plain opened out. The Ethiopians behind became irrepressible, and in the wildest excitement they scanned the country for game. A Thomson's gazelle there: piercing whispers, stop the lorry, a herd of oryx. We were crawling off through the thin bush to shoot when round the corner came the Dedjasmatch Nasibu, Governor of Harrar, in his private touring car and with his suite of ten lorries.

The Dedjazmatch was doing a whirlwind tour of the Ogaden before Wehib Pasha arrived.

As he climbed out of his car the first thing that struck me about Nasibu was his youth. Later in Harrar I noticed that his hair was grey, though Mlle. Hall told me that he was only thirty-seven years old. He was tall and well built, with a hard handsome face.

He was dressed like any white man who travels in the tropics; only with a good deal more elegance and care for colour. A khaki silk shirt with a light mauve tinge to it, rather darker shorts, stockings and rather light leather bush shoes. The mauve in the make-up would have looked effeminate on a European, but exactly suited a dark skin. His topee carried in front the button of the Ethiopian state official, coloured in concentric rings, red, yellow, green. A silk handkerchief was neatly pinned round his neck against the Ogaden sand, and he wore fawn gloves and carried a riding switch.

For one who had been travelling day and night he looked the picture of neatness. I felt as filthy as Baal-Zebel, the God of Flies, when he invited me to take coffee with him.

Coffee cups with golden rims were brought out of one lorry, a kettle out of another, whisky and glasses out of a third. In five minutes we were drinking and talking in the shade of a tree.

"I am a pessimist," said Nasibu. "What has the League done? Why have you stopped us buying arms? Do you want to destroy the influence of the Emperor by proving to his chiefs that the League has no value?"

"And how can we hold out against gas?"

It was the first time that an Ethiopian had mentioned gas to me. "How do you know that they will use it?" I asked.

"We know that they have gas in Somaliland at this very moment," Nasibu answered. Then with his switch he traced in the sand the whole of the plan concerted between him and Afewerk for the defence of the Ogaden. The outpost at Tafere Katama, to be overwhelmed. Gorahai, with its sentinel post at Gerlogubi, to hold out and if possible to drive back the enemy. Bulale to guard the thick bush road from Ado and the so-called "neutral zone." Gabridi-hari for the defenders of Gorahai to fall back upon if the position in the plain became untenable against the mechanised arm. Daggahbur, the last defence.

It astounded me. Here were the most aggressive fighters in Africa talking defence in every line. The waterposts of the Ogaden to be occupied and held against planes, tanks, armoured cars and worst of all, artillery!

"They will beat us," said Nasibu, "but we will hold them as long as we can." Nasibu knew, as did Ato Ambai and the Emperor, that war goes to the machine. "We are supposed to be brave," he said simply, "our courage is our only weapon. In the end, we depend on you."

"Against the aeroplanes and the tanks we are digging trenches all over the Ogaden. It is no use attacking any of their posts—what can we do against their machine-guns? Better for the camps in the Ogaden to hold out to the finish. Afewerk will see to that. His motto is—'Over my dead body.'"

And the Dedjazmatch left, with a present to me of his reserves of champagne and Vichy water.

That afternoon the thorn closed round us again. Lorries had covered the bush near the road with a thick red frost of sand. It lay in drifts where the ruts had gathered in rare Ogaden rains. The tigrit, a tiny wide-eared buck, held up its delicate front hoof to look with bewilderment at us as we plunged past through the dust clouds. One single tortured species of thorn here, multiplied millions of times and packed together on red sand. It grew with spiral branches, fully spined, to the height of a man's shoulder, and to the width of six to seven feet across. At its flat top it was a perfect circle, traced from centre to circumference with branches like the colours in a boy's marble. From above, it was as if some lunatic giant had taken up a round die and stamped the Ogaden up and down with it, to drive people mad with the uniformity of this bush and suffocate them with its long thorns.

As night fell there was nothing but the gaunt shapes of bush, dull with dust. Suddenly we went into a gully and up again. In the darkness I saw a tethered camel and a man stooping over a fire on a steep hillside. There were voices after the long desolation and we were asked for passes at a thorn fence. "Nonsense," said Ali Nur, and we drove full tilt into the hill fort of Gabridihari.

It took ten minutes to shake and beat the dust out of me that night. I was taken to a square hut owned by a bearded captain of fifty: he slept across his door. "We built these houses ourselves," he said proudly. "when Gabre Mariam came down and took this place, and the Bandas went away by the Italian road."

Balambaras Abebe, the thin commander of Gabridihari, came down to present me with two bottle of tej. In spite of the fact that he had no front teeth, Abebe was able to discuss the war with emphasis. They ought to have attacked the Italians straight away after Wal-Wal. An expedition like Gabre Mariam's would have swept Eastern Somaliland clean and raised the Mijjarten Somalis, who hated the Italians. The League of Nations. . . . My God!

A little boy outside the hut started crying "I want to go back to Harrar. I am frightened."

Five old rifles and a new Mauser hung over my bed that night. They were the family heirlooms of the captain of fifty, won in the civil wars and the fighting with the Somalis, and one of them bought at Addis Ababa. But the oldest was his father's, taken at Adowa.

Gabridihari looked over the wide Ogaden plain. There were three hundred men within its boundaries. Like all the southern Ogaden camps it was planned in an oval, with about one hundred small square huts, made of mud circling the outer edge. There were no trenches and the only defence was a hedge of thorn and a shallow ditch, which Abebe thought was sufficient protection against air raids. The view and the field of fire was magnificent.

The telephone no longer worked. "The posts were old," said Abebe, "so they fell down."

There were no buildings in the centre of the hill; fires were feared. "Tanks?" I asked—"Tanks won't climb this hill," said Abebe with the startling assurance of the ill-instructed. As a matter of fact he never waited to see if they would. When Afewerk died he ran away faster than they could follow.

So far I had counted six hundred troops south of Jijiga and five machine-gun rifles. I was not impressed. The harsh morning was set to burn the bush when we drove away to Gorahai past ten wells. From the little hill of Gabridihari, which commanded for miles the road north and south, donkeys came tripping to fill the petrol tins which glittered from wooden crates slung across their backs. An Indian woman from Aden, heaven knows how she got there, waved a British good-bye and artfully attempted a military salute.

The donkeys brayed. I looked at the half-wit Abebe, but he could not do it as well as they could.

In a minute we were out on a level plain. Animals were grazing—camels, cattle, horses. The grass was long and whispish, but thick. We passed our first Somali village a kilometre to the west: round frameworks of wood covered with skin or sacking made the Somali huts, and a composite herd of all the creatures that bleat surrounded them. To the south a little point stuck up in the middle of this huge grass-covered flat: nearer, it divided into two small sticks, nearer still it was a radio mast and a long pole flying the Ethiopian flag.

Yellow beehive huts, fresh-made, sprang out of the Gorahai plain. To the left a few trees marked the oasis. We drove up to the camp, entered over a deep trench with a fire step, manned by Ethiopians in trim khaki. Ten men on either side of the road presented arms: a small cannon jerked its nose out of a camel-thorn camouflage.

In the middle of the camp, under a large brushwood canopy, very high and cool, sat Gerazmatch Afewerk.

And the first thing that he did, with a great courtesy I admit, was to place me under open arrest.

Physically, Afewerk was better than his photograph.

He was wearing now the simple field dress of an Abyssinian officer, which suited him better than the costume of the court. That is to say, he was wearing a Japanese solar topee, a British warm, Ethiopian jodhpurs and Somali sandals. A heavy revolver hung at his side.

His manner was slow, steady and somewhat defiant. He showed at once that he was a man of weight and force. His Kafa ancestry made him much more African outwardly than the other chiefs that I had seen—the heavy way he sat under the canopy, the dark short eyelashes that curved back from his eyes, which rolled a little when he said anything positive. While he was talking he moved his heavy neck, with a scarcely perceptible rhythm, from side to side.

An orderly ran in with a board, planed level and clean, to which was pinned an order sheet written in strong Amharic characters. Afewerk read it through carefully, signed it, removed the two lower pins and signed some other documents disclosed beneath.

It was only six-thirty: these were instructions drafted the night before, addressed to various subordinate officers in the camp and to the commanders of Gerlogubi and Gabridihari. Afewerk, I believe, issued orders of this kind every day and saw that they were obeyed.

There was something quite un-African in the system and cleanliness of these documents. Afterwards I found that Afewerk was thorough in other ways: I suppose that he must have been the first African commander to dig latrines for his troops.

"Why must I stay in this shelter?" I asked him.

"Those are my orders to you," said Afewerk. "The Emperor has wirelessed me that you were coming. But he did not tell me what you were permitted to see. I have radioed Addis Ababa to ask for instructions. Meanwhile, you must stay here.

"I will tell you anything you want to know," he said, "but you must take no photographs. And now, tell me, what is the use of the League of Nations?"

"A law court for the world should be the same as the law court in Ethiopia. In my country no one is allowed to come to court with a stick. But while your court talked Italy kept on sending arms to her colonies. She despises the court of the other nations. She says she is the biggest nation."

He had six hundred soldiers at Gorahai, he said, and he told me the history of the camp. It was only three weeks old: his previous headquarters had been at Gerlogubi. Up to the beginning of August he suspected the Italians of preparing a move into the Neutral Zone south of Gerlogubi, and he stood ready for it.

In August, however, he heard that Hussein Ali, leader of an irregular Somali banda of about six hundred men, had been promised machine-guns and "perhaps a tank" by the Italians if he would occupy the wells of Gorahai and the Mullah's Fort, not held at that time by anybody.

The object of the Italians was to cut off not only the Ethiopian forts to the south, especially Tafere Katama, and Gerlogubi, but those to the east as well, from direct communications with Jijiga. "No food would have been able to come through and we would have had to withdraw all our posts," said Afewerk.

At Ado, Danot and Mersi, posts which the Ethiopians had been forced to evacuate for lack of water, the bush had overgrown the lorry track. It was impossible to revictual Gerlogubi by the alternative route from Daggahbur to the south, which passed through Harradigit.

"So I ordered the occupation of Gorahai," Afewerk finished. "Look at it." I did. From our canopy in the middle I could see the Mullah's Fort, a round stone building which had been patched up to house the Gerazmatch. An Oerlikon anti-aircraft gun stood in an embrasure nearby. "That is mine," he said proudly.

Afewerk was a historian. "The Mad Mullah," he explained, "came here before he died, at the end of your war with the Germans. He was very powerful here and has left many sons. We wish that we could fight in the way that he did, but you cannot do that against the air."

Next I was shown, from a distance, the radio; its operator, a young man from Addis Ababa, took down the daily French and Italian Press for Afewerk, as well as receiving and transmitting military messages.

The dispenser followed: he had been trained by the Swedish Mission at Harrar. He told me that malaria was very slight now and that the only maladies he had to worry about were those following the gordit bite. Later I was allowed to move to his dispensary, where there was a bunk for minor operations and shelves full of clean chemists' bottles labelled in Latin. All in a long hut, made of yellow straw and lined with canvas to keep out the Ogaden sand.

This blew in gusts across the camp all day.

And all round the circle of the camp, far apart, were the yellow beehive huts over the soldiers who kept Gorahai; to sleep and cook in by day, but to be abandoned every evening at a blast blown by the Gerazmatch's buglers. Then they took their places in the trenches, and patrols went out into the limitless plain.

On either side of the Mullah's Fort were two emplacements

—for two heavy machine-guns, I found later. They were nicely sited to cover the whole circle of Gorahai plain.

The wide centre of the camp—it was about a hundred and fifty yards across—was used for the ceaseless instruction of troops. A gully ran across the south end: trenches for tanks were being dug in it.

The Gerazmatch left me to harangue his troops, and I managed to take a few photographs.

I hated him at the time. I knew very well that he had not wirelessed the Emperor, and that he simply wanted to stop me seeing anything. To him all foreigners were spies.

"I have caught a spy," he said to me that afternoon, looking steadily at me to see if I would wince, "a Somali. He was in the gully. But I cannot kill him. I fear God. He does not know what he is doing. The people who sent him here are more criminal and more clever than he is. So his punishment will be to dig more trenches and latrines and mend the Mullah's Fort. But his masters . . . if I ever get them!"

But as I looked at his beautifully organised camp: the trenches against air raids, skilfully built on the zigzag pattern, the placing of the guns, the huts distributed around the circle at spaces which would prevent a general conflagration: the measures of hygiene: the regular and detailed issue of orders, and his personal explanations to the troops: his rapid communications—for as well as his radio, his car and two horses stood by all day at the Mullah's Fort, ready.

All done in three weeks.

And as I see his face now, full of force and sarcasm, heavy with authority, vigilant and steady, when he stood at salute with his troops before his country's flag at sunset.

And when I remember his contemptuous voice, "The Italians can rob all my country—when I am dead. I shall not care. I shall not *know*."

I thank God that made me and Africa, and bound us together in such a bitter union, that once in my life I met this man.

In the evening, the savage and uneducated Ethiopian, Afewerk, son of a slave race and servant of a grasping

Emperor, saw to it himself that issues of coffee and grain were doled out to his garrison, and that they had firewood, before he sat down to his own dinner.

He invited me to join him. Ali Nur, as a junior officer, sat on the ground at the table leg. With flabby rolls of injura we ate a dish of meat, onions and chillies, followed by mangoes and oranges. He talked with great contempt about the League of Nations and British policy—"I get it all on my wireless," he said by way of explanation, "and it makes me sick." As my own views were identical but I was addressed as a specimen Englishman, I found it difficult to take up the dialogue. "Well," said he, relenting a little, "I've had a message from the Emperor this evening. He says you can be shown all our arms."

When dinner was over we left the Mullah's Fort. First, some Italian rifles and boxes of ammunition—"We got that from the Bandas": and as we left, a large box of Epsom Salts—"Good for my soldiers," said Afewerk, with a seriousness that made me start.

We went all round the camp: three hundred men were in the trenches, with modern rifles and eleven automatics. Ato Wolde Mariam, the machine-gunman, was called for, and took me into the two machine-gun emplacements, where he showed me how to pack up the guns for transport, adjust them for low shooting in the plain, or cock them against aviation. "Now," said Afewerk, "come and see me."

He led me into the side turret of the Mullah's Fort. The Oerlikon anti-aircraft gun barrel took the moonlight. "We have only this one against the planes," he said, "I handle it myself. The people who sold them to us said they were wonderful; but they were Europeans and probably cheated us." He shuffled about with the fittings at the base, and the Oerlikon became an anti-tank gun. "It has an armour-piercing shell," he explained.

Afewerk was firing his Oerlikon against twenty planes two months later when he received the wound that killed him.

As I went to bed, Somalis in the uniform of the Italian *bandas*, fringed turban, lithe bare chest, long dust coloured skirt, rifle and cartridge belt, came up to report. There were about fifty in the camp, used by Afewerk for scouting and tribal espionage.

He returned to his room in the Mullah's Fort and worked on an order sheet. "I must go to Gabridihari," he said, "the man there is no good."

There were four wells at Gorahai, one of which was in the Fort itself and another outside the camp supplied the Somali herds. The other two lay in the donga south of the camp which we crossed next morning at six on a drive of more than two hundred and fifty kilometres to the Webbe Shebeli. Looking back on the camp by the way that the Italians would come, I saw that it lost its individuality soon in the enormous yellow plain that surrounded it. When I came back to Gorahai two days later, even the telltale trees which marked it at short distance had been cut away and replaced by tank traps. To the west there shone in the morning sun the white hills across the Fafan. Herds of bored camels scattered about the skyline and a hundred gazelle pulled the blond grass, which flowed along under a south wind with a promise of dust clouds. It was the old Italian road that we took. In half an hour we came to a bitter well, protected by thorn fences at Maranale; so keenly do the Somalis prize water here. Then moving up to higher ground and thicker bush, we passed the waterpost of Shelabo where twenty Ethiopian soldiers with old rifles watched over the Somali chief Hussein and his keen-eyed tribesmen. Hussein is a son of the Mad Mullah and was not trusted by the Ethiopians: the soldiers here, leaning against the mudguards of our lorry to take provisions of grain sent by Afewerk, told me that they distrusted two of the four posts of the Bagheri, the Mullah's old tribe, and the Rer Delil Ba Hawiya, "who camp in any place and spy." The rest of the Ogaden tribes were good.

Another small post held the Bulei well, which we passed at midday. Here a road branched off to the Italian frontier post of Ferfer, from which afterwards Gorahai was occupied (November). We were axle-deep in dust here. Driving as we were in intense heat, with both the windows up, it yet managed to cover everything inside the cab, pouring in suffocating clouds through the holes for the brake-pedals and the clutch. Behind, the men were russet devils. I wondered when any traffic could have passed to plough the dry veld so deep.

And suddenly we were in the valley of the Webbe Shebeli, my first Somali river, which runs broad and sluggish between wide green banks covered with magnificent African palms. Sandbanks showed in midstream but the river was not shallow. The air was fresh again after the dry windy heat of the endless Ogaden thorn above. Gradually we drove lower and lower into the valley. Dry hills with crumbling precipices rose on the left and on the right stood the white kopjes on the far side of the Webbe Shebeli, dull and dirty now in the change of light before sunset. Between lay fine cotton country.

We climbed the northern side of a hill in the plain and found Tafere Katama, which means the Strong Village. It lay on a flat space at the back of the hill. The same huts, but not as tidy as Gorahai. Scattered trenches. Five hundred troops in new khaki. The old five-pounder which I had seen at Daggahbur; four machine-guns on a lorry; four or five automatic rifles. Such was the armament of the post which held the southern defences of Ethiopia. Women were bringing up water from the river in old buckets. Nagadras Basha, a stout man who was always in need of advice, received me with four bottles of tej. I was bedded near the little wireless station.

Basha felt sure, so did I, that Tafere Katama was impregnable by tanks, and he said that he was not afraid of aerial bombardment. Trenches and holes in the rocky hillside were protection against that. But he was terribly afraid of gas. What if they used gas?

We lay right up against the Italians at Tafere Katama. Ethiopian morning prayers were at five-thirty. The garrison lined up on either side of a flag-post flying the Ethiopian colours, and joined in an antiphonal chant, standing bowing and kneeling for twenty minutes. After this unusual church parade I walked out of the camp to the brow of the hill.

Across the plain, down river, over a wide country covered with bush (but it seemed no thorn), stood another tall hill with a fort on the top. Through glasses soldiers could be seen stirring about and the Italian flag was run up. I could see at least one gun, probably a fifteen-pounder. This was Moustahil, Italy's outpost on the Webbe Shebeli, where the Ethiopians said there were about seven hundred Somali troops, two white officers and a powerful wireless. "They have many strange guns," said Basha, who could not specify further.

The river plain below was continually patrolled. The Ethiopian commander or his servant always had their glasses fixed on the enemy. A donga, darker red than blood, in the middle of the plain was accepted by the Ethiopians as the provisional frontier.

We left for Gerlogubi by the same road. I was very tired, but found the peppermints given to me by Leonard Barnes three months before restorative enough. Fatigue is always swept away by the ancient British cure-all. In middle afternoon we were once more near Maranale, and turned right for Afewerk's old headquarters.

"The road here," said Ali Nur, "was made by the Abyssinian side of the Boundary Commission before Wal Wal."

Before we reached Gerlogubi there were three more bitter wells at Morera, deserted by all except the bush pig. The gawkish but elusive geranuk, antelopes with long bodies and short necks, flitted through the thorn without a sound. The road presented a chain of twists and turns to our driver, whose wrists weakened long before Gerlogubi. The thorn, laced with a wicked scarlet parasite and crowned everywhere by mimosas in pale flower, crowded us in again on every side.

At Gerlogubi we were met by Balambaras Tafere. He came down to the brushwood gate as we drove in over the stony surface which surrounds Gerlogubi. Two bombholes, profound appendices to the Wal-Wal dispute, lay beyond the outer works of the camp. The bush had been cut back for forty yards around the camp stockade and trench: otherwise the camp would have had no field of fire.

"Only four miles away," said Tafere, "is the Italian post of Afdub, where three hundred Somali *bandas* are camped behind barbed wire and trained all day in machine-gunnery by Italian officers. We hear it all here," he added, a frail officer with a delicate voice, "but what do we care? We are going back to Gorahai as soon as the war begins."

Ali Nur said, "One hundred and fifty *bandas* are at Ubertaleh, which is behind Afdub, and another hundred and fifty at Afira, which is behind Ubertaleh. Three thousand soldiers, with fifty white men and aeroplanes, are in Wal-Wal and Wardair to help them."

Again the neat grass huts made by Afewerk: though here they were scattered more freely all over the camp. The trenches too were cruder; without a fire step and protected at the top by branches only. Evidently, Afewerk had been practising and learning before he constructed Gorahai. There were eight wells.

Tafere chose night to take me round the fortifications. I was surprised to find the trenches well manned, for when I arrived there was hardly an Ethiopian visible. The proportion of automatic rifles to ordinary pieces was remarkable. In a nest which I had already noted as empty I was astounded to discover some bird had laid a machine-gun.

I heard a flat sound like the patter of naked feet on hard earth. I looked at the machine-gunner's face. It was Wolde Mariam, my old friend in charge of the Gerazmatch's machine-guns at Gorahai. He evidently served both camps—and what if they were attacked simultaneously? He looked sheepish.

When I got back to my hut I found Moosa roaring with laughter. The pock-marked cook had till then been sour, silent and hideous as the grave. But Gerlogubi was a turning point in his life: he never frowned again.

"There are only forty soldiers here," he said. "When you leave one place they leap up behind you and in another place, then jump in trenches and pretend they're more soldiers. Askaris noirs, they no good, they can't fight Askaris blanches, only forty here, they'll run faster when the Italians come."

Moosa slapped his great behind with mirth. He was clearly the type of slave who would enjoy his Bacchanalia and serve the white man humbly for the rest of the year.

And with another laugh he said, "Tafere send you biscoot to eat. Très sec. Biscoot indigene." Charmed by the change in Moosa and by the trick played on me, I decided to count the men in the morning. I got up very early.

It was true. There were only forty. The machine-gun was being packed into a lorry and going back to Afewerk at Gorahai.

There was no point in going on to Ado and Mersi.

Between the line of wells which runs through Gorahai and Gerlogubi eastward to the Italian positions of Wal-Wal and Wardair, and the other series along the Tug Fafan through Sasabaneh, Anale, Bulale and Daggahbur, there is no perpetual water.

When rain falls it lies in so-called ballehs, wide depressions in the rock, in which the Somalis have dug deep holes. But between rains the water dries up; no posts on the ballehs can be permanent. Ado and Mersi had been given up and the road to them was thickening with young bush. We went back to Gorahai.

Fitorari Simu, the same who was to lead the cowardly flight from Gorahai after Afewerk's death, had just arrived with an advance party of his battalion of "regulars" from Harrar. An outpost had been fixed at Faf, across the Fafan, and another at Danan farther east, half-way between the Fafan and the Webbe Shebeli. The Ethiopians, Afewerk especially, lived in continual fear that Somali bandas would come up overnight and occupy waterholes which they were not holding with soldiers. Afewerk at this time was determined to hold all the water that he could, from the Webbe Shebeli to the neutral zone north of Wal Wal.

When we arrived he was showing Fitorari Simu the camping ground for his troops and already fixing the positions for the machine-guns.

He was very pleased. He had caught another spy. An Eritrean Askari who had fought for Italy in Tripoli had served three years under Afewerk and other Ethiopian commanders in the Ogaden. Afewerk, with Ato Kibrit of the Ethiopian secret service, had found that he sent messages to the Comte de Rocquefeuille in Jijiga, who had already been arrested on charges of espionage.

Heavy chains were put on the tall Eritrean's right arm and he was tied to a solder guard. He looked cheerful enough as he mounted behind us, smoking a cigarette. Three malaria cases, thin and brittle-eyed, were hoisted into the lorry, under white shammas. I shook hands with Afewerk and drove away, never to see him again. Our road lay north again, sleeping at Sasabaneh in the open among the thorns.

Reaching the Bulale road junction we took a new track which Ali Nur boasted he made, by lorry-butting and clearing, in five days. Large herds of cattle showed brown and white through the bush, and the pink Ogaden earth turned to dirty grey as we approached the greatest wells in the Ogaden. We drove through an immense herd of four thousand young camels, which were going on the regular daily service to the wells. These animals return to water every sixteenth day, and the wells therefore supply about sixty thousand animals. The largest well is sixty feet deep. Seven channels pass through the hard earth to the bottom; up each of these nine singing Somalis, glistening with water, throw conical gourds with a twist of the hand from man to man till it reaches the top. There the gourds are emptied through cotton cloth before the water is put in the mud camel troughs. There are many other wells for men and cattle at the sandy edge of the Tug Jerrer.

Across the river bed was an Ethiopian force in camp, under Fitorari Wodjáku. This delightful elder welcomed us to his tent and poured tej for us out of a massive curling ox-horn into horn cups. Ali Nur bowed before him, for Wodjáku was of ancient family: but the Fitorari would not allow him to kiss his feet; instead, with a deft movement of the hand he caught Ali Nur under the chin and forced him to kiss his cheek. Then he sat down on cushions beside his Hotchkiss machine-gun, and burst into unrestrained gossip.

The huts in his camp were raised on little feet, to avoid the loathsome gordit. Wide mimosa trees screened them from the upper air. Bulale was a new camp, and the first guard trenches were being dug there when I arrived. Old Wodjáku said I must, I really *must* take his photograph and give it to his son. The boy was training in the Imperial Guard at Harrar and he must understand that his old father had got to the war in front of him. Wodjáku was the most charming host: apart from the tej and the honey and the guineafowls and the potatoes that he showered on me, he rolled about with laughter at my feeblest jokes and nodded his head gravely at the wisdom of every serious statement. His tej-side manner was superb. No, he had no automatic rifles. He had about two hundred soldiers and was expecting more. Men were going down with fever.

In the afternoon we drove through dense bush to Harradigit. The track was disused and dangerously overgrown. A man broke his back when thorn branches swept him off the lorry. Harradigit was a wide bare balleh, with an eagle shuffling round after a snake on the rocks near the brush. At one side of the three thorn-covered wells in the middle, two wrinkled old men, half naked, sat mourning. Now and then groans issued from some perished sound box in the middle of their bony frames. We enquired of them the occasion of their suffering, and the old men replied:

"The lions have been to this water and the cattle are too frightened to drink." But when Ali Nur sat down at the well-side and offered them a basin of milk, the two old men perked up and said, now they were strong again, that they would be able to go back to British Somaliland.

"But that's a long way," I said, "and you are incredibly old."

"You are wrong," answered the two old men, patting their parchment bellies. "We are young now that we are full."

Two others, Ethiopians, came strolling across the balleh out of the bush. They were tall, handsome young men who lived at Gurati camp. They had been out shooting. A tigrit was slung across the shoulders of one of them. Most of the Ethiopians in the Ogaden were good game shots. We took them to Gurati, two kilometres farther on, where was another balleh, pierced by three shafts in the rock.

The water in these holes, they calculated, would last them fifteen days, and after that they would have to withdraw. Men reached the water by clambering down long poles. Ato Kidane, with about sixty rifles, held the last outpost in the area of parched ballehs; but his camp had room for far more and he assured me that when the rains returned they would come back in great force. Kidane gave me tea in his hut, and, to delight me, incense from a tree that grows around Harradigit was burnt in a brazier by the doorpost.

Next morning we were back in Daggahbur, where the telephone was again working with Jijiga. Malion invited me to breakfast on a rice dish, half-way between porridge and kedgeree, very tasty. He explained that soldiers eat this in the morning when they expected to eat nothing through the day: otherwise they eat nothing in the morning.

"They say they do not want to become greedy," added my smug interpreter.

Malion fed my mouth with his own hand as we sat on the floor round this excellent dish: it was a sign of friendship which means much in Ethiopia.

As we drove to our base in Jijiga, the driver, who was half Greek, half Ethiopian, told me how much money some of my friends received monthly. He got $100, which is about £8: junior chauffeurs for the Ogaden lorry fleet, about $40 or £3. Soldiers in the army from $8 to $12. Fitorari Shefara, Governor of Jijiga, $200 a month (about £16): "But Shefara," he said, "has twenty gabars who bring him about a hundred sacks of mashila (guineacorn) a month, which can be sold at $10 each." A gabar is, in Ethiopia, anything from a serf to a labour tenant: varying with the backwardness or reform of the provincial administrations. Balambaras Ali Nur got $100 a month, with four sacks of mashila. Garage boys, who accompanied every lorry, were given $3 a month and one sack.*

A telephone post had been installed in a zareeba, half-way to Jijiga. The commander's function was to look after the single wire, which the Somalis, said my driver, sometimes cut *"pour jouer."*

As the entered the long valley east of the Harrar hills that leads to Jijiga, something square like a solid steel curtain hung from mid-sky to the eastern horizon. On its cold fringes danced lightning: it threatened a downpour. The road suddenly became a skid-surface and, all our escort cowering, we switched off into the bush to find a drier route. It had rained here the night before. The first rain that we had seen or smelt in the Ogaden. The whole bush had suddenly burst into greenness, flocks and herds sprang from nowhere. We passed a party of Somalis, clapping their hands and dancing like lunatics round a water bottle which lay on the ground, very small but definitely over-flowing. "It pleases them when it rains," said the driver simply.

As we swung into Jijiga market place I spotted young Mohamedally on his anti-constipation prowl. That night Ali Nur, released from the tiresome duty of not letting me see things that I shouldn't, drank like a lord and beat up

* The dollars referred to are Maria Theresa thalers, then about twelve to the pound.

the night watchman. I too relaxed, upon the iron bed of Gerazmatch Afewerk, while Moosa and the interpreter each received a bottle of champagne.

The Ethiopians had been enjoying themselves while I was away. They had arrested a Frenchman.

The Comte de Rocquefeuille had lived for three years at a house in the Karramarra Pass, between Harrar and Jijiga. During that time he held a mica concession from the Emperor under the impressive name of *Société Minière d'Afrique Orientale*; but the Ethiopians, watch and pry though they might, could never see any mica coming out of the mine.

On the other hand, they noted that the Comte de Rocquefeuille and the Italian Consul in Harrar used the same unattractive Somali milkmaid. She seemed to spend her whole time touting milk backwards and forth between these two Europeans.

They caught her and found upon her person a metal medicine tube with a letter inside, typewritten and unsigned, addressed to the Italian Consul at Harrar, with a photograph of the Jijiga garage. She said that it had come out of the cow, or some such nonsense.

Ato Kibrit (Mr. Matches) of the Ethiopian OGPU established the fact that the Comtesse had tubes of that kind in her house. The final problem facing the Ethiopians was, how to get hold of the Comte. In Ethiopia foreigners are protected by the Legations and it is improper for Ethiopian officials to enter their houses.

But for every problem the Ethiopian OGPU had an answer.

The Jijiga flying squad, in their old Ford, drove shakily up the Pass of Karramarra. Outside the Comte's house they had a breakdown. One of their number went up to the door and knocked. The Comtesse came out; politely —"Would your husband help with our engine?" While his nose was still inside the bonnet, the flying squad jumped on top of him and carried him off with his Comtesse to Jijiga. The house was ransacked and thousands of documents removed.

The Ethiopian secretary of Jijiga garage was arrested, and with him the Ethiopian secretary of the Posts and Telegraphs of Jijiga, and his deputy. At one neat blow the Ethiopian OGPU halved the Ethiopian bureaucracy.

"They will all be hanged," Ali Nur told me, "and we will take them over to Harrar in our lorry." Rain kept us in Jijiga the next day, but on the morrow we left. A full load. Ali Nur, the driver, myself, Moosa, the interpreter, ten soldiers, the Somali woman, and the four other prisoners (including the Eritrean) chained two and two.

Moosa, whose fair and flattering contempt for all men except his master had gratified me throughout the voyage, was now revolving commerce under his banausic skull. His proposal to the other servants now was to buy ghee, which is melted butter in whisky bottles, at Jijiga, and sell the stuff high in Harrar. In Harrar you could buy fruit, a box of oranges for one dollar, and sell it at a huge profit in fruitless Jijiga. And so you could go backwards and forwards, adding to your box of thalers until you were a very rich man.

The interpreter, a patriotic young Ethiopian, said no, far better to spend your wages on ammunition. At the dealers' tables in Harrar square stood, like assorted sweets, boxes of all the mixed cartridges of the world: Lee-Metford (the gun that Ali Nur and the Ogaden swore by) sold at three or four to the dollar.

Rain fell heavy on us in the Pass of Karramarra. We only just got over the rivers that separate Jijiga and Harrar. The prisoners, who were to be hanged, helped to push us through every obstacle and at moments of enforced rest, when the lorry fixed immovably in the river-bed, went for long walks together down the bank. Their guards did not seem to worry. "They will come back," they said.

Terrified Indian families, whose gay-coloured silks hid their wet eyes, met us fleeing to Jijiga. The trading population of Harrar was panicking. Somebody had said that the League of Nations would meet on September 4th and the news had been magnified in the market. The local politicians and all Arabs with any experience in international affairs roundly asserted that on September 4th the League of Nations was going to tell the Italians to bomb Harrar.

And on the night of September 3 the whole population left the town for the hills to watch the operation of the Covenant in comparative safety.[*]

[*] One old woman died in a trench constructed with her own hands against air raids. She leapt into it and it collapsed upon her without more ado.

For me September 3 provided a quite new experience. We passed over the rivers, with a lot of tearing at the lorry's sides and more than a lot of singing. But the Ethiopian chikka, the mud that clogs the feet of animals and sprawls like grease under the wheels of automobiles, put hill-climbing off the map. The rain stormed at us all night: our tents and bedding were at Jijiga. So I hauled out three benzine boxes and a mattress into the open where the air was fresh, and slept in the water without a covering. Ali Nur and the boys were immensely impressed by this feat. I was rather impressed myself. It dried off under the Union Jack of the Harrar Consulate, and internally it was cured by Chapman-Andrews porridge.

Next afternoon I went down to see a special train passing up to Addis. It contained a Sikh detachment for the defence of the British Legation, commanded by Major Charter. It seemed quite a small detail in the day of September 4: I never thought then that I would be marrying behind their machine-guns in seven months' time.

The Times recalled me to Addis Ababa.

The first Ethiopian troop trains passed us at Ardem, at Khora and at the Hawash: three holding twelve hundred men and their womenfolk and children. They were Hapte Mikael's men from Kulo and Konta in South-west Abyssinia. Their coaches were steel cattle trucks, with narrow grilles at face height: no uniforms were to be seen. Soldiers, women and children sat beside the permanent way in the evening at the Hawash, roasting their shimburra or dried peas and eating them very hot out of a fold in their shammas. They drank coffee. They were friendly and communicative, like all the common soldiers whom I met in the Ogaden. Little ochred day-tents were rolled up in the trucks behind them. I had seen others pitched by the Imperial Guards instructors in the maize-fields of Harrar.

Everything was in movement in Addis. Vinci had recalled the Italian Consuls throughout Ethiopia and was quarrelling with the Ethiopians about the routes which they should follow. Mombelli, Secretary of the Italian Legation, had just taken his wife down to Djibouti. It was obvious that war would break out any moment.

Muzzi Falconi was in hospital in Addis recovering from his bullet wound. Vinci was beginning to walk through the streets without an escort.

I discussed with Virgin and the Emperor my tour in the Ogaden and Harrar. I had counted about seven thousand troops, allowing for the small posts at Danan and Faf, near Gorahai, which I had not seen; and including the twelve hundred who had just been sent down to Diredawa. Only about a third of these had modern arms. On an average they had two hundred rounds a man. I had only seen eight heavy machine-guns and about thirty machine-gun rifles, one anti-aircraft gun and two small cannon. A hundred and forty lorries.

The morale of the men was very good: so was their health. Malion and Alinur struck me as capable leaders, and Afewerk was clearly in a class by himself. The organisation of defensive positions was better, I found afterwards, than anything else in Ethiopia, and the command more united. But what could they do against the Italian armament in Somaliland?

How could Gorahai hold out against artillery bombardment or Daggahbur and Jijiga against tanks? What would be the effect of aviation on the small round camps of the south, Gerlogubi, Tafere Katama, Gabridihari?

Even in numbers the Ethiopians were inferior to the Italians on the best organised of their fronts. There were about fifty thousand Italian and native troops ready in Somaliland, with an abundant mechanised transport (Monfreid counted it in thousands), batteries of field artillery by the score, sixty landing grounds, good roads and an inexhaustible supply of ammunition coming up them. Graziani was Italy's greatest Colonial General.

Against this was set only the Ogaden force. Bale had just mobilised and Dedjaz Bayenna Mared had sent a few thousand troops down to Imi on the Webbe-Shebeli. But the Dedjaz himself was in Addis. Ras Desta could raise between fifteen and twenty thousand troops in Sidamo to carry out the threat to Dolo in western Somaliland. But it was a very distant threat—two months away at least. The troops had to march hundreds of kilometres down the

Ganale Doria, the Dawa and the Web before they were near Dolo.

Giardini, the Italian Consul in Harrar, used to boast openly that the Italians would be in Harrar before the first fortnight of the war was over. Once he even said three days. He ought to have known; his espionage had penetrated as far as Gorahai.

Mine had gone farther. Nasibu and Ato Ambai at Harrar also agreed with me secretly. We all believed that the Italians would be in Jijiga before the arms embargo had been removed.

If their southern war had shown any of the sparks of genius they could have reached Jijiga almost as quickly as I did with Alinur. Italy has nothing in Somaliland to be proud of; the Ethiopians much.

VIII

AERIAL EXCITEMENTS HAD THEIR DAY at Addis as well as Harrar, as I found on my return.

The single theme on which the Press was theorising in every hotel, bar and dosshouse was "what arrangements shall we make for the bombardment of Addis Ababa." In a search for the same solution the Emperor joined. While most of the others arranged for cars to take them up Entoto or rented safe houses near the Italian Legation, the Emperor decided to establish an air warning, consisting of three shots from an old gun in the Gibbi.

A practice was staged. The population was ordered to leave the town or to take refuge in the shelters which they had constructed. The gun exploded. The town panicked, for the word practice has no African equivalent. Taking the signal for the real thing, some stayed days in the hills round Addis Ababa. Petty larceny abounded, and the municipality heard that something on a bigger scale was being planned by the criminal classes.

A day and night watch was set upon the gun, to provide against another untimely detonation. The gay brown ladies of Addis Ababa, in whose quarters the conspiracy was believed to be hatching, were ordered to prepare to accompany the soldiers to the front: alternative, fine of five dollars for the Imperial war chest.

They were to suffer more. When Ethiopia signed the Red Cross convention, the emblem of that International Association had to be removed from their doors. For hitherto it had been the symbol of their "tej-houses." The Red Cross meant, as an Ethiopian explained to me, "good Christian cheer here."

We were in the last month of the rains. Italians were

moving troops towards the frontier. The position of War Minister in Ethiopia is immensely powerful and Mulugeta was becoming restive.

In the middle of September, Mulugeta was sick of all this twaddle about diplomacy and guerrilla tactics and truckling to the League and foreigners. He decided to mobilise on his own. The mobilisation order was printed and left, ironically, upon the desks of the Emperor's European diplomatic advisers. Colson immediately protested to the Emperor. Haile Selassie had not known of it. The order was suppressed. But it was only a beginning of the impatience of the old men.

Mulugeta became intolerably aggressive and rude in the State Council. He insisted that every European should be expelled from Ethiopia—"they are all spies and friends of Italy," he said. Mulugeta, the Adowa veteran, the grizzled hero of the civil wars, deep-drinker and autocrat, hated all *ferengi*.

As a concession to him the Emperor ordered the troops already in the North, those of Seyyum, Ayelu, and the Dedjaz Haile Selassie Gusca to stand by. All those owing war service had already been assembled: they now had to collect their wives, children, servants, mules, if they had one, and as much food as possible.

Extraordinary figures were spread at this time in Addis Ababa regarding the strength of the army which the Emperor could raise. Full details for each province, totalling in all nearly one million one hundred thousand men, emanated from the Imperial Secretary's office. The object, which the Ethiopian Government achieved, was to leave Italy in ignorance of Ethiopian vulnerability.

Something of ancient pride inspired this mild mendacity. The Ethiopians did not like to admit that they were weak. The Emperor himself was in a dilemma. He knew that he needed arms: at the same time he believed, rightly, that to seem optimistic and confident was the best policy with Europe. The League, he was beginning to see, was not made for Little Powers that were mealy-mouthed.

He was still ready to offer Italy his final concessions—the Assab-Dessye road project, sale of the Aussa, and exchange of the Ogaden. But now he too was concentrating on military preparations, as the period of the great feasts which celebrate the end of the rains came round.

All his commissariat arrangements, the establishment of granaries near Dessye, at Gondar and Debra Tabor, were completed. The troops had already been mobilised in Gore and other outlying provinces. It remained to prepare the final act of preparation and mobilise the people of Shoa with the war drums of the Imperial Gibbi.

As the Tigre Province began to dry and the wind over Addis veered to the north, he thought over the bareness of the armies which would have to defend Ethiopia: the few machine-guns, the wretched rifles, the low supplies of ammunition. The arms embargo was crumbling, but it had not yet been swept away: his whole plan of armaments for the north had to be remodelled because of it. He needed money.

He had postponed the importation of arms until late in the summer, so that Ethiopia should not be accused of aggressive attentions. When he had tried to import them the embargo had been imposed. When he had hoped to use the money of the Rickett Concession to repair the damage, the diplomatic combination of the Great Powers had prevented him from selling what was his own.

There was one course left, to ask for a munitions loan.

It was on the day of the King's Maskal that I was invited to the Little Gibbi. The Emperor had just been informed that the Italian Government rejected the scheme of the Committee of Five.

"This is the final effort of the League of Nations," he said, "to preserve peace by discussion between the parties. Negotiation in anything like a reasonable atmosphere approaches its end."

And he proceeded to give his idea of the sanctions which he hoped would be used to combat aggression. An embargo on the export to Italy of vital raw materials: the closure of the Suez Canal to Italian traffic connected with the war. Finally, he asked for the collaboration of the other powers with Ethiopia by the provision of arms and munitions, motor oils, lubricating materials, aeroplanes and officer instructors.

He leant forward earnestly to say that he wished to make

a special appeal to Great Britain. Serious he was at all times, but I never saw him so emphatic.

"It must be fully clear by now," he said, "that the policy of the arms embargo, however high its motives, has worked only to strengthen the comparative position of the aggressor, who is thereby encouraged against the Power who can get no arms. If a condition of the arms embargo had been that Italy also undertook not to send more troops and material to Africa, then it would have been fair enough.

"I therefore feel justified in asking that the arms embargo, which has served its purpose," he added sarcastically, "shall be withdrawn and I make a further request of Great Britain. I ask for a munitions loan, the amount to be negotiated in London, guaranteed by the Government interest in the import of salt and other monopolies, and by the Government shares in the Franco-Ethiopian railway.

"I make this request, like all requests, in the interests of peace. If Ethiopia can use such a loan as well as her own funds, Italy will think again before attacking a Power fairly armed and backed by world opinion with the threat of general sanctions. I can think of no step of more immediate advantage for peace."

Long afterwards, when the last appeal was being made to the Assembly, I learnt what the Emperor had spent upon the war. Armaments, the roads to Jimma and to the north, uniforms, granaries, commissariat, radio, had cost him a little under two million pounds.

Fantastic stories have been spread about his personal wealth before the war: deliberate lies have been printed about the amount of money which he took away with him to Djibouti.

The Emperor of Ethiopia was not vastly rich: he lived like a gentleman within his bounds and spent the State's money upon the State. His tastes were, for an Oriental monarch with autocratic powers, modest as well as modern. He liked good wines, books, music, his private cinema, horses, the chase, his children and his dogs: before the war he had thought of importing motor-boats to use on Lake Zwai. That was the limit of his personal extravagance.

When the war had ended, his fortune no longer existed. The villa at Vevey even, where he had hoped to keep his children if anything happened to him, was mortgaged to an armaments firm: all that was left of his money abroad was a trust fund of twenty-five thousand pounds for the education of his children, for whom he would have made any sacrifice.

The silver that he took away from Addis was the Ethiopian Government account at the Bank of Ethiopia, capable of keeping him, his family, his entourage and his representatives with foreign powers in sub-bourgeois comfort for three years. If he had left it in the Bank of Ethiopia, Victor Emmanuel, the new Emperor, would undoubtedly have taken it for his. But nobody would have regarded this theft as an act of impropriety.*

Haile Selassie did not remove the reserves of the Bank of Ethiopia, as it was in the power of the absolute ruler of Ethiopia to do. The reserves of the bank covered the note and nickel issue of the bank; legally the reserves were the property of the public who held the notes and nickel.

It was easy for the Italians to steal these. All they had to do was to close the bank, and collect the outstanding notes at a heavy discount in their own favour. For the worthless lire which they paid noteholders they could get, on presentation of the notes, pure silver behind the doors of the Bank of Ethiopia.

The request for a munitions loan was made more than once by the Ethiopian delegation at Geneva. Collier, of the Emperor's bank, was in London throughout the war trying to raise it. If it was considered at all, it was considered simply on its commercial merits. It was asked for as a sanction; it was tested as a bargain. Could five per cent come out of Ethiopia?

The Emperor, out of his own resources, was able to hold out until two months before the rains. He was able to keep fighting forces in the field for six months. Another two million pounds would have protracted the war into the

---

* I wrote this on what I considered first-class authority in Addis. It is not in fact true, as even the Government account was left behind in Addis, and only a few small personal accounts were withdrawn from the Bank of Ethiopia.

rains, which began in the middle of June and which stopped all operations in the plateau until the middle of October.

The one measure which could have maintained Ethiopian resistance and so enabled sanctions already imposed upon Italy to gather full weight, would have been a munitions loan: either from the League Powers, or from Great Britain. One would have thought that the Powers which crucified Ethiopia upon the arms embargo would at least have sought for some means to make amends. One would have thought that the collective security system, about which they made such moving speeches, and the establishment of a common victorious front against aggression was worth even more than two million pounds.

The rains peter out in Ethiopia amid scenes of high religious fervour. The Ethiopian feels very near to the soil and his primitive gods when the wind veers into the north. Large yellow daisies sprout in millions over the fields, and the Shoan plain, outside its grey patches of eucalyptus, is splashed with astounding colour.

The Emperor draws closer to his people: he appears at two public festivals. His foreign advisers saw him little during the week between. Like his people he was putting on the ancient Ethiopia and preparing for war.

Market days were every day. A huge traffic in old cartridges, gourds, pack-saddles, pots and pans for the journey of the Shoans to the far north. Coffee, dried peas, and the grain of 'tef made the necessary provisions for the journey. Roll upon roll of khaki went from Mohamedally's. The chiefs were buying themselves the most expensive and showy apparatus that they could find: powerful revolvers in brilliant leather holsters were the favourite choice. A revolver was, so the Europeans showed, symbolical of high command. Gas masks at a high price were advertised in the vernacular press.

A spate of art encouraged the people. From the startling blue sky tortured, three-motor monoplanes fell to earth in dozens before the artful shots of three or four Ethiopians ensconced in ideally umbrageous trees. Gnashing hyenas devoured aviators. Pistols were discharged into tanks by heroes in hundreds.

On September 23 came the King's Maskal, or the Dance of the Priests.

The dim gebir hall of the great palace was opened to foreigners. It is at this festival that the Emperor appears to his chiefs and priesthood, and admits the triumph of the Ethiopian Coptic Christian Church over African paganism and popular fallacies.

Haile Selassie presided on his bed-throne, escorted by two Likamaquas, his battle impersonators, and surrounded by the Diplomatic Corps, all of whom, including Vinci, kissed his elegant hand. The windows and immense doors of the hall were covered with strips of orange silk, and the floor was strewn with reeds and strong-smelling mint leaves. The palace servants under the implacable Likaba Tasso, in shimmering light green satin surcoats and jodhpurs, carrying their whipping wands and long red swords, ushered in a hundred priests. These, under faded Ethiopian flags and fringed silk umbrellas, sang in a chorus to five choirboy altos dressed in white robes and two tenors, whose solos were part of a composition in praise of the Emperor.

The songs over, the priests advanced towards a table in the middle of the hall, where lay the Gheez bible; slowly dancing and swaying rhythmically, crossing their silver-topped staves and shaking copper rattles to the accompaniment of two sweetly-toned leather drums of urn shape. David must have skipped with similar dignity and enthusiasm before the Ark. They showed no emotion in their faces, for their eyes were lost in a measureless profundity. The Emperor kissed the Bible in token of his loyalty to the true faith. Posies of spring iris and marigolds from the school gardens were presented with palms to the Emperor and the members of the Diplomatic Corps. Vinci was loaded with flow'rets.

Six days later the Emperor showed himself to the common man. The whole population of Addis Ababa and those of nearby Shoa turned out with long poles, emblems of a more gross and ancient religion, from whose tips dangled yellow Maskal daisies. In the square of Giorghis more poles were stuck into the ground, and round this beflowered erection the Emperor had to pass in a ceremonial circle, to welcome in the year and the campaigning season anew. The whole fighting array of Shoa turned out in frenzy and their traditional gay clothes of war. Thousand after thousand passed the Emperor's throne, led by the grizzled Adowa professionals who specialised in martial caricature. Capering, shooting and cutting up their ghostly enemies, they told the Emperor that it was high time that he did likewise.

At the Maskal one is free to give advice to the Emperor. The Dedjazmatches shouted that "he should not meddle more in the affairs of the outside world, but look after his country." Common soldiers followed with the cry for more rifles that was to distinguish all the parades before the Emperor for the next two months. "What can I kill with this bastard of a tabanja?" shouted an old peasant, and broke it in two pieces on the ground.

The Imperial Guard marched by, and the young boys of the Swedish Cadet School. Red Cross cars: radio vans: machine-guns mounted on lorries; the modern equipment of the Emperor was very quickly and quietly passed. Old Mulugeta, in his feudal magnificence, wearing his Ras' coronet rode by: he carried a long spear tipped with silver and wild horsemen surrounded him in a body. In a final wave, the Ethiopian rains came down and smothered all the colours. But in the north, in Tigre, the earth was dry and flaking.

Something had happened to make the Emperor feel the warrior spirit of his people, their primitive ceremonies at the season's change, more intensely. On Thursday, September 26, he had received a telegram from his Delegation at Geneva. It ended with a statement that opinion in Geneva was unanimous that war was inevitable.

With the full concurrence of his counsellors, including the foreigners, the Emperor decided to inform his Delegation that he would order the general mobilisation if their estimate of opinion in Geneva was correct. Considering the seriousness of this step, they were requested to repeat their statement. The Delegation replied that war was thought to be not only certain but imminent. He received their reply on Sunday, September 29.

On September 29, the same day, he informed the

President of the Council of the League of Nations that general mobilisation could no longer be delayed. He signed the decree of mobilisation for his own provinces and locked it in his desk.

We had a dry day.

October's first week was full of alarms for a windy Press. On the last Sunday of September the Emperor signed, but did not issue, the order for general mobilisation. He had agreed to postpone, to silence Mulugeta and his party, until the politic moment arrived.

Knickerbocker, for his part, beat his drums in every village of Ethiopia, and flashed his beacon fires from hill to hill. In recompense for this journalistic enterprise his colleagues agreed to present Knickerbocker with a small toy drum.

I do not know whether Signor Mussolini reads, as he regularly writes in the Hearst Press. But it was interesting to note that, among his excuses for aggression, he claimed that the Ethiopian general mobilisation was a hostile act against which he had to defend himself. The Ethiopian general mobilisation was not ordered until five hours after the Italian bombardment of Adowa.

Signor Mussolini must have been very startled by the toy drum.

In point of fact the Tigrean guards of Ras Seyyum had been withdrawn thirty kilometres from the frontier for many months. Only a few scouts stood along the dry bed of the Mareb on October 3, when the Disperata squadron droned over to Adowa and the tanks forced the crossing opposite Adowa, Entiscio and Adigrat.

Seyyum had long been ready for a war of withdrawal until the armies of Kassa and Mulugeta arrived. On October 1 he received orders from the Emperor to stand by.

On October 1 the Italians entered what was generally admitted to be Ethiopian territory at Moussa Ali, a lava mountain sown with caves, on the edge of Ethiopian Danakil: a landmark, waterless and hard, on the Mohammedan slave route from old Ethiopia to the Red Sea. The frontier had never been delimited, but lay according to treaty sixty kilometres from the coast. An

Italian motorised column penetrated inland, carrying its own water, ninety kilometres.

The French of Djibouti, on whose northern border Moussa Ali lay, noted the facts on their desert aerial patrol. The pilot, turning down the grey right wing to inspect, saw on the harsh serrated slopes of Moussa Ali, in yellow stunted scrub, a square. Nearer it became lorries in laager, peopled by bare-chested men in shorts. The tricolour rosettes of the Republic circled inquiringly against the bare plate of the sky, to see the green-white-red flag flutter in Imperial pride below.

The French Minister in Addis informed the Emperor of Ethiopia, as a friendly act, that Italian forces had entered his territory.

There are no telephones to Moussa Ali. The Sultan of the Aussa, overlord of the place to whom all Danakils owe a vagrant allegiance, is a small man with a short kilt and a long knife. Even if he had wished to, he had no means to inform the Emperor, who thanked the French minister tor his service.

Haile Selassie had always believed in asking the Diplomatic Corps for their help: the method was bearing its fruit. Even the friends of Italy responded.

Lively little Vinci (now representative of Italy in Hungary) kept on walking round the town on his own feet, unescorted. This was an unusual form of locomotion for a Minister: even the Greek did not sink below the level of four wheels.

So the Ethiopian Sûreté set to work. Whenever Vinci strolled abroad, an honest black walked ahead saying that a great man, a *tillik sau*, was coming. Another bigger black walked behind with a large stick in his hand, to settle accounts with anyone who might attempt an incident. The Ethiopians, few of whom knew what Vinci looked like or who he was, one and all have an immense respect for great men. They bowed and stepped aside for the little Minister.

Plans were drawn up for the treatment of Italian subjects on the outbreak of war, which was now inevitably close.

Obsessed to the last with the superiority of diplomatic values, the Emperor did not want to make any public show of his mobilisation. He did not want to say it with drums: also, he seemed to me to think it rather silly. Colson differed and prevailed. For Colson was the only man at the Emperor's side who knew the value of the picturesque in propaganda.

On October 2 we had one of our nervous spasms. The Emperor was going up to the church of Mariam Entoto at an unbelievably early hour in the morning. We believed that he might declare the general mobilisation.

The last day of Abyssinian peace opened lovely and clear. Already at six the sky was frank blue, a light lisp of wind caught at the eucalyptus, still green and supple from the rains that were over. I woke early, with that flicker of excitement which decides one to turn out of bed rather than sleep another three hours. No drilling. No noise. No dust. The kites were sitting drowsily in the trees, the servants lazily brushing shoes on the wide ramshackle stairs of Mendrakos' Hotel. Collins called and we went up to Entoto.

The mountain stands about nine hundred feet above Addis. Except where the steep shelving road winds over rock, like a worn watercourse, it is green and covered with the bluegum. On its summit is the church of Mary, where every year, after the rains are broken, the Emperor comes to the celebration of the Mass. Three separate terraces enclose the octagonal church, in whose dim interior, divided into two sanctuaries of graded holiness, hang pictures of the saints in rapture, and the damned in the reverse. A gold-mounted rifle lay in the Holy of Holies.

Entoto was Menelik's first capital, an eagle's nest from which to scan the wide Shoan plain, where even then the Gallas were possessors. The swell of the foundations of the houses which he built could still be traced in the rich turf. It was at Entoto that the order of war before Adowa was set up, written in heavy Amharic letters on a wide wooden board.

The road to the mountain-top was full of pilgrims and the curios. At its side sat wakeful women selling long strips of red cloth to deck the trees and stones round the church. Everything was clean and new—the air, the sky, the fields and a fair proportion of the people. Everybody was happy; at the first gate of the church a roaring trade was being done in laxatives. These consisted of earth from a sacred well adjacent and were sold in small paper twists.

In the second gate of the church people were offering gifts to complete their pilgrimage, raisins which left in water made the wine for consecration, fair heads of wheat for the other element, woven cloth for the clergy.

A shaggy-looking man in a goatskin, half hermit, half shepherd, had a fit during the service and was carried out. For hours the Coptic priests and deacons sang under their fringed umbrellas before the pictures of the Virgin, while little boys in high crowns shook incense, blandly gazing on the crowd who stood in the outer sanctuary. There was a move to the doors half-way through. The Emperor had arrived and was coming through the main gate.

He came up Entoto in his smart Rolls-Royce, followed by palace servants on mountain mules. His figure is fixed in my eye still, as he stepped out of his car and walked to the church briskly. The scarlet gold-tasselled umbrella was held over his head: he looked neat, fresh, gentlemanly, very George Herbert-like in a white suit and mantle, with an elegant walking-stick of ebony. It was a peaceful day, and his look seemed to crown it. Smiles to us and his Ethiopian friends in the crowd. There were no uniforms in his suite. The carabineers who usually travelled on the running-boards of his car wore clean new shammas, hand-woven with a loose ripple across the material, but no khaki was evident. It was as if a country gentleman were walking round his quiet estates in England with his game-keepers.

As we drove back down the mountain, the huge Shoan plain opened out in front of us, bright yellow with the daisies of the Maskal. These flowers, like large sulphur marguerites grow, I believe, only in Ethiopia at the turn of the year. They signal the dry season, when people go back into the fields to work for another harvest, and the mules of the Nagadis take the road again for the interior. Peaceful circulation begins in Ethiopia when they return. Everybody knew this year that they were to bring devastation.

By his dress the Emperor meant to show that there would be no mobilisation yet. We did not guess that we were enjoying the last day of Ethiopian peace.

A sentence typewritten on a worn and faded ribbon was pinned on the Hotel notice-board that evening. "Mm. les journalistes are invited to an important ceremony at the Palace to-morrow, at 11 o'clock. Lorenzo Taezaz."

The Bank of Ethiopia, now dissolved by decree of the Italian Government, opened its doors at nine every morning. But in Ethiopia there is never a physical run on the bank, even during riots.

Time passed slowly at the Bank of Ethiopia. Even time's regulation was absent; there was no clock. In the middle of the wall facing the door a sort of dummy existed, for part of the wood panelling above the counter was carved into the shape of a conch-shell. I frequently looked at this place where the clock ought to have been, but the wood only responded with an expressionless and unhelpful shine.

It took half an hour to cash a cheque. The cheque-book was very large and cumbersome and it took some time to pull it out of your pocket. Then you signed a cheque-form for so many Maria Theresa thalers, and handed it to an Armenian cashier, who retired to consider whether it was a fraud.

In collaboration with a Goanese accountant, a British Indian clerk, and the biggest ledger you have ever seen in your life, your past record at the bank was balanced out anew. If you passed this test, which took time owing to the enormous complications of the book, the various employees of the bank wrote chits to each other to establish that they were as innocent as you. Finally, you received your cash in a box at the other end of the bank, and signed one or two more documents to prove that you had kept faith to the finish.

Thalers are near-pure silver coins, bigger than a crown. Ten would be placed on top of each other in the box, and piles of similar height would be arranged in quadrilateral formation round the first. If the cashier wished to simplify matters, and if he did not like you, he would hand it to you in a bag and you would count it and be damned to you.

When you knew the managers of the bank, Wright and Press, the latter a relation of Sir Samuel Hoare, you cashed out in two minutes. But for the rest, the basis of the bank (as of all Ethiopia) was rigidly anti-rush.

On Thursday morning the bank was full but the scene could not be described as lively. The international cashiers, clerks and accountants were comfortably fixed in bottom gear, just growling along. In the office of Wright and Press I found Lorenzo getting out money. De Grenet of the Italian Legation was also filling his sacks.

The office of Wright and Press was an ordinary-looking place, two windows, two desks, a safe and a seventy-year-old map of Shoa, on which the plateau altitudes were laid in a sombre shading worthy of Wilson. Lost in wonder at its art, you forgot that it completely disregarded topography.

The only other decoration of the room was a hippopotamus skull, which lay on the floor fixing Wright's desk with a hollow glare. The Ethiop who cleaned out the office in the morning stuffed his cloths into the eye sockets. Its gigantic mouth barely concealed soap and tins of floor polish. We used to call it Vinci. As we called anything comic and sinister in equal parts.

I was sitting on Vinci when Lorenzo came over to me. Lorenzo is the only Ethiopian among my friends who can speak with a cigarette in his mouth. He did not take it out for what he had to say this time. It was as if he were wishing me his ordinary good morning. "The war began this morning," he said, "they bombed Adowa and crossed the Mareb." Something jumped. It was me or Vinci.

The streets slowly emptied. The approaches to the Palace hill, the cobbled avenue from the station, the more modern tarmac road from the Little Gibbi were a flurry of shammas, picked out with many bristling rifles. The brass-bound Fusil Gras was shouldered in all the streets. Long before eleven the great courtyard of the Old Gibbi was full of armed men. Five thousand soldiers of the town squatted with their guns held across their shoulders, in front of the great war drum of the Empire, the Negariet of the Negus Neghesti. Four servants carried it out, while a fifth followed bearing a crooked club with which to strike it. The drum, which is a half-globe of dark brown lion-skin, was rested on its rounded base on the steps below the Throne Chamber. Two powerful jet-black Ethiopians from the Western provinces slowly raised on each side two silk national flags on long eucalyptus poles. The Lion of Judah, bristling archaic hair, waved in picturesque defiance on his green-yellow-red ground. The drummer began a series of deep single beats to summon all the unarmed people, whose first intimation this was, if the rumours of their chiefs be excepted.

From the platform behind the drum I looked at Addis Ababa over miles of grey eucalyptus, dusty roads, dull brown tukuls behind wood fences, turbulent seas of corrugated iron, and more eucalyptus shading dirty, grassless compounds. Amazing town—squalor and natural beauty sprawling side by side. For all its irregularity the African lived in Addis Ababa a happier, freer and cleaner life than in any other town of the continent. Accra, Free Town, the "locations" of Cape Town and East London, Djibouti passed through my mind: all these gifts of the white to the black were far more crowded, stank more, more gravely offended the eyes than the gift of Menelik and Haile Selassie to unconquered Ethiopia.

Under the hollow triumphal arches, past the empty Parliament House, round the bright domed churches, a hurrying people answered the drum. Not it, but the report that it was being beaten spread with a speed measurable by the eye over the whole town.

Notables gathered round the drum. A rough kitchen chair was hauled out of somewhere: the journalists pressed down the steps for the news. I caught the eye of Lij Andarge Masai, the Consul at Djibouti; he looked very happy, he had handed in a well-documented report on the Moussa Ali movement the night before when he arrived from Djibouti. He told me that two Spanish girls, Lolita de Pedroso and Margaréta de Herrero, had come up in the same train.

Grey-haired chiefs in front of the squatting soldiery suddenly drew their swords from the right thigh and ordered them to rise. The drummer stopped beating. The men moved slowly forward with their arms extended, in every hand a rifle. The Court Chamberlain, Ligaba Tosso, a fine ferocious figure, stood on the chair, the mobilisation decree in his hand. The drummer cried "Listen, listen, open your ears. The symbol of our liberty wishes words to be said to you. Long may he live, and the enemy within our gates may God destroy."

Absolute silence in the centre; on the outside of the crowd the stewards of the Palace were beating still noisy elements into a state of receptibility.

The Ligaba, in a grating voice, read the Imperial Decree.

The Emperor, who wrote it, bases everything on history: in life a reforming traditionalist, in diplomacy an authority on precedent. The preamble to the Decree was a clear statement of Italian efforts since 1896 and the first Adowa to break Ethiopia. It culminated by measuring the steps of the Italian Government in the preparation of its aggression during the last year.

> "Italy prepares a second time to violate our territory," it read. "The hour is grave. Each of you must rise up, take up his arms and speed to the appeal of the country for defence."
>
> "Warmen, gather round your chiefs, obey them with a single heart and thrust back the invader."
>
> "You shall have lands in Eritrea and Somaliland"
>
> "All who ravage the country or steal food from the peasants will be flogged and shot."
>
> "Those who cannot for weakness or infirmity take an active part in this holy struggle must aid us with their prayers."
>
> "The feeling of the whole world is in revulsion at the aggression aimed against us. God will be with us."
>
> "Out into the field. For the Emperor. For the Fatherland."

The whole people rushed forward to the steps, madly shouting, waving their rifles and crushing Ariel Varges, the cinematographer, who had clustered with his kind at the bottom of the steps to capture the scene. Some shouted, "Till now we have had doubts of our Emperor, but now we know that he is with us." The younger ones, "Not a man will stay here after five days, we will all join our brothers in the fire."

Some of the younger ones, I fear, stayed behind. Gabre Selassie, the insolent taxi-driver, waved a borrowed sword with the boldest, but never got further than the Dessye gate. Joseph, my interpreter, brandished my typewriter violently. He never found a more penetrable weapon. Most of the generation after Adowa, the men of the civil wars, were telling the truth. Five days, of course, was a misjudgment of time, permissible to Ethiopians—but they were ready to die. Little Lorenzo now had to do his job. He fell back on the steps of the Throne Room, pursued by an undignified horde of whites, in which the Diplomatic Corps were represented. A secretary of the German Legation trod violently on Paris Soir's toe. Paris Soir said he would hit him if he did it again. The representative of another famous French newspaper tried to wrench the communique out of Lorenzo's hand: a Czech was feeling in his pockets. The little man was more or less hoisted up by the pressure of the journalists on his circumference.

"The Imperial Government have received a telegram from Ras Seyyum," he read. "Adowa was bombed early this morning by Italian aeroplanes, with loss of life and property. Fifteen projectiles have been counted. The bombardment continues at Adigrat, where a hundred houses have been destroyed. Ras Seyyum reports that artillery can be heard in action in Agame, where full battle is engaged."

While he was reading, Count Ciano's and another plane were bombing Adowa a second time. Seventy-eight bombs had been counted by Ras Seyyum. As Count Ciano said to the infantry officers, "My job is much more comfortable than yours. I fight sitting."

The news broke the journalistic circle and spread through the mob like ripples in water. All, their voices strained with shouting and faces contorted with violence and rage, ran to the north tower of the Emperor's lodging. He was there on the top balcony, still in court clothes: he stood in perfect calm and dignity, neat and fresh, with the Duke of Harrar and his Ministers around him. On the balcony below was the vast, hawk-beaked figure of the Minister of War, satisfied at last.

I saw Colson in his wide hat, standing in front of the tower under an oleander tree, a turn of steady ironic pleasure on the mouth beneath the grey moustache: his policy had won by a head, the aggression had just preceded the mobilisation.

Tearing their knives out, the mob shouted "Death to the Italians; finish it once and for all. We thank you for your decree. God give you long life." The Emperor, gently commanding silence with his hand, replied, leaning on the balcony,

"I am happy to see you before me with knives, swords and rifles; but it is not I alone who knows, but the great world without, that Ethiopian warriors will die for their freedom.

"Soldiers, I give you this advice, so that we gain the victory over the enemy. Be cunning, be savage, face the enemy one by one, two by two, five by five in the fields and mountains.

"Do not take white clothes, do not mass as now. Hide, strike suddenly, fight the nomad war, steal, snipe and murder singly. To-day the war has begun, therefore scatter and advance to victory."

At this the whole wild assembly clapped sharply three times, shouted "Glory to the Emperor" and plunged away through the narrow Palace gates, through the Ras' gate and the gate for men of rank and the other gates which they should never have entered. There was a surging block of mules, men and rifles in the gates until midday.

By lunch-time the idlers were in the same places on the pavements of Addis again, discussing the speech of the Emperor. The journalists were back in the hotels.

At 11.30 Major Dothée, Chief of the Belgian Military Mission, conveyed the instructions of the Imperial Government to the Italian Minister and all members of the Legation to stay within their compound and leave only under escort.

When they came out, they had to drive at a slow pace, accompanied by four mounted police.

Italian subjects or protégés were ordered to concentrate

at the Legation, and their properties were placed under seal by the Ethiopian Government.

Perfect order was maintained. The Emperor's authority was so strong that from this day until his flight no foreigner suffered injury; only one missionary was temporarily tied with his own dogchain.

IX

ON OCTOBER 6, WHEN THE SUN was half-way up the sky, the advance guard of Maravigna's Second Army Corps marched through the fields of dourah and maize which mark the small plain of Adowa in the Tigrean mountains, and occupied the town without resistance. Only men without arms and the immobile brooding priests of Ethiopia remained. Ras Seyyum was far away with his force of sixteen thousand; far away, watching at half distance the progress of the Italians to the mountain line which he had been ordered not to hold, and the sluggish conspiracies of his rival, the Dedjazmatch Haile Selassie Gucsa, who had been left to guard the fief of Makalle in the rear, but whose troops were carefully being seduced from his allegiance. The Italians set up a marble statue to the dead of 1896, saluted King and Duce, and sat down to wait. Since the opening of the war on the 3rd hardly a blow had been struck by the loyal Tigreans. The occupation of the Adowa—Entiscio—Adigrat line by three Army Corps of Italy, its abandonment by the Emperor's chiefs, proceeded according to the well advertised plans of both sides.

Dedjazmatch Ayelu, the governor of the fierce shifta region of Wolkait and the Setit, where guerrilla warfare is engrained in the population, assembled his men around Amba Bircutan in the far North West; ready to strike down upon Om Ager in the western corner of Eritrea, or to the right, across the Takazze river if the Italian advance should venture on too fast. At the head of a telephone line he could within four days make contact with the Emperor. For the Ethiopians relay messages and slumber between calls. Ayelu had been a fighter since boyhood; of the northern rulers he was, though a sick man, to prove himself the ablest. A patriotic brigand leading brigands pure and simple, he and Girku were to keep the Adowa Army Corps in play until February and stave off for many months the threatened invasion from Om Ager across the sullen muddy river. His work was lightened in the cover which the thick bush and woodland of his mountain provided, fingering out into the long dry grass and fever of the Takkaze valley.

The Ras Kassa, once the greatest horseman in Ethiopia, who bred racers on the mountain plains which he owned above Addis, drummed in throughout the provinces of Amhara and Beguemder, from the wooded sides of Lake Tana and the shelving uplands of Debra Tabor, a huge host. One hundred and sixty thousand men, women and children servitors are said to have assembled at Gondar for the war. With his two sons, the great Ras, once a claimant to the throne which Tafari occupied, but the loser because a simpler personality, rode away from the shadows of the ruined Portuguese castle and the overgrown stony alleys of Gondar upon thoroughbred ponies. Part, the smaller part, of his armies made straight for the Takkaze by Dabat and Davark (where outposts had been stationed since July). Kassa led the rest slowly and quietly, unseen by enemy planes, in scattered parties to Lalibela, where eleven monolithic churches in the valley opening out into the Galla borderlands are all that are left of the splendid religion which decorated Ethiopia in the thirteenth century after Christ. The old theologian loosened his big toes in their narrow iron stirrups and stooped lightly from the cantle to kiss the single carved stones. At each of the eleven, beautiful and simple as a graven diamond, weathered little by rain or time, the priests of Kassa's army blessed the Gondaris who were to fight in barren Tigre. Leaning on the silver-topped branches of their praying sticks at the dim rock entrances cleft out of the mountain side, they intoned the victory which jealous Europe was not to concede to Ethiopian arms.

It was near the middle of October when Kassa's vanguard left his province of Lasta; the tracks had hardened, the mules had no longer to pick their way delicately through the liquid mud. They moved up the alignment of the

Imperial Road, Bietry's making, crossed the pass of Amba Alagi which sticks like a devil's tooth into the dizzy air and underwent their first bombardment on October 14 and 16. Most sanely took cover; but some of the men and women dashed foolishly about, shaking the glittering petrol tins in which they carried food and the Chianti bottles which Italian trade, a practical monopoly, had brought to Gondar and Lasta, where they were used as gourds. There was a little loss, many soldiers whispered together and went home: others had squandered their millet and dourah and had perforce to leave. With an army much reduced Ras Kassa went on into the southern Tigre by night marches only, scattering his men like chicken feed over a wide area of country. Henceforward the planes searched in vain: by day caves hid the Ethiopian commanders and bushes the Ethiopian fighting men.

The restriction on their movement now began which made it impossible for the Ethiopians to develop a free guerrilla war. As far as they could they *felt* their way towards the war. But slowly, very slowly. . . .

The Ethiopian northern front had not nearly filled in. Kassa himself was nowhere near Amba Alagi. Mulugeta had not left Addis. The arms embargo, the cumbrousness of Ethiopian mobilisation, the menace of the aeroplanes conspired to reduce every Ethiopian movement to something near zero.

It was only after the fall of Makalle, in November, that Kassa was able to assemble his whole army north of Amba Alagi. And it was because Makalle had fallen so tamely that Kassa was forced to lie south of it so long. The Ethiopians always believed that the Italians would at any moment advance from Makalle. Kassa was therefore ordered to guard the Imperial Road, Tigre's main commnuication with the south . . . until Mulugeta arrived.

That is why the Ethiopians scarcely moved for two months after the war had begun: during which time the Italian steamroller passed heavily from one end of the Tigre to the other. The dead eventless period intervened when Europe only saw the Italo-Ethiopian war as a series of submissions, non-resistance, ceremonial occupations, roadbuilding and Italian propaganda flickering dully across sham-pacific newsreels. The war became a political parade without horrors, and in this unreal atmosphere the Hoare-Laval plan was negotiated, to kill for ever prospects of an Ethiopian success.

Its uneventful form was given to this period by the fall of Makalle without a struggle. Makalle was captured because Dedjazmatch Haile Selassie Gucsa submitted to Italy.

The withdrawal from Makalle, until the end of October no part of the Emperor's plan, altered the whole face of the northern war. I think it is true to say that it saved the loyal Tigreans for another day: and that if Gucsa had not been forced by events to go over when he did, he deserved the abuse which Vinci poured upon him for the prematurity of his decision. It was Wodaju Ali who spoilt his conspiracy.

Wodaju Ali had been Ethiopian Consul in Asmara and later Director of the Municipality of Addis Ababa. Of no high birth he held only the civil title of Nagadras or "Caravan Head": a man made by the Emperor, like most of the Ethiopians who speak foreign languages, he was one of the Kingsmen who watched the activities of those governors who might deny the Imperial authority. A fortnight before the war he had flown to Addis from the dry landing ground at Makalle, to report that the Dedjaz Haile Selassie Gucsa, a woolly-haired savage of the north, was concerting revolt with the Italian Consul in his fief.

The Emperor did not act. He refused to believe the story; thought that the Kingsman was jealous of the Baron. Earth defences had been constructed north of Makalle by Konovaloff: the Dedjaz had two Oerlikon anti-aircraft guns, thirty machine-guns and machine-gun rifles, four pieces of mountain artillery. His private army, ten thousand strong (he had actually boasted of twenty thousand to the Italians) was meant to held the centre of a line, whose left was Seyyum south of Adowa and whose right Kassa Sebhat in Agame, against the Italians when they left the Shire line. The Emperor, who erred often on the side of generosity, had already given the Dedjaz too many material tokens of trust to disgrace him at this crisis.

In spite of the fact that he personally disliked him.

Haile Selassie Gucsa, a heavy-drinking boy, was presumed

in his Tigre village to be the son of Ras Gucsa Araia, lord of all the province, by a fleeting baronial union. The old man, smitten by a paralysis for which his humble amours were held responsible, and childless of all other beds, had summoned to his chief place and recognised the young boy before his death in 1932. The Emperor, new to absolute power at the centre, accepted the position. Haile Selassie the son of Gucsa was given the fief of Makalle; Seyyum, his uncle, the fief of Adowa and Axum. Land does not always descend from father to son in Ethiopia: it tends to remain in the family, but it is for the highest feudal lord, the sovereign Emperor, to decide major cases of division.

The young Dedjaz came to Addis in 1932 where, though his fuzzy hair, boorish manners and brutishly complacent face did not impress the Court, he was given for dynastic reasons the daughter of the Emperor to wed; at the same time the Crown Prince married Seyyum's daughter. Tigre was thus bound more tightly to Shoa—had not the princess died of the young man's neglect two year later.

In 1933 and 1934 Haile Selassie Gucsa had visited Asmara, for Eritrea with its railway trains, its champagne, its steamer to Djibouti, made an easier route for the Tigrean lords between Addis Ababa and their provinces. To travel in comfort as a rich man should, why take the long caravan road through Central Ethiopia when the Italians smoothed the other way?

In 1933 and 1934 the young Dedjaz had visited Addis in order to increase his landed holding in Tigre: the Emperor had refused.*

Even so Wodaju Ali could not persuade the Emperor of his treachery.

Nor were the Italians themselves certain that he would come over, though he had pocketed their money like all the other chiefs.

Wodaju Ali returned by plane to Makalle on the 9th.

Italian reconnaissance planes wheeling over the harsh rocks of Tigre reported troops moving north of the town that Wednesday; the little Ethiopian Potez machine slipped through at dusk like a green moth. Haile Selassie

* On the ground that he had not yet shown capacity to govern that which he had.

Gucsa had acted already, for he knew that Wodaju Ali would arrest him, whether the Emperor had agreed or not. That afternoon he drummed in his men and told them that they were to march with him against the invader: only the chiefs knew that he was going to submit to Italy. Relieved that this was to be no new-fangled guerrilla war, many of the soldiers were ready to march. The traitor followed next night with his servants and bodyguard, under the moon, tearing down the telephone wires which on crazy Ethiopian posts supported Seyyum's one connection with the south.

Wodaju's men raced after the army. Throughout the night detachments were warned that their leader was going to surrender them to the *ferengi*, who would disarm and kill them. They doubted and turned. When the sun was up on Thursday and the reconnaissance machines set out again, they were astonished to see small parties of Abyssinians between their new-captured ridge at Edagahamus and the corn plain of Makalle. Some were marching north, others south, others east and west, in a pattern incomprehensible to the Italian aviation. Edagahamus, whose sharp ten thousand foot barrier to the south was occupied that very morning, was reinforced.

Towards sunset, young Gucsa marched in under a white flag. The Italian press of Friday morning reported several thousand followers, the Italian communique of the weekend fifteen hundred, the Ethiopians one hundred and fifty-eight.

The Italians were not only surprised; they were angry. Haile Selassie Gucsa had changed sides almost too late for his own safety, but much too early to further their own strategic plan. He had been told to wait until they were near Makalle, and he had revolted with only a small part of his army long before they could begin the advance on Makalle.

If he had waited, he could have broken the Ethiopian front and the Italians could have turned and cut off Seyyum. But now no front was formed; they did not even know where Seyyum was. They only knew that he could no longer reach Addis on the telephone.

And so the first phase of the war ended. De Bono

solemnly entered Adowa on the 14th, by which date the natives had learnt the Fascist salute. Desultory bombings upon the remnant north of Makalle, whose erratic countermarches were now intelligible to the Italian high command. . . . Early in the morning of October 15, Axum, the holy city, was entered from Adowa without a fight. The "keys," such as they were, were transferred to the Italians by the Nevraid or High Priest at G.H.Q., where priests intelligently improvised a Coptic chant in favour of the Italian conquest. Certain of them were to be murdered afterwards for disloyalty to Italy, but on October 15 they sang in harmony.

As the line straightened out through Axum, Adowa, Entiscio and Edagahamus, Marshal Badoglio, Chief of the General Staff, arrived at Asmara to report progress.

He found that the High Command knew nothing of the whereabouts of Seyyum, who was "probably somewhere on the Gurungura river south of Adowa" or of Kassa "who was probably fortifying Amba Alaji." He heard them say that Ras Mulugeta, the Minister of War, was on the march, when he knew very well that Mulugeta was still in Addis.

The one hundred and ten thousand men who were facing Seyyum's sixteen thousand, the two hundred and thirty guns, two thousand three hundred machine-guns, ninety-two tanks, thirty-five thousand pack animals and eleven thousand lorries and cars were all waiting to be disentangled before they advanced for the next step, Makalle. Feebleness of direction had already led to desertions of Eritrean Askaris to the Ethiopian side— two hundred and fifty in western Agame on October 9, a battalion next day. The confusion was to become worse, for De Bono had promoted his son to a position of financial trust in the Commissariat; the Italians were only to take undefended Makalle, where Gucsa's family were having a rough passage, a month later.

War was carried on only by the Dedjaz Ayelu, whose bands jumped on the River Takkaze, now at this place, now that, like a dog on a snake's brittle back. He hit twice in these days at Om Ager; then he tried the fords east along the Eritrean frontier, but thought them too closely guarded by Eritrean M.G. companies and planes to risk a heavy attack. He lost a few men, then pulled the rest back through the grass and dense bush; he felt rather ill and sent for a doctor, who was flown north to Dabat from Addis. He underwent a cure, biding his time and the forces of Ras Imru from the south. His instructions had been to attempt an invasion of Eritrea on the Takkaze frontier, where no roads connected the scanty Italian forces with their base: but he could not do it, and he sensibly refrained. Amba Bircutan, his base, was bombed, and little harm done.

Only the planes, the Disperata squadron under Ciano, the young Mussolinis and other less sensational fliers ventured out daily over barren Tigre, attempting reconnaissance and aerial cartography, and occasionally dropping bombs along the alignment of the Imperial Road.

For Bietry, the Swiss engineer who had been paid to survey the route from Addis to Dessye and Mai Chow for the Emperor, had arrived in the Tigre in time to go over to the Italians with Dedjazmatch Haile Selassie Gucsa. Italy used his knowledge throughout the war to bomb, to gas, to machine-gun from the air, and finally to pursue along the ground. The finest road that the Emperor ever made served only the Italians; without it they could never have taken Addis Ababa before the rains.

Meanwhile the Abyssinian workers, feudal levies from every rich man's land where the road passed, were to the disciplinary blast of ox-horns draining off the mud from the alignment south of Dessye, clipping away the side of Mount Tarmaber, levelling the soft edges of the plateau where barley grows above Debra Brehan, piling stones upon the black cotton soil of Sholameda, where ancient cedars and junipers upon a gentle hillock hide the wooden church which is the election place of the Shoan Kings. It was a long business, but until it was completed the Emperor was unwilling to move his Imperial Guard north of Dessye. He thought that they would be starved if there was no speedy road to feed them from his central granaries.

In Addis we journalists were told that we would go north when the road was ready. Knickerbocker bought a caravan with every convenience. Fox Movietone cleaned its scarlet motor bicycle. Others proposed to buy dozens of mules. Reuter (Collins) and I tried out a few lorries and at last settled on a Ford, to either side of which boards marked "Reuter" in plain Roman capitals, and *The Times* in the old Gothic of my youth and our Armenian sign painter's latest edition were solemnly fixed. Gainfully I chose the left. In Ethiopia the rule of the road is the right, and whenever we pulled up *The Times* was the side which got the fuller publicity, in floreate Armenian Gothic.

The Italians were also road-building, in their individual style.

By October 27, twenty-four days after they had crossed the Mareb, all-purpose roads had been thrown up to the new line in the Shire range. The order for the final advance on Makalle was given.

The same day the Ethiopian Council, sitting in Addis, decided not to defend Makalle. Wodaju Ali received the Emperor's instruction on the telephone and was told to attach himself to the army of Ras Seyyum. Seyyum and the Dedjaz Kassa Sebhat in Agame were also to be informed.

While the Emperor's communications existed he was implicitly obeyed. The two Army Corps, Santini's I and Pirzio Biroli's Eritreans, advanced with leisurely system, road-making as they went. The Italian Juggernaut was in careful progress again.

Santini hugged the caravan ridge to the east of the plateau, making for Dolo along the route which, a few months later, was Italy's chief highway in Ethiopia. The Eritreans were divided into three columns, which covered the three mule-tracks of Central Tigre—the main track leading to the Tembien, a wildly broken region to the west of Makalle, another track through the Abaro Pass and the third straight through the Geralta, dry and tumbled, directly north of Makalle.

Resistance nowhere along the line. The first week in November they tired of road-making and moved forward more rapidly over the ground, without mechanical transport. At Gundi in the Geralta they clashed with the enemy.

An outlying post of Seyyum's was covering the preparations for the withdrawal from Makalle. Seyyum himself had decided to fall back into the Tembien, down the Gheva valley.

Not even minor resistance confronted Santini. While his Army Corps pursued the mountain ridge to Dolo, whence the track turns suddenly due west to Makalle, foreign journalists dropped down the steep mountain-side and took a short-cut across the plain. So peaceful was the scene at the taking of Makalle. The town could be seen a thousand feet below the ridge, said they, with startling suddenness.

The usual Ethiopian town—a Gibbi on a hill, a big circular church in a compound, representing the two powers of Ethiopia. A dirty causeway, square houses topped with dull brown grass or tin, on which had fallen the dry leaves of the eucalyptus. Dried mud for the market. All the possessions of the supporters of Dedjazmatch Haile Selassie Gucsa were stolen or scattered in the street.

Only the night before Gerazmatch Zagaye, one of the traitor's friends, had led a small patrol up to the town. Machine-gun fire was opened on him from houses on either side . . . a few men dropped dead, for Wedaju Ali was not yet ready to leave. Before dawn he had withdrawn south of the town and west by the torrent Gheva.

Dedjazmatch Haile Selassie Gucsa, an American journalist and the photographer of *The Times* entered Makalle on November 9 without resistance. Coptic priests offered their silver hand-crosses in reverent silk handkerchiefs to be kissed, and the flag of Italy flew again on the Fort of Enda Jesus.

The Emperor's orders had been carried out, the soldiers of Seyyum had been drawn off to the south-west without leaving a trace. Kassa Sebhat offered no frontal resistance to Santini. After a skirmish at Azbi with a Danakil column he likewise withdrew.

Behind the Italians, and along the caravan road hastily rolled and spaded by thousands into a track wide enough for lorries in dry weather, came their enormous land fleet. The Tigreans in the fields screeched Li-li-li at the sight. Some had never seen cars before . . . they had only seen the Emperor's aeroplane.

Thirty thousand troops, with lorries and mules, tanks, armoured cars, machine-guns and artillery moved magnificently down the Dolo track. Thirty thousand of the Eritrean Corps over-ran the tougher centre of the Tigre to keep the right wing of the thirty thousand whites clear. Behind came all the services of the huge host which was here to wage a colonial war, including a heavy artillery which even Marshal Badoglio was ready to abandon.

The services of these two Army Corps concentrated in the narrow bridge-head of Tigre at Makalle became so deeply entangled that there was no advance for over three months after the capture of the town on November 8. Only the passages round the huge mountain to the south of Makalle were occupied: the Doghea Pass south of Sheliket and the craggy course of the Gheva were held by Italian troops. They clasped as it were in their arms the great tableland of Amba Aradam, where the decisive battle of the war was to be fought.

But at this time they were incapable of fighting any battle in front of their lines. General De Bono's machine was too involved to unroll.

Over the thorn and stones of the Tigre and its scattered patches of thin cultivation, the status of slavery was abolished. For roads had to be made. Those who had lounged about in the big man's compound, supplied with a regular daily amount of bread and beer by his womenfolk, now had to earn an honest living. It was wonderful to see their shining faces, wrote the Italian Press, when they realised at last that they were free. . . . The enjoyable prospect of ten hours a day knocking mule tracks into lorry roads warmed many a dark man's heart as well, for the African loves to earn his bread by the sweat of his brow.

The Eritrean Army Corps began to send small columns through the Tembien, and Seyyum with his adviser Konovaloff left the district for the south. They were still awaiting impatiently Ras Kassa with the Gondar levy.

And he was finding, with every new day as the planes droned over Tigre like a ceaseless shuttle, how cruel was the task of a chief who wanted at the same time to shelter and to control his men. Even now, the Gondar and Lasta levy covered an area of four hundred square kilometres, so sparse was the cover in the Tigre. How could one move so huge and shapeless a thing along? — and at night?

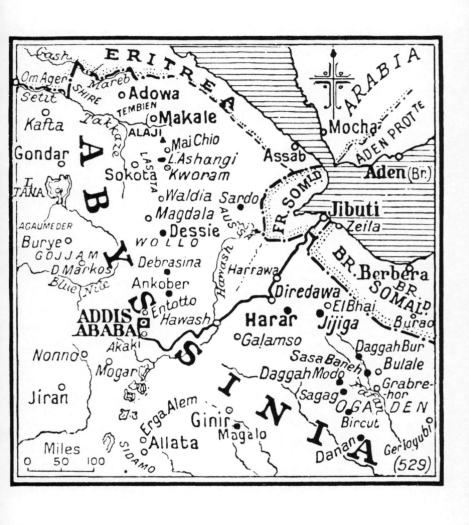

X

ADDIS ABABA HAD SETTLED DOWN again to its African calm.

October, the first fortnight of the war, saw the dispatch of Vinci for Djibouti and of the Yamahal Sarawit under Ras Mulugeta, the seventy year old War Minister, for Dessye and the north. Thirty thousand words of press nonsense went out on an average day from the radio station which the Italians had planted outside Addis, and of which the Ethiopians took the increase. There was little thoroughgoing war news; the Press Bureau turned quickly into an engine of internal propaganda. Aerial bombardments and reconnaissance were rapidly recorded, but we had precious little official news about movements on the ground. Because there were none.

There were a hundred-and-thirty journalists in Addis, eighty of whom had "collect" facilities at the Radio Station. Of the eighty about fifteen would visit the only regular source of news, Colson the American adviser, at midday and at six, when he came back from the Gibbi. We sat in the glass veranda while he sorted the papers in his pocket, and eventually shuffled out the thing which the Ethiopians would publish as a communiqué six hours later. The rest of the day we dashed frantically about in cars between the Legations, the Foreign Ministry, the Palace and the radio, scratching together from the barren rockeries of Ethiopia a few frail seeds from which we hoped would flower exotically a story. Taxis jumped from ten to fifteen dollars a day, real hot rumours from the locals sold at double pre-war price, benzine raced up and down again like a thermometer in the mouth of a man with delirium tremens. What with heavy outlay and wretched returns, we all got to dislike and suspect each other if we were keen journalists; to despise and cut each other if we were not.

A censorship was imposed. A Belgian youth, member of the strange new Belgian military mission, was appointed censor. Under his baffling edict nothing but "government communiqués or false military news" would penetrate the outer world. Meetings of the Foreign Press Association were called to face up to this boy, stirring speeches were made, but the proceedings always ended in a fight between pressmen. All sorts of queer characters crept in under cover of a press card—photographers who said they could write, Pan-African organisers looking for material in Shoa, spies of all nations. Evelyn Waugh once kept the minutes: the accounts passed from hand to hand. A standing surplus could not be expended by me, the permanent secretary, on anything but notepaper: but as there was no object on which notes could be sent, since the Association never reached agreement on any topic, I had regretfully to use our lovely notepaper, stamped "Association de la Presse Etrangère" and designed by the Armenian Imprimerie Artistique, for typing my messages to *The Times*. Fifteen dollars worth lasted me six months: the Committee, a packed body, were agreeable to this economy when I transferred to them some of the envelopes.

For just one ecstatic moment we thought that we had reached agreement on how to bludgeon the censor. Unity was visible at the Association: Collins the President no longer had to bang the table, I no more had to shriek "order" at the treble. No sounds of fisticuffs in the doorway. Stallings was no longer standing up to Linton Wells, the Americans had stopped repeating that the German Press was not free. Even the French did not protest that their sentiments were being flouted. Setting our noses to paper, smelling afar off the blood of the accursed Belgian, we drafted a ferocious resolution and wired our owners that drastic action was afoot.

So it was.

Next morning we visited the censor with our message of doom. The insufferable youth was sitting in his office, wearing a new stock; a golden horseshoe inverted, emblem of hope and happy fortune, pinned into position below his exuberant Adam's apple. Around his table sat renegade journalists, American, French and German, who had come to settle the censorship question in a more friendly manner. All had their hands on the table, all smiled. Our deputation withdrew in wretched order. It was then that, disillusioned, I decided to misappropriate the funds.

Everybody was afraid of an air raid. The Diplomatic Corps met and forwarded to their Governments the information that there were six thousand foreigners in Addis Ababa and five hundred in Diredawa, would they please ask Mussolini not to bomb these unaggressive whites and yellows: Mussolini answered yes, but nobody believed him. The American Minister daubed the Stars and Stripes on his roof. Windy journalists took to the hills. An Ethiopian who valued freedom of circulation under bombardment painted a small Red Cross on the crown of his old Panama. The town emptied, then gradually filled up again.

The old Belgian Military Mission disappeared and the new Mission took its place: the Belgian Minister refused to receive them. The Swedish officers were forced by the Swedish Government to resign their commissions: they stayed.

Huge trainloads of foreigners left Ethiopia; the station at Addis was flooded by the tears of Greeks and resounded to the lamentations of the Levant. Interested persons detected what they called a "change of temperature" in the feeling of the Ethiopian for the white. Ugly looks were noted, but I saw none uglier than nature. To suppress talk of this kind the Municipality published an edict which was read not only in Addis but along the railway zone, proclaiming that the *ferengi* who were enemies were gone; the *ferengi* who remained were friends and must be treated as friends should be treated.

Not strictly true. Vinci was still at his Legation, with sixteen of his staff. Italian Consuls were straggling over the country. Dr. Dagnino, his wife and his two radiotelegraphists arrived from Debra Markos across the Blue Nile: they declared that the roads were still very wet, but that the country people were considerate and provided water and food free. The only trouble that they had was with the Customs north of Addis on Mount Entoto, who wanted to inspect some of their kit. . . . Corbeon came in from Dessye: the same story. The Commercial Agent of Mogalo in the south, Dr. Agostino, started in a leisurely manner for the railway: an amateur entomologist, he spent weeks butterflying *en route* and mapping out a course for Graziani if he ever wanted to strike the railway above the Hawash River. Antonio Prasso, son of the owner of the Prasso concession in Western Wallega, took an affectionate but expensive farewell of the local governor, whose price was five hundred thalers, and walked east to Addis with a caravan bulging with platinum, gold and assorted correspondence. The Italian missionaries in Kaffa, the southwest, sewed their more intimate documents into the seats of their trousers, and struck north-east ominously crackling. In Addis, Vinci sat down to wait, his gates guarded. He came out once into the town, to dine with me: visited the other Legations occasionally under escort. His staff settled down to finish the cellar, while the Ethiopians thought out the note which was meant to rid them of this embarrassing representative of the new diplomacy. Jesus Afewerk was told by the Emperor to leave Rome.

Vinci said he had no instructions. In Rome, six days after the bombardment of Adowa, which was caused by the Ethiopians' aggressive withdrawal of her troops thirty kilometres from the frontier, it was officially stated that Abyssinia was clearly responsible for the rupture of diplomatic relations, as it came about on the initiative of the Abyssinian Government. Surely these unprecedented arguments should be couched in an unprecedented diplomatic language: I recommend Esperanto to high-spirited aggressors.

At ten on a Thursday morning, October 10, Vinci received a polite note requesting him to leave as quickly as possible. A special train would be put at his disposal. Reasons given were the Italian aggression in the Tigre and his improper use of the Legation wireless for the transmission of messages to Rome, forbidden on October 3. Vinci indignantly denied the second accusation, but did not risk himself on the first. He delayed a little: asked the Ethiopians to speed up Agostino, which meant in effect to stop him butterflying. The little man bounced up and down with fun at his novel position, while his staff sold out their racing stable at 40 or 60 dollars, £3 to £5 a horse.

On October 11, Vinci sent a note informing the Ethiopians that Rome permitted him to leave: and the Ethiopians announced a special train for the morrow at eight a.m.

I visited Vinci that evening and spent till midnight with him. He was very worked up. The little man's voice, naturally grating, softened to a coloratura when he spoke of Agostino—"poor Agostino, I cannot leave him behind" —poor Agostino, busy entomologist. As he thought of that net vagrant Vinci's eyes, naturally sparkling with Fascist life, welled unusual water. Then he jumped up and took me out on the veranda, to show me something, he said.

There in the moonlight young Lanzoni, his secretary, was burning the cipher under the trees. A huge bonfire, stoked persistently with a eucalyptus stick and fed with benzine, blackened the steps and stank to high heaven. Jack, the pet monkey, grunted his delight and extinguished outlying flames with the firm pressure of his scarlet behind. But that was not what Vinci had to show. Dramatically he indicated a line at the top of the steps and said, "When they come to-morrow I shall refuse to advance beyond that. I shall tell them that they can only take me further by force." The boy stood on the burning deck. I promised to come early in the morning and record the behaviour of his Naughtiness the Italian plenipotentiary.

Morning at five-thirty. The Italian Legation alive and packing. When I came in they were climbing up the bluegums to hack down the wireless aerial: they were burrowing in the cellar to remove essential parts of the transmitting apparatus. Mombelli, who preferred peaceful penetration to war, was sad and silent. Prince Ruffo spoke joyfully of the possibilities of a return to Nizza.

The old Legation car stood at the steps; the Minister's favourite cheetah was lashed on to a lorry. Six Ethiopian taxicabs, clamouring for and eventually getting twenty-five thalers for the trip to the station, were there to carry personnel and luggage. The usual rate was five thalers return, but it was known throughout Ethiopia that Italy overpaid.

The Minister himself, a little chubby figure in a little

floppy Homburg hat carried his effects to the car, and at six forty-five a member of the unrecognised Belgian military mission arrived to invite the party to leave.

The night before, Vinci had told me that he would yield only to force. But he must have had a strengthening vision in bed, for now he said that he would yield in no case, force included. Meanwhile, he stood behind his line, as children do in games like Catch as Catch Can. A quarter of an hour later and four times during the next two hours, he was visited by various Ethiopians who, with remarkable restraint, repeated the invitation to leave. When Major Moskopoulos, chief of the Secret Police, Gerasmatch Kefele and the Belgian paid the third, Vinci turned fiercely to me and said, "Do you think I would change my mind for three moustaches?"

This stubbornness was catching. Colonel Calderini the Military Attaché, suddenly said that he too would stay in Addis Ababa, on the (ludicrous) grounds that Agostino was an officer of the Reserve and therefore needed the support of the Military Attaché . . . for setting butterflies I guess. Young De Grenet the second Secretary also would not leave the deck, until Vinci told him to.

At nine the staff left for the station, bar Vinci, Calderini and Cesare the valet, who growled and went inside the house. The British and French Ministers had been on the platform since eight. Barton was furious: he waited another hour, then drilled his shoulders and drove home. De Grenet enjoyed a fit of mild hysteria at the trainside and escaped into a public lavatory, saying he must rejoin his chief. A burly Belgian followed hot foot and disarmed him of a revolver which he was carelessly brandishing. At eleven the train left without Vinci.

It was only in the late afternoon that the patient Tasfai Tegan persuaded the three Italians to quit their Legation. Vinci was almost in tears, Calderini white, Cesare the valet couldn't make head or tail of it. Evidently word must have been passed that Vinci could await Agostino: but his removal to the wooden chalet owned by Ras Desta on the slopes of Entoto mountain alarmed him. The Ethiopians for their part were afraid that he would injure himself and wanted to keep him under surveillance. The Emperor, smiling, told his advisers that food was being sent to the house from the Imperial Hotel owned by George Mendrakos, whose cuisine was notoriously unpleasant. "Perhaps they will go," he said. The three recovered rapidly on a regime of French newspapers brought by Tasfai, and on cut-throat.

A fortnight later, when Agostino's scientific work was over and he was approaching the line at Hadama, Vinci and his supporters left for the coast in a closed sleeping-coach. The only evidences of life were pieces of orange peel thrown from the window when the train was in motion, but as it pulled out of Mojjo, Count Vinci shouted a boyish good-bye to me from behind the shutters. Agostino was at Hadama, his bottles full. A military escort and Italian priests and nuns also accompanied this original diplomat, who was sent on from Diredawa next night behind a faster engine.

Mulugeta at last fixed the rent of my house, a hundred and forty thalers in consideration of bombardment risks, and on October 17, when the roads were fairly dry, he was ready to move north. His force, the Yamahal Sarawit, or Army of the Middle, was numbered at eighty thousand. It was to leave for Dessye and there divide, part to stay with the Crown Prince, who was Governor of the Wollo province with his capital at Dessye, part to go farther north with Mulugeta to Makalle.

The Army of the Middle was literally the army of Middle Ethiopia, of Shoa, the central province, the septs of Wallega to the west centre round their capitals of Gore and Saio, and Kambata to the centre-south west where the Great Lakes begin to settle on the Rift Valley. Shoa included the Imperial Guard, dressed in khaki of British cut and carrying British knapsacks, but black and barefooted: it included too the tribal levy of the Shoan chiefs, wearing the shamma of the Amhara, which fluttered clear behind the running infantry, and is called by Ethiopians the "white cloth of Shoa." Of the Governors of Wallega, Bidwoded Makonnen, the Emperor's near relative, had not yet come in, nor had Dedjaz Makonnen Endalkatchu of Gore. But there were various parts of Wallega which belonged to Ras Mulugeta and whose armies he had summoned. Dedjaz Moshesha Wolde of

Kambata too had brought his large army (said to be thirty thousand, nearer twenty thousand) into the capital. Though poorly armed, they were fine fighting material, and their lithe trot round Addis under the green-yellow-red flags of Ethiopia the day that Vinci refused to leave quite overshadowed, for us, that absurd event.

On October 16th, too, the Gofas started entering the town from the south, after a two hundred mile march from their desolate province. Led by their Governor, Dedjaz Abebe Dimtu, and by his three sportive lion cubs, they camped on the outskirts, while the other tribesmen were drafted forward to avoid repetition of the tribal bloodshed which had occurred the night before after a boasting match. Red Cross units saw their first war service in this affray.

The Gofas' fearful reputation was borne out by their fantastic dress, which was either bright brick or glaring ochre: for Abebe had heard of camouflage against the air, and wished his men to resemble geological formations. They were to be seen wandering the city in twos and threes, and they were extremely unpopular. The population declared that they feared neither God, nor man, and would not pay for what they took from the shops. As huntsmen nomads of the Amhara colonial type, they knew the value of progression under cover. Their favourite method of shooting is the sitting posture with the rifle in the right hand, barrel inserted between the great and second toes of the right foot. The left arm and buttock are thus left free and with these they propel themselves forward unobserved. Boastful Gofas profess ability to move two miles in this position without rest or refreshment.

The Emperor had decided that Abebe and the Gofas should do their creep in the Ogaden: Mulugeta wanted them to follow him to the north. Mulugeta wanted to throw all the Europeans, including the Press, out of the country: the Emperor told him gently that it was impossible. For internal peace, the only thing was to get Mulugeta off to the war at once. The Emperor fixed next day, October 17th, for his review: after that he would have to leave the town.

A great tent, scarlet within, was set up on the grassless plain below the Old Gibbi. Carpets lined the earth, and gilt chairs were placed upon a temporary dais.

The Emperor, in khaki field uniform, took his seat upon the highest chair next morning at ten. His ministers, all except Blattangeta Herrouy, the Foreign Minister, carrying service rifles, squatted on the ground below him. Fearsome yells, reminiscent of Maskal, announced the head of the procession. The Emperor's guards loosened their swords and rhino-whips as the leaders of the Yamahal Sarawit approached the tent-entrance. The ramshackle buildings on the edge of the plain were filled with spectators who bellowed encouragement to the vanguard of Ethiopia. Dust rose into the pale air and confused the wheeling hawks.

It took four hours, from ten-thirty to two-thirty, for the army to pass the Emperor's dais. It proceeded in jerks, some running by, others marching in order, others stopping to shriek a précis of their warlike achievements or to demand new arms of the King of the Kings of Ethiopia.

The troops ranged from the Imperial Guard, followed by Vickers guns on well-trained mules, to fierce fighting men from the provinces armed with nothing better than sticks and empty cartridge belts. These capered in front of the Emperor in a cloud of dust, clamouring for rifles and ammunition, their idle sticks erect like a hopfield in winter. Those whose firearms were too old for action threw them with a deafening racket to the ground, or cracked the butts with their hands until they were flogged off by palace officials and the municipal police, all of whom now were wearing khaki and carrying carbines.

Splashing the procession with deeper noise and more penetrative colour came the negariet, or war-drums, male and female, large and small, which were balanced on the backs of lightfoot mules and beaten in a menacing tattoo by Ras Mulugeta's scarlet-turbaned drummers. These, old professionals, looked straight ahead in the intensity of their rhythmic effort; sweat and dust started from their faces, but their eyes were glazed and yellow with a sacred activity. They bestrode their mules' hindquarters, only their legs dangled down in physical relaxation, nearly trailing on the beaten ground. Behind them came the levies of Chelia and Konta, then the licentious Gofas, smeared irregularly with ochre and pink. These, as they passed by under their local chiefs, to whom alone they concede a small authority, were inclined to treat the Emperor simply as an arsenal.

I squatted under the canopy with the Ministers, and enjoyed many anxious moments. Men drew their long swords, straight like a crusader's or curved to a fishtail point, and swung them backward dangerously as they went through the fearful motions of attacking, dispatching and dissecting an enemy. Their swordsmanship was skilled to the miraculous. The men following madly behind were untouched: the Palace servants in front lashed them off without injury. And as they shrieked, lept, flashed swords, cracked butts in dozens and covered us with earth, the Emperor conversed amiably with their chiefs who stood by his dais and, slender brown hands to their mouths and the sovereign's ear, whispered low words of encouragement before joining the long column. This moved out of the town to the vibration of war songs and row of drums.

Only one accident.

This sole disaster of the day was experienced by a chief whose silver-bridled mule, frightened by the Ras' drummers, bolted over a wide meadow towards the palace. Faithful retainers hurried after their lord and the chase, thus stimulated by Ethiopian feudal devotion, only ended by that dignitary falling heavily to earth.

Ras Mulugeta himself passed the throne about noon, preceded by hornblowers dressed in European uniform, their gigantic antlers lifted high. Drawing his sword of modern temper, the towering grizzled figure with the face of an eagle approached the dais and the Emperor slowly rose and saluted. Mulugeta was in a different dress from that of Maskal: the Ras's peaked coronet was discarded for a khaki helmet, and his chest blazed with decorations from his European journeys; instead of the velvet surplice broidered with lion mane and the silk jodhpurs he wore field uniform. Typical of Abyssinia's indomitable and intemperate old age he set his sword to earth as a formal sign of fealty and proceeded to give words of blunt advice.

Curtly: "Do not interest yourself overmuch in politics," he said. "Your weakness is that you trust the foreigner too much: kick him out. What are all these fools of the Press doing here? I am ready to die for my country, and you are too, we know. War is now the thing and to conduct it you had better remain in the city of Addis Ababa. Send all the foreigners packing. I swear you perfect loyalty."

The Emperor replied in the learned philosophical tones which he knew always baffled the old general. No man, he said, reposed his money or his confidence in a servant that he did not trust, and he was in that position with regard to the Ethiopian people. He gave the same advice about the wearing of khaki, the abandonment of white shammas, guerrilla tactics, scattering before planes and tanks that he gave on mobilisation day. The troops should not use the wide radial style of encampment traditional to Ethiopia, but should settle under cover of trees and in hidden caves and gorges. "Every man who dies for Ethiopia," he said, "will be a holy saint and martyr, and I am ready, too, to pour out my blood, with my family, children and dynasty."

He thus showed to the Ethiopians that he did not intend to follow the advice of the War Minister: that he was going to the war.

Dedjaz Mangasha Ilma, Director of the War Ministry and the Emperor's uncle, led off the vanguard to Bole camp on the plain towards Debra Brehan and Dessye. The Gofas were barred the town for misbehaviour and calculated ferocity. Ras Mulugeta followed with his great tent.

At Bole, however, he preferred to use a hut, roofed with corrugated iron, where he sat for a day or two dealing out severe sentences to disobedient soldiers. Moshesha Wolde with his lean-faced Kambatas was also with him. The army scattered northward to Dessye, by the two caravan tracks and the new Imperial Road. Other troops arriving from Gore filled the Akaki plain.

Dedjaz Abebe and his Gofas had been told by the Emperor that they would be used in the Ogaden; Mulugeta with typical tyranny ordered Abebe to follow him to the north. He was interfering now in all directions: he had even chained up the Ethiopian Director of the Finance Ministry because Colson had opposed his mobilisation plan. Measures of pardon extended by the Emperor to his old enemies, Fitorari Birru and the eunuch commander Dedjazmatch Balcha, had strengthened Mulugeta's conservative following.

Dedjaz Abebe told Mulugeta sharply that if indeed he

owed allegiance to anybody, he owed it to the Emperor. So far as he felt like being obedient, it would not be to Mulugeta. The Emperor intervened gently: to show that Abebe's political theory was the more orthodox, he invited him to a gebir with his ochred spearmen. Abebe later went to the cinema run by the Greek Georgitis. While the young baron celebrated his victory with his womenfolk following intently the film, "Peg de Mon Cœur," his three lion cubs and his indolent slaves curled up on the veranda outside and slept for three hours solid.

Mulugeta's army drifted off. We watched the curious procession pass the British Legation gates by twos and threes. What could they do? They thought that they could do everything.

Barefooted, in their ragged dirty jodhpurs, their swords sticking far away behind them, they moved along with a steady stride. If they had had time they had bought wide sun-hats made of dried grass: their rifles were slung round their necks with rimpjes, or carried by a little boy. Most had no servants but their wives: some had mules, and if they had mules they could take tents. The men themselves went ahead carrying the tent-poles, from the ends of which dangled sandals and a few pouches and calabashes: more pouches, holding food, hung around their persons. The woman leaning forward in her long broad skirts to haul the mule, brought up the tent and sacks of mashila or dried peas. All carried a little sack of piastres and pesas for the country-side: on every man there was a cartridge belt, whether full or empty.

On the 21st Mulugeta himself left. Until he reached Dessye, in spite of his age (he was well over seventy), and his confirmed alcoholism, he proved himself an indefatigable marcher. Leaving at dawn, he would do twenty-five miles a day until four o'clock, when he encamped. Behind him followed his seven secretaries and their servants, carrying on their heads the tables and chairs which he would use for writing dispatches to the Emperor and autocratic orders to the country-side through which he passed. His military adviser was a Cuban machine-gunner, Delvalle, educated in Texas, and for some time a member of the A.B.C., the secret Cuban revolutionary organisation.

Haile Selassie had given orders not to spoil the fields or

bludgeon the peasants on the way north: but the farther from the capital was Mulugeta the more disobedient did he become. His troops, saving their rations, lived almost entirely on the country. Whenever they saw a field of beans, corn or maize, they were down on it like a troop of monkeys: it was stripped and eaten raw. To hell with this new-fangled commissariat, thought Mulugeta, as he trudged along.

There were pauses when he sent back messages to Addis; when he waited for troops who were left behind. Delvalle set his army at between sixty thousand and seventy thousand, but the old Ras himself did not know how big it was. Among the high-spirited rabble were troops of the Imperial Guard in better formation: machine-gun detachments with good mules, and a few mountain guns. About ten thousand of the Imperial Guard went north over Entoto, where they divided in thick columns along caravan tracks, part to the Blue Nile for Gojjam, part to Warru Hailu for Dessye.

For mile upon mile of North Shoa stretched the trail of brown ants, sensing the direction in which they had to move; eating up everything.

At Dessye the Crown Prince and his tutor, Dedjazmatch Wodaju, mobilised Wollo: it was a difficult process. Wollo was riddled with sedition paid from the Italian Commercial Agency at Dessye. The old Wollo chiefs, adherents of Lij Yasu whom Haile Selassie dethroned, dared not refuse, but they intended to delay. No rifles . . . no food . . . no money. . . . When Mulugeta arrived in Dessye on November 4, there were floggings. Delay was killed by the ancient Ethiopian method.

On November 7 the Crown Prince could safely fly to Addis to report the success of the Wollo mobilisation and learn from his father the other principles on which Addis should be ruled when he took over control of the city. The road to Dessye, built and improved by Ayenna Birru, the young Wallega Galla trained at the Camborne School of Mines, was nearly ready. It was in that long transitional state notorious in Africa: nobody knew exactly how ready it was.

Pressing his thousands of ants into motion again, Mulugeta continued northward, with much more care than before. He felt that he was now in the zone of aeroplanes. Men had to be sent ahead to blow horns from mountains if they saw the Italians coming through the sky. Only small groups could follow.

It took a month and a half more for him to reach the north. From Dessye to Lake Ashangi, even to Amba Alagi where he knew the planes were always flying, there was cover, but he did not like the population. From Amba Alagi there was no cover. The old man became nervous.

Already the Gallas around the Lake and south of it had given trouble: they were paid from Makalle now to do so. They must be given a lesson. Leaving a large part of his force at Waldia, Mulugeta marched rapidly on the celebrated "shifta" village of Cobbo. Unexpectant Cobbo, south of Lake Ashangi, came out with its tej and its dergo, customary gifts to a passing army, when Mulugeta marched in towards the middle of November. The old man, who could act when he wanted with a brutal speed, divided the male population into the sheep and the goats. He had evidence of treasonable relations between some of the Galla leaders and the Dedjazmatch Haile Selassie Gucsa.

The men he wanted he forced to join his army. The others were flogged to death or near it. When Holmes reached Cobbo at the end of February and asked for tej, a solitary old man told him that they no longer made tej in the village. There were no men left to drink it.

A large garrison was established at Koram near the Lake to deal with the "shifta" trouble. Caves were excavated for the chiefs. Very gingerly, Mulugeta went forward to Amba Alagi. He was not sure of the water, nor of the Italian planes, which he had not yet seen. Small parties followed each other slowly to Amba Alagi, betrayed only by their mule trains.

On November 13 and 14 the Italians with ten planes bombed the road from Antalo to the high pass of Amba Alagi, where they noticed khaki uniforms. They thought that it was the soldiery of Mulugeta, but it was not. Exactly a month before the pass had been bombed for the first time. It was the same army that they had attacked —that army of the careless front and hurrying end; the army of Ras Kassa.

It took the Italians three months before they understood how the Ethiopians marched. Step by step: small parties: rough estimate of the water supply as they progressed through unknown territory to the front. Never great herds of pack animals to show the airmen where there were agglomerations of men. Caves and bushes: garrisoning of the points occupied.

Kassa's army took precisely a month to file across the Amba Alagi ridge into the Tigre; and even then he was using for his main force the other caravan route to the west, from Sokota to Fenaroa.

Mulugeta, who had been told strictly not at any cost to mass before the enemy, but to hold firmly the Imperial Road from Dessye to Makalle, left another garrison at Amba Alaji and directed them to dig trenches. Bidwoded Makonnen, the all-powerful ruler of Wallega, took over this position.

Mulugeta saw his first planes fly over on the 28th of November, when Lake Ashangi was reconnoitred. On the 1st of December, other planes noted large masses of Ethiopian troops moving over the Pass: they could not know that these, the men of Mulugeta, had been ordered forward in haste to prevent the Italians pressing Seyyum out of the Tembien. The rearguard was heavily bombed on December 10.

It took Kassa a month to enter into the Tigre. It took Mulugeta, hurrying at the end, almost the same time. Bitterly the two elder Ras in the north reported to the Emperor their powerlessness to move under the Italian reconnaissance planes.

"They chain us up like prisoners," they said.

Air supremacy was already beginning to disintegrate their armies.

Mulugeta had no field radio: all his messages to his commanders were taken by runners. Scattered over a large area for fear of the planes, it was long before they could receive or respond to an order. They did not know, when they moved along, where their other parties were. They were never in the villages—that would be to expose themselves to bombardment. To keep together they lay near the road, mile after mile: or along the mountain tracks which ran east and west of it.

At no time had order been a quality of Ethiopian armies, but now even the mass movement which had carried them along vanished before the planes. Mulugeta, with the old instinct of Ethiopian leadership, sensed the change. Somehow or other, he must gather these scattered bands together under his ferocious eye.

Two months had passed since he had left Addis. The Ethiopians only owe service for two months in the year. It did not matter, he thought, so much about the Gallas whom he had pressed into the army, but the Shoans and Wallegas and Kambatas would have to be paid. He would have to open the chests of thalers in his baggage.

XI

IT WAS THE SOUTHERN WAR which worried us most at this time. The Ethiopians had already suffered severe reverses in the Ogaden. The little camps in the thick camel-thorn waste, under the burning sun, were drenched with blood. The air had mastered its easiest targets. . . .

In the south Graziani opened the war with a splash; with the capture of two camps and the bombardment, as he thought, of two support headquarters.

Gerlogubi, with its forty men under Balambaras Tafere, was overwhelmed on the second day of the war. The Italians had nearly four thousand troops at hand in the Walwal area to do this.

To the far west Dolo was a half-Ethiopian, half-Italian town on the Juba river. Climbing over a clay wall, the forces of civilisation occupied the section which was still savage.

Gorahai in the east and Mogalo in the west were bombed heavily three times each in October. In the Italian view, Mogalo was the support headquarters for the Ethiopians who occupied the crumbling banks of the Webbe Shebeli at Imi. But they also concentrated on the Italian Commercial Agency, where the Ethiopians announced that they had found a large store of ammunition.

At Gorahai Afewerk was delighted with the results of his bombardments. He had carefully constructed a contempt for aeroplanes in his men. He still ate his food with the knife made out of a bomb-splinter, to show that these noisy "pomps" which never hit anybody could be put to sensible uses when the planes went away. Now he made a cap out of another.

Since my visit he had dug another series of trenches round

Gorahai, with shallow bomb-proof shelters. Fifteen hundred troops were assembled here. His radio kept in touch with Tafere Katama and Harrar every day.

Six Capronis bombed on October 4, 5 and 11. The fort held steady as a rock. Afewerk fired his solitary Oerlikon from the exposed turret of the Mullah's fort while the bombs rained around him.

On the 5th, three hundred projectiles were dropped, a hundred of which Afewerk noted with satisfaction failed to explode. Five men were killed and fifteen wounded by two direct explosions on a trench, which Afewerk attributed to chance. On the 11th the wireless operator, a feeble civilian, ran away; but he was captured and put to work again: report—"slight injury to wireless."

Tafere Katama, the fort on the Webbe Shebeli facing Moustahil, was bombed on the same days. Shellabo, halfway between Tafere Katama and Gorahai, a petty post, was bombed on the 11th.

The effect of these bombardments on the Ethiopian soldier must be imagined. First, a belief at the back of his mind that the aeroplane was a devilish instrument, uncannily accurate when it was directly on top of you: and when you looked up it seemed always to be on top of you. Afewerk's steady propaganda in Gorahai had done much to counter this, but the other camps were less indoctrinated.

Second the failure of all Ethiopian arms to bring a plane down. Bitterest of all, the feeling that one could never send *one's own* planes back to strike the Italians. And then . . . the infernal explosions and someone with his guts pouring out into the trench.

Afewerk maintained morale. But he had to ask for reinforcements. The first that came to him was the rain.

In the Ogaden it rains intermittently in September and October, after the rains have stopped on the high plateau. The dry sandbeds become torrents for a day or two, and the pink earth along the Ogaden tracks a spongy pulp. A mechanised column sinks into the mud and sometimes remains engraven in the earth after it has dried, so quickly does the mud turn into rock again in the Ogaden.

Italian mechanised columns were ready for the attack on Tafere Katama on October 14. Rain fell there and at

Gorahai. On the 15th rain continued. It was decided to attack by foot under the cover of the Somaliland aviation.

Tafere Katama and Shellabo were simultaneously attacked by the Dubats, the Somali irregulars who held the Italian frontier posts of Moustahil and Ferfer which faced these two objectives.

The Dubats, sly as cats in the bush, crept up to Tafere Katama: when they were in position in the cover surrounding the fort to the south, below the rocky hill, the fort was bombed intensively by ten planes. The Ethiopians scattered and hid, as they had been instructed to do: and the bandas rushed in with machine-guns. The fight lasted for two hours with severe losses on both sides, but the Ethiopians, caught by surprise and scattered, were outnumbered and out-machine-gunned. Shellabo, a much smaller post, fell in exactly the same way—the same number of planes, the same number of Dubats.

The occupation of Shellabo on the road behind the frontier post ought to have cut off the survivors of Tafere Katama. But many of these struggled through the bush, with water only from the Webbe Shebeli in their small gourds, until they reached Gorahai, a journey that took them seven days. Whether it was true or not, Afewerk reported that two of the planes that attacked Tafere Katama were shot down when they flew low to machine-gun the camp.

Something happened which prevented the planes from stooping over Gorahai or any of the Ogaden camps again. They had machine-gunned Gorahai in their first raid. Now they kept at a safe altitude—three thousand feet or more.

Gabridihari, behind Gorahai, was bombed. All the posts on either side of it, Gerlogubi, Tafere Katama, Shellabo, had fallen. Afewerk's scouts reported that the waterhole at Maranale had been taken, only a few kilometres from Gorahai where the old Italian road from Ferfer joins the Ethiopian track to Gerlogubi. New small arms and ammunition, the pick of the material which had come in from Berbera when the arms embargo was abandoned, were sent down to Gorahai, together with a few more men.

The Italians wrote afterwards of the anti-tank guns and the sixty machine-guns that Afewerk had at Gorahai. The only anti-tank gun was the Oerlikon that he handled. His machine-guns were at most four; he had about forty machine-gun rifles.

To overwhelm Gorahai the Italians prepared an enormous column, Six battalions of Dubats, a hundred and fifty lorries, four field batteries, nine tanks and twenty armoured cars. It advanced along the Ferfer road.

Afewerk, who got good service of espionage from his Somalis—he was the only Ethiopian on this front who understood the organisation of intelligence—heard of its preparation and made his own. Five hundred of the new "regular" troops which had arrived from Harrar at the end of August were sent into the bush on the eastern edge of Gorahai plain, to shelter there and attack the column when it left its lorries to encircle Gorahai. The men carried everything with them, water as well as food.

On November 2 Gorahai was bombed mercilessly from the air by twenty planes. Again and again their whole cargo of bombs was loosed on a circular target only a hundred and fifty yards wide cut visibly in the ground below. It took them half an hour only to reload and return.

Afewerk was struck in the leg by a heavy splinter as he served his Oerlikon. It was a serious wound and he could not be cared for at Gorahai. Daggahbur was the nearest Red Cross unit, two hundred and twenty kilometres north.

Afewerk knew that if he went back all his men would follow. Ethiopians do not last out the battle if their chief falls. However resounding the victory, they must take him back to consecrated ground. It is their last duty to him, and the braver he is the more they admit the obligation.

The Gerazmatch decided to do without medical aid. He had insisted always on the necessity of sacrifice, and he was the man to play his part.

He sent a wireless message to Nasibu informing him that he was severely, perhaps mortally wounded, but that he would hold on to Gorahai. Meanwhile reinforcements must be sent under a good leader, fit to take over command of the fort which he had organised.

Only Ali Nur and Fitorari Simu, and Afewerk's personal servants, knew of his wound. He continued to fire the Oerlikon. The soldiers noticed that he did not leave his gun turret. He could not. He could scarcely crawl.

On November 3 Gorahai was bombed again by twenty

planes. The gun was handled, though the pain was becoming intense. The Italians, who were getting to know the place now, also bombed the Somali waterhole near the fort, scattering the herds and killing the Somali women who were taking the day's water there.

On November 4 the twenty planes returned to their fearful work of devastation. Ali Nur, who is a brave man, told me it could no longer be borne. The whole earth heaved about and rocked under explosions which seemed to break the ears. One could not see to shoot under the deep pall of sand. Nothing but sand, flashes of red lightning, thundercrack explosions, more sand, groans and shrieks of wounded men, the earth heaving in foul yellow obscurity and a noise like the falling of mountains.

And all at once the Oerlikon, whose repetition had kept them steady in their places, ceased to fire.

Afewerk had fallen unconscious. He was sprawling over the breech of his gun, his hands tumbled to the ground. His wound was beginning to gangrene.

Poems have been written about Sir John Moore, but there will be no poets in Ethiopia to celebrate his counterpart. For in his unenlightened way Afewerk was a great soldier and a noble spirit: like Moore he cared for his troops and explained to them the meaning of the innovations that were for their own good. One innovation only he could never teach them: recovery after the loss of himself.

Afewerk is forgotten as Ethiopia is forgotten. The great soldiers before whom Europe bows are those who have hundreds of aeroplanes, oil, petrol, artillery heavy and light, thousands of machine-guns, lorries and tractors, trained staffs, wireless, Army Corps after Army Corps. If they succeed, like Badoglio, they are acclaimed as the geniuses that they are always said to be: if they make little headway like Graziani, circumstances are said to have been against the display of their genius. Perhaps the General Plan of the campaign did not allow them to move—or the troops at their command were only twice those of the enemy.

The Gerazmatch Afewerk had none of their advantages, no material on which to work: in spite of which, he built up something.

But enough of this tedious subject. The wounds of this

unknown black man are beginning to smell even more than he used to smell alive. Let us bury him quickly and forget his unfortunate intrusion into Valhalla, which only the white materialists are fit to occupy.

The secret of Gorahai could no longer be kept. They carried Afewerk out, his lips firmly compressed, and placed him with great care upon a lorry. They counted their dead and wounded: twelve killed outright, seventy dying or seriously hurt. Ethiopians do not consider light wounds. Fitorari Simu, when the planes had gone, ordered the retreat; though Afewerk had told him to stick to the fort.

A broken force, in spirit as well as body, they took their leader out on his bumping lorry to the north. Gabridihari also, which had been bombed twice, followed the rout. The "regulars" in the bush followed in better order.

The Italians entered the empty camp on November 7. The yellow grass huts had been burnt to the ground. Afewerk died, I believe, before his lorry reached Daggahbur. All his army broke out into uncontrollable weeping. I have not bothered to find out where he was buried. After all, I was a journalist, and who in England wants to know?

Colonel Maletti was ordered to pursue the Gorahai garrison to Daggahbur, with six tanks, eleven armoured cars, and between two and three hundred Dubats. Clearly the Italians had hopes of an unlimited advance using Somali troops only.

An excitable Italian press announced the capture of Sasabaneh (where there was no Ethiopian position) and even of Daggahbur.

Gorahai became what Afewerk always feared it would become: a perfect air base.

The fall of Gorahai and Gabridihari, and the Italian claim to an advance on Harrar which I did not know then was extravagant, gave my ideas about the war a nasty jerk. I knew that Harrar could be taken any day now that the Ogaden rains were over. The dry bush and hard dusty earth rolling sweetly to Daggahbur and Jijiga gave easy passage to the mechanised arm. It was like sending a toy tank over carpet.

The Italians said that they were at Gabridihari . . . at

Warandab . . . at Sasabaneh . . . at Daggahbur. Halfway to Jijiga in two days, according to them. Three motorised columns operating. The Ethiopians in headlong flight to Harrar.

I knew that there were only seven thousand Ethiopians to stop them; scattered under different leaders, they were probably demoralised.

And then on November 11th, while the padré in Addis was preaching a good sarcastic Armistice Day sermon to the Legation, the Anglo-American colony, Reuter and *The Times*, the Ethiopians ambushed an Italian motorised column at Anale.

Actually it was the end of the Italian offensive from the south. Both sides ran back fifty miles to report. In the waterless territory of the Ogaden re-appeared that vacuum which it did not abhor. The Ethiopians were abashed by their victory: the Italians astonished by their defeat.

It happened thus. The day was very hot. Colonel Maletti with six tanks and his Somali irregulars in lorries left Gorahai soon after its capture. The Ethiopians were in full flight from Gorahai and Gabridihari northward. Maletti followed them along the Tug Fafan. His small tanks were put in lorries and covered with tarpaulins: their drivers sat tanning themselves on top of them and enjoying a tankman's holiday.

Somewhere near Anale the wide plain east of the Fafan is broken by dry river beds heavy with sand. This is an area of occasional wells, of Borgut, Sasabaneh and Anale itself. The little tanks dismounted and led the column. The Ethiopians might have stopped here to take water. One must be careful.

The Ethiopians had stopped. Their tyres were flat and their radiators steaming. They laid their wounded out on the ground near Anale.

Fitorari Gongol was marching south of Daggahbur with five hundred men. His objective was Gorahai: he was the reinforcement that Afewerk had demanded. He did not know that Gorahai had already been abandoned. Before Anale he heard the distant noise of rifle-fire and told his men to divide into the bush on either side of the red road.

They took cover and advanced quickly fifty yards from the open, blotted by the opaque thorn.

Maletti had caught the Ethiopians at Anale. They scattered like buck, leaving the jacks under their damaged lorries. The tanks roared after them over tufted sandhills, zigzagging round the treacherous crumbling dongas, and crushing thornbush. The tanks, slit narrowly in front for eyes, were half blind in the dust which their tracks knocked up. The sun was burning hot, for it was nearly eleven o'clock . . . on Armistice Day. The drivers, sweating, shoved up their lids and shot forward, spitting a chain of fire.

They drove, with a fearful grind of tracks, straight into the troops of Fitorari Gongol. He was leading them himself and fell wounded to one of the first bullets from their linked machine-guns.

His servants fell at his side, firing and tugging at their swords.

The tanks passed over them, moved again to left and right. The Ethiopians understand cover Perfectly. Not a man could be seen in the dirty dust-clouded bush.

A tank moved up to a little hill to inspect. It fidgeted this way and that. Twenty Ethiopians were lying in the roots of thorn trees forty yards away. At the top the driver stopped. Nothing visible. A head in a suffocating crash helmet bobbed up from the tank. "We thought it was a cruel animal," the soldiers told me, "we dared not shoot."

The driver got out. It was a two-man tank, Fiat-Ansaldo, double machine-gun 1935 model. The machine-gunner got out, as the Ethiopians held their breath and pressed closer into the thorns.

"Kill them," whispered their officer. Twenty shots from the Fusil Gras. "They fell very slowly to the ground, like sand off riverbanks," the soldiers told me.

They did not dare approach the tank which had killed, they thought, their Fitorari Gongol. Another tank came up, stopped its engine, could not see in the track dust. It shouted to the other tank—no reply. "We think they wanted to know what was wrong, and could not see," said the soldiers.

Again the men got out. Another volley, and they slipped to the ground. But the Ethiopians dared not approach. There might be more men in the tank, they thought.

A third tank came up and in a businesslike manner the driver got out to fix chains on one of the others. His machine-gunner was meant to cover him, but the guns were fixed in a traverse of 15° pointing in the wrong direction. The driver fell dead: they think that they wounded the machine-gunner, I don't know how.

Many of the Somalis in the lorries were shot down as they tumbled off them into cover. A wicked fire out of the bush mowed them through before they could use their guns. The Habash is the master of the Somali any day.

Both fled.

The Somalis, because the invincible tanks had been conquered; the Habash because the incomprehensible had happened and, master-key to the Ethiopian morale, their leader lay on the ground. Picking him up carefully, they bolted back to Daggahbur.

It was a victory that left the Ogaden once more to the hyaenas and the vultures. It was the end of Graziani's Ogaden offensive, though at that time I thought it was simply an incident in it. The Somali *bandas*, who had always believed that tanks could lead anywhere, refused to move in the Ogaden sector. Graziani's white troops were then too poor to go ahead, so he thought.

With the wretchedest troops properly armed, he could have pressed on to Harrar. There he could have lived on the rich country and smashed the railway. He dared not. He thought that the Ethiopians were a hundred thousand strong.

The Italian bodies were mutilated and distributed among the local Ogaden. The machine-gunner who could not drive the tank died of starvation and thirst after three days of the sour camel's water of the Ogaden.

No one knows what happened to a fourth tank, which the Ethiopians said with alarm was bigger and had a cannon. The other tanks lay on their hill a fortnight.

Stokes, a young Englishman of the Bible Churchman's Mission, drove a Red Cross lorry down past Anale and picked up Ethiopian wounded. They turned on him and tried weakly to kill him, thinking him an Italian, but he brought them back. He saw the tank tracks in the Anale sand, but no tanks.

I decided to go down to Harrar. Lolita was there already, and Margarita came down with us to join her.

It was very unexciting on the line. The Italians and the French directorate of the Franco-Ethiopian railway had come to an agreement about the railway. The enemy planes which had formerly appeared at odd points along the single-track line stayed now at Italian Assab.

For their part the Ethiopian Government now knew for certain that they would be unable to import more arms through Djibouti. By a process of hard bargaining in Paris, the Laval-Mussolini pact of January, 1935, was working itself out into its uttermost unmentionable details.

Taylor was with us. Taylor, the gunner who had turned geographer. Captain R. H. R. Taylor, now Assistant Military Attaché at the British Legation in Addis Ababa, had served as surveyor-general on the Anglo-Ethiopian boundary commission whose work culminated in the Battle of Walwal and before that on the Anglo-Italian boundary commission which had delimited the short frontier between Italian and British Somaliland. He knew the tracks and wells of Somaliland, of the district inhabited by the Ogaden tribes in particular, with the science of a phrenologist. Every bump in that scrubby skull had its name for him.

Taylor is a big heavy man and when he is in boots he thuds abroad. A leading figure in the Plughole hunt, he disguised a paternal mind underneath a close-cut head, glasses of Teutonic steel simplicity, and moustaches which forked skyward in an enormous growth which would have shamed Wilhelm II in his heyday. Taylor believed in no nonsense, no fancy stuff. His favourite dialectical method was scorn, executed in a slow but steady double bass. His tobacco pouch, emblem of critical serenity, was often in evidence. So was an elaborate collection of keys. Taylor was a methodical person, everything had its hole and corner. In recognition of his girth and capacity we called him the Firkin.

At the Hawash bridge we took different sides of the train for purposes of military espionage. Between us we spotted an anti-aircraft gun, three machine-gun posts, and disconnected strands of barbed wire entanglements. Three hundred men under a Swiss and his wife, Captain and Mrs. Wittlin, defended the most strategic point on the Franco-Ethiopian railway. Mrs. Wittlin had sores on the legs. Some of the men were down with fever exhaled from the featureless Hawash gorge. Others were out shooting the prolific game. The Greeks were snoozing in the bar under the purple bougainvillea.

Along the railway line the dirt-track under mimosa, meant to replace the railway if that were bombed, had only been half-finished. The alternative telephone had been half erected. Any Italian flight of planes could have landed troops and taken the place in a single morning, wiped out the garrison and gone home in the afternoon. The moral effect would have been enormous. But as I have said, the Italians in this war did not take a single risk. Theirs was the progress of a machine, sometimes out of gear, but always avoiding a reverse. Their Cæsar was a mechanical Cæsar, innovating only to improve a military method, not to make a daring coup which would strike alarm in the heart of the enemy.

Signor Mussolini believed in white prestige; nothing more. By that he meant white military invincibility, not the spread of Roman culture. He found white prestige such a delicate thing that a single small defeat could wipe it away. So he took no risks. He ran his Juggernaut very carefully and efficiently, on benzine.

At Diredawa, all quiet. Continual friction between the French garrison, Senegalese who were there to guard French interests in the railway works, and the Ethiopian governor of the town. The French had tried physically to stake out claims to an area round the station. The governor would not have it. Altogether a lot of bad temper, diluted with a lot of whisky.

A third element in the strife were the new Diredawa police, uniformed in blue, and tough customers.

Before leaving Addis Margarita had taken the precaution of asking for permission to travel to Harrar. Permits to go from point to point are usual in Ethiopia at any time: in war they are often potent weapons of delay. But

Margarita was popular, and they wrote on her press-card with a biblical simplicity, "Let the woman go to Harrar."

I had no permit. But after sitting half an hour on the governor's doorstep and scrawling various patterns of the Italo-Ethiopian war in the dust of the Diredawa pavement, and after visiting three offices for three different stamps, standing five drinks and telling an obstructive servant he was a bastard,* I got a far more elaborate permit to Harrar.

Collins had a different pass, equally valid. Lolita was in bed with fever at Diredawa, so we left the two Spaniards there at Bollolakos Hotel, and went up the mountain road to Harrar, lovely ledge in the khat-covered hills.

Harrar, too, was full of journalists. The Hotel de l'Imperatrice, a bathless establishment with a solitary lavatory, sheltered the distinguished French. Tharaud (Paris-Soir), Helsey (*The Journal*), Lavoix (*Havas*) leant every day over their balcony and imagined that an anti-European atmosphere was rising among the Harraris. But the only atmosphere that rose was due to the Greek drainage system: in every way possible, the proprietor made them pay through their noses.

Another nest of the press was Mademoiselle Hall's, which lay outside the town on the Diredawa road. The Halls were charming people who had a bath. Their Ethiopian blood gave them perfect easy manners, their German the quality of deliberate cleanliness. The two sisters, Mlle. Hall and Frau Schumacher, were descended from a German missionary and they had the old missionary virtues— equity, industry, peacefulness, order. Mlle. Hall had been the Governess of the Princess Tsahai, the Emperor's daughter. Their brother bought arms for the Emperor and did his banking in Europe; but their life was less adventurously bound to Harrar, where their *pension* was now prospering.

Denny of the *New York* Times, Paula Lecler, Collings of *Liberty*, sat in peace round an oval table in this establishment, where they ate German food and listened to Frau Schumacher perform upon the guitar, singing the while.

* This is not so beastly as it sounds. "Min a batu" meaning simply "Who is your father?" is the usual way of making an Abyssinian servant get a move on.

But the most extravagant and noisy of the journalistic menageries was that assembled at the British Consulate, a three-storeyed white house in a lovely sheltered garden standing on a hill a mile outside Harrar. The keeper of this zoo, Chapman-Andrews, had dealt with Kurds and Iraqis in his time without flinching, but a fortnight after our arrival he removed to the Swedish Hospital for a rest-cure.

The pressmen in their separate cages were as follows, 1. Herbert Ekins, of the United Press. Ekins was a flash expert on China and Manchukuo. He could send any big story back in a split second. He held the most extraordinary views about the numbers of troops which Nasibu had assembled in the Ogaden. He was convinced that Graziani would enter Harrar before the end of 1935. Betting was his favourite sport and his formula, uttered in a high impulsive voice was this:—

"I lay you all that General Graziani will enter Harrar by the Jijiga gate in Nasibu's Ford V8, with Dedjazmatch Nasibu in his entourage, £10 by December 1st, £25 by December 15th, £50 by Christmas Day."

The Jijiga gate was a corrugated iron erection on the Ogaden road just below the Consulate. A few people were bright enough to take his bets but most, including myself, were too alarmed by the circumstantiality of the terms to utter a word. Ekins, we felt, must be in the know.

2. Lawrence Stallings of Movietone and Nana. Stallings wrote "What Price Glory" and "The Big Parade": a poetic genius of immense verbal power, with the dislike of the Confederate States for coloured men, he ran about loose in Ethiopia. As loose as his mechanical leg would let him. Stallings lost his leg in the war and had suffered hell from osteomyelitis. I had enjoyed the same disease as a boy, and together we used to swop wonderful stories about the decay of bones at the marrow. Stallings' leg lay heavy on his mind. When he was not talking about the old leg and the new substitute, his suffering sublimated into abuse of the Emperor—"the little Jew pedlar who's lost his licenee"—or the rest of Ethiopia—"the booggies* and the dirty slaves."

* A booggy is a black man

He seemed to regard me as responsible for British policy. "Why does England go round begging for Allies? Why don't you get up and shut the Italians up for yourselves?" Stallings as well as being anti-Ethiop was anti-Fascist.

In his more wrathful moments Stallings could be suddenly domesticated by a careful selection from the works of Shakespeare, whom he considered a typical exponent of the older and more glorious policy of England. What a bun is to an elephant a speech from the Histories was to Stallings. I used to read *Richard II* to soothe him. Himself he knew thousands of lines by heart and became immediately inspired with romantic fire in pronouncing them. Not counting swear words, which he seldom used, his range of denunciatory diction was enormous. He could and did write beautifully, painting a huge canvas with sombre or with gorgeous tones. Light and shade were handled with the emotion which, in the world, worked itself out in his temper.

He once told me that Nasibu had five hundred thousand troops in the Ogaden supplied with water from petrol tins. His generous wide brain under the poetic sombrero believed implicitly in every story to which it gave language.

3. Tovey, expert cameraman of the *Daily Express*. Stout, stocky and dogmatic. Took very good pictures. He ran the mess, as the Consul's table was called, round which the menagerie assembled. He used to take Ekins' bets.

4. Genock, of Paramount News, a very quiet cinematographer, looked after the drinks. Genock was young, learned, knew everything about electricity, cars, aeroplanes, navies, modern novels. In his reserved way he was amused by the behaviour of cages number 1 and 2.

5. Drees, photographer of *Planet News*. A lanky youth in a high double-breasted waistcoat. He took pictures with a battered old box which did not in the least resemble a camera, and which he seemed to handle with minimum care. Yet his results in *The Times* were the best pictures of the war. Drees had won prizes for his grace and mobility in many a Palais de Dance. The others were always trying to crush him, but he was irrepressible. When attacked he often replied with a cutting Cockney repartee which amazed me, so fragile was the frame from which it emerged.

The new animals came in two by two. First Taylor and myself. Then Collins and his pet monkey Angko, the only one of us with the face to admit his cageability. Angko was rather unfairly put outside, while the others gathered round the table to eat, under the keeper's eye.

Between the two agencies, United Press and Reuter, war immediately opened. Carefully at first. The initial battleground was Angko, whom Collins said he liked, but Ekins said he did not like because it gave him fleas.

At the second course there was a fearful row about betting. All the animals started betting and shouting at the same time. Taylor and myself, good steady animals, the grizzly and the opossum of the collection, looked on in a baffled manner.

The keeper, Chapman-Andrews, noted down all the terms in his diary, but even the awful feeling that their wagers would be remembered did not restore peace at feeding-time. Afterwards we separated by couples to different parts of the Consulate and told each other how inaccurate we thought the other people were.

Finally, there were open clashes about other people's methods. An appalling guerrilla war broke out, every correspondent and photographer sniping from behind the rock of his own probity.

The battle of the press at Harrar completely overshadowed the war in the Ogaden, which was not engaged on the ground for two months after the battle of Anale.

On November 17, fifteen wounded of Anale arrived in Harrar, including Fitorari Gongol. They were all severely wounded, bullets all over the place. They had rushed into machine-guns. . . . French nuns who nursed them called them our *grands blessés*.

The Ethiopian has the most remarkable powers of recovery.

Within a week our *grands blessés* had smuggled raw meat into their wards, with tej. At nine o'clock at night, when the flowers are withdrawn in English nursing-homes and the patient feebly sips his sleeping-draught, the Fitorari and his men settled down to a terrific blind. Belching, singing and swearing, they feasted until midnight. The horrified nuns who ran in to try and restore order were addressed in terms which obliged them to retire. Sobriety did not return to the French Hospital in Harrar for twenty-four hours.

Gongol's men took to drinking because the Emperor inspected the Southern Front.

For several days Mischa Babitcheff, the Emperor's chief of aviation, had been teaching the Ethiopian Air Force to fly in formation of three. Mischa was an able pilot and they were quick learners. By November 19, the Fokker three-motor and the two old Potez biplanes, though of wildly different speeds, were able to stick together over long stretches in something resembling a wedge.

November 19 was the day fixed for the departure of the great journalists' caravan to Dessye. Holmes of the *Daily Worker* was going off to cover for *The Times*: Lowenthal, a German Jew who had prospected for gold in Wallega, accompanied him for Reuter. All the press were concentrated round the lorries, either Dessye-warding or saying good-bye.

The Emperor, who by now knew that the foreign press was introvert, drove quietly to the Akaki aerodrome with his secretary and suite, and took off for Jijiga.

A rigid censorship was imposed when the press discovered that the Emperor had slipped through their clutches. One enterprising correspondent got four words over to his London editor, *"Big Boy Skychiefed Frontwards."*

The Emperor had decided that he must visit Jijiga to stop the decay in the Ogaden. Till now he had been waiting in Addis for the last detachments from the south-western provinces, and for the drying of the Dessye road. All the governors had come in loyally, to his great satisfaction. His control over the country was perfect. He could now go to the war.

At Jijiga he asked for a full report on the battle of Anale and the flight from Gorahai which preceded it.

He created Afewerk Dedjazmatch of the Ogaden. For the first time, a title was given posthumously in Ethiopia. Afewerk's son, who survived him, was created a Gerazmatch.

Ali Nur, the Balambaras who had taken me round the

Ogaden and fought at Gorahai at Afewerk's side, was created a Kenyazmatch.

After rewards, drastic punishments. . . .

Fitorari Simu, whom I had met my last day at Gorahai, had ordered the flight from Gorahai and was sentenced to death by Nasibu for cowardice. He and another officer of the so-called "regulars" were to be shot the morning that the Emperor arrived.

He commuted their sentences.

Simu was publicly flogged before the troops whose rout he had led, and after thirty lashes was given two bayonet stabs in the back. The other Fitorari was flogged. The property of both was confiscated and assigned to the young Afewerk.

The Emperor's visit galvanised the Ethiopians of the Ogaden. If Anale improved matters his arrival in Jijiga restored their confidence entirely. He gave no orders for an advance or grand offensive. It was clear to him that the strategy of the small round camps like Gorahai, Gerlogubi, Gabridihari, had failed. They offered too narrow a target to concentrated bombardment. Daggahbur, where men could scatter over a large area, was almost bombproof. He told Nasibu to stand his ground there, and try to make similar camps in the no-man's land further south.

On the afternoon of the next day he drove back to Harrar with the linked machine-guns of the tanks which the Italians denied that they had lost at Anale. He visited and gave presents to the wounded, who were preparing even now to celebrate. With his usual gentleness and consideration he called on a sick Spanish journalist to whom he owed little. I burn for shame as I see his smiling face then, when he walked in the half-dark under the pink oleanders which framed the courtyard of the French Hospital at Harrar. I think of him in his wretched exile, neglected and forgotten by the people who had promised to aid him. When did he neglect any of the press, however humble, who came to Addis to disturb his peace and make his war complicated past bearing? What white man's request did he turn aside? Yet when they had forced him into failure they dropped him like a stone.

Next morning he flew back to Addis from Diredawa. The first two Italian planes appeared over Harrar, and circled three times over the Radio station which had once been Ras Makonnen's palace. I stood in the tower which dominated the town and the fruit groves outside, and watched them spin above. Joseph was very worried and rushed up with my rifle.

XII

THREE ANGLO-SAXONS were allowed by the Ethiopian Government to go over to Jijiga, where Nasibu's headquarters lay.

Collins of Reuter, Denny of the *New York Times*, and myself jolted one afternoon, in separate cars, to the little town at the head of the Ogaden. Seven hours of mountain road.

Collins put up at Mohamedally's. Denny and I woke up the new Kenyazmatch, Ali Nur, late at night. He gave us his own, his best room; talked long about Gorahai and the planes.

All was dark in Jijiga. The only man out, beside the night watch, was the old professional in the market place.

This man sleeps in the middle of Jijiga market place, entirely surrounded by sacks of guinea-corn and mealies. The sacks are those unsold during the day, and the owners pay the old man one piastre (about a penny) per sack for looking after them at night.

The old man pays the police a quarter piastre per sack to let him sleep out of doors after curfew. He is regarded as one of the wealthiest private citizens of Jijiga. He faintly growled as we approached him.

We were invited to a meeting of the Ogaden Headquarters' General Staff.

Nasibu's morning was full of detail. Half-an-hour with a soldier's wife, arguing with her whether she should be allowed to join her husband at the front or not. "My good woman. . . ." Imagine the wife of a Tommy being allowed to enter Haig's H.Q. in France and keep him for half an hour demanding, often with threats, a permit for a trip to Passchendaele.

Next came Elias Nasser, the Cypriot who ran the hundred and fifty lorries in the Jijiga garage and repair shops. Every detail, certainly to the destination of the last lorry and probably to the repository of the smallest tool, had to be passed by Nasibu. Hours. . . .

After Nasser, judgments. Shirkers, drunks, thieves, ravishers, unmannerly soldiers who shot at their fellows in the lines, all came up to the Dedjazmatch for trial. He not only directed every arm and service; he was courtmartial and arbitrator rolled into one. Nasibu was quick and authoritative, but even so his time was spent.

As we came up, we saw his tall figure on the wooden upper balcony of the white-washed Gibbi at Jijiga. On the ground below stood a man in chains. Nasibu, neat in his khaki tunic and jodhpurs, dismissed the case with a quick sweep of the forearm. But there were others behind. . . .

We were summoned up to the General Staff room; a bare chamber, wooden floors, cheap wooden ceiling, pictures of the Emperor and Empress in coronation robes. A few wooden chairs and a bare wooden table. Nasibu came in looking rather tired, swung on his khaki mantle, sat in a chair and received us silently. We sat down uncomfortably and Denny burst into broken French. . . .

A khaki-clad secretary entered with a leather satchel. The Dedjazmatch had to sign permits for somebody to enter Jijiga and for somebody else to leave Jijiga, and for a third to stay in Jijiga. Another permit for the Egyptian Red Cross to import a certain amount of this kind of medicines and a certain amount of that.

The General Staff were admitted.

I did not realise it at the time, but it was the General Staff who walked in, preserving Indian file. I hope that if they read these words they will forgive me for my lack of recognition. I learned to like all these three of the General Staff. They served Ethiopia well.

Leader of the column was an elderly, stout, short man in

off-white trousers and gym shoes. He wore an old zip-fastener shirt in blue artificial silk, the skin of his face was greyish and seared, though still heavy, and his hard round head was partly covered with white stubble. At first I took him for a retired Greek confectioner and wondered what on earth was the pass that he wanted Dedjazmatch Nasibu to sign.

In front of the Dedjazmatch he paused, brought his gym shoes together with the dud equivalent of a click, saluted with a podgy but expressive hand, and bowed as smartly as his figure would allow, too smartly for his uniform. Evidently no Greek: too much a soldier for trade. Turning towards me he wafted away my hand in a warm, emphatic grasp—"Wehib Pasha," he said, with such stunning unexpectedness that I sat back hard in the wooden chair without uttering a word.

A tall thin man followed him. An ungainly shape, narrow waist and wide bony hips; ill-fitting khaki all over, slacks and puritanical tunic without insignia. From his head, which was smaller than Wehib's, and covered by a featureless uniform cap, a long nose protruded and occasionally twitched a little at the point. His chin, which receded, did not support the nose but maintained the general angularity of Farouk's appearance. He wore large boots, no arms, no belt, and I fancy no braces. The eyes were smallish but extremely quick, lacking lashes almost entirely. The mouth was prim. Facially a martinet: and I learned later an intelligence officer of great experience. Major Farouk Bey had, I believe, been Turkish Military Attaché in Athens but had fallen out with the Kemalist régime. Since then his awkward figure had butted its way round the Levant, refusing to rub off its corners; the mind of Farouk remained intensely critical of anything which did not come up to its own high standard of discipline and concentration. Wehib Pasha had invited him out to Ethiopia, where he found no mental kin.

Farouk sat down without saluting anybody, and throughout the conference which followed opened his mouth only to cut one of us short.

Third, a black man with a short moustache, fully accoutred for war. He wore the uniform and tabs of the Turkish General Staff. He clicked his heels, really clicked them, before Nasibu. His large revolver was secured to his burly person by a piece of rich velvet piping. A huge whistle bulged from his breast-pocket, lashed round his shoulder by a heavy scarlet cord. Like the ear-splitting long-distance horns of the heroes in Celtic romance, I am sure that one blast from this fearsome machine would have summoned all the oppressed tribes of Africa and Arabia.

And that was Tarik Bey's object. Tarik was a pure Sudanese, and he bore his tribal marks upon his cheeks. Picked up by some itinerant Turk, he had received a military education in Constantinople. Well over fifty, he looked in his thirties still. He had fought in Tripoli for the Turks, in the Dardanelles and the Caucasus for the Turks, in Anatolia for the Turks: in thrilling unhoped-for victories and overwhelming defeats. Now he had come back to Africa, to fight for his home against the invader. He stood up and made a brisk speech.

"Here am I, Excellency, at your service.

"I have fought all over the Turkish world. I am back in Africa because I love it and because Ethiopia attacked is the last corner of free Africa. I have enlisted one hundred and fifty specialists from all over the Levant; Ethiopians and Sudanese and Arabs. All of them know what to do, how to handle machine-guns, wireless, telephones, mines; they are at your service."

He bowed forward, "and maps," he added. He went to the door where an anonymous and disembodied hand was ready with a large paper package.

Undoing the string, Tarik Bey revealed about thirty maps of various parts of Ethiopia, published in England. After two months of war these must have been the first to reach Ogaden headquarters. Tarik Bey put them on the table in front of Nasibu. I don't know whether his homeland was included in Tarik's strategy, but they definitely included a map of the Sudan.

Nasibu opened one and looked rather cautiously at it.

The Ethiopian has many points which mark him out above other Africans. More discipline, more seriousness, more tactical sense, more administrative ability, a written language, an inherited pride in his race. But he cannot read a map. I only met six Ethiopians who could—the

Emperor, Wolde Giorghis, his secretary, Lorenzo Taezaz and Ato David of his Press bureau, Lij Andarge Masai, and Ato Worku Yetitako of the radio. There were probably a number of others: Nasibu was not one of them.

Detecting the embarrassment of the Commander-in-Chief, Tarik folded up his little present to Africa and passed it back to the Hidden Hand. "Now we will be able to organise our campaign," he said, and sat down.

We asked Nasibu about his recent journey to Daggahbur, when he and Wehib Pasha had been bombed.

This was the signal for a long but courteous wrangle between the Dedjazmatch and his chief adviser. Nasibu said that there were eight planes. "Pardon me, Excellency," said Wehib, with a sweeping gesture of his fat hand, "but I counted precisely eleven." Nasibu, who is a crack shot, had used his machine-gun on them, therefore he knew. "Ah," said Wehib artfully, "but then you can have concentrated on only a part of them."

Until then Wehib had been fairly restful and quiet, but now he rose to heights of romanticism. For Wehib Pasha is a romantic. His wide forehead, leonine head, copious French and Parisian flourish of the hands, can all thrill together to a military subject. The well-rounded descriptions that proceeded from him ended at every full-stop on a note of positiveness which brooked no criticism or interruption. Old Wehib evidently had a great contempt for the air. Against a proper system of defence, said Wehib, the air is powerless. From Dardanelles to Daggahbur, what could the air do against trenches? asked Wehib, flourishing his hands like a propeller.

Tarik, a realist, broke in to say exactly what the air could do. "When I was in the Caucasus," he said, "your British planes caught a train of artillery in a defile and smashed them to pieces. Planes can be used against vast concentrations, towns, strategic centres, ports, agglomerations of civilian morale—but where are these in Ethiopia? And these Italian pilots aren't nearly as good as the British who bombed us."

Farouk twitched his nose a little. Sharply: "The Australians were better than you British. What we want are Australian flyers here."

Wehib Pasha continued, undisturbed by his friends. Trenches . . . defence . . . trenches . . . defence. Daggahbur could not be taken, and Jijiga could not be taken. The morale of the troops was very high, and the Somalis who fought for the Italians had given up the struggle . . . one heard were murdering their officers.

And the charm of it all, as I think back on it now, is that old Wehib was so very nearly right. The air bombardments of Daggahbur, from November to April, had no effect whatsoever: even when gas was used. Eleven dead. From November to April Graziani made no more progress in the Ogaden. Ethiopian morale mounted to bursting point.

The General Staff decided to issue a communiqué. It was the first, last, and only communiqué issued by the Ogaden General Staff. It was issued especially for us. It all arose out of a question which Collins asked about Walwal.

"Congratulations," said Collins, "on your reconquest of Walwal."

"Long live Ethiopia," I echoed, feebly.

"What do you mean?" asked Nasibu rather testily, thinking that we were making fun of him. "Haven't you retaken Walwal?" asked Collins. Nasibu's gracious manners, swept aside in a moment of irascibility, returned. "I'm afraid I can't claim as much as that," he said, smiling.

Collins had arrived before us in Jijiga. The telephone was still open, and while the telephone is open there is news. Two Belgian officers who formed the Rival General Staff at Jijiga had met Collins and said to him, "You know the news? Walwal is ours." Collins in amazement said "Really!" and the Belgians confirmed their own story.

The Belgians of course were never in a position to confirm anything. Whether they were serious or not, and they were generally serious fit to burst, they had nothing to be serious about because they never knew anything. But we did not know that then, and the recapture of Walwal was duly flashed about the world.

"But this is ridiculous," said Collins.

"Well, what do you expect of the Belgians?" asked Wehib scornfully, "they get more pay than we do, but we don't let them into the General Staff. They're dreadful."

"Grocers," said Farouk, with an air of finality.

"Look here," we all said together, "you must tell us something about the position. Where are you? Where are the Italians?"

"A communiqué is required," said Farouk, sharply.

Wehib Pasha and Tarik agreed that a communiqué was an excellent idea, and finally even the Dedjazmatch was willing to shed a little light on the Ogaden. Farouk, as the most metallic mind, was commissioned to write it, and the meeting of the General Staff broke up.

We descended the outer staircase of the Gibbi. One of the Belgians was waiting in the crowd of petitioners at the bottom. With the painful labour of the born weary Willy, he slowly used his handkerchief to flap the flies off his elegant shorts and the nasty dust off his khaki stockings. He was complaining of the heat. Nobody took the slightest notice of him. So far as they seemed to know he might have been one of the local Boy Scouts.

He was in fact Nasibu's most highly paid adviser.

"Come and see the tanks," said Farouk, shuddering.

We went off to the repair shops. Tarik's specials stood at attention as we passed. They were a rum lot, but he was to make a fine corps out of them. These few trained by Tarik, held in the camps that he made later in the Ogaden and supported by Fitorari Malion and his men, kept the Italian advance of April back for days. They only gave in when they were completely encircled. Courage, spirit, heroism in war is not enough: victory goes to the mechanical Cæsar these days.

Farouk had evidently Victorian views about pose in photographs. "You can take them only from the angle I tell you," was his stiff attitude.

Two little tanks came romping out of the garage, one towed on an injured track, the other skilfully driven by an Ethiopian chauffeur. He was wearing the furry crash helmet that the Italians had worn at Anale when they were shot down.

They had found a camera in the tanks. The Ethiopians had developed and printed the films. The four tanks together, all crews smiling and young . . . the lorry going forward to its finish at Anale, a sail over the tank which it carried . . . more smiling sunburnt young men enjoying the African adventure. . . .

Gabre the chauffeur drove his tank round: he jumped up and down in his seat for glee as he turned the machine round by stopping one of its tracks. "Enough," rapped out Farouk, "photograph."

The tanks were lined up stiffly and squarely. Abyssinians manned them, sitting bolt upright and staring with a soldier-like vacancy into that part of the great beyond which started at the end of their noses. This denoted proficiency. Two Ethiopian guards at either side of the tanks, grimly at attention, bayonets fixed, represented conquest. The Ethiopian crowd, already excited by the tanks in circulation, mobbed them when they came to rest. Farouk Bey seized the rifle of one of the guards and rushed the disorderly Ethiopians at the point of the bayonet. The photographs were taken in comparative calm.

See them here. The rigidity of the attendant Ethiopians and the quadrangularity of the mechanised arm are Farouk's idea of what a military picture should look like. Outside the frame the Ethiopians were all pushing and scrapping with each other as a result of Farouk's bayonet charge. Imagine that, too, if you can.

It was late that night that I spoke to Farouk more intimately. He came over to Ali Nur's house, into the little courtyard where the oleander trees grew. We were eating hard-boiled eggs and Denny's American canned herbarium, for Denny travelled with all the vegetable products of the world in tins. Farouk sat down stiffly, then as suddenly relaxed. . . .

He told us everything.

Farouk managed the commissariat for the Ogaden. He superintended the distribution of lorries to this place and that, for the transport of troops, food or ammunition. Later he trained men in artillery manipulation and fire discipline.

Even then he noticed a tightness of money. The Ethiopians had not the finances for a long war. Means to borrow on their national resources were denied them in Europe, and Farouk was bitter about it.

He had been working out the average pay of a soldier in the Ogaden. It was between eight and nine dollars a month. He had found that a soldier's food should cost him five dollars, but as the soldiers bought their food for themselves they always paid more to the traders for it.

He wanted the Government to supply food to the soldiers direct, not merely the transport which would take it down to Daggahbur and beyond. In addition, each man would get one dollar a month pocket-money.

The Dedjazmatch, with an Ethiopian's fear of rapid improvisation, did not like the proposal. It would have saved the Treasury between two and three dollars a month for every man, but Nasibu wondered whether it would not be going too fast for the common soldier.

This individual was already putting up with many novelties. He was fighting in the Ogaden, where he had only twice fought before. He was fighting a defensive war, such as he had never fought before. He was receiving food from the base, instead of taking it with him and returning when it was finished: a new system. He was taking cover, and well, from daily air bombardments, experienced for the first time. He had seen tanks and armoured cars and was to feel gas, new weapons to him. But the Dedjazmatch did not look at it that way: a novelty was a novelty, and should not be assumed until it was forced upon one.

And so money ran short, men got less pay, they exchanged cartridges for food; the circle entered on its first revolution towards the emptying of their ammunition pouches.

Tarik Bey did field work. He was going down south of Daggahbur now, where the shelters and trenches had been dug by the Ethiopian, Ali Nur. Nasibu's idea, a sensible one, was to fill up the gap between Daggahbur and Gabridihari caused by the fight at Anale, cautiously, one waterhole at a time.

Sasabaneh was now occupied: though it had already figured widely in the battle reports of the most distinguished correspondents, Sasabaneh had not yet been known to either belligerent except as a big fat name on British War Office maps. Tarik Bey found that it offered good cover, a high commanding position, rocky approaches, water. What more could one desire in the Ogaden?

Borkut and Anale were occupied. Camps were constructed here too. Tarik's specialists were assembled at Tarik's Farthest South, and Malion, my old friend of Daggahbur, took over the command here.

The Ethiopians of the Ogaden decided to sit down and wait for reinforcements. Graziani began to turn his attention to the pressure from Ras Desta on the west. The Emperor's son-in-law, soft-spoken but conceited ruler of Sidamo, was moving down the streams that form the Juba at Dolo, and then flow to the sea through the far west of Italian Somaliland. A fever-stricken area, where rivers turn to swamps overnight that are dried always by a torrid unquenchable sun, where huge palms wave slowly over seeming lazy crocodiles. A land of flowing water, of massive cover that can swallow armies as they march in fretted shade along the rivers with the high-sounding names, Dawa Parma, Web Gestro and Ganale Doria.

The hill of Gabridihari was fortified with barbed wire and sand-bagged redoubts, and about a thousand Eritrean Askaris were established there. It protected Gorahai, advanced bombing base for the Ogaden, twenty kilometres south on the wide crumbling plain along the Fafan. From then until April, only the Italian birds of the sky were to move into the Ogaden. The period of daily bombardments of Daggahbur, Sasabaneh, Bulale and finally Jijiga began. Heavy bombardments, doing no harm. As I left Jijiga report of one came from Daggahbur. On November 29th Daggahbur was bombed by eleven machines, and more than two hundred bombs were dropped, including two over six feet long. Killed and wounded, nought.

The Ogaden was proof against the air. Even when gas was used from sprays the defence did not crumble as in the north. The Emperor's visit, the rewards and punishments, the supply of arms from Berbera—all wrought a wonderful change after Gorahai; especially the supply of arms, spent though that was by the middle of April. As long as the Ethiopian felt that a lorry could in two nights bring him more *tiyit*, another cartridge, he was ready to fight on.

With the simultaneous appointment of Badoglio as Commander-in-Chief in Eritrea and the Emperor's three-day drive to his new headquarters at Dessye, the northern war began in earnest.

The last of the provincial armies which had come up to Addis to show their loyalty to the Emperor had been dispatched to the front. The morale of the Ogaden army had been restored after the disaster of Gorahai. A series of sanctions had been imposed against Italy by the Assembly of the League of Nations, and for the time the correspondence with the delegation was over.

The Emperor could now go to the war.

An Ethiopian Emperor does not leave his capital in the hopes of fighting a war without a battle. He comes back either victorious, like Menelik, or defeated: not before. When Haile Selassie went north it was for action.

His delegation at Geneva had often wired to him advising the guerrilla war—"never meet them frontally, always yield." "But a time must come when I *must* fight," he had said, with some annoyance, to Colson.

Total withdrawal from the Tigre was already showing poor results. Seyyum had been forced to withdraw even from the Tembien. The Tigrean population was firmly under Italian control. Villages which supported the occasional raids of Ras Seyyum were blotted out, and the feeding of his army was becoming a painful problem, solved sometimes by desertion. In Makalle, the traitor Haile Selassie Gucsa, whom the Italian and foreign press were allowed by the Italian censorship to ridicule freely, was nevertheless providing his masters with perfect dark-skin cover for propaganda among the Galla of Tigre in the south.

Gucsa knew all the Galla well: the tribes of the Wojerat, the Azebu and the Raia living around Amba Alagi,

Tigre's great boundary peak that dominates the Danakil desert on the west; and in the rich level lands, broken by few gorges, of Lake Ashangi to the south. When he ruled in Makalle before the war Gucsa had made many contacts with their local chiefs, who owed an ill-defined allegiance to Tigre.

The Galla of the Wojerat, the Azebu and the Raia were beginning to give the Emperor trouble.

It was part of the Italian propaganda in this war that the Galla were peaceful peasants, original owners of the Ethiopian soil, now brutally enslaved and exploited by the Amhara governing class. This story was made to fit all parts of Ethiopia: like the suits of cheap tailors, which can be bought in all sizes but identical proportions, it could dress up the highest mountains or the lowest plains that the Negus ruled over. It was far from being the truth.

Ethiopia was invaded by the Galla in the sixteenth century, and the Amhara were driven back into the plateau.* These ferocious nomads only failed to conquer the whole of modern Abyssinia because they were incapable of organisation on the scale of the people whom they defeated by sheer weight of numbers in the plain.

In Ethiopian legend, they introduced the war custom of the mutilation of prisoners and of the dead, rapidly popularised throughout Ethiopia.

A terror of the Gallas, based on history, myth and baby stories is bred into every Ethiopian child. Even in those of mixed birth, who predominate. In a country of loose marriage like Ethiopia, where divorce can be obtained at the will of either party, mixed Amhara-Galla parentage is more the rule than the exception.

During last century, when the Galla owned and ruled all the rich borderlands of the plateau, Wallega, Shoa, Wollo, Yeju, Lake Ashangi, the Amhara possessing himself of the rifle used his superior power of organisation again to recover his mastery over this mass African movement.

* The Galla had come up from the south—probably from somewhere near the great lakes, and were in what is now British Somaliland by the beginning of the century. They then spread out fanwise over Aussa and Harrar, up towards Shoa, and over to Jimma and the Wallega country.

Starting in Shoa, where a compromise was reached between the races, the other provinces were reconquered.

The extent to which they were ruled by the compromise-race of Shoa varied with their distance from the central province. Lake Ashangi was furthest away of all. Here the Galla remained nomadic and intractable, unmixed in blood with the Amhara and retentive of the language and the peculiar habits of the first invasion. The Wojerat, for instance, had mixed with the Danakil and lived half the year raiding their neighbours, half the year engaged in the cutting of, transport and sale, indeed sometimes the theft of salt, a staple of Makalle. On their rare rest-cures they lived in twelve villages and eschewed trousers.

Azebu and Raia were a little more settled, but in the Ethiopian view barbaric still. They lived in a few biggish villages of which Cobbo, south of Lake Ashangi, the same Cobbo that was grimly mobilised by Ras Mulugeta, was the southernmost. Cobbo was famous for its piracy—for its *shiftanet* as the Ethiopians called it: among the *nagadis* or caravaneers it was notoriously the nastiest place to pass between Addis and Makalle. A tangle of tracks show that the caravan route here was endlessly changed to avoid the "tolls" of the Galla community. Trousers were to be seen here, but were rather an ornament of the prosperous than the uniform of the masses. Trousers were highly prized, and were often removed from unwary travellers.

These Galla all owed allegiance to an Amhara overlord, most of them to the nearest ruler of the Tigre, the lord of Makalle. "Owed" was the operative word. Allegiance was a debt that stood for ever on the Amhara books. The Galla never paid a farthing until an explorer went among them. An Ethiopian explorer: for that is the title which must be given to Dejazmatch Aberra Tadla.

If you take away his compasses and his maps and his superiority of firepower and his money from Stanley, or his ship and his instruments and his furs from Captain Scott, and paint them brown, you have the Dedjaz Aberra. He was sent like them to an unknown part of the world, where the people were nasty and hostile and the climate novel to a degree. Letters were seldom received from home. Like Afewerk, who had shown the Ethiopians how to live in the Ogaden, the Dedjaz Aberra learned to like the place.

For everywhere, under the Emperor Haile Selassie, the Ethiopians were beginning to explore, to understand and to consolidate their Empire. That is why they were attacked. . . .

Aberra's occupation now was to see that the Galla kept the peace while the Ethiopian armies were beginning to face up to Makalle. Mulugeta's supply lines would lie across Galla country and the army must not be attacked from behind.

In Gucsa and the Italians, guided they say by Signor Gasperini, an old Colonial civil servant, he found a combination that beat him.

They had money.

Thalers were poured out from Makalle. At one time I know that it was fifteen dollars, at another time it was reported to be thirty dollars a man. For every Galla who was willing to come to Makalle, or would receive a trusted man as chief, fifteen dollars and some rounds of ammunition, with willing permission to steal and kill what he liked provided it were on the Ethiopian side.

With their rifles and money they formed *shifta* companies, which grew ever larger. Timid at first, their courage increased with their size. At the end of November they were only just beginning to mass: petty theft was their first warlike operation. The Emperor saw the sign. He went north.

The same day that he left Addis, Marshal Badoglio succeeded General De Bono as Commander-in-Chief: on November 28.

He replaced De Bono because De Bono's strategy was copybook.

De Bono's entry into Ethiopia had been a simple affair. A matter of concentration at the three bases of the three Army Corps, deployment and advance without resistance, roadmaking to the points next occupied, Adowa, Entiscio and Adigrat. A long rest. Advance to Makalle, sluggish at first because the troops went no faster than the roads built to feed them: at the end, with a burst of speed that did great damage to the Italians' animal transport.

Makalle was won only at the cost of a grave displacement of balance on the Italian front. Two army corps were used where only one was needed. The army corps of Adowa was left behind, its line of communications to Makalle only covered at the extreme southern end by the Eritrean Army Corps which was now turning west into the Tembien.

An uninspired plan of campaign, incapable of ever bringing the Ethiopians to battle and expensive to the peaceful victor. Every area entered had to be thoroughly scoured. Instead of breaking the enemy's morale by sudden blows, De Bono tried the more costly and less glorious method of indoctrination.

He waged a more humane war than his successor, but it was a war whose timetable might be disturbed by the cumulative weight of sanctions.

It was after his departure that the more ferocious and terrifying processes of warfare were employed; that Cæsar sent his aeroplanes on long-distance bombing raids into the centre of the country and against the civilian population, attacked the Red Crosses deliberately, used gas with ever-increasing efficiency, and cornered and smashed the Ethiopian armies in the field.

Badoglio had to reorganise much that his predecessor had muddled: meanwhile he kept up Italian prestige by a succession of aerial stunts. It took two and a half months for the changes in command and disposition to be made that he considered necessary. Because of the mood of the man opposed to him, he was then able to attack the Ethiopians at short range.

While Badoglio said "Action!" the Emperor was thinking "No more Retreat!" Haile Selassie gave out orders for a move forward as soon as he arrived in Dessye. With his young son the Duke of Harrar, his old tutor the Dedjazmatch Haile Selassie, and Fitorari Birru his ex-Minister of War, the Emperor, who liked modern conveniences, occupied the Commercial Agency of Italy which stands on steeply rising ground above the main dusty causeway leading from Dessye to the North.

He went to the war in every point a European gentleman. At his table four courses of well-cooked European food were served, with Ethiopian *wot*, chicken spiced with sauce of chillies, to crown the banquet. A cellar was laid in. In the front hall lay a selection of solar topees, and, in a corner, stood a series of walking-sticks for going to church, which the Emperor attended daily, for visiting in the town, for walking on the mountain, for inspecting the troops and the Red Cross hospitals.

His best Arabs were brought up to Dessye. The Emperor had a good eye for a horse, and liked to discuss their points with Kosrof Borgossian, the chief of his stable. His Arabs and his cars were kept in the grounds of the Commerical Agency. The Emperor of Ethiopia had the gift of appearing at all times, even in the middle of war, completely detached and poised above the mêlée, pursuing his quiet, rather delicate and well-dressed life without noting overmuch the noise which surrounded him.

In the house he worked day and night, organising the last detail in the construction of the two northward roads, that to Korem and the branch road to Lalibela. Seeing that the food caravans went through Dessye regularly. Negotiating with troublesome chiefs. Writing to his wife and his Council in Addis about his League policy . . . air raid precautions . . . the decent treatment of Europeans. Codifying and improving his regulations for the Ethiopian tactic against western arms—all except the spraying of mustard gas, which he did not foresee.

The only evidences of war, besides his khaki uniform, were hidden away behind the house. Here, under branches of mimosa and bluegum, was the anti-aircraft machine-gun which he had learnt to handle. The Emperor had a liking for arms of precision: accuracy, the neat bull's eye, were to his taste. Next to the gun was his dugout, with a store of ammunition. Above, the mountain-side of Ethiopia, rock and sweet grass. . . .

Heavy bombardments in the centre of the country began with the first week of December. Dessye and Gondar, the two bases for the feeding of the northern Ethiopian armies, were attacked. The object in both cases was demoralisation, but at Dessye the Emperor was a special target.

On Friday, December 6, six aeroplanes circled over the Portuguese palace of Gondar and the overgrown cobbles which form its streets. After a double turn they released their bombs, over fifty of middle size and innumerable incendiaries. Four women and six children were killed, for the fighting men had gone to the war with Kassa and those who had deserted dared not appear in the town. Many tukuls were burnt, for the old capital of Ethiopia is more thickly housed than it is populated.

On Friday, December 6, at about eight in the morning, the Press (I was in Addis) were beginning to stir out of bed in Dessye. Lowenthal and Holmes, representing Reuter and *The Times*, were settling down to eat when a distant hum was heard. Said Lowenthal to Holmes, as he forked a sausage from the plate at the tentside, "That must be the plane which is taking Mrs. Wells (wife of Linton Wells, *New York Herald Tribune*) back to Addis." Contradicting him flat, the plane dropped a bomb near enough to Lowenthal's breakfast.

Eighteen planes circled over Dessye. The journalists who were camped in the grounds of the Seventh Day Adventist Mission, turned into a Red Cross hospital, scrambled all over the place. Some lay flat, others did the instinctive thing that everybody from a Galla upward does in an air raid—pressed their backs against the trunks of bluegums not in the thought, for they did not think much, but in the hope of not being seen. At moments of alarm one ceases to think. Between thought and simple sensation there is a middle, semi-passive condition, which in air raids is hope. If I had been there I would have backed up to a tree and gone on hoping.

Old Mills of the Associated Press was as cool as a cucumber. One or two like him walked round taking photographs.

Forty bombs were dropped straightaway on the Adventist Compound, mostly incendiaries; one of which narrowly missed the petrol stores of *The Times* and Reuter. Five struck the hospital building itself, destroying the roof of the surgery and two wards. The instrument-tent of the field-unit which Lady Barton's Committee of Ethiopian women had fitted together was blown to pieces. Only the Belgian censor was wounded within the hospital grounds: miraculous event, which gave the Press new courage.

Incendiaries were scattered all over the town. Every Ethiopian of standing has a gun. All the guns were whipped out, and the hollow hills echoed to the violent detonation of every musket imaginable to man. In the Red Cross camp servants of the journalists took out their revolvers and blazed away into the pitiless blue, whence rained the stinking fire.

Smoke swelled up softly from huts along the causeway, for there was little ground wind in the cup of the hills which contains Dessye, and the bluegum grows thick in the green valley bottom. Circling again the planes dropped bombs, most of which narrowly missed the Crown Prince's Gibbi and the house of the Dedjazmatch on twin hills to the south of the town. Heavy bombs aimed at these fell into the central plain below them, where markets are held usually but which were then empty.

The Emperor took his machine-gun and rattled away. His suite, instinctively Ethiopian, surrounded him closely, and he showed great anger. "Haven't I told you not to mass?" he said. "Do you want to make me a target? Take cover, and let me fire."

Twenty-one high explosives were dropped ranging from twenty-five to two hundred pounds. About a hundred and fifty incendiaries. The casualties were very heavy, for the bombardment was quite unexpected. Fifty-three were killed, many by burning in their huts, and about two hundred injured in crowded Dessye. One woman and her two children were blown to pieces on the causeway. Thirty amputations were done at the Adventist Mission when they had collected the scattered instruments again. The people of Dessye were crazy with fear and rage: as the planes circled round, the town seethed like a furious hive.

When the planes had gone the cinema men and some correspondents left their compound in lorries to see the town. They were met by concentrated rifle fire. Havas stopped a bullet in the knee. In their desperation the Ethiopians believed that these were Italians landed from the planes, come to rob them of their town.

The Emperor left his machine-gun very hot, drafted his telegram of protest to the League, took his cloak and stick and visited the hospitals. A plane was set aside to take the wounded Europeans to Addis. The Belgian censor was decorated. The radio was ordered to give press matter first consideration.

Instructions were handed to the chief of Dessye and telegraphed to Gondar—"Clear the town every day."

I went over the area of the bombardment ten days later.

According to the Italian version, the action was confined to military encampments and the fortified enclosure, (meaning the Italian Commercial Agency artistically crenellated in brick), where the Emperor was known to be. The hospital and Press camps were not specially bombarded and could only have been hit accidentally if located in military camps.

There were no military encampments in Dessye, though there were plenty north of Dessye whose tents, widely scattered on flat plains, were bombed by the raiders on their return, without serious harm. It was evident that apart from the incendiaries which were meant for the huts of Dessye itself, the main objectives of the heavy bombs were the Commercial Agency to the north and the two Gibbis to the south of the town.

Of both objectives the Italian projectiles fell wide. Their bomb-sighting can have taken no account of the currents caused by the scoop of the winds along the rim of the cup in which Dessye lies. Uniformly, their bombs fell wide of their targets . . . in the plain three hundred yards north of the Gibbis . . . in the Mission camp three hundred yards north of the Emperor's headquarters.

It was not a deliberate attack on the Red Cross, like those which were to follow. It was an attempt to burn a large civilian centre and a rather poor potshot at the Emperor.

A bottle was dropped by one of the planes, which went equally wide. It contained a note, scrawled in pencil. *"Long live Italy, long live the Duce, long live the King. We carry with our three colours the Lictor's badge, the civilisation of Rome. Greetings to the Negus. Ask him if he has digested his biscuits."*

A few hours later the Emperor had collected all the biscuits which had not exploded and piled them up in front of his house. Setting his foot on one of the biggest, he was photographed by a nervous Press. They thought of time-fuses, and used the fastest exposures.

When they had gone, he settled down happily to weighing and measuring the bombs, investigating their contents, and precisely recording the results in his notebook. The bomb-holes were also measured, and details were collected about the range of the various shellbursts.

Either the Ethiopian is a quick learner, or his Emperor was a clever instructor. Sure enough, five Italian planes came back next morning to bomb again. The Emperor did not fire his gun. He sat with folded hands in his dugout. Ethiopians did not squat in their tukuls. They had already left the town at daybreak.

Hardly anyone was touched.

And nobody was touched again in Gondar, for many months.

XIII

IT WAS ON SUNDAY, DECEMBER 8, I think, that Ozanne, the polished correspondent of Havas, presented to Colson a wire from his Paris office which gave in fair detail the lines of the Hoare-Laval proposals.

The Ethiopian Government had not been acquainted with these proposals. The Italian Government had. The men who were running the League of Nations machinery at the time, Sir Samuel Hoare and M. Pierre Laval, conceived that this was the best procedure: to secure the approval of the aggressor first, as the party to the dispute most worthy of consideration, and then to inform the Ethiopian Government.

Later in the week the proposals came over the Legation wirelesses to Barton and M. Bodard. Even when they were officially handed to the two Governments, the Ethiopians got them after the Italians. For the French Legation pleaded a "defect in the wireless apparatus" which caused them immense trouble in receiving the full text.

Colson said to me, "We felt that we were treated worse than the dirt."

The Emperor was at Dessye, over four hundred and twenty kilometres of crazy road away, nearly two hours by ten-year-old Ethiopian aeroplane, a day or two by languid telephone relay or frayed Ethiopian wire.

The French knew that Bodard had no personal weight with the Emperor: so they wished to use an English agent who had. And the British Government willingly agreed. And the plan went wrong because the personal contact necessary between the Emperor and Barton did not exist, and could not be brought about.

Barton and Bodard visited Blattangeta Herrouy at the Ethiopian Foreign Ministry. Sirak Herrouy, the cricketer from B.N.C., acted as interpreter for his father. The great plan was unveiled: the united flags of Britain and France dropped from the monument commemorating the assassins of collective peace.

On its base was engraved the map of Ethiopia. All Tigre except Axum was given to Italy. The southern Ogaden was given to Italy. The whole of Southern Ethiopia was handed over to Italian colonisation and economic supremacy. Some of Ethiopia remained to Ethiopia. "A Premium to Aggression" was carved upon the monument in Roman capitals.

Bodard withdrew, while Barton had to go through with the unpleasant duty of reading the dedicatory address. The Ethiopians say that it was done with a decent formality appropriate to the occasion.

After all, you could not apply pressure to old Blattangeta Herrouy. The man immediately sank into one of his blank periods. However hard you sit upon a stone you cannot dent it. So why injure your behind?

In the early days of the Ethiopian Foreign Ministry the Foreign Minister, I have been told, used to sit at a table and put the Notes which he received in a pile on the floor. There they got covered with dust.

When, months afterwards, he had read them, he used to spike them on an iron spike which hung on the wall behind him. The sort of spike used in shops for bills and receipts. This did not mean that he had answered the notes, but that he had perused them.

Ethiopia, to her misfortune, had advanced beyond that, though it would have been a marvellous finish for the Hoare-Laval plan.

The Emperor when he left for Dessye gave full powers to his Council at Addis to decide questions of this sort. In fact, they were incapable of decision. The text was sent to the Emperor. They were all very angry about it, but they did nothing. The younger Ethiopians were for answering "nonsense," but Blattangeta Herrouy's mind continued to draw blank.

We had our first experience that week in December of the incapacity and vacillation of the Emperor's councillors when the Emperor was removed. These were the men who bungled the defence of Addis in April, 1936.

Colson for once lost his temper with them, and sent a four-page wire to the Emperor in Dessye insisting that he should fly up to see him immediately.

An aeroplane took him up that evening. Next day and the day after, Ato Tasfai Tegan, the Director of Foreign Affairs, Karl von Wiegand and Lady Drummond Hay flew up. A draught seemed to be setting in towards Dessye. I was caught in it on Sunday afternoon.

On Sunday morning the radio closed at noon and did not reopen until Monday morning at seven-thirty. When we were in Addis, we used to picnic out on Sundays on Entoto, or somewhere in the woods off the Dessye or Addis Alem roads. Here I practised a technique which I studied in extreme youth: how to catch butterflies in the fingers without hurting them.

The discreditable Ford lay outside Collins' flat and we were stuffing it with food when Ato Worku Yetatakou, Director of the Radio, and Ato Makonnen Hapte Wolde, Director of Commerce, suddenly appeared and invited me into a dark corner. Ato Worku looked stout and impressive. Ato Makonnen was seen slowly and significantly to wink.

Makonnen, a thin Ethiopian who enjoyed poor health, was in control at this time of all the Imperial communications. He worked long hours: it was he who before the war had been systematically breaking down the internal tolls of Ethiopia. He was loyally sly. His skinny eyelids, thin face and persistently subtle expression reminded me of a milder, more subordinate Trotsky. A small straggly goatee was of the piece.

"An aeroplane will be ready for you at four. Tell nobody that you are going, not even your friends. Say that you are going to a funeral."

Hockman, the missionary doctor, had died of a morbid interest in unexploded bombs in Daggahbur. A student of aviation and war despite his Protestant associations, he used to take his stop-watch and glasses out at Daggahbur and calculate the time that it took an Italian bomb to drop, tuning up his powerful red Indian motor-cycle the while. When the aeroplanes had gone, he dashed round the town picking up the rare injured—he was leader of the Red Cross unit—and spotting what, by a gloomy misnomer, he termed duds.

The duds and the injured were all carted off to the Red Cross hospital where the injured were soon put to rights, for Hockman was a fine surgeon. Next came the turn of the duds, which were Hockman's especial hobby. He hammered them on the nose, twisted their tails, broke open their shells, and sorted their insides out. Ethiopians and duds, for him, were very much the same upon the operating-table.

One day he hit a dud too hard on the head and died in ten minutes.

He was a great loss to the Ethiopian Red Cross and to many others. His friends, who had begged him to abandon his practices, arranged a funeral for him that Sunday.

Packing a small suit-case and hiding it under my overcoat I told Wolde the houseboy not to worry if I did not come back, and my other acquaintances more dolefully that I was off to the cemetery.

"Say you are going to a funeral," said Ato Makonnen. With this disconcerting prognostic in my ears I drove out to the aerodrome at Akaki, to find a two-seater open Potez, ten years old, being hauled out on to the tarmac by an Armenian mechanic.

At four-thirty the Minister of Aviation, in ordinary Ethiopian day dress, stepped briskly out of his new American tourer, handed instructions in Amharic script to an employee at the hangar and introduced me to Lij Asfau Ali, a pilot in a grey uniform. He looked smart, handsome, young and friendly. He spoke French, though he had never been out of Abyssinia, where he learnt his flying.

"We haven't had a fatal accident yet," he said, and his cheery smile put me at ease in the matter of the age of his machine. With a laugh, an Italian parachute was clamped round my waist, and swaddled in an over-size Ethiopian flying-suit I was hoisted into the rear cockpit.

"How do you open this thing?" I asked in a fit of cowardice, pointing at the Italian manufacture. But the plane was already revving and pulsing and flapping its wings with senile debility, and I never heard the answer. Even now I do not know which string to pull, but I was keener to know then.

A machine-gun followed, and in three minutes we were soaring over the scented eucalyptus. Below appeared the gilded mausoleum of Menelik. Zukwala, the sacred mountain, loomed eastward like a gigantic serrated sea-urchin. The summits of the Entoto ridge were pointed with circular Coptic churches, terraced and enclosed. Between them bright grass and bare rock showed in exotic conjunction. The air grew cold as we said good-bye to the southern Shoan plain, and waited for the geographical revelations to follow. My helmet, made for Ethiopian hair, blew loose at once. I had to fly the rest of the way clutching it in one hand and the machine-gun in the other, so to hell with the parachute.

Descriptions of Ethiopia leave the impression that the country is divided into two parts—dry wastes skirting the European colonies, springing up of a sudden to eight thousand foot precipices which form the impregnable castle of the Abyssinian plateau. Not quite a true picture: but only from an aeroplane can one see how nearly true; and how cruelly the rivers have spoiled a geometer's neat dream.

Soon something gave the Potez a big bump, and I leant over the side to look. We were travelling over a great plain from which a frightful precipice sheered away into a horseshoe basin, where trickled a tiny foaming stream. It flowed away to the Blue Nile lying under cloud to the west and blue distant Gojjam, through mile upon mile of violent gorge and wild uncultivated valley bottom. As far as the eye could reach to the north were other yawning cauldrons where the confluents of the Nile were boiled, and other giant trenches of rock through which the waters poured west. We soared high, the sun flashing upon the threaded streams and showing the towering walls of mountains alternately grey and rose . . . in light or shadow from the lonely distant west of Africa.

On each plateau there were cultivation and a crude

irrigation, good enough to live by: each supported a squat toadlike *tukul* kraaled with a thorn fence or stone and speckled around with grazing goats and cattle. On the checkered table, green for wheat and millet and brown for pasture, were the smaller *tukuls* of the freemen peasants owing allegiance to their chief. For their land, they paid war service and a small due yearly. They were all of his family, or freed slaves of his fathers. To show their freedom, they did not live in the shadow of the big *tukul*, but scattered all over the amba. We flew over Northern Shoa into Wollo, of which Dessye is the capital.

The provinces are divided by a sheer fantastic gorge, streaked with another stream Mofer Wuhu making for the Nile. Each flat mountain-top was ringed with cactus euphorbia or wild lemon, to prevent the cattle from falling a sacrifice to the gods of the cliff who specially protected the Ethiopian fastness. I could see no paths leading down the cliffs, and if there were a passage between mountains it was along some fearful razor edge daunting even the mules of Abyssinia. One after the other there passed under our breathless little machine the massive mountain baronies to which contact with the outer world was unthought of.

This was the dry season. In the rains the gorges roared full and great banks of cloud shifted from place to place like incalculable flabby amœbas under the microscope. The natural baron sat in his natural castle, eschewing his neighbour and gloating over his crops.

My impression of Ethiopia until I flew over it was of an undivided mountain plateau shelving suddenly into the Danakil plain. But the Galla who invaded this region four centuries ago found land to live upon between their own dry Kenya uplands and the plateau of the ambas which they could not conquer. An hour later we were over a green rolling weald whence a river flowed not west, but east. "Galla," said the pilot, and eastward could be seen mountain and plain alternating, but the mountains smooth and forest-covered. A green world between the Amharic fastnesses and the sandy wastes of Danakil.

We climbed down again to cross a wooded neck between

two wooded peaks, dark green as Christmas trees. An oval lake lay pale, only a thousand feet beneath us. Through the evening mist we could see a large house on a square earth platform, many small *tukuls* clustered dependently about it, and natives drove donkeys laden with water-gourds from the shimmering lake.

A dive over another peak and we circled backwards and forwards into a huge rich plain where small tents shot up to us, coloured in red earth. As the sun set we landed beside the Borkenna river, fifteen miles from Dessye by the hairpin mountain road of Kombolcha.

Twelve journalists in Dessye were eating their heads off with boredom in one of the most quietly beautiful situations that could be imagined. They sat round camp-fires making toffee, drinking whisky and playing expensive card-games with the Belgian Military Mission.

The town is scattered at the bottom of a cup irregularly formed by the surrounding hills. Two smaller hills, completely detached and clambered by those circular roads seen only in Sicily and fairy-books, carry the rambling Gibbi of the Crown Prince and the unfinished modern mansion, twin-pinnacled, of the Dedjazmatch. Through a deep breach in the mountain wall to the south-east the Borkenna, silvered with fish, cascaded away to the airfield and Danakil. The gap was called by the locals "Chicken-Jump" — "because even a chicken, which cannot fly, can jump across it."

On the west lay a long ledge of mountain: and on its extreme slope the Italian Commercial Agency, just above the dusty causeway which prolongs Dessye from south to north.

Dessye must have been the strangest of headquarters for an army that ever existed. At the Agency gates, kept tightly shut by Ethiopian gatekeepers, proverbial for their ungenerous suspicion, there was always a crowd of chieftains and retainers, all in khaki or the home-grown ochre substitute, waiting for days to say good-bye to the Emperor before moving north. Sitting, squatting, standing, picking their hard feet, sleeping, but generally chaffering, they all had advice to give or requests to make. In the Ethiopian system, feudal though it was, the smallest freeman loved to inform the Emperor in person, or ask the Emperor in person, about something. Although this wasted much time it was a clear and useful check upon the power of the great Ras and Dedjazmatches. Ever so gradually at Dessye they were allowed to filter into the Agency grounds and say their piece.

It was the sight that I was used to in Addis Ababa . . . the long line of petitioners squatting in the plain outside the Great Gibbi, who wailed "Abiet!" until the volume of sound penetrated the quarter of the Emperor's Justices.

The avenue marching steeply up the hill was flanked with machine-guns and the Emperor's lorry-park, concealed behind geraniums. At the top, in front of the Agency, were the bare headquarters, two tents where ciphering, radio transmission and reception, the publication of *communiqués* and the preparation of war strategies were done by three men sitting on three chairs and working on six wooden boxes. . . .

News was sparse, and when it came it was pinned to a eucalyptus bole.

Colson had not gone to Dessye for nothing.

The day after my arrival that part of the Press which was not climbing the mountains was summoned to the Agency.

The Emperor was on his stoep with a document in his hand. Holmes, of the *Daily Worker* and *The Times*, Lowenthal, of Reuter, and Wallega, Colonel Otto Zettlin, of the Lithuanian Government Press and the Lithuanian Light Horse, Rasmussen, of the Danish Politiken, and myself gathered in line below. Gallacher, of the *Daily Express*, took a photograph of this literary flotsam and jetsam. It was published under the caption, "The Emperor addressing some of his men," and it looked rather like it.

The statement which the Emperor made is, I think, one of the best pieces of work that he and Colson did together.

"We desire to state," he read, *"with all the solemnity and firmness which the situation demands to-day that our willingness to facilitate any pacific solution of this conflict has not changed,*

but that the act by us of accepting even in principle the Franco-British proposals would be not only a cowardice towards our people but a betrayal of the League of Nations and of all the States which have shown that they could have confidence up to now in the system of collective security.

"These proposals are the negation and the abandonment of the principles upon which the League of Nations is founded. For Ethiopia they would consecrate the amputation of her territory and the disappearance of her independence for the benefit of the State which has attacked her.

"They imply the definite interdiction for her own people to participate usefully and freely in the economic development of about a third of the country, and they confide this development to her enemy, which is now making its second attempt to conquer this people. A settlement on the lines of these proposals would place a premium upon aggression and upon the violation of international engagements.

"The vital interest of Ethiopia is in question, and for us this takes precedence over every other consideration; but in reaching our decision we are not unmindful that the security of other peaceful, weak or small States will be made doubtful if such a recompense should be accorded to a State already condemned as the aggressor and at the expense of the State victim of its aggression."

The Emperor of Ethiopia was determined to press the League policy to the uttermost.

Sir Samuel Hoare when he resigned office, and even after he had resigned office, repeated that these were the best terms that Ethiopia could ever get. I think he was wrong: the best terms that Ethiopia could have got was the raw material embargo on exports to Italy and the munitions loan for which her Emperor asked. These would have been terms more faithful to the Covenant.

Granted even the grosser standards by which Sir Samuel Hoare admitted that he judged Ethiopian advantage, Ethiopia, conquered as she is now, lost nothing by rejecting the proposals. She rather gained.

They improved the conditions under which Italy would be able to attack her.

They brought the aggressor even nearer to the capital of the country; they put a premium upon any future aggression of his. They offered Ethiopia no guarantee that she would not be attacked again.

In fact, they guaranteed that she would be attacked again. For they asked her to sign away her claims under the Covenant that her territorial integrity and independence should be protected by fellow-members of the League.

That done, she could never appeal to the Covenant again.

And that is why the Emperor and Colson rejected the terms.

The Emperor went out to the war against the Italians a learner.

Conversation at his table turned rather on matters of military detail than on sweeping movements involving constant reference to the geography of East Africa. At dinner he spoke about the calibre, range, traverse and efficiency of the machine-guns on the tanks captured at Anale and Enda Selasi, about the speed, range and petrol capacity of this or that plane or the suitability for different purposes of this or that camera or this or that breed of camel. One had the impression of a tireless yet outwardly impassive mind, seeking always for precision in points of detail and building up a whole out of the smallest elements. Once a detail was established from an expert source it was established for ever, and this gave the Emperor his dignified imperturbability.

Next day was Christmas Day.

Holmes, Lowenthal and I decided to take out the old lorry and drive some distance north along Bietry's road, by which the Emperor intended to move northward to Korem.

The servants, Addis Ababa bred and without arms, did not want to come. A journey, however short, towards the front somewhat alarmed them. The muleteers insisted on ten more thalers to "buy grass" for the mules—a fruitful source of peculation in this grassy land. We settled the difficulty by giving separate sheep to the Christian and the Moslem servants and a little tej to cheer the heart and blind the eye of our soldier guard. Before nightfall we had covered eighteen miles of road along the valley and mountainside to Lake Haik, pitched camp, and ranged the lake rim massacring duck unsportingly for supper. In the middle of the lake was a green island and a white monastery, reached only by a reed raft shaped like a long sweep. The placid water was full of duck, geese and moorhen, and important-looking pelican floated a hundred yards from the shore. Three pink flamingos stood in delicate gawkish silhouette near the margin. There was not a sound but the cruel report of our guns echoing in the unpeopled mountains, the call of the children round the lake to the cattle, and as evening fell with a light mist on the waterside *tukuls*, every now and then a shout from the Galla to frighten the wild animals away. The war seemed very distant.

The part of Wollo through which we were travelling is a typical mix-up of the races which make Ethiopia. We woke next morning early in the enlivening air of the plateau; an old Moslem squatting like a tree-stump near our camp was watching us with silent ethnological interest. When he could be persuaded to speak, he wanted to know everything about the tent, the truck, the clothes, the soap and water. What was it all *for*? He asked questions like my old tutors at Oxford. Meanwhile in protective bewilderment he slowly told his beads. So we took advantage of his curiosity to ask him others in return.

Everyone near the lake, he said, was Christian and paid service to the monastery and to a church at the northern end. Everyone who lived west of the road which ran parallel to the lake on its western side was Moslem. He spoke, to our surprise, Amhariña not Galliña. For a long time he insisted that he was pure Amhara, but at last he admitted that four generations back he was pure Galla, speaking Galliña. It was interesting to us to note the triumph of ideas over tradition: he had abandoned his natural tongue without abandoning his assumed religion.

We found that the whole Galla population in this part of Northern Wollo was the same. They spoke Amhariña and the men wore the shamma, and jodhpur pantaloons of the Amharas. Only the women kept up the braided head-dress of the Galla country-side.

The old man had once possessed a little land but it had been confiscated because he was a partisan of the Negus Mikael, Lij Yasu's father. He now lived, an African old age pensioner, on the generosity of his village and, he artfully suggested, of the passing traveller.

Slaves, which in the Negus Mikael's time cost sixty dollars now cost twice as much, he said, and no one in his village was rich enough to possess one: he remembered the time when caravans of slave-dealers used to pass up and down his valley, but now one could only buy secretly from house to house, which reduced one really to buying and selling the children of people already in slavery. Detection, he added, was severely punished, with a fine of five hundred thalers and two years' imprisonment in Dessye. "A-he-e-e-e" he said, regretfully scratching himself for bygones that were bygones.

On the subject of the Italians the old man was accommodating. He did not like them, but if they came to his country by force he would like them. As for himself, he would not go and fight like those others who had rifles and had gone to the war behind their lord, who lived near the court of the Crown Prince. He preferred to support the armies with his prayers. "But will you not fight for Ethiopia?" we asked. "Where is Ethiopia?" he replied, so we gave it up.

All the southern armies had gone up through his valley, but he told us that there had been no looting or spoiling of the crops, and that what had been taken had been paid for. Evidently old Mulugeta had mended his ways after Dessye. The Italian aeroplanes had passed over one day when a convoy of mules, horses and men was in the valley. In high excited treble he described how all had run this way and that with extreme rapidity, and how he and his village had left their huts on the brow of the hill and taken shelter under convenient spreading trees. Bombs had dropped and no one was hit: clearly the aeroplane had gone down a lot in his estimation.

We travelled twenty-five miles farther into the province of Yeju and by questions put to soldiers' servants trekking back from the front to fetch more food we learnt that the road continued another eighteen miles to Gherado, where the Imperial bodyguard were encamped, and that the same distance north of them was part of the Dessye army. Each apparently was working full blast on its separate roadhead, moving north and south simultaneously. The rain washed it all away a fortnight later, so they had to start another road.

While we travelled in Wollo it was much the same picture . . . the valleys pocketed into little fields with frequent irrigation . . . the villages a cluster of a few huts on the shoulders of the hills, each hut surrounded by tall euphorbia compounds. When the road passed high above the villages in a mountain pass, whole threshing floors spread with the chillies that Abyssinians use to spice their food stared up in startling brick-red under the sun.

Here, along the steep sides of the River Mille, we came often upon wild cotton growing luxuriantly, and in the fields wheat gave way to more elementary African goods, guinea-corn and maize standing, when uncut, twelve feet high. From lofty nests on poles above the cornfields little naked boys kept the rapacious finches in constant circulation, and reconnoitred for monkeys. Villages were few and big. Urgeisa spread out with many coffee groves over miles of stony river-bed. An Amhara woman came down to talk to us, her lips, finger-nails and the palms of her beautiful hands reddened with berry-juice.

We had to return before the Imperial bodyguard stopped us on our unlawful excursion. So we faced south again over the hairpin mountain road, and turning back regretfully, I looked once more at the way to the northern front. On either side were the camp-fires, old and grey, of the armies which had gone before to victory or destruction. A fine romantic figure sauntered along the road, with grizzled moustaches and beard, wide sombrero, rifle slung aggressively across his back, belt full of cartridges, and shamma tied around his waist. Yeju was said to be full of *shiftas*; the Galla were banding together where the hills slip into the Danakil plain. The old soldier, therefore, walked ahead to deal with any such foolish interruption, and his great curved sword jerked behind him like a wild-boar's tail with the youthful springiness of his stride.

Two servants followed leading a gaily saddled mule, all pommel and cantle, and carrying food and water-gourds.

I had seen his like all along the road. To judge from his lithe step, game carriage, and cunning look, he at least had no doubts which side would win.

XIV

MULUGETA, WITH HIS BOOKS of international law, his secretaries and their tables, his decorations war-like and civil, his Cuban machine-gunners and part of his army arrived south of Makalle the second week of December.

Part of his army he had left at Lake Ashangi, part on the barrier peak of Tigre, Amba Alagi, under Bidwoded Makonnen. Trenches had been dug on the north face of the mountain which puzzled the Italian airmen reconnoitring these high altitudes. Was this the limit of the Ethiopian advance?

Mulugeta felt less sure of the Wollo army, which had only left Dessye after long arguments at the beginning of November. He trusted Dedjazmatch Wodaju, the commander, but not his officers. These, Mohammedans a generation back, allied by blood with the defeated faction of Lij Yasu and his father, the Negus Mikael of Wollo, had long been rotted by the Italian money which poured from the Commercial Agency in Dessye.

The Wollo levies were left on the hill of Buia, above the wide plain of Buia through which flows the thread-like stream Zamra. Mulugeta had a great contempt for the fighting qualities of Wollo: his bloodiest victory of the civil wars, rifles cast aside and red long-sword to tough rhino-hide buckler, had been won over a Wollo army near Dessye. They, too, were frightened of the hawkish old man. He resolved that, under his harsh eye, they should look after the mules and food-supplies in the plain, where there was pasture, water and cover. Buia at the junction of the two main southward caravan tracks from Makalle and Dolo remained to the end the head of his food-supply and of his telephone to Addis Ababa. It was on the line of the Imperial road planned by Bietry; and therefore was well-known to the Italian aviation. To the Wollos, then, the servile task of commissariat.

Mulugeta's arrival disengaged Ras Kassa, who till then had held his positions south of Makalle. For the Emperor, when he decided to let Makalle fall without a struggle, was determined not to go back farther. Contact with the Tigre population must be maintained at all costs: if it were lost, abandoned too were the hopes of a successful guerrilla warfare behind the Italian lines.

To this end Seyyum held on alone on the borders of Tembien, whose capital Abbi Addi was occupied by detachments of the Eritrean Army Corps on December 6. Kassa held the whole region of Selva, south of Tembien, and of the River Gheva, as far east as Antalo which is immediately south of Makalle.

During this period of waiting for Mulugeta, Seyyum and Kassa were reduced to inactivity. The one had come to the limit of his withdrawal south, the other of his march north. The routine of both was first of all to conceal their armies and themselves from the omnipotent air. They were only to attack the enemy if he passed farther: they whiled away their time with the ruses that the Ethiopian sits for hours round the camp fire planning, unplanning, replanning and prematurely rubbing his hands over....

One of the prettiest of these tricks was played by Kassa on November 18, after his arrival near Antalo. His object was to restore the morale of his army already sapped by the bombardment early in the month in the high pass of Amba Alagi.

In the mountains half-way between Antalo and Amba Alagi is a defile, steep and tree covered, for at the bottom is the water of Mai Mescic. Squadrons of planes at a time had inquired into the area, where the tents were taken down at the shivering dawn, according to the Emperor's instructions, and the men hid. Only the mules, by their stubborn self-exposure, had shown the Disperata squadron that there were men about. Kassa rewarded their inquisitiveness.

On November 18, for the third day in succession, the encampment stood untouched below the trees. In the centre, the large tent of the Ras. The Disperata squadron could resist no longer: with the 14th squadron at their side, they flew down to the level of the crests and lashed the empty canvas with bombs and machine-gun bullets.

About eight thousand Abyssinians let fly at them with anything from an old Fusil Gras to a Belgian automatic rifle. Hidden all the way round the defile they caught the Italian planes in a cross-fire.

Ethiopians have told me that it was a great moment to see the planes fly straight up at the shock: then plunge about wildly machine-gunning and bombing at enemies whom they could not place. They shot again and again at the planes, hoping to see one fall: but the planes flew away one by one, beaten but not broken.

They would have been happier if they had known that they had driven off the sons of Signor Mussolini . . . that Count Ciano, the Duce's son-in-law, lost part of his left oil-tank in the attack and only just landed at Makalle in time . . . that another pilot was forced down at Hauzien, and that a machine-gunner sergeant died of his wounds.

Afterwards, they folded up the tent of the Ras, they said, and thanked God. For the next two months the planes flew much higher, and they felt that they could advance.

At about the same time as the Italian High Command claimed that they had thoroughly combed the Tembien, Kassa appeared on the southern border of the province and joined hands with Ras Seyyum. Mulugeta took over the area south of Makalle, between which town and Adigrat to the north there were scattered the I and later the III Italian Army Corps.

The Ethiopian Army of the north was nearly doubled by the arrival of Mulugeta. It became a force capable not only of waiting but of penetrating the enemy's lines. Together, Kassa and Seyyum faced the Eritrean Army Corps which had "combed" the dry tangle of mountains, precipices, ridges and narrow, waterless torrent-beds where their joint head-quarters lay. Numerically, they were the superior of the Eritreans: and Seyyum knew the Tembien.

At Dessye it was decided not to launch a direct attack on Makalle; though henceforward the recapture of Makalle was the objective uppermost in the Emperor's mind.

Advantage, he thought, must first be taken of the weaknesses left in the Italian line by the strategy of De Bono, which could only be repaired by his successor over a period of time and which, in fact, took two months to straighten out.

De Bono's most resounding error was to use two of his three front-line Army Corps for the taking of Makalle. The only result of this disproportionate use of force was that the First Army Corps of Maravigna, which had taken Adowa, was left with the gigantic task of extending westward along the Shire mountains to Axum, Selaclaca and the desert region of Adi Abo . . . holding the fords of the Takkaze southward over a stretch of nearly twenty miles . . . keeping touch with the old head-quarters of the Eritrean Army Corps to the east at Entiscio . . . protecting front line communications to the south-east towards the unconquered Tembien, "combed" but still shaggy. All this while the other two Army Corps sat almost within talking distance of each other around Makalle.

The Takkaze was the weak flank of the Italian line. Makalle was untakable. Nor could it be approached or encircled from the East, where the Italian position was also strong.

Mulugeta was told that he was a holding force. He must occupy a powerful position and simply by sticking to it keep the Italians in Makalle.

He found Amba Aradam.

The Ethiopian high plateau is not a continuous tableland. It is striped and torn by gigantic gorges which divide it into a series of steep table mountains. These mountains are called by the Ethiopians *Amba*, once part of the undivided plateau, formed by erosion of rivers through the channels which lead always to the great streams of Ethiopia, the giant's trough of the Blue Nile and its major tributaries, and the Takkaze. There are always springs in the *Amba* sides, which cut other trenches down to the bigger river channels. The whole mountain mass appears to be supported by flying buttresses of the natural rock. From below, the plateau of Ethiopia swings in separate fortresses to the skies.

Amba Aradam lay, a huge platform of rock, twenty kilometres south of Makalle. It was eight kilometres long and three kilometres across at its widest point: nine thousand feet high. Innumerable caves gave protection from the air, and there were five water-springs whose channels opened five doors into the wild table-land of Amba Aradam. Pasture for mules and cattle lay behind in the plain of Antalo and farther back at Buia.

Slowly the old man occupied the mountain. Small detachments went up to find the best caves: his baggage was moved into them. Then he went up with his heavy boxes of thalers, from which he sometimes paid his army. The water-springs were divided among the troops, who came up nightly in fifties and hundreds. The pathetic heavy pieces of Ethiopia, the cannon captured at Adowa in 1896, were dragged up the mountain and shown a magnificent view of Makalle, which they could never reach. Old Mulugeta did not know their range.

It was about this time that the Italians first noticed "enemy groups" on Mount Aradam, which their aviation "dispersed." Mulugeta went very gradually, and it was a long time before they realised that an Ethiopian army thirty-five thousand strong had slipped between their outposts. A Red Cross unit manned by an Austrian Nazi doctor, Schuppler, and two Irishmen, Brophil and Hickey, arrived at Amba Aradam early in the new year and spread out their Red Cross ground-flag. They were promptly bombed.

After five, when the planes that dawdled daily over the mountain went back to their base, a meat market was opened on the sides of the *Amba* by the trades-people of the Enderta, a tribe of slippery allegiance who after the desertion of Haile Selassie Gucsa had been induced by Wodaju Ali to take a special oath of loyalty to the Emperor. Meat and chickens, bought in sharp competition with the other customers, the Italian soldiers in Makalle, supplemented the grain brought up every day from Dessye which the women of the camp made into bread for the men. The Emperor's supply system worked perfectly until the end of the war.

On the extreme right of the Italian front in the Tigra, where their lines were weakest, General Maravigna in Axum did not see much cause for anxiety. He had defeated small Ethiopian detachments cut off in the valleys north of the Takkaze. But the bulk of the enemy were very remote. Dedjazmatch Ayelu of Wolkait seemed to be attacking continually, without being able to cross, the fords of the Setit far away to the west. The nearest Ethiopian concentrations were at Dabat, thirty-five miles north-east of Gondar, in the shadow of the Semien mountains: they were bombed heavily on December 4 and 6, when the machines reported that they seemed to be making north-west to the province of Wolkait. After that they were lost.

They were, in fact, the troops of Ras Imru of Gojjam, purified by the desertion of all treacherous elements. They were not making for Wolkait: Imru, a genius at improvisation, persuaded a detachment of his soldiers to march in the open in broad daylight at right-angles to the route which they were really following. He wanted to bluff the Italian Command into the belief that they were going north-west rather than north-east.

The planes bombed them heavily on December 4. After the planes had gone, they marched back to camp. The ruse cost them three killed and ten wounded. On the 6th they repeated it without casualties. After that the Italian planes searched busily but found nothing. They were looking in the wrong place.

They did not know that the Potez machine which they chased and machine-gunned without damage at Dabat on the 4th was a courier carrying new orders to Imru of Gojjam and Ayelu of Wolkait. Ayelu was told to abandon unprofitable attacks on the Eritrean frontier, Imru to combine head-quarters with Ayelu and march to the Takkaze. If possible, he was to pierce the Italian line at its weakest point there.

Mai Timchet—"Water of Easter"—is the ford by which caravans have always crossed the Takkaze from Adowa to Gondar. Further west there is fever and little water once you have crossed the river: the long rustling grass, hard and dry as metal rods, in the sultry levels beyond, hides only shiftas, the bandits who live by shooting game and robbing caravans. Experienced *nagadis* lead their mules only along the Mai Timchet route . . . and march with the Fusil Gras always ready. . . .

Imru and Ayelu were, together, the most wary and capable commanders of the Ethiopian war.

They got together, laid their plan, mobilised and marched their men and made good their military objectives in eleven days. They operated from bases over a hundred miles apart by tedious mule-tracks: their men travelled on bare feet. They had no aviation to do their patrolling or reconnaissance for them. One of them, Ayelu, had first of all to wind up another campaign; the fruitless guerrilla on the Setit. The advance which they made was another hundred miles. Yet Imru and Ayelu did it all in under a fortnight.

On December 13 Ayelu was able to disengage his right, well-armed as Abyssinians go, and to send it under a Fitorari to the ford of Mai Timchet, where a small "fort" made of stones by the Eritrean Askaris guarded an easy crossing, for the Takkaze was very low. Travelling at night, the Wolkaits reached the ford at about four in the morning of December 15, ran over the river and killed off the enemy garrison, almost without a sound. They pressed up the mountain trail to Edaga Sheikh where they fell upon another post at daybreak. They numbered about two thousand, the defenders about five hundred. Aeroplanes were called up at once by radio from the field at Axum, but they could not be used. When they arrived the fight was already hand to hand. The Ethiopian swords were out.

Another column, also about two thousand strong, had crossed another ford about nine miles down river. It met with no resistance and came with terrific speed up a mountain track parallel to that followed by the first and gradually converging. These were Imru's troops. When they suddenly appeared behind the position of Edaga Sheikh, the Italians and Askaris still fighting there had to withdraw immediately up the Dembeguina Pass.

Both columns chased them almost at spear-distance up the pass to the next post of Enda Selasi, five miles farther and about thirty miles west-south-west of Axum, on the main rib of the Shire range running towards the Takkaze.

Again the aviation could not intervene for fear of hitting their own men.

Enda Selasi was cleared at the point of the sword. It controlled the tracks to the river over a distance of twenty miles, but it could not be held against the onset of the Ethiopians. A little success, and Ethiopian soldiers, properly controlled, will charge anything.

Aviation failing twice, infantry reinforcements and tanks were ordered out from Selaclaca to stop this irresistible advance.

They left at seven-thirty a.m., in unorthodox battle order, lorries manned by Blackshirts and regulars in front, and then ten tanks. The lorries were soon ambushed, the troops being shot down as they tried to jump clear to cover. Two prisoners were taken. The tanks followed, but the Ethiopians knew that they were coming by the noise they made, and rolled big stones across the track.

The tanks were only two or three miles outside Selaclaca when they were attacked by the head of the Ethiopian column, which had advanced twenty miles from its third success at Enda Selasi. On either side of them was a broad valley, cut by fissures when the track was abandoned, and covered with thorn bush and huge rocks. They attempted to keep in formation under the enemy fire, but the driver of the leading tank was killed: all the other tanks jammed behind him.

The little Fiat-Ansaldo 1935, which I had already seen in a captive condition at Jijiga, is a handy machine to manage, but if it gets fixed it can shoot only within the traverse of the two linked machine-guns sticking out above the driver's head. A traverse of only fifteen degrees. When the ten tanks were jammed together they could only shoot at the tanks in front of them. It was impossible to turn the tracks and find a more fruitful field of fire.

Some of the tanks, trying to shuffle out of the column, slipped into fissures at the side of the path. Two burst into flames.

The drivers got out with revolvers in their hands. They were riddled by a hundred bullets.

Mad with success, the Ethiopians fell on the tanks with their long curved sabres. Two Italians still cowered in one, crying out "Christos! Christos!" They joined the other two prisoners, sole quartette of the Italo-Ethiopian war.

Next day the hollow of Selaclaca, Imru reported, was occupied. They were only ten miles from Axum. In twelve days, by forced marches, use of the night and of the flank-attack and by constantly keeping the enemy in play with a small well-disciplined force, the Ethiopians had penetrated the Italian right to a depth of forty-five miles, taken ten tanks, avoided all planes, and killed according to their own claims one hundred and fifty white and two hundred Eritrean soldiers. They captured twenty-eight machine-guns: the rifles, ammunition and uniforms of the dead were shared out among the bravest of Imru's and Ayelu's mobile advance-guard.

It took the news four days to reach the Emperor by telephone at Dessye. He sent a message to his other commanders in the North "Why do you not do likewise?"

The whole of Imru's army moved across the Takkaze.

Precisely the same manœuvre followed a week later, on December 22, in the Tembien.

Stirred by the Emperor, Seyyum and Kassa decided to act.

The same size of force was used—four thousand well-armed men. Their leader, Dedjazmatch Hailu Kabada, was a high lieutenant of Seyyum, the junior of the two commanders. His objective was Abbi Addi, the capital of the Tembien, but he too was ready to push on as far as he could.

The forces facing him, like those who faced Ayelu's lieutenant, were Askaris scattered over newly occupied defensive posts. Two columns were used, to make sure of Abbi Addi as the others had made sure of Edaga Sheikh.

Surprise did not figure so brilliantly in the Tembien attack.

On December 19 an Askari patrol met a group of armed Abyssinians a little south of Abbi Addi. The fight, according to the Italian communiqué, was sharp, an N.C.O. and an Askari being killed and fifteen men wounded on the Italian side. But the enemy were dispersed. . . .

The tumbled ravines and ridges of the Tembien enabled the dispersed to recollect. The Tembien was still unmapped by the Italians: their aerial cartography was a failure in this wild region, whatever its success elsewhere. Dispersed Ethiopians could not be followed up. . . .

A column from the south-west, unnoticed, and the supposed dispersion from the south met in Abbi Addi the following Sunday, December 22. The fight began at daybreak and lasted for nine hours. It was clinched by a rising of the population in support of Ras Seyyum. The forces of Askaris and Italians who could be mustered in time to resist the Ethiopians were numerically a trifle less than their enemy.

When Abbi Addi had been penetrated the Eritreans withdrew from their barbed-wire and stone barricades between the tukuls, and aviation was called up to support them: also what Seyyum in his dispatch to the Emperor described as machine-gun companies. Hailu Kabada avoided punishment from these arms, of which he had no counterpart, by hanging on to the tail of the enemy. He pursued to Work Amba, the "Golden Mountain" north-east of Abbi Addi where he stormed another Italian position.

His conquest was to be of great value. Work Amba blocked the southern end of the Warieu Pass, around which fighting was to break continually during the next two months and through which the Eritrean Army Corps communicated frontally with the Second Army Corps of Maravigna in Adowa. Abbi Addi straddled the main caravan track running north and south through the Tembien *massif*. If the Ethiopians ever were to strengthen their positions to the north they would encircle the Eritrean Army Corps: as long as they simply stood their ground, the threat of encirclement hung over the Eritreans like a dark cloud.

Encirclement by an Ethiopian army might be no great danger where the ground was known, where artillery could be manœuvred from point to point with speed, and where the enemy could not come to grips before he was seen. But in the Tembien all, except the positions just abandoned, was unknown. Only mountain artillery could be used, and that with labour. The tortured formation of the country, mountain and gorge ever supervening on gorge and mountain, broke any force of size into small groups. Behind every turn of the cliff stood surprise and the Ethiopian, ready to destroy the invader at short range with the Fusil Gras.

Hailu Kabada and Seyyum were pleased with their victory. They reported twenty Italian "officers" and many Eritreans killed. Others came over, or were made prisoners by the population in Abbi Addi, where twelve machine-guns were taken and hundreds of the rifles and the ammunition that Ethiopians fight to the death for. "It was a hard fight," wired Seyyum to the Emperor, "but God protects your humble servants. The Lion of Judah has conquered."

Marshal Badoglio published a different version of the battle, which according to him ended in the complete success of his troops. "The Abyssinian forces were thrown into confusion . . . over seven hundred dead and two thousand wounded . . . seven of our officers killed and six wounded, a hundred and fifty N.C.O.s and Askaris killed and a hundred and sixty-seven wounded . . . our troops are continuing their operations south of Abbi Addi without, as yet, encountering any resistance from the fleeing enemy. . . ."

It was not often that Badoglio published deliberate falsehoods in his communiqués. He was, on the whole, a truthful old man, inaccurate only where figures of Ethiopian slain or the numbers of Ethiopian armies were concerned.

But this communiqué of his was the sheerest nonsense. The Ethiopians not only entered Abbi Addi: they held it. There was neither fleeing nor fighting south of the town. Italy was in no position to know the Ethiopian casualties, which were in fact heavy: they were picked up by their own people, who scoured the battlefield alone. . . .

In other words, the Ethiopians won.

The two series of engagements that go by the name of Enda Selasi and Abbi Addi are interesting not only as deep penetrations of the Italian system. They have more lasting significance in that they show that man for man, and infantry organisation against infantry organisation, the Ethiopians were better than their enemies.

In both series, the numbers on either side were not far from equal. Aviation played a very small rôle. Artillery did not have many opportunities, except perhaps to check the Ethiopian impetus after Amba Work.

The Italians had the modern advantage of the defensive. They used the heavy machine-gun: the Ethiopians had next to no machine-guns, though a few of them carried Belgium Mauser machine-gun rifles, light and versatile instruments for mountain fighting.

The Ethiopians won because, fighting on near equal terms and in manageable numbers, they exploited to the full their mastery of cover, their pliability, and an obedience to command less evident when they were fighting in greater masses. Later, as the armies moved up, they became static and unwieldy, irresponsive to orders, clogged by their cumbrous train of mules, women, servants, children, pots and pans. But not yet.

As Imru followed his vanguard into Shire, Kassa and Seyyum moved into the centre of the Tembien.

Imru, the Italians think, originally intended to attack Axum fair and square. They believe that he came up to Selaclaca to look over the ground for himself, and realised that Axum was impregnable.

He immediately exploited the success of Enda Selasi in another direction, more daring still.

The penetration to Selaclaca gave him free entry into the back areas of the Second Army Corps; the only free entry along the Shire mountain ridge. To his west was the waterless rock desert of Adi Abo, to his east Axum and Adowa firmly entrenched and wired.

He divided his forces. Half his army lay still in the Takkaze valley, the rest except for about eight thousand occupied the posts which the Italians had abandoned. Eight thousand, with the Ras at their head, made straight for the Mareb, boundary between Ethiopian Tigre and Italian Eritrea. The river at this season was an exhausted trickle.

Imru knew all about supply depots. Adi Quala, the supply depot of the Adowa Army Corps, was his objective,

In the disorganisation prevailing under De Bono, Adi Quala had been left undefended. Second Army Corps' already portentous duties have been outlined already. To add to them defence of the supply depots within Eritrea itself would have been to lay upon Maravigna a strain which he was not fitted to bear.

As it was, he had been expected to hold the door of Selaclaca locked against the Ethiopians: even that he could not do.

There were no means to stop the attack. Imru was already within sight of Adi Quala. If troops were sent back from Adowa, Adowa or Axum would be attacked by Imru's reserves. They could not be weakened.

In desperation, Badoglio turned to the air force. His instructions to them were that Adi Quala was to be defended *at all costs*. They knew what that meant.

On Sunday, December 22, squadrons, I do not know how many, rained yperite on Imru's advanced party. For the first time in the history of the world, a people supposedly white used poison gas upon a people supposedly savage. To Badoglio, Field Marshal of Italy, must be attributed the glory of this difficult victory.

Some were blinded. When others saw the burns spread upon their arms and legs and felt the increasing pain, whose source and end they could not understand and for whose cure they had no medicine, Imru's men broke and fled. The moral effect was even more terrible than the material. From their easy perches in high heaven the Italians could see with their own eyes, and with a feeling of rich treasure trove, an Ethiopian force jerked suddenly backward, horrified and scattered. Bombing had never shown such fine æsthetic results. Total dispersion.

With a sudden taste for gas they poured the residue from their machines on the reserves of Imru, in the Takkaze valley.

At the new year, gas bombs were dropped on Mulugeta's forces on Amba Aradam. The Red Cross Unit, which treated thirty cases for burns, was bombed with high explosive.

Experiments in the burning of Ethiopians from the air were opened on all fronts. At Bulale in the Ogaden, gas-bombs were dropped on December 30 and 31, and the Red Cross Unit which dealt with them was bombed with high explosive on the same occasion.

It was just before the Swedish Ambulance at Malka Didaka on the Ganale Doria was blown to pieces, that they too received their first gas patients.

The yperite or mustard gas used was outlawed by the Geneva Convention of 1925, of which Italy was a signatory. It is an invisible liquid and the smallest drop burns the skin. The burn spreads indefinitely and causes intense pain.

Simple medicaments can arrest its action: otherwise the burn gangrenes and the end is death.

Only late in the war did the Ethiopian Government import medicines to treat yperite burns. Money was scarce, and had to be spent on arms.

In this early period yperite was dropped in metal containers, like milk from the dairy.

Imru withdrew his damaged force to Selaclaca. Adi Quala was saved, and the Italian High Command saw how the Italo-Ethiopian war could be won.

XV

SINCE THE EMPEROR'S VISIT TO JIJIGA, when the universal sentiment of cowardice that the Ethiopian soldiers felt was expiated upon two of their leaders, spirits were higher. Taylor, our Military Attaché in the south, made an inspection of Daggahbur and found the defences good. Anale and Sasabaneh further down the valley of the Fafan were turned into Ethiopian camps. Munitions were coming in. The Italians showed no disposition to advance through the Ogaden.

Graziani had turned his attention elsewhere. It was his complete ignorance of what Ethiopian forces lay between his north-western front at Dolo and Sidamo, the Ethiopian province of Ras Desta, that disturbed him. Desta's intentions of diverting the Italian Army of Somaliland had long been publicised but the means by which he was to do it remained a total mystery.

To Olol Dinle, the Sultan of the Shaveli with whom the Duke of the Abruzzi had entered into relations on his geographical expedition down the Webbe Shebeli, was left the initiative of operations on that river. His tribal banda, one or two thousand well armed Somalis, were aided by Italian officers, wireless, armoured cars, tanks and by Dubats of greater experience. By the middle of December he had penetrated as far as Gabba, near the fort of Dedjaz Bayenna Ma red at Imi.

Between the Juba and Imi the Italian command, which wished to create a defensive line across the whole of central and eastern Somaliland while it dealt with the menace of Ras Desta, created an artificial desert in the bush. At Yet and two other strong points all the Somali herds were collected: northward, the wells were systematically destroyed.

And Desta?

Desta was trusted by the Emperor, who believed that he was a capable soldier. He was given one or two anti-aircraft guns and about a hundred machine-gun rifles: a certain amount of money was sent to him to buy lorries and further supplies in Kenya. Very few of the lorries were bought.

Sidamo, Ras Desta's province, is a broad peninsula of the Woina Daga, or middle highlands, lying to the east of the Lake chain in the Rift Valley. Though our geographers call it a plateau, it is no part of "the plateau" to the Amhara. Its mountains have none of the character, abrupt and riven, of the Amharic centre of Ethiopia. It is divided off from the plateau of the Ambas, the endless flat-topped mountains, by the wide primeval valley of the Wawash.

Deeply wooded, rolling hill country, it grows coffee and is inhabited by the most quiet and static of the Galla race: an Amhara garrison with an important ruler have held the province since the time of Menelik, for it is one of the richest in Ethiopia.

Erga Alem, a market place in the north of Sidamo, with two landing grounds for planes, was the newly made capital of Ras Desta. Southward of Erga Alem the rolling mountain started and continued through the tangled fastnesses of Jamm-Jamm to Adola, where it steeply descended. The whole region is full of coffee, wild and cultivated. At Wadara, south of Adola, the country flattens out and continues through wood to Negelli, which is the limit between Ethiopian forest highland and the true African plain.

From Erga Alem to Adola the country, traversed by caravans of skins and coffee, is impassable to motor traffic. But another road goes due south of Erga Alem to the Kenya border, skirting the western edge of the Sidamo highland: and from Mega continues east, then suddenly northward over the River Dawa Parma at the crossing of Malka Guba to Negelli, a large African village. Lorries could pass by this road in the plain.

Because Desta was going to use mechanical transport, he chose Negelli as his base. A long road, much the same type as those in the Ogaden, took one all the way from

Malka Guba to Dolo, between the rivers Dawa Parma and Ganale Doria.

Negelli itself was in a cul-de-sac: to go either south-east to Dolo or south-west to Mega, the single track south to Malka Guba had to be used. Northward the road petered out in the forests of Wadara.

According to his own computation, Desta had about twenty-five thousand men at his call. The garrison of Sidamo was about ten thousand Amharas and Amhara-Gallas. Richer Gallas of the province also carried arms. Rifles were distributed to about five thousand of the peasantry.

When he moved south to Negelli through the woods with his wireless, Desta realised that he had one advantage over the other Ethiopian armies. He was working in an area where there had never been an Italian Consul: where there were secrets worth keeping. He told the Emperor, trying out his new machine, that he did not want any journalists down at Negelli.

Another advantage he discovered when he arrived there. The two rivers that flow through African plain from Negelli are shaded by enormous palm trees their whole length down to Italian Dolo. Both Dawa Parma and Ganale Doria, between which ran the lorry road, provided perfect cover all the way to Italian Somaliland: and his troops would never lack for water.

Along the high ground between the rivers there was wild olive and thick mimosa, extending on a thin grey line, the Woina Daga, which the Ethiopians love to live in.

All the territory to the south of Negelli is inhabited by still nomad Galla: the "pagans" of the Borana and the Laban acknowledge their local "kings" and less regularly the Ethiopian huntsmen who came among them, looking for lion, elephant and buck. The borderland Ambara of this country correspond in their dark shaggy way to the "pioneers" of "civilisation." They are tough, courageous, unprincipled and disorderly. They poach in wide open spaces, not gold, but wild life.

These Fanos, as they are called, made excellent scouts. Desta, fearing their indiscipline, did not wish to use them. But his Fitoraris Adama and Tadama, old garrison chieftains in the south, insisted; the Fanos were enrolled and offered pay.

Desta marched towards Dolo, moving his headquarters a third of the way to Filtu. Most of his men were moved forward on his right wing on the Dawa Parma, for he wished to threaten the extreme left of Graziani on the Kenya frontier. He himself held the higher land between the rivers. On his left one of the Fitoraris moved under the palms of the Ganale Doria. Dedjaz Bayenna Mared of Bale combined with the Fitorari's left wing to man the post of Lama-Shillindi, some eighty kilometres north of Dolo on the Web Gestro, third of the great palm-invested tributaries of the Juba.

Concealment being the main principle of Desta's advance, the presence of two Red Cross units with their innumerable emblems and copious ground-signs seriously embarrassed him. The Ethiopian Field Unit under a Canadian missionary doctor Hooper was therefore kept at Negelli and the large Swedish Unit No. 1, with an abounding material, was carefully guided off to the Ganale Doria, where much the weakest point of Desta's army lay and where he did not wish to do more than hold the Italians.

At the time of the defeat of Anale, nobody knew where Desta was. It was only known that he was moving. Graziani was worried. He determined to make a personal survey of the front which Desta might attack with ease— because there was water all along it.

On November 12 he went up the Web Gestro to Waladaia, some twenty kilometres north of Dolo. Next day he explored the southern bank of the Dawa Parma from Dolo to Malka Rie on the Kenya border. Dolo and Lug, the bases of this line of defence were held now by Somali battalions.

A week later the method used at Tafere Katama was tried out again on Lama Shillindi—the air attack in force, followed by an infantry surprise. For Lama Shillindi in the thorns near the Web Gestro marshes was the only Ethiopian post which the Italians could place in November, 1935.

The surprise was complete. Graziani's mule column, instead of travelling directly up river, where the Ethiopians kept outlook posts, went through parched bush, up dry river-beds, by a long detour to the east. It travelled only at night with Somali guides and arrested any natives who saw it. Water-points were carefully avoided. On the morning of November 22, twenty planes bombed Lama Shillindi, whose Ethiopian garrison scattered, according to rule, in the bush. Dubats were sent in with machine-guns like a flash from the east and the Ethiopians were driven over the Web, abandoning their ammunition. They could not find their chiefs to reorganise and resist: they fell back on Irdolei, another zariba sixty kilometres up-river.

After their victory the Italian force occupied Lama Shillindi and Dimtu farther north; but could not find the enemy again. Graziani felt that he could not waste time and men on small expeditions of this sort: with the menace of Desta increasing, said rumour, daily, he must prepare a greater shock.

But first he must discover the whereabouts, the base, the strength and spirit of the enemy.

Vital though they were to reconnaissance, mapping, and (though they could not tell it then) to the destruction of Ethiopian mobility, the Italian Air Force did not distinguish itself at the beginning of this war as a fighting organisation. It took very few risks. Its successes—Gorahai, Tafere Katama, Lama Shillindi—were the success of mass-fire on a small target. It flew very high where no anti-aircraft reaction was to be expected. The almost daily bombardments of Daggahbur throughout this period, November, December and January, were executed regularly at eight in the morning: the Ethiopian learnt very soon that punctuality was a European fetish and went out into the bush at seven-thirty every morning on his daily chores.

When the bombing of large towns came into fashion, the altitudes chosen were much too high for accuracy. Really good direct hits were scored only on the Red Cross, where anti-aircraft fire was not to be expected. It was only after the defeat of the northern Ethiopian armies that the Italians realised how absurdly they had exaggerated the anti-aircraft reaction of the enemy.

But on this occasion the Italian Air Force, under General

Bernasconi, the Schneider Cup trainer, did something novel, hardy and useful.

Their mission was to discover what they could about Ras Desta. It was known only that he had left Negelli for Dolo, and that his troops were marching down-river. Otherwise the news brought in by Somali spies was, as ever, contradictory.

"The Somali is a spiritual creature," Farouk Bey had told me. (Farouk has some experience as an Intelligence Officer: he worked in Palestine during the Great War.) "He comes in, looks at you, and sees exactly what you want. Then he sits down with the calm of a clairvoyant and tells it to you."

Graziani preferred to trust the air.

At dawn on December 5, General Bernasconi took a squadron of seven planes from the base at Dolo up the Web Gestro's western bank and returned along the high country between the Web and the Ganale Doria. He flew at one thousand five hundred feet but saw nothing. (Incidentally, if he had flown up the eastern bank he would have been shot at.)

Next morning he reconnoitred the westward bank of the Ganale Doria and the Kenya frontier, with the area in between; following at first the lorry route from Dolo.

The squadron must have travelled over a hundred kilometres when they spotted Ethiopians on mules who darted into the bush. None of the normal shooting against planes followed. Bernasconi took a great risk. He flew down to three hundred feet to draw fire.

Fanos, who had long chafed at the discipline of Desta (who ordered no firing against planes) and who believed that they could bring anything down, blazed away from the bush. Three hundred feet was too good a chance to miss.

Desta's secret was out. Firing followed all along the line to Filtu. The bulk of his forces was mapped and fixed: and the Italians placed them with a little exaggeration at twenty thousand men.

Negelli, Desta's provision base, was bombed for the first time, and an Italian pilot was shot through the heart. His squadron came back to report that Desta's army seemed to be established over a wide area, in. positions from which he might attempt invasion along the Kenya frontier.

Desta's first scouts appeared near Malka Rie that week. Graziani covered the whole line of the Dawa Parma, from Malka Rie on the Kenya frontier to Dolo, with barbed wire entanglements, sand-bagged machine-gun posts and trenches. White troops for the first time in the war were brought up to Dolo and an immense transport—over a thousand lorries—collected between Dolo and Lug. The Division of Fascists Raised Abroad was called into service at last, and a lorry bridge straddled the Dawa Parma and the crocodiles at Malka Rie.

The Italians were ready both to defend and to invade.

Every day fifteen planes flew over the region between the Dawa Parma and the highland that Desta occupied. His camel trains were bombed and scattered. His army could move no farther without food. On December 12 Negelli was bombed for the second time by two squadrons, and by now the Ras knew that the south was closed to him.

His reaction was to attempt the initiative again. The war for Desta was still in its chess period, and though his movements were more restricted he could still move about. He transferred troops from the Dawa to the Ganale Doria and the Web: from the north-west to the north of Dolo. Perhaps he thought, too, that he could feed them better where the planes did not follow, or where they were scattered more evenly over the wide arc on which he wished to operate.

By December 20 he had re-occupied Lama Shillindi in force and without a struggle: the head of his column on the Doria was at Semlei and Amino, sixty kilometres up-river from Dolo: on the Dawa his men had come right up against the British frontier, which was now patrolled by the R.A.F.

Swedish Red Cross Unit No. 1 camped at Malka Didaka, twenty kilometres up the Doria from Amino. There was no need now for secrecy: under the flags of Ethiopia, Sweden and their Service they began at once to tend the wounded, for there had been serious bombings from the air and clashes on the ground with the outposts of Dubats. The troops around them numbered four thousand.

For eight days they watched the planes flying up and down the Dona, bombing the river's edge and machine-gunning the great palm-belt without cease. Monoplanes passed over their camp every morning: they dug no trenches or air-raid shelters in order not to suggest that they were afraid of air attack. It was a pleasant life for the Swedes as they bathed in the wide river, baked in the sun, slept under the palms, did their work in the camp. Pastor Svenson daily read his Bible and prayed that the war would end. Mustard gas cases came in towards the end of December. The Ethiopians were terrified by the burns. Desta, now only twenty kilometres away, reported them to Addis—it was only a few days after the experiment had succeeded at Adi Quala, but was he to know?

The feeding of Desta's army was becoming incredibly difficult. Posts were fixed by him on all three rivers to stop desertions. The army began to live on the roots and berries which were to be its staple food for a month.

All the transport routes were now known to the air arm, and were mercilessly bombed with high explosive and gas: both Desta and Addis Ababa regretted that the money which should have been spent on lorries had enlisted the sharp-shooters who gave his secret away. . . .

And on December 31 we heard to our horror that the Ras Desta had wirelessed: "The foreigners' Red Cross at Malka Didaka has been totally destroyed by aeroplanes." It made a great story in the Swedish press.

The Swedish Red Cross tents were the only ones visible by day on the Ganale Doria: they were marked clearly with the Red Cross. Their guard, Hylander told me, was two miles away. At seven o'clock on December 30 the Italian planes appeared over Desta's men on the Doria scattering a pretext in pamphlet form. Signed Graziani, it read: "In violation of the Convention of 1929 the Ethiopians have decapitated an Italian airman taken prisoner of war. Prisoners of war should be respected. By reprisal the Ethiopians are going to get their deserts."

At seven-fifteen three planes flew, seven hundred feet high, over the camp from the east. There were no soldiers near, no firing. The camp was roped off. Hylander, leader of the Unit, was in the operating tent, at the table, with two Ethiopian assistants at his side. A bomb exploded beside the operating tent which was marked by a ten-foot Red Cross, and the canvas was riddled with four hundred and fifty bullets. Hylander was struck in the side and his assistants killed outright.

Four more planes came from the west. Lundstrom took his Bible from his tent and sat in the cab of a Red Cross lorry. As he was reading his jaw was blown off. Three more planes came from the east, bombing and machine-gunning the unit. By now twenty-eight patients had been killed and fifty wounded, two lorries destroyed and palms had fallen heavily all over the camp.

The survivors crept out of their holes as the planes flew away. All their apparatus was smashed to pieces. Lundstrom was dying. They abandoned their ruined camp and took him to Negelli, where he was buried. One by one they came back to Addis by plane.

The bombardment of the Swedish unit was studied and deliberate. It was meant to clear foreign witnesses out of the way while illegal methods of war were being used by the Italians.

On December 30 they dropped yperite bombs at Bulale and bombed the Egyptian Red Crescent camped in the Tug bed. Here their activities were better synchronised. The gas was only documented by the War Office: the Egyptians were too startled to notice it.

On January 5 five more planes bombed Hockman's old unit at Daggahbur and destroyed its equipment: missing Stokes and Dawkins, the two English missionaries who ran the hospital. After that gas could be used on the Ogaden.

And the pretext?

Flight-Lieutenant Minniti Tito was forced down by engine trouble while he was reconnoitring Daggahbur on December 26. He landed in bush some way from the camp and his fellow pilot ran away. Somalis caught Tito while he was examining his machine. He was killed, decapitated and mutilated: his head was taken by the Somalis to Daggahbur, as evidence of their loyalty to

Ethiopia. The rest of him was divided among a large number of these simple nomads.

> "It is now time to demand from the Government," wrote the Italian press, "a harsher and more inexorable conduct of the war, more in keeping with the barbarity which has always been displayed by the Abyssinian soldiers and their voracious chieftains . . . they must employ all the modern and lethal weapons of war from the use of which Italy has in generosity hitherto abstained . . . against savages war must be waged without quarter. Fortunately both science and technique offer the necessary means to the civilised peoples . . . an eye for an eye and a tooth for a tooth . . . we must win as soon as possible."

Victory and the road to Negelli were not far off.

Over a thousand lorries were assembled behind the barbed wire of Malka Rie, with two weeks' provisions for four thousand men. Sixty water-tank lorries holding altogether seventy-five thousand quarts were added, with caterpillar tractors to carry benzine and heavy trenching material and wire. Twenty thousand men stood ready at Dolo with machine-gun companies, artillery and tanks.

Olol Dinle at the end of December occupied Danan, and the protection of Graziani's right flank was believed to be complete. From Walwal to Gabba on the Webbe Shebeli it was held by camps, and in the centre by the artificial desert.

In the first days of January Dubats were sent forward to Areri on the Ganale Dona to push out an Ethiopian advanced guard of three hundred, behind trenches. The Dubats were driven back, but armoured cars on the second day cleaned out the camp. A hundred and thirty killed and wounded. Two days later Amino, another small camp, was occupied in the same mechanical way: machine-gunning the crude trenches from behind steel plating was easy enough.

January 12 was the day fixed for the "contact" battles of Graziani. He sent out three columns along the three rivers Dawa, Ganale and Web. Blackshirt Forest Militia followed the Dawa along the Kenya frontier to fend off the fugitives from the north. Dubats set out along the Web to recapture Lama Shillindi.

The third and central column entered Amino and carried the attack on to Semlei, where the wooded approaches were defended desperately against tanks and Dubats, and finally the Eritrean infantry. Aviation participated, bombing all land defences disclosed by the forces attacking on the ground. For the third column had to do far the hardest work of the three. By the evening Semlei's trenches had been penetrated by tanks and armoured cars and occupied by Eritreans.

On January 13 and 14 and on the morning of January 15 the main position of Desta himself was defended with more than desperation. All the troops that he had left, about eight thousand, were ordered to hold the lines of trenches on the highland until the death. The Italian communiqués claimed for these days four thousand dead; by the mechanical means used at Semlei, troops made contact, aeroplanes bombed, armoured cars and tanks penetrated hastily-made defences, troops followed up to occupy and to assess and bury the dead. Half the Ethiopians must have taken Desta's orders seriously. Yet most of them had not eaten for days, so chaotic was their commissariat after the bombardments of December.

In his final hopelessness Desta sent out his horsemen against tanks.

The Ethiopians had ammunition for two days' modern warfare, if they were sparing. They could do no more. They fought two and a half.

On the 15th, with nothing in their pouches or their stomachs, what remained of Desta's army turned in headlong flight to the north-west and to the Dawa Parma.

Graziani ordered out his pursuit column from behind the barbed wire of Dolo and Malka Rie. The gigantic snake of metal, guided by its aeroplane antennae which warned it of every enemy movement, set off at seventy kilometres a day for Filtu and Negelli. Four thousand men in a thousand lorries, with cannon, armoured cars and aviation, chased the broken remnants of Ras Desta's army.

The Ras himself with his Belgian adviser Frère fled in his two staff lorries with his servants and bodyguard. On the way he met Hooper, coming down to replace the shattered Swedish Unit. "Turn, turn," cried Desta, "the whole army is broken and they are upon us with thousands of camions." Hooper turned round with some speed and all three made Negelli.

They arrived at Negelli on the 18th, two days before the Italians. Hooper went up into the mountains at Wadara. The Ras, discarding his war-drums and his baggage, took all the arms that he could find and followed.

On the 20th, twenty-seven planes bombed Negelli—where there were no soldiers—for forty-five minutes. The great mechanised column rumbled in without a shot fired. General Graziani issued champagne.

During the nine days which preceded the capture of Negelli, the Somali aviation made a hundred and forty-one bombing raids, forty-nine reconnaissances, and dropped forty tons of explosives in six hundred and sixty-eight hours of flight.

Wadara was reconnoitred but no attempt was made to push into the mountains beyond. All that barred the route was Desta with five hundred men and a light trench across the caravan track.

His Fitoraris, who had held the rivers Dawa Parma and Ganale Doria to right and left of Desta, reached him after a wearing retreat, nearly a month later. All that was left of the forces which had contested the rivers with the Italians were fifteen hundred men, nearly dead for lack of food. Desta's first act was to enchain Adama and Tadama. They, he said, had retired without receiving his orders, and without bringing back all his hundred machine-gun rifles.

In his autocratic manner, he grudged the loss. Ethiopians are made that way. He still thought that he might hang on to southern Sidamo against the immense mechanical means of the enemy; if only he had his hundred machine-gun rifles.

It is strange, but till the end of the war he was left without sensing the loss. He was never attacked.

The possession of Negelli was not exploited locally by the Italians; and it was three months before they even exploited it elsewhere.

At Addis, fearful alarm in the Council of State. Total

mobilisation was declared; only those who held land from the Emperor or his chiefs (or the modern equivalent, a salary from the Treasury), had been affected by the mobilisation of October.

In its preamble the new decree made no mention of Sidamo and Desta: it simply described the illegal actions of Italy, the bombing of the Red Cross and the use of gas. These were the grounds for a conscription unparalleled in Ethiopia.

Two weeks later, the first conscripts were given an advance of pay by the Crown Prince and dispatched in lorries to Erga Alem. Dedjaz Makonnen Wosene of the neighbouring province of Wallamo was ordered into Sidamo with a few thousand men. Dedjaz Gabre Mariam, the old Governor of Harrar and once Ras Tafari's Captain of the Household, was sent down from Dessye.

In January the Council of State were still capable of energetic action. But all their spirit had gone three months later, when it came to the defence of Addis Ababa.

And the reason was that in January they were in touch with the Emperor at Dessye, but in April they could not find him anywhere. However modern Ethiopia had become, the leadership principle bound the Empire together.

In the north, there continued the period described by Signor Mussolini as an "indispensable pause." Badoglio was taking stock.

First encouraging sign, he noticed that the Ethiopians were beginning to mass near his lines: not in deep columns it is true, but over well-defined areas they were beginning, in their own words, to "sit down."

The Ethiopian Ras conceived it to be their duty to come up as close as possible to the enemy front; to create what they considered a defensive position: and to raid the supply lines or advanced posts of the enemy. They all believed that if they could block the Italians long enough, husbanding at the same time their ammunition, Europe would at last come to their aid. All except Mulugeta, who believed in nothing but drastic field punishments.

None of them realised that a surprise might be prepared against them; that they were just too modern to fight an Ethiopian war yet not modern enough to fight the moderns.

While their concentrations were too broad for them to maintain the effective control of a Menelik over them, they were not too broad for the enemy to define and map their boundaries. Mulugeta was now only twenty kilometres south of Makale, a position impossible to take by assault, so elaborate now were its defences. Kassa and Seyyum were only fifteen kilometres south of the Warieu Pass into the Tembien, where the Blackshirt October 28 division and associated battalions were equally impregnable. Imru was facing Axum at fifteen kilometres: he knew that he could not take it, but he felt instinctively that he must be in a position to *watch* it.

Finally they were obsessed with the idea that the *Amba* was invulnerable and that white men could not climb.

By waiting in Makalle Badoglio had encouraged the natural inclination of the Ethiopian to draw nigh. He was going to use mass against mass: to pin and to pulverise the enemy. His preparations were conducted in great secrecy and suggested to the Ethiopian that he was intending to withdraw.

Except for the revictualment of the forces holding the Warieu and Abaro Passes on the edge of the Tembien and of the Geralta, he used no roads through the centre of the Tigre. Makalle was only supplied by the Adigrat-Dolo motor road to the extreme east of the Tigre plateau, far away from all Ethiopian concentrations except the small force of Dedjaz Kassa Sebhat. The road was metalled by private contractors.

Seyyum began to feel his way forward again: the post at Work Amba was used for reconnaissance and Italian patrols south of the Warieu Pass were cut off at the end of December. He renewed relations with the people of the Geralta north of Makalle but found them much more timid than before. They had been disarmed. The churches on their boundary with the Tembien were burnt as the small Italian garrisons retired, leaving an enormous gap for infiltration between the Gheva and the Gabat confluence to the south and the Pass of Warieu to the north. Twenty-five kilometres across lay the deserted tangle of rock and thorn valley. Was it a trap? Did they wish the whole force of Seyyum and Kassa to pour through it?

Seyyum in fact did send troops through under Dedjazmatch Gabre Heyot and a Fitorari, (Gabre Heyot was a celebrated Ethiopian machine-gunner who led many daring raids in the Tembien). On January 2 they reported they had cleaned out a little post south of the Abaro Pass in Geralta and that Gabre Heyot had taken two more machine-guns with ammunition. Five days later Seyyum, following through with his main force, had taken all Southern Tembien and a tank from the enemy.

He was at this time making the greatest strategical mistake of the war; due in the main to the fact that the great dumb Ethiopian mass of fighting men were now assembled in his rear and clogging his movements to left or right.

Seyyum's duty at this moment was not to penetrate an obvious void, not to worry himself in such a local way with the position of Makalle. He should have moved north. But Makalle was a question of honour to the Ethiopian governing class, to the Emperor and his northern Ras; and to his Belgian military advisers who had never seen the Tigre or an Ethiopian army in the field.

Never at this period did the Ethiopians under Seyyum and Kassa attempt to attack the supply lines of the forces to the north of them who would one day hem them in. The whole mountain area north of the Tembien, whose magnificent valley entrances from the Takkaze ran across the revictualment of the Warieu pass, was never touched again.

By the middle of January, Kassa too had moved forces up to the eastern boundary of the Tembien south of Warieu, thus pushing the Tigreans of Seyyum more forcibly ahead.

Mulugeta had assembled most of his men on Amba Aradam by the first week in January. He was in contact with Kassa, Seyyum and Konovaloff, and agreed with them that Makalle must be surrounded. For his part, he would tackle the Doghea Pass, southernmost point of the Italian advance below Makalle, commanding the caravan track to the south and the alignment of Bietry's Imperial Road. His patrols—for Mulugeta used patrols—had explored the area as far as Shelikot.

He might have known, by the violent artillery bombardment which greeted the bulk of his army when they arrived on Amba Aradam, that the Italians south of Makalle knew his intentions well enough. Mulugeta had spies in his camp who reported all his movements to the enemy. The European education which he had always denounced in Ethiopia was defeating him now: his cleverest friends were corrupted by it.

The moon was eclipsed on January 9, and a raid was staged—the one big night raid to be recorded in the Ethiopian war—upon the machine-guns in the Doghea Pass. Even so it was not the obscurity but the religiosity of the occasion which stimulated the Ethiopian to a night manœuvre. His priests, forecasting dole for the *ferengi*, worked him into a hysterical condition which denied the claims of sleep. For one night the Ethiopian went without his eight hours' unbreakable repose.

He found the searchlights staring in his face and his comrades broken by machine-gun fire. Mulugeta could carry out no surprises on the Italians, who had money enough to pay for their information.

A message was sent to Kassa—"I am turning my mountain into a castle." Del Valle, the Cuban machine-gunner, led one or two raids into the outposts directly south of Makalle to mask the activity on Amba Aradam— but it was seen from the air. Caves and trenches were dug in every fissure of the gigantic rock, and the castle was turned into a granary as well. And punishments. . . .

Azebu Galla, who had responded to Haile Selassie Gucsa's agents, and had come to Makalle to receive their rifles, ammunition and money, camped ingenuously one night in the middle of Mulugeta's livestock. He and his men were caught next morning and taken before the Ras. In his fury he ordered them forty lashes a man; after which their faces were branded in a raw and sizzling circle. "Now let them go to Makalle and draw their silver," said Mulugeta. Del Valle intervened. "But what will the League of Nations say?" "To hell with the League of Nations," said Mulugeta, and sent the cripples off under escort.

Amba Aradam and the Tembien were bombed daily from the air, but only eight dead were counted during the first week of January. More severe, however, was the bombardment with mustard gas of the two routes by which supplies were brought up from the south. For the first time yperite was used upon the pack animals which fed the two armies. Badoglio wished, by a process of starvation, to make the Ethiopians come nearer and fight it out, or quit.

As Mulugeta and Kassa massed their armies, so did their animal transport litter the tracks behind them. For the first fortnight of January the high mountain route from Amba Alagi to Antalo, and the lower track from Sokota to Fenaroa and the Tembien were bombed pitilessly.

The gas still did less damage than the high explosive. It still fell in containers which, bursting over a restricted area, did not infect the grass generally. But hundreds of animals were killed. Extensive pamphleteering was done against the Haile Selassie dynasty when villagers were seen along the routes. Lake Ashangi and Korem at the base of these routes were bombed with particular severity. The restlessness of the local Galla population, now safely provided with arms by tracks east of the Ethiopian positions on the plateau, was developing into open war.

Farther south part of Waldia village was blown to pieces on January 16: fourteen old people were killed and thirty-five were wounded after seventy minutes' continuous attack, reported the Ethiopians, but when the British Ambulance Unit arrived there were thirty civilians dead and fifty wounded. Gas was not used; for Burgoyne's Red Cross liaison unit, which lost two tents in the attack, was stationed then at Waldia.

On the 15th and the 17th and the 18th of January Korem was bombed. On the 18th a reconnaissance plane appeared over Dessye. Colson, who was leaving that morning by plane for Addis, ran up the hill to see the Emperor fire his gun. Ethiopia was a country where small incidents count: and Colson strained his heart. He had to leave Ethiopia two months later. The last and greatest of the triumvirate of foreign advisers, Colson could make the Ethiopians in Addis do anything. The Emperor respected him more than any other European. Colson was a bedrock man, graven with hard corners out of honesty, common-sense and force. Had he been in Addis during the fateful April days the Emperor would have gone west, not to Jerusalem.

But the object of the great bombardments along the mule-tracks in January was not to knock the breath out of

Colson. It was to destroy the northern armies' supply: to strike terror into the Ethiopian villages along the road: to show the Gallas that now was the time to murder the people and steal the stock that were making for the north. Likaba Tosso, the Emperor's fierce Chamberlain, reached Korem a little later and found that the *shiftas* or brigands as the Amhara called them, the "free Galla" to themselves, were strong and well-armed enough to attack his army in the field.

Over Korem the great new Savoia 81s dropped pamphlets as well as bombs. The Italian method was indoctrination of the civilians of Ethiopia by terror. It did not matter much to the whites whether high-explosive or literature struck the individual: it was the picture of force driving home the lesson into the whole community that satisfied them.

The pamphlets read:

> "People of Eritrea and the Tigre, listen. War brings both good and evil, even churches being sometimes damaged and destroyed. But do not think that this damage or destruction causes the least care or regret to the Italian Government. When by the Grace of God peace is restored, every church which has suffered harm will be renovated and improved."

Those who read in Ethiopian villages are the priests: property owners who take great pride in their property, to save which they submitted to the Italian forces throughout the Italo-Ethiopian war without a patriotic qualm. It was a subtle propaganda: civilian morale was rotted by the spread of terror through those interested to spread it.

Threading the caravan tracks north and south with high-explosive and gas, the Italians bombed the two headquarters of the north, Amba Aradam and Abbi Addi, simultaneously on January 18.

Next morning the end of this immense aerial preparation was evident. From the north and from the south, from the Pass of Warieu and the River Gheva, Italian troops closed in upon the Tembien gap.

The October 28 (Blackshirt) Division and the Diamanti Group of four battalions were thrown into the action from the Warieu Pass. What the Ethiopians calculated as about ten thousand Eritreans attacked them from the south-east.

The Diamanti Group, who had been in Eritrea and the Tigre for over a year, were ordered to lead the less experienced Blackshirts out of the Pass on to Shum Aberra at the side of Work Amba on January 20. A small Ethiopian post which had held it slipped away to report, and Kassa, at great speed, sent off five thousand men who cut off the Group's animal transport.

The Diamanti Group were now in a position of some difficulty, since they had lost most of their stores and all the animals used for carrying them across the Tembien. They wirelessed to the October 28 Division for supplies, but none came.

More Ethiopians fell upon a section of the October 28 Division which issued from the Warieu Pass and annihilated them. An initiative of the Eritreans from the south to extricate the stranded contingent on Shum Aberra ended in another bloody battle in the gorges of southern Tembien, and the retirement of the Italian native forces.

On the second day the Diamanti Group evacuated Shum Aberra and, towards evening, made their painful way back down a stony valley to Warieu, with their mountain artillery and mortars. But now every Amba was swarming with Kassa's Gondaris: when they were near the Pass, the Diamanti Group were surrounded on every side. Their artillery, four batteries, were ready just in time for the charge in the dark.

Fifteen mountain pieces were taken by the Ethiopians within an hour, for this was their most irresistible mass charge of the war. Wave after wave descended in the dusk from the rocks, racing up to the artillery crews with the drawn sword and wrenching machine-guns out of the hands of the men who fired them. They lost men in swathes, but it was impossible to stop the black cataract. The mountain air, fresh and darkening, rang with the high battle-shriek of the Ethiopians whipping themselves to risk any kind of death. The black men ran forward shooting straight in front of them and boasting in a wild falsetto of the number of people they had already killed.

The first Blackshirt reinforcements to come up were charged in the same way and ran, abandoning their rifles.

More of the October 28 Division, heavily armed with machine-guns, issued out to draw off the survivors, who fought a desperate rearguard action.

Of the four batteries only one gun remained, fired by a one-eyed colonel. The Ethiopian could not take the trouble to capture it. (The Ethiopians' worst vice as a fighting people was that pursuit, the completion of a battle, meant nothing to them. They could lay an ambush, they understood ground; once the charge was over and the booty assembled, they drew off to drink.)

Nobody took any notice of the one-eyed colonel as he fired into their midst. The Gondaris were stooping over the dead, taking their rifles and cartridges, their brand new lire notes, their regimental scarves, their revolvers. Fire-arms, money, anything warm (for the Tembien is cold at night), or novel (for the Ethiopian is always consumed with curiosity). Konovaloff counted seven hundred white dead in this valley alone.

The Blackshirts had no difficulty in rescuing the rest of the Diamanti Group. Through the dark echoed the songs of the stagnant and drunken victors, who brought up their womenfolk round the camp-fires on the field of battle. They dragged the heavy material up the sides of two Ambas held the day before by Italian outposts.

Next morning they were subjected to a terrific bombardment from the Warieu Pass and from the air: the Italians calculate that their air force, which had throughout the last two days spent all its efforts on the Tembien, bombed and reconnoitred the labyrinth of rock south of Warieu for two hundred flying hours on January 22.

But the air for once meant nothing to the Ethiopians, who, after their victorious debauch, were completely out of hand. They now decided to attack the Warieu Pass itself. Throughout the day in spite of the aircraft and artillery fire, which was new to them, they hurled themselves at Warieu. The Blackshirts had recovered their morale and mowed them down.

For three more days the Italians used light artillery to try and blow the Ethiopians out of their new positions, but without effect. The first attempt to crush Kassa had failed, and the Eritreans in the south, who had made some quiet progress, returned to their starting point.

To Kassa's headquarters they brought all the machine-guns and rifles that they had lifted from the battlefield. At the cave mouth everything was counted and counted again, so wonderful was this victory. Over a hundred machine-guns; two thousand, eight hundred and fifty-four rifles. And on the positions which they had taken there were fifteen mountain guns and about ten mortars. Kassa, the Old Testament scholar, felt truly that he had smitten them hip and thigh.

The Ethiopians never counted the dead, their own or the enemy's. But at Rome, where this, the second battle of the Tembien was claimed on tortuous grounds as a victory, twenty-five Italian officers were reported killed and nineteen wounded, three hundred and sixty-nine white soldiers and three hundred and ten Eritreans killed and wounded. The Rome communiqué describing the battle was the most untruthful document that she issued during the war.

The Ethiopians were to cap it later by claiming fifteen thousand dead in the Tembien, a figure, they declared, which made necessary the formation of special interment squads. *Quelle délicatesse.*

From this battle the Italian High Command learnt that it did not pay in Tigre to launch an offensive except in overwhelming mass. At the most twenty thousand Italians and Eritreans had attempted to break a rather larger force of Ethiopians and had only just got behind their old defences in time.

A more powerful artillery, too, was needed to dislodge the Ethiopians from the broken mountains which they occupied south of Warieu.

Finally, the simple flank attack on the Ethiopian was found to be useless. Only one way remained to clear him off the field: the attack from the rear.

Badoglio, who was expecting large reinforcements of Alpini and Alpine artillery, could afford to wait a little before he translated his experience into action.

Kassa and Seyyum, for their part, were so delighted with their victory that they imagined that they could stay in the Tembien for ever. Learning from the discomfiture of Ras Desta, they were unready to move into more open ground nearer Makalle. They wirelessed to the Emperor that they were not going to face the enemy's tanks. . . .

But in their holes in the cliffs of the Tembien, or camped in the bushes of its tangled stony ravines, the Ethiopians felt assured that no one could beat them now. They had vindicated themselves in a battle of masses (to exact numbers they were always insensible), and against artillery (they did not distinguish between the different sizes of cannon). Well and good. They did not bother to inspect their cartridge-belts, and count the gaps that the war had already made in them.

XVI

WE KNEW THAT THE EMPEROR WAS GOING NORTH, but we did not know when.

Holmes, of the *Daily Worker* and *The Times*, and Harrison, of Reuter, were all that were left at Dessye of the journalists' caravan. They were going north with him: Korem, south of Lake Ashangi, was to be his next base.

The Italians also knew that he was going north at any moment. After the second battle of the Tembien, their planes turned again to the Imperial Road surveyed by Bietry. On the 4th Korem was bombed again. On the 9th Dessye was bombed, and on the 10th it was bombed again: on the 8th, 9th and 10th the whole northern road from Dessye to Lake Ashangi was pricked with bombs. On the 11th Dessye was reconnoitred, and the villages northward were bombed for the fourth day in succession.

By now conditions to the north of the province of Wollo were chaotic. The Italians were scattering pamphlets saying that Haile Selassie was dead from Amba Aradam southwards to Korem. The *shiftas* had grown to great power and had defeated a part of Ligaba Tasso's army. The route to Lalibela was closed to all travellers, however poor, by the predatory bands. Local governors could do nothing: only at the great centres where there were armies, like Korem and Waldia, was it safe to live.

Absurd subjects occupied the Emperor's attention. The Reverend Harold Street and Mr. John Trewin, two missionaries in Wallamo, had been arrested by the local authorities for moving about, they said, at forbidden hours. The Reverend Harold Street was chained up with his dog-chain and Mr. John Trewin was allowed to walk freely because there were no other gyves to be found. What were they to do? wired the Council of State.

The French were still intransigent about the railway. Although the Ethiopian Arms Treaty of 1930 specified that the Emperor should be free to import all the arms that he needed, and under the Railway Convention he could use the railway for the transport of anything in time of war, the French would not allow him to import war material through Djibouti. He had to arrange for a protest in Paris.

While the Italian planes were trying to find and destroy him, the Emperor had to dispatch all the business of state between these two extremes of seriousness.

His four Italian prisoners, captives of Enda Selasi, enjoyed themselves looking after the Emperor's garden. It was while they were cleaning out the beds below his veranda that the Emperor received two urgent messages from his northern Ras.

Kassa said that he must have reinforcements. Mulugeta described his position on Amba Aradam. Food was getting short and the men restive. The bombardments of every day were fraying everybody's tempers and killing the stock in the plain of Buia. His Galla soldiers were deserting. He could not go on sitting on Amba Aradam, he must either go on or come back, fight it out or withdraw to the positions prepared on Amba Alagi.

The Ras of Gondar was the greatest baron of the Empire, second only to the Emperor himself. Kassa was Haile Selassie's cousin: he had greater claims of blood upon the throne, indeed. He considered himself a more direct descendant of Solomon, but he had waived his claim because he was not such a wise one.

His requests, however, had to be granted. The whole force of Dedjazmatch Moshesha Wolde was ordered to detach itself from Mulugeta and place itself under the orders of Kassa in the Tembien.

The Emperor quite rightly realised that he could not decide back in Dessye what Mulugeta should do. He could only divine what, with his knowledge of the Ethiopian's qualities, would be the best way to do it. If he had to retire, he must not wait until the Italians were engaged with him: to do so would both seem and be a defeat, and his army would become a rabble. Mulugeta was told that he could go forward if he did not risk an open battle. But never to repeat the mistake of Desta and wait to be fully engaged before he withdrew.

It annoyed Mulugeta beyond measure to be deprived of the fifteen thousand men of Dedjazmatch Moshesha Wolde: the garrison of Kambata, like all the south-western provincial pioneers, were fine fighting men, lean and conversant with the realities of war. He kept them as long as he could; and though he himself had stressed the need of attack or withdrawal, did neither.

Kassa awaited the reinforcements of men and ammunition which were to make up the gaps in his own army caused by the free-for-all battle in January. Until they arrived, he firmly decided, he would take no initiative.

When the northern part of the Ethiopian armies was in this state of stagnation and feudal jealousy the plan of Marshal Badoglio was put into operation.

The famous series of three battles which were to follow, Amba Aradam, the Tembien and the Shire, were won by their overwhelming mass.

Mass of men, mass of fire, mass of artillery, mass of aviation. The mass of a civilised people, six times in population greater and incalculably more advanced, smashing the wholly inferior mass of an African State.

In every point the Italians were superior: but the most important point was numbers, and the second most important point was rifle ammunition.

As fighting men, for courage, cleverness, endurance: as artillery, for accurate counter-battery work or improvisation: as a modern army in the field, the Italians cannot be judged. These three battles, when the whole Ethiopian front was blown away in a typhoon of bombs, shells and machine-gun bullets, provide no indices of Italian advance as a battle organisation.

But they show a most striking improvement in Italian administration behind the lines.

In English military theory, which is reputed to be overcareful, each division is believed to need a road of its own for supply. Badoglio, for the battle of Amba Aradam, used one road between Adigrat and Makalle to feed two Army Corps. Evidently he had time to prepare and to store food. His road was not subjected to bombardment. He could use it in day-time, for there was no need to be afraid of the air. The toy artillery on Amba Aradam could never reach his line south of Makalle. His final preparations were concealed from the Ethiopians south of him by the Italian aviation, which bombed and gassed the whole area of Amba Aradam and Buia intensively, destroyed the stock of Mulugeta and kept his men pressed under cover.

On the 10th of February everything was ready for the capture of Amba Aradam. The two Army Corps, the First and the Third, lay on the base line of the Gabat half-way between Makalle and Amba Aradam, ready to advance. The aerodrome of Makalle was packed with planes and bombs, and a special aerodrome had been constructed just north of the Gabat, only ten kilometres from the great table mountain. The artillery ready for action numbered over two hundred pieces and ranged from 75 mm. quick-firers to 149 mm. Howitzers. I believe, but am not sure, that heavier artillery was used behind.

Amba Aradam had been perfectly mapped by the Italian Air Force. All the routes round it were known better to the Italians than to the Ethiopians. The chart of Amba Aradam was divided into minute squares and every piece of artillery knew its range and its objective. The slightest error was immediately corrected by aeroplane spotting and wireless reports.

Amba Aradam could be penetrated by five valleys to the south rising from the plain of Antalo: its northern face was almost impregnable. Badoglio's proposal was to encircle the mountain with an Army Corps on either side and enter it from the rear.

It was a field day. Everything was mapped out on the Italian side. Even the umpires, the journalists, long oppressed by the severe censorship of Badoglio, were given their observatory.

Mulugeta and his twenty thousand men on Amba Aradam knew nothing about it. They sat in their caves and clefts in the giant's castle, or lay in the trenches which the Italians supposed were constructed for battle. Their whole war-life had been one of subjection to the aeroplane. Every cave, hole and trench was there to shelter them from bombs. If one lay very quiet, covered in one's dirty earth-coloured shamma, the "aeroplan" would at last go away and the "pomps" would cease to fall.

On February 11 the "3rd of January" Division of the First Army Corps was ordered up to Shelikot, some eight kilometres from the base of Amba Aradam which was its objective. Shelikot was already held by the Italians and there was no fighting. The Sabauda Division of the same Army Corps meanwhile moved out towards the mountains to the left of the "3rd of January." Next day the Sabauda went further to Anseba in the mountains without encountering any of the enemy. The "3rd of January" pushed on four miles to Afgol, where the caravan road enters the series of plains behind Amba Aradam, the first of which is the plain of Antalo.

They found first the advance guards and then the main force of Dedjazmatch Wodaju, Governor of Dessye. The Wollo army was not numerically strong; it was less than twenty thousand men. Nor were its chieftains the most loyal to Haile Selassie. Already their interest in the succession had been aroused by the reports, dropped from the air, that Haile Selassie was dead.

But Wodaju was a faithful and determined servant of the Empire. He drove the whole mass into battle, and they fought desperately if with little accuracy of aim until three in the afternoon. Another Italian Division, the Pusteria (Alpine troops) were ordered in to equal out the mass: the Marshal was taking no risks. With the Third Dvision of the First Army Corps, the Sabauda, forcing itself into their right flank and with their chief Wodaju seriously wounded, the Wollo Army fled.

Disloyal chiefs made their way back to Dessye along the western caravan track, through Sokota and inland. Wodaju was carried up to Amba Aradam next day and reported the advance in force to Mulugeta, who summoned Bidwoded Makonnen's army, the Wallegas, from the south.

Other Ethiopians came in from the west to report that the Kambatas, Dedjaz Moshesha Wolde's army, had fought with the Italians in the mountains toward the river Gabat.

But Mulugeta, who had got it fixed in his mind that the Italians would never advance in huge force against his impregnable mountain, saw no need yet to hurry his retreat.

The Third Army Corps, the "23rd of March," and the Sila divisions, were now level with his left flank, but he was sublimely unconscious of the fact. It rained heavily that night, and the Ethiopians had learnt to depend on rain for their defence. On the evening of the 14th, when no Italian infantry had appeared near his mountain (for they were resting), but the planes had bombed him into cover all day, Mulugeta reported to the Emperor that his men (among whom he did not include the detestable Wollos) had met the enemy only in small skirmishes.

At seven next morning the old Ras was pulling on his field boots and wondering how long the Galla would stick these air bombardments, when the whole mountain thundered about his ears. He retired deeper into his cave. Amba Aradam from one end to the other was a cloud of dust. Again, the infernal explosions. Every human being on the mountain ran to his peculiar funkhole, obedient to the Emperor's orders and to four-month-old Ethiopian practice.

Shells from two hundred guns fell neatly all over the mountain. The Ethiopians, who had never conceived such a weight of artillery, took them for bombs from the Italian planes which were spotting for the guns above.

Not a shot was fired from the tremendous Amba. Not a man remained on sentinel. They lay, wrapped head and body in their grey shammas, like immobilised pools of mercury in every hole and depression.

Towards midday Mulugeta was worried. The cannonade, and now a real aerial bombardment, continued intermittently. But between the heavy salvoes that crushed rock and the thin thorn below, he could hear furious rifle-fire south of the Amba, where he kept his mules and cattle.

For it was on Saturday afternoon that Bidwoded Makonnen did his duty as an Ethiopian chief.

Though he heard the bombardment of Amba Aradam in the Tembien, Kassa did not move. He was waiting for the Kambatas—who never came. He was like many other Ethiopians, including at times the Emperor himself, fearful of taking the initiative, for the Europeans might trip him up. If Kassa had moved south of the Tembien and attacked the Third Army Corps in the rear, Badoglio's next battle plan would have been in grave danger.

But how could he know? What was the Third Army Corps to Kassa? What Ethiopian chief ever knew how many of the enemy was opposed to him, or maintained liaison with any of his peers to know what help he wanted?

The only means to make Kassa move would have been a wireless message from the Emperor in Dessye: and the Emperor knew nothing from Mulugeta suggesting that he needed help on such a scale.

Only Makonnen did his duty: for only he realised the fact that Amba Aradam was being encircled by a huge force. Taking his sons and four thousand of his best men, he led the Wallegas straight into the machine-guns that were descending from the east, in a threatening half circle of molten heat, into the plain of Antalo.

Nobody that I met has ever been able to tell me where Makonnen fell. Some say in the burnt-out village of Antalo south of the mountain: others say against the barbed wire on the caravan track at Afgol. He was a chief in the prime of his powers and he led his men against two divisions: he slowed up the Italian mass-advance just long enough to enable the old Minister of War to leave his mountain trap.

It was the noise of his mad battle to the south that woke Mulugeta from his illusions. Stirring from his cavern, he saw to his horror that white men to the south-west of Amba Aradam—it was the "23rd of March" Division which had marched over his unregarded west—were entering two of the valley clefts which opened into the mountain. They were feebly resisted, for all except a few were still huddling in holes.

Mulugeta raised a terrible din. All his hornblowers blew and the War Minister himself drew his sword from his side. Messengers ran here and there to set the points of dirty mercury unrolling. Throughout the Amba the Ethiopians jumped to their feet, too late, for the first defences were taken.

There was no barbed wire for the Italians to pass. After

the first trenches there were no second trenches. Rocks and holes everywhere, steep precipices, twisted channels that once carried water, but little deliberately placed to oppose an enemy. It was child's play for the machine-gun, which rattled merrily into knots of black men, just awakened, and for the hand grenade, which cleaned the caves. Mulugeta organised a late resistance in the eastern part of the Amba which was not penetrated yet—thanks to the dead Makonnen.

At five-thirty on Saturday afternoon the "March the 23rd" raised their flag on the summit of the Amba. Mulugeta was grateful for the darkness that followed. Abandoning all his equipment, his uniforms, medals, books, papers, his ceremonial dress, his glory of the civil wars, he fled with Del Valle through the gap made by Bidwoded Makonnen. His army was a chaotic remnant, scattered in all directions. Many were caught in the mountains, and shot in cold blood. The Italians grossly exaggerated the force opposed to them. Including Wodaju and Makonnen it was only forty thousand, less than half of whom were on Amba Aradam. But the number of dead that they claimed was not far from the truth. Six thousand . . . as nothing, compared with the deaths that were to follow.

Six small cannon were captured by the Italians: Mulugeta's total artillery. In small groups under the petty Shoan chiefs, drilling their way clear with the dozen machine-guns left to them, the Ethiopian Army of the Centre moved towards the south. Only the remainder of Makonnen's Wallegas kept together. The rest spread out in fear of the planes which they expected in the morning. For while there was night they knew they would have peace.

The Italians were scouring the mountain, killing off the men who were trapped in the caves and wondering at this huge bastion which the Ethiopians had held but never defended. Their victory was described as a magnificent feat of arms. But it was not. It was a perfect piece of destructive organisation, executed on a people of whom only a handful knew what organisation meant.

With all the animals, mules, horses and cattle that they

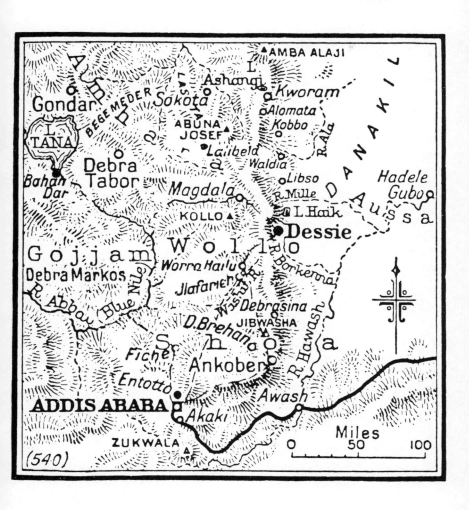

could collect in the plain of Buia, the Army of the Centre went through the night, centripetally bound. At morning, Marshal Badoglio launched half of the Eritrean aviation, two hundred and fifty planes, in pursuit down the Amba Alagi track.

Seventy-four tons of bombs had been dropped on the Ethiopians of Ras Mulugeta during the encirclement of Amba Aradam, which took the Italians six days.

The first day of their flight the carnage was appalling: forty tons of bombs were dispersed upon them in the first five hours of the morning; on the 16th and the 17th of February a hundred tons of high explosive were dropped on the fugitives in the most intensive aerial bombardment that the world has ever seen.

Amba Alagi, the great peak which sets a rugged fullstop to the mountains of Tigre, was reached by the first of them on February 19. Not only the aeroplanes murdered them during the day on the forty kilometre mountain track: the Galla in the hills on either side ambushed their small detachments and mowed them down with Italian bullets, day and night. A part of Bidwoded Makonnen's army tried to hold the trenches on Amba Alagi, commanded by the younger of his two sons. The elder had fallen at his father's side. He told me that they were gassed out of the defences.

Mulugeta felt almost finished. With him were Del Valle and Major Burgoyne, an English officer who was serving with the Ethiopian Red Cross. Struggling along they passed Amba Alagi to the east, trusting that the aeroplanes would not follow. Mulugeta could not find his son, of whom he was very fond. A messenger with torn clothes came up. "Master, your son has been murdered and mutilated by the Galla on the edge of the mountain."

In his last black rage the old Ras turned round to avenge his son. The Galla surrounded him, and planes, recognising the khaki in the middle of their allies, flew low to bomb. Mulugeta fell near his son: his bodyguard carried him off the field, over the rocks and short grass which concealed their enemies. So died the last of Menelik's high officers, the man who had stopped more lead in his rhino-skin shield and killed more men with the sword than any in Ethiopia.

Burgoyne too fell to the bombs and the Galla, who stripped him and cut him about.

Starving and waterless and rotting with wounds, a few thousand men struggled into Korem on Lake Ashangi at the end of February. Many came to the British Red Cross Unit to be attended in the first days of March. The Emperor, who moved north at speed when he realised the importance of the assault on Amba Aradam, heard every bitter detail when his car arrived at Cobbo. Mulugeta and his son dead: Makonnen and his son dead: Wodaju wounded: the whole centre of Shoa shot to pieces and the Italian way clear to Amba Alagi.

Their mass-destruction north of Amba Alagi finished, the aeroplanes began their search for the Emperor again. On the 24th of February they bombed the road north of Dessye, on the 25th south of Amba Alagi to Koram, on the 26th they smashed up the Dessye aerodrome and next day dropped high explosive and, for the first time so far south, yperite along the road from Amba Alagi to Cobbo and Waldia. The drastic operation of the 27th was carried out by ten of their largest machines.

Advancing still in cautious battle formation, the 1st Army Corps reached Amba Alagi on the 28th. Not a shot was fired on them. They occupied the crest at eleven in the morning and raised the flag of Savoy.

Haile Selassie reached the three caves slit in the side of the rock at Korem. He moved into them his wireless and the furniture of his Secretariat, his camping equipment and anti-aircraft machine-gun; finally a set of sewing machines and piles of satin and cotton sheeting. Twenty lorries accompanied the Emperor, with his little set of cannon and his reserve munitions.

The arms were put in another cave. The British Red Cross Unit followed to Alomata, where they encamped a few miles south of the Emperor's new headquarters on March 3, and dealt with a hundred and thirty mustard gas cases—burns of all description on head, arms, legs, faces, of which the Ethiopians were terrified.

Badoglio did not repeat his error of January and attack the Tembien with forces inferior, however slightly, to those of the Abyssinians. The natural attraction of the battlefront had drawn them near to one of the Army Corps: he sent another Army Corps behind them to make sure of victory.

The day after the battle of Amba Aradam was over the 3rd Army Corps left the mountain which they had occupied and turned directly west to Gaela. Aerial cartography had prepared the way for them over this rugged territory but had not smoothed for them the minor difficulties of passage. As they went they made a rough road for motor supplies to follow. The improvisation failed and was improved upon.

For the first time in military history an entire Army Corps was fed from the air, by parachute. Experiments of the Italian aviation in this method of supply had already led the Ethiopians on Amba Aradam to report that the town must be invested, for was it not being fed by aeroplanes? The Eritrean Army Corps, meanwhile, stood ready at the Warieu Pass under General Pirzio Biroli. This was composed now of an Askari Division, the "October the 28th" Blackshirts Division, and a "gruppo" of Grenadier battalions and Alpine artillery.

Kassa and Seyyum kept nearly all of their troops at this time in the southern Tembien. Seyyum had withdrawn all except three of his bands from the Geralta, where they had made the routes from the Abaro Pass and from Hausien to the south very difficult for the Italians for the last two months. Both of them were hugging their dream that the encirclement of Makalle was the event to wait for. One must attend the order of the Emperor to go forward: one must prepare the advance when the Kambatas had come.

The bulk of their two armies were at Abbi Addi and south and west of Abbi Addi. Advance posts held the ambas up against the Warieu Pass, of which Work Amba was the chief.

Until they were attacked in the rear across the Gabat neither Kassa nor Seyyum had the faintest idea that an Army Corps could approach them from the south, or indeed that there was an Army Corps at Makalle free for that purpose.

They had heard of an attack on Mulugeta, but not yet that he was being pursued. The news came to them across the Gabat, by the direct route from Amba Aradam. Its messenger never reported the march of the 3rd Army Corps, because he had passed far north of the 3rd Army Corps. The arrival of the 3rd Army Corps at Dibbuk on the Gheva, on February 26, was a harsh surprise for Kassa: and even when it was on the river two days passed before he understood that it was an Army Corps, not a force like the Askaris which had attacked his right in January—and so deliberately retired.

His entire interest was directed towards the north, where Pirzio Biroli had prepared for him a surprise of extraordinary daring and skill. In the early hours of February 27, when all the Ethiopians throughout the Empire were sleeping, a company of Alpini and mountain-climbing Blackshirts were sent out from the Warieu Pass to climb the steepest side of Work Amba. They were loaded lightly, with rifle, dagger and hand-grenades. They reached the top just before dawn, walked through the first circles of the garrison of Work Amba, who snored in their shammas around the white ashes of their camp-fires—for the Ethiopians roll themselves up at night and lie heavy. Then they scattered their whole cargo of grenades. The garrison of Work Amba, about five hundred men, woke in sudden panic believing that the mountain was taken, so violent was the noise of battle near its centre. They fled down the Amba sides.

The loss of Work Amba is symptomatic of the effect which the Italian aviation, and the precautions which the Emperor had enforced against it, had already made upon Ethiopian morale. Had they been alert, these men—who after all had won the first and second battles of the Tembien—would have resisted and probably have driven the Italians off the mountain. But the fearful noise, they said, which woke them up was so like bombs that they felt that it was all over, that they must retreat. Their first instinct had broken their ordinary reactions to leadership, and leaderless they became fugitives.

The most cruel effect of aviation on the Ethiopian was that it destroyed his traditional response to his leaders. Instead of assembling for mass security around their leader in the instinctive flow that one saw around the Emperor at the first bombardment of Dessye, they scattered now in a frantic dash for individual security. The controls had already been snapped between Mulugeta and his men the last day on Amba Aradam.

Italian air supremacy made of the Ethiopians a rabble which could not think for itself. It demolished, in fearful explosions and vibrations of the solid earth, the aristocracy which was the cadre of their military organisation. The people's support of that framework was very physical. It kissed its feet, hung on to its mule, crowded behind it in the streets, touched it when it walked, helped its limbs in every activity. The aerial supremacy of Italy abolished all these contacts in war for ever.

Kassa was furious at the loss of Work Amba. He ordered that it should be retaken immediately. Six times the forces of Gondar were sent into the assault of the Amba during the day of February 27, and by evening three thousand had fallen dead to the Italian machine-guns, while their artillery from Warieu plastered the approaches where the Amhara hordes gathered for the charge. The simultaneous advance of the whole Eritrean Army Corps kept Kassa concentrated entirely on the north. It was only on the 28th, when the 3rd Army Corps had taken part of his baggage in the Andino region of the Tembien that his servants came running to tell him of the mass of men to his south. He fought on for another day, while the Eritrean Army Corps enveloped the other forward Ambas that he had taken in January; for the Army Corps were now supported by artillery heavy enough for their task.

At this time Kassa and Seyyum had between them thirty-five to forty thousand men, next to no artillery, and about forty machine-guns in the hands of various chiefs. Of the artillery and machine-guns which they had taken in the second Battle of the Tembien they had shot off nearly all the ammunition that the victims of that massacre had left them. They knew that they were surrounded by almost twice their own number. They were covered daily by about a hundred and fifty aeroplanes, which bombed their slightest reaction along the Tembien valley paths. Nearly two hundred tons of high-explosive were dropped in the preparation and during the progress of the Army Corps' advance—twice the appalling weight which had struck and shattered the fugitives of Amba Aradam.

None of the forward positions near Warieu could be held. The fighting men, after two days in which the enemy aviation had bombed their herds as well as them, were starving. Munitions, already short after the battle of January, were running out.

On Amba Aradam, let it be recorded, there were between two hundred and fifty rounds to a man, according to his degree. In the Tembien there were far less.

On the 29th Kassa summoned Colonel Konovaloff, the White Russian military adviser who had worked with him and Seyyum since July, when the Emperor had sent him up to prepare for the invasion of the Tigre. Konovaloff advised an orderly retreat, before it was too late.

An orderly retreat in Ethiopia does not mean that columns are formed and men withdrawn gradually, a gallant rearguard action raging all the while. It consisted in this case of orders sent to all chiefs during the afternoon of February 29 to fight until nightfall and then come back to a point near the Takkaze where they would be given food.

Part of Kassa's reserves, who were assembled peacefully round his livestock, had already been surrounded. At night the flood to the west began. The aviation could not intervene, nor could the Italians follow fast enough. All the camp equipment was abandoned, the captured guns, the radio, everything. The wounded in the Red Cross unit were left in their caves. Hickey and Schuppler of the Unit left in the same party as Konovaloff and with Kassa's two European radio operators.

Next morning the two Italian Army Corps met behind Abbi Addi. Kassa had pulled his men out just in time. The Red Cross wounded were murdered, so Hickey's boy told him.

Kassa's Gondaris, sick of the war and hungry, went off across the Takkaze to their homes, pursued and harried by the cavalry of modern times, the Italian aircraft. Kassa and Seyyum, with a long caravan of Tigreans and Shoans from Kassa's fief of Fiche, were not noticed as they moved steeply south along the Takkaze to Sokota. They had, like all Ethiopian chiefs, to fall back on the Emperor to explain the cause of their failure. Only the King of Kings could give their broken-hearted forces a new courage, and perhaps more ammunition.

The Askaris that had come over from the Italians to Kassa fought to the death, though leaderless, against the 3rd Army Corps on the Gheva fords. One by one the machine-guns toppled them over and their tall fantastic tarbooshes rolled, red bobble and all, down the rocks.

It was now the turn of Ras Imru, last and most brilliant of the northern Ras, the self-made administrator of Harrar, Wollo and Gojjam, most modern of the Ethiopians.

Imru, though his men were the first to undergo the test of mustard gas, was the only Ethiopian in this war who knew how to carry out an offensive with small means. His was the worst-armed of all the northern armies, but it did the most.

Since December Imru had been in the possession of the whole of southern Shire. First he penetrated as far as Selaclaca: then came his astonishing raid into Eritrea. Profiting from the diversion which this caused, he cleaned up all the Takkaze fords and provided himself with several alternative routes of supply. When one trail from the Takkaze was gassed to injure the livestock, Imru's men used another.

Gradually he forced the 2nd Army Corps under Maravigna to withdraw outposts until they were only five kilometres from Axum. He paid his men regularly, although many of them had no claims to pay.

In the matter of payment Ethiopia was as in almost every phase of its life straddled between the old and the new. Theoretically the regular household troops, like the Imperial Guard and the soldiers around each Governor, were paid, though not necessarily in the field. Sometimes the Ethiopians thought that no present pay was better: then, in hopes of pay to come the soldiers would fight longer. This view predominated among the northern Ras: the idea that a cave full of boxes of silver would always keep the army in a state of loyal expectation satisfied Mulugeta especially, who sometimes doled out a dollar or two to his men on Amba Aradam and slipped, for every regular paid, a dollar into his own wide pocket.

As for the men who owed military service, they could not claim money for two months. The two months over, it was always possible to argue that they must go on fighting without pay for the good of their country, and at the Emperor's command.

Imru and Ayelu disliked this lack of method. They standardised payment throughout their army and they also standardised loot. Any capture was divided regularly among the band that made it, and did not have to be carried laboriously to the cave of the commander-in-chief, which is the common Ethiopian practice.

By the middle of January Imru had established his force in a line south and east of Axum, with whose clergy he entered into relations about the strength of the place, its artillery, aviation, and so on. The numbers of the Italians here were, he found, rather more than his own, which were about twenty-five thousand. He was improving his knowledge of Axum when the good priests were shot by the Italians.

Imru felt strong enough to take up a defensive position near Axum. Trenches were dug for the safe repose of his troops during aerial bombardments. Crude precautions were issued against yperite—"You soldiers must be always washing." When his men were nicely established, he sent two bodies of his troops out on a raid into the enemy's baselines.

No white men saw these raids except the victims of them. But Imru's messages to General Headquarters were on all other occasions scrupulously true. The Italians, on the other hand, made no mention of any casualties on February 13, when Imru's parties reached their objectives, until a month later when they denounced the mutilation and death of fifty-seven innocent workmen and one woman on that date.

This is Imru's own story.

On the night of February 11, a thousand of his men were sent down to the Mareb, where they looted during the day the cattle of the population that had submitted to Italy. Next evening they returned by the Asmara-Adowa road, keeping carefully to the side and passing one or two guard-posts where there were lights. At Fort Rama, a blockhouse of stone surrounded by barbed wire on a hill only twelve kilometres from the Mareb, they saw there was no light. While a part of them entered the barbed wire, another part let fly at the other end of the fort. The garrison, which had never expected an attack, rushed to the point where the noise came from and were nearly all shot in the back. During the battle a dump of shells blew up beside Fort Rama, which had always been believed to be a safe depository. It killed five of the Ethiopians and the Italians accounted for forty-five more. A hundred were wounded.

According to Imru's men four hundred and twelve Italians, white and black, were killed and the whole fort cleared. They found uniforms, rifles, machine-guns and food enough to satisfy them for a long time, and were home in the early morning. Their figures of Italian dead were perhaps exaggerated, for it would have taken the Ethiopians hours to count as many corpses as four hundred and twelve.

Another party had climbed down the northern side of the Shire ridge on February 12. Imru knew that he could not repeat the surprise later. The Adowa-Asmara road would be guarded too well. His parties were sent out at the same time. Five hundred men with a proportion of automatic rifles marched off to Damogelila on the Adowa-Asmara road that night and waited for their opportunity to shoot. A convoy passed to Adowa: they enfiladed it at a turn of the road when the lorries presented a good mass target and were going slow. Then they charged with the sword. It was all done at great speed, and they told Imru that they had killed two hundred and fifty-six men. What interested him even more was that they brought back, through the dark, over one hundred thousand cartridges—"All that we could carry, but there are many still in the camions."

Putting the shells and the cartridges together, Imru realised that he must prepare for an offensive.

Imru was a good general. He had already shown that he knew how to fight the Italians. Mulugeta, Kassa and Seyyum all sent their men against outposts and patrols in front of the Italian lines. But Mulugeta never tried to cut the road between Makalle and Adigrat: Kassa and Seyyum never got behind the Eritrean Army Corps at Warieu.

Imru, on the other hand, had made it his chief occupation to raid behind the 2nd Army Corps at Axum and Adowa. He now went further: he tried to discover the plans, numbers and dispositions of the enemy in the offensive which he divined was near. He was the only northern Ras who organised a service of military intelligence.

From his friends in Eritrea he learnt that the Italians were making a new road to the Mareb frontier on his left. He had always believed that his left was safe, for between it and the Mareb lay the bare rocks, lifeless and waterless, of the Adi Abo desert. But when he heard that there were thousands of troops with tanks assembling on the border behind Adi Abo he felt that he must act at once.

The Ras Imru was completely out of touch with any other Ethiopian army, except that of Dedjazmatch Ayelu who was with him. When he sent messages to the centre they took anything from five to eleven days to complete their course, for the messenger had to run to the nearest telephone, in the province of Gondar. Imru knew nothing of the defeat of Kassa or of Mulugeta. If he had realised that they were both lost he would not have risked a battle.

As it was, he decided to attack the 2nd Army Corps before reinforcements challenged him on the left.

On the 27th of February the 2nd Army Corps moved out of Axum towards the hollow of Selaclaca, to the south of which the hills covering the tracks to the Takkaze had been "fortified" by Imru. In other words, Imru had dug trenches and tank traps and placed a few machine-guns. I believe that he had no artillery.

Two divisions, the Gavinana and the "21st of April" led the advance out of Axum: they were followed by the Gran Sasso Division and by heavy artillery. Ras Imru sent off the whole of his right, about eight thousand men, to attack the Italians from the south. There was heavy fighting throughout the day.

To his surprise, artillery began to batter his defensive

positions. He did not know that the Italians had so many heavy guns. He had no means of knowing, for they had arrived that morning from Makalle, where they had been used for the assault on Amba Aradam. But he did the right thing: he moved his left out of the danger zone of the artillery in an attempt to encircle the enemy. Next day they moved nearer to Selaclaca and brought their light artillery into action on his centre.

On the 2nd of March the rifle battle was so hot that the Gran Sasso Division was brought up. It prevented in time an Ethiopian envelopment and threw the Ethiopians back on their hill base. In its turn it was in difficulties and had to be rallied by its commander, the Duke of Bergamo. Again and again Imru, with his instinct for battle, ordered out the positions that were being bombarded to the attack. For now both the aviation and the Italian artillery were pouring hot destruction where the tracks joined below Selaclaca.

March 2 was the bitterest fight that the Italians experienced in their northern offensive. The Ethiopian tentative at encirclement had failed because Imru had not enough men to carry it out. He now launched all his men in a series of diabolical attacks upon the field guns and the machine-guns of the enemy. (Often the Italians report the field artillery had to fire at point-blank range.) Machine-guns were seized by the dark hands of Imru's soldiers as they fell sawn in half with bullets. The contempt for death that the Sudanese showed at Omdurman was as nothing to this: the Ethiopians knew what machine-guns were.

They fought right on into deep night.

By midnight the Ethiopians, except for Imru's personal guard, had only about twenty rounds left. They held on a little in the morning of the 3rd, then flooded back to the Takkaze. The heights of the Shire ridge were littered with five thousand dead. During the last battle of Italy's mass offensive in the north, the 2nd Army Corps, which already had a numerical superiority over Imru, spent on his Gojjamis ten million cartridges, fifty thousand shells.

In three days the 2nd Italian Army Corps had fired as much modern ammunition as the whole Ethiopian northern line possessed at the beginning of the war.

As the survivors fled back over the Takkaze they were bombed from the air and sprayed with mustard gas.

I did not hear of Imru again until the end of March, the night before Colson left. Colson was in bed, his face white as the sheets he lay in: it made one sick to watch him struggle for breath. He was my greatest friend in Ethiopia and I was sorry he had to go: he looked so ill, I wondered if I would see him again.

I was saying good-bye when he told me something which meant that it was all over. I was to tell it to no one, "and that means," with a comic weak drawl, "no one," he said. They had just received a telephone call from Gondar saying that the Italians were only a day's march away: that they would have to surrender because there was nobody to defend the town. There were only five thousand soldiers, and they at the north-eastern end of Lake Tana. "But where are Imru and Ayelu?" I asked. "That is Imru and Ayelu," answered Colson. "The other soldiers went home because they said they could not fight against gas."

"It's getting the Emperor under the skin, too."

When the whole northern front was broken the 4th Army Corps appeared at Selaclaca.

Let the 4th Army Corps stand as an organised and living definition of Badoglio's northern offensive, in which it never participated.

The 4th Army Corps represents the excess of Italian effort to defeat the Ethiopians. It was, indeed, the final element in the "indispensable pause" proclaimed by Mussolini two months before Badoglio struck.

Badoglio, when he framed his offensive, was taking no risks. Every Ethiopian army in the north must, if possible, be attacked by twice the number of Italians.

> Mulugeta's 35,000 to 40,000 by the 1st and 3rd Army Corps.
> Kassa's 35,000 to 40,000 by the 3rd and Eritrean Army Corps.
> Imru's 25,000 by the 2nd and another Army Corps.

The offensive, therefore, had to be delayed while a 4th Army Corps was created out of the Cosseria Division, the "1st of February" Blackshirt Division and an Askari battalion, and while roads were constructed to take it to the front. It arrived late.

And it was not needed. The 2nd Army Corps was fully capable of defeating Imru by itself: alone and unaided it enjoyed the numerical superiority over an ill-equipped enemy that was considered necessary, in this war, to the success of Italian arms.

The 4th Army Corps in another sense was typical of the Italian effort. It was perfectly administered. It was supplied at difficult moments on the march over the rocks of Adi Abo with all its food and water from the air. In even more trying conditions than those which the 3rd Army Corps had to face, the daring experiment succeeded.

In the 4th Army Corps is represented both the administrative advance of the Italian army and the strange lack of confidence which they still had in themselves as fighting men.

One charitable explanation might be given for the excess of force used by Badoglio in the Tigre; that he wished to encircle the enemy. But as it was, the enemy always slipped away after his defeat and suffered loss only to the Italian aviation.

Nor was the enemy less broken by the impact of one Army Corps than by that of two. Imru indeed took less men out of the battle against one Army Corps than the other Ras saved from the encirclement of two.

The real reason was that the Italians were taking no risks.

Their victories astonished the world at the time. The brilliance of the aggressor more than anything in those fateful days of March convinced the undecided mass in Europe that he was invincible, and therefore not to be opposed.

But in fact, he only succeeded because he employed mass everywhere, and because he made the war in Ethiopia at crippling cost to himself.

Cæsar converted himself into a vast machine and rolled over the Ethiopian armies that were mad enough to come near him. Like all machines, he can best be described in figures and measurements.

1. Amba Aradam - 2 Army Corps, supplies of 22,000,000 cartridges, 219,000 shells, over 200 cannon, between 200 and 300 aeroplanes, 176 tons of bombs, details of gas unpublished.

2. Tembien - - 2 Army Corps, supplies of 7,000,000 cartridges, 48,000 shells, 800 radio stations, 100 to 200 aeroplanes, 195 tons of bombs.

3. Shire - - 2 Army Corps, supplies of 10,000,000 cartridges, 50,000 shells, over 100 tons of bombs, details of gas unpublished.

With the whole northern front swept away, first by overwhelming mass of bombs, shells and rifle-fire, and, as the Ethiopians retreated, by bombs and poison gas, there remained only one Ethiopian army in being in the north, that commanded by the Emperor himself, lying now at Korem.

Only twenty-five miles separated these forces from the Italian First Army Corps at Amba Alagi. The Third Army Corps was ordered slowly forward to Sokota on the Emperor's west, in order to cut off all retreat to Gondar. With the Danakil desert on his east, he could, if he wanted to withdraw, take only the Imperial Road by which he had come from the south, or climb south-west into the edge of the plateau.

Whichever way he advanced, he would meet an Italian army.

This period is really Holmes' story. Holmes, who spent three months at Dessye, went north with the Emperor and the British Red Cross to Korem at the beginning of March, with Harrison, the Reuter correspondent who had replaced Lowenthal.

Holmes was eyewitness of all the bombings and gassings which followed. He is writing a book about it: I can only give the bare details of the period as I received them from him . . . with comment to the discredit of the British Government, who were able to conceal as long as possible the fact that poison gas was being used on blacks.

The British Red Cross Unit assembled on March 2 at Alomata, and an advanced party went forward to inspect a camping site on Korem plain, a few miles north. The rest of the Unit, which was attacked by *shiftas*, moved three miles up the valley (the whole of the Korem area was filled with *shiftas* now, and they had already attacked a transport column of the Dutch Red Cross, killing several of their native guard). On March 3 the Unit gathered at their new camp on Korem plain. The same day, between Alomata and Korem, Holmes reported to me by radio that they had dealt with a hundred and thirty gas cases. This was immediately published in *The Times*. From then onwards the British Government knew that if they wanted evidence on gas they need only refer to the British Red Cross Unit, address General Headquarters, Korem, Ethiopia.

Barton was in constant touch with the Unit.

Italian planes had previously flown over the Unit. They knew exactly what kind of lorries it used, how it moved from day to day, what were its ground signs, its Red Cross Flags and its Union Jacks.

On March 4 an Italian plane flew over the new camp at Korem. Its mark was S62, and its pilot was Vittorio Mussolini, son of the Italian Dictator. It had a full load of bombs.

A criminal strain must run in the family.

At an altitude of between five and six hundred feet he circled round the camp.

Not a shot was fired at him. He said that he was shot at, but he was not telling the truth.

He dropped forty bombs on the British Red Cross Unit.

One hit the ground sign, forty feet wide, in the centre of the Red Cross. Another destroyed the operating tent where Melly and McFee were working. It was blown to pieces: how they escaped, I do not know.

Another destroyed the tent which Holmes and Harrison shared—they had come over in the Times-Reuter lorry that morning. Another set the lorry on fire.

Two Ethiopians lying in a ward-tent nearby were split

up the middle by the explosions and, one hopes, died at once. Their guts trickled out.

A second Red Cross tent was also destroyed. Altogether three patients were killed and several wounded.

The doctors, dressers, and as many of the wounded who could move ran out of the camp to shelter in ditches.

It is hard to believe that the pilot could not see that these were Red Cross doctors with armlets, and that he was attacking wounded men. He appeared to spectators to change his course and pursue them, throwing bombs which exploded either just outside the ditches or fell into water. Holmes, who was the last to leave, was thrown down by the force of their explosion. Then the plane flew away.

The Unit withdrew to a ravine, where they carried on their work under cover. The ruined site of their Korem camp was bombed again on March 5, and again on March 6. On the 8th the Unit was able to move into caves above Lake Ashangi. Melly, the leader of the Unit, reported ten tents destroyed and twenty-five unusable as a result of the three bombardments. Two weeks of medical stores were left.

Like the bombardment of the Swedish Red Cross near Dolo and of the Ethiopian Red Cross on Amba Aradam and at Daggahbur, the bombardment of the British Red Cross was cold-blooded and deliberate.

It had the same object. It was intended to drive away the Red Crosses from the front while the Italians were employing illegal methods of warfare.

They now began to weave a web of gas all over Lake Ashangi and the plain of Korem.

The League gave them the cue for which they were waiting.

On March 4 the Committee of Thirteen sent a request to both parties, inviting them to open negotiations for the cessation of hostilities within the framework of the League, and in the spirit of the Covenant.

This, at a time when the Emperor's last army was in the field; when it was clear that sanctions must be increased now, if ever the system was to survive.

No machinery was set up to bring the two parties together.

Ethiopia had to agree to negotiate: Italy, seeing her advantage, agreed to negotiate.

On March 23, twenty days later, the Committee took note of these answers, and requested its chairman, assisted by the Secretary-General of the League of Nations, to get in touch with the two parties and to take such steps as might be called for in order that the Committee might be able as soon as possible to . . . within the framework of the League and in the spirit of the Covenant . . . and so on. . . .

After that we, in Ethiopia, heard no more about the negotiations within the framework of the League and in the spirit of the Covenant.

And while the Committee were drivelling, the Italians put in their most intensive gas campaign of the war.

They centred it on the Emperor himself, who with his anti-aircraft gun at his cave-mouth, shot at the planes as they passed over Korem. They sprayed the whole of the sides of Lake Ashangi with mustard gas. They used now the method which Californian farmers, I believe, use to destroy the insect pests on their fruit trees.

In a disregarded speech which the Emperor of Ethiopia made before the Assembly of the League of Nations on June 30, 1936, he described this refined method of maiming and killing people.

"Special sprayers," he said, "were installed on board aircraft so that they could vaporise, over vast areas of territory, a fine death-dealing rain. Groups of nine, fifteen, eighteen aircraft followed one another so that the fog issuing from them formed a continuous sheet."

For about ten days Holmes reported simple bombardments. On March 14 he reported the gassing of the Ashangi plain. From that day on the spray of yperite on the plain of Lake Ashangi, on the plain of Korem, on the Emperor's caves at Korem, on the livestock and the native paths did not cease.

At this time the Emperor sent a letter to the Empress saying that he could bear it no longer; that it was horrible to hear the screaming of his men during the night, which at Korem was generally quiet, and that old friends had come to see him whom he could not recognise on account of the terrible burns on their faces. Holt, the Senior British

Military Attaché, who visited Korem at this time noticed a change in the Emperor's attitude.

He was still as courteous as ever. But he seemed disgusted past bearing with the behaviour of Europe. He began to see that he had been tricked by the West: he was beginning to return to his own people, and to prepare for a last battle in the field.

His messages to his delegation, which went through the hands of Colson and Spencer in Addis, became at the same time more curt and impatient.

During this period the use of gas was constantly reported in *The Times*, but the Government of Great Britain did not consider it worth their while to examine the Red Cross Unit which they knew had dealt with gas cases.

On March 19 the Korem correspondent of *The Times* reported that there were sometimes eighty cases of yperite burning treated daily by the concealed British Red Cross Unit.

On March 22 *The Times* reported that the Emperor was appalled by the effects of mustard gas, and that the Princess Tsahai, his daughter, had sent a telegram of protest to the Women's Advisory Council of the League of Nations Union. It read:

> For seven days without break the enemy have been bombing the armies and people of my country including women and children with terrible gases. Our soldiers are brave men and know that they must take the consequences of war. Against this cruel gas we have no protection, no gasmasks—nothing. This suffering and torture is beyond description, hundreds of countrymen screaming and moaning with pain. Many of them are unrecognisable since the skin has been burned off their faces.

On March 24 *The Times* published another appeal from the executive secretary of the Ethiopian Red Cross, Dr. Lambie, in which he reminded Londoners that Charing Cross might one day be gassed as easily.

And finally, on March 30, the question was raised by Lord Cecil in the House of Lords. In answer, the Viscount Halifax said, as reported in *The Times*, that *"he wished it were in his power to give the assurance that there was no foundation for these reports, but he had no information. . . . It would be quite wrong and quite unjust to prejudge a matter so grave and so vitally affecting the honour of a great country. . . . The first step must be to obtain the observations and comments of the Italian Government."*

When he was asked whether the representative of Great Britain in Addis Ababa had been asked for any information from trustworthy sources as to the truth or otherwise of the reports, the Viscount Halifax replied that he thought . . . *thought* . . . that had already been done, *but he would make sure.*

The Government of the United Kingdom had had a whole month to inquire into the use of gas, and they had made no inquiry. Not even when the Emperor himself had protested to their representative.

They still professed ignorance on April 2, when the diplomatic correspondent of *The Times* could write *"The use of poison gas has not been witnessed by an authoritative British observer, but such first-hand information may yet be available."**

And on December 31, 1935, three months before the debate in the House of Lords, Captain R. H. R. Taylor, R.A., Assistant Military Attaché at the British Legation in Addis Ababa, visited the wells of Bulale in the Ogaden, which had just been bombed. Either an unexploded bomb, or part of a bomb, was sent to Aden and from thence to the Gas Experimental School at Porton, where it was proved to contain crude mustard gas—the forbidden yperite.

On March 9 the Kenya and Somali boys who had served the British Red Cross as orderlies and dressers went back to Addis Ababa. They had been engaged on the understanding that the Red Cross was a safe institution to work for, and they had found that it was the reverse. They therefore demanded to be repatriated.

The Unit itself was able to go on working under increasing

* At Rumleigh House, Bere Alston, Devon, resides Major F. R. Woollcombe, R.A. (retired). In points from letters in *The Times* of April 14th, he writes:—"The fact remains, that in my opinion we have had no authoritative proof yet of the use of gas!" Had Major Woollcombe been on the spot he could have had plenty of authoritative proof.

difficulties until March 22, when its stores had run out and it withdrew from the front, taking Holmes. Throughout this period the Emperor was negotiating with the Galla chiefs who headed the *shifta* bands of the neighbourhood.

They would come into his cave, below which could be heard the song of the sewing machines, and receive from him new clothes and money for their return to loyalty.

Striped shirts, mantles and newly-tailored trousers are an esteemed combination among the *shiftas* of Lake Ashangi. They handed in hundreds of rifles which they had received from the Italians.

The planes droned over every day. On March 5 two fell into Lake Ashangi. Another was downed on March 14, and the Ethiopians claimed two more between March 23 and March 25. They were flying lower now.

One, we were told in Addis, fell to the Emperor's Oerlikon.

The Dutch, too, withdrew with the British Red Cross. The last Europeans on the Ethiopian side went up to the cave to say good-bye to the grave-faced Emperor. They could do no more for him. At that symbolic moment he must have felt his abandonment by the West.

The only white man who stayed with him was Konovaloff, the White Russian without a passport and without a country.

His army was left without medical aid, except for a young Ethiopian doctor who was related to the Emperor.

After all the promises of the West, all the Articles of the Covenant, all the speeches of Sir Samuel Hoare and M. Laval, all the protestations at the British General Election, that was what the West left with the Emperor of Ethiopia. A landless refugee, and the medical training of one Ethiopian.

It had done more for the other side, for it had given them the scientific means and the time to break his heart. They knew well enough, although they called him a barbarian, that he was sensitive to other people's suffering.

Holmes arrived in Addis with the Unit in the evening

of April 2. I showed him the rambling reports of official doubt . . . and asked him to write a special piece for *The Times*, It was too late of course to have any effect: the Emperor had lost his last battle.

XVII

EVER SINCE GAS HAD BEEN REPORTED in concentrated quantities in the north, the Ethiopian Women's Work Association, which was run by Lady Barton and the English Church chaplain, Mr. Matthew, had been experimenting in the manufacture of gas masks.

They at last evolved a type resistant to the most noxious gases, based on the first masks used in the Great War against the poisonous cloud from Germany. These head bags of flannel, done up in little canvas cases, had mica slits for the eyes and were tied round the neck with tape. They were lengthened especially to cover the shoulders, and the air, drawn through the flannel, which was steeped in solution, was expelled by the mouth through a short rubber tube. The whole was coloured a rich chocolate brown for camouflage.

A dozen experts with their sewing machines were engaged in the town to make up the gas masks, which were cut by Lady Barton, the Princess Tsahai, and other of the Ethiopian ladies of rank who formed the Association and who had not yet fled into the country for fear of an air raid on Addis.

For the morale of many homes was already broken by the reports of gas from the north.

By April 6 the women in their white overalls and the shirt-sleeved machinists had finished their work. Twenty sacks, containing the first eighteen hundred gas masks made by the Ethiopians, were piled into the lorry of one Madros, a burly and surly Armenian.

Next morning Arthur Bentinck, brother of a former Minister at Addis Ababa and representative in Ethiopia now of the Duchess of Hamilton's Humane Killer (not to be confused with Signor Mussolini), climbed on to the top of the lorry in the pouring rain. He was followed by his trusted servants Alemayu, Igezu and a diminutive cook who was known as Zinb, which is Amharic and also Onomatopœic for the common house-fly. I occupied the seat next to Madros, and we set out in the mud for the north.

Our instructions were to reach, if we could, General Headquarters. Nobody knew where the Emperor was, but it was hoped that we would find out. We would go by lorry to Dessye, and then find our own best means to go further. We had letters to the Crown Prince.

A lot of bunk has been written by propagandists about the heroism of the final Italian march on Addis Ababa — the horrors of the road, the landslides on the mountains, the appalling mud which clogged the wheels of the motorised column, the cheerfulness of the troops in spite of every obstacle. . . . I feel that the association of Bentinck, Zinb and Company was much braver. Even surly Madros became quite cheerful after eleven damp days with us.

We sunk over thirty times in the mud and had to dig ourselves out. The only outside aid that we were given was that of Madros' two servants, who ran in front of the lorry to signal where the road was dangerous. We hated these horrible men. They always conducted us into waterholes.

But we kept up our spirits throughout. Bentinck, who had been in the Saar Police during the plebiscite, sang "Deutsch ist die Saar," a stirring tune, on the top of the lorry as we bumped out of Addis on the northward road.

The next two days we drove in chains over the Shoan plain. It was a peaceful journey over a country little offended by the war. We shot our food. The plain was full of horses and big pink lilies headed the fields of wheat around the villages. At Debra Brehan, when we asked them whether they had seen aeroplanes, they answered, "Yes, they are white."

Beyond Debra Brehan, where the road circles round the mountain shoulders, making for the eastern gap, we entered a lovely country which the natives, Shoan and Galla mixed, call "Cold Field" because of the altitude; but now it swayed ripe green with wheat and barley. The only signs of war were the ruined churches, whose bare bones still protruded from the hill-sides; burnt by the Mussulman invader Mohamed Grañ over three hundred years ago, they slept now in the peace of ill-recorded history. Outside the houses, well made of grey stone with oblong roofs of thatch, and round their grey rock compounds and in front of their lych-gates, grew the tall yellow flowers which the people of these uplands use against earache when the wind blows cold and hard from the eastern summits. Houses grew less as we clambered up into the mountain mist, and the flowers grew richer. The edge of the Gib Washa range, through the gusts of driving rain which licked our faces, was a measureless garden of wild flowers, white thick thyme, yellow clustered bushes of daisies, deep blue flowers with a stem like burrage and a bloom like forget-me-not. The grass could hardly press its way through. The whole carpet of the world was white, blue and yellow. The rain came down in a final curtain of dismal lead; our lorry nearly slipped down the steep hillside from a road of mud and water, and for a day and a night we camped in the track while the skies emptied themselves upon us, and the clouds lay in soft immobility around. We carved runnels on all sides of the tent to draw off the flood, and I climbed down through the intoxicating colours to bucket water from an icy stream that sprinted narrowly below. We had our comforts. Every herb on that mountain smelt sweetly and the Ethiopians gathered them in armfuls to make a springy carpet for the tent. Nothing to do but lie in bed eating wild duck with our hands from the pot, soothing ourselves with rum and enjoying the full practice of our noses.

Next day the skies cleared, and Madros returned from the Galla hut where he had fugged for twenty-four hours. We went ahead to relevel the Imperial Road with spades and pickaxes, and cautiously passed down the mountain which drops by hairpin bends cut in the precipice of Tarmaber to Shola Mieda and the grove of Debra Sina, the most historic monastery of Shoa. The rain had played havoc with the road. Whole sides had shelved away sheer, and the centre was scored feet deep with new watercourses. We had to get out again—we spent most of this day walking—and rolled rocks into the channels, picked away their banks, hung in a body on the side of the lorry which shaved the rock-face as it eased itself squeakily to the plain.

Peering over the edge, we descried the wreckage of a lorry far below. Madros laughed scornfully. This other lorry belonged to a Greek, who four weeks before perished through doing a stupid thing. You have to back to pass the pinched corners of Tarmaber. Halfway round a hairpin, he stopped as usual: but instead of putting his gear column into reverse he carelessly slipped it into second, and plunged down the cliff with a speed worthy of the men who dropped upon the Persians at Marathon. Ha, ha, said Madros, laughing nastily, which was the only way he could laugh.

He then drove us with the help of his two revolting boys, both of whom had pink-eye, straight into the black quagmire of Shola Mieda, where we stuck for the night and laboured under the glare of our "Ever-readies."

It was Good Friday, and the Coptic monks were fasting in their olive and cedar grove. A Polish engineer, the only engineer camped on the road, came up for a friendly chat and did not get it.

We talked to him freely about his road.

With morning came an old priest selling eggs, and our boys, all Christian except Zinb, tied single rushes round their heads in preparation for Easter. We passed on, continually repairing the road, into the Danakil borderlands of Ifat Ephrata and Mahfud, where occasional rivers in hot channels under huge level mimosas, like giant's bridge-tables, pass slowly to the Hawash. Dry reeds strangle their flow: the country was suddenly very hot and the road dry as we pitched up and down tightly folded hills. To our right, always in a conical haze above the yellow waste, rose Mount Agelu, the highest peak of Danakil. To our left, the wall of the plateau.

Around us the vegetation took on the dusty yellow and lifeless mimosa green of the tropical lowlands. Flowers only were a flaring brimstone, scarlet finches rustled wings over tall dry heads of grass. The butterflies were huge white swallowtails in copious numbers, which flounced uncarefully through the bush like windborn paper. But there was no wind.

The Galla of these parts wear Danakil dress, the tight short kilt of brown tied by a belt round the waist, and the knife shaped like an "S," curving away to the hilt and blade. And, like the Danakil, one rarely saw them. They looked cautiously through the undergrowth with a spear in their hands. Guineafowl crossed the road and I stopped to shoot, but the driver was nervous—"There are *shiftas* in this part now," he said. We went on till the hot sky turned to the sullen yellow of the African desert evening, and camped in the market-place of Lij Yasu.

The market-place, a lonely square in the bush, fenced on three sides by Menelik's seal, the slim eucalyptus, lay not far from the village of Fitorari Dingil, who with a garrison of a hundred Amharas kept the peace throughout this long unpeopled area, from Debra Sina to Dessye. We did not see him, and slept in the open without guards. At midnight I woke up to hear shooting on the hill across the road, and Alemayu and Igezu answered blind with British rifles. There was silence under the brilliant night, and I turned over again.

We drove through Easter Day with the rushes round our heads. After the long dry waste of bush the Amhara villages seemed to be creeping back on to the road again. Or rather they lay on the brown hills and watched us. Men whom we met on the road told us that they had heard "ba silk," by the government telephone which passed near us, that Janhoi, His Majesty, had gained a great victory over the Italians, which they had celebrated by a raw-meat feast. But the men who worked on the road refused to carry on . . . they would not repair it.

We hoped to be in Dessye that night, the sixth of our journey. But the lorry stuck again in an unexpected marsh, where small butterflies in a confetti of light colours, thousand after thousand, sat sipping the stagnant water. A string of lorries passed us travelling fast towards Addis Ababa. As they picked their way through the dusty bush we counted twenty, filled with machine-guns, ammunition, food, and one or two mountain guns. They carried two hundred soldiers, including Del Valle, Ras Mulugeta's machine-gunner. Some of them said that the Crown Prince had already left Dessye, others that he would quit that evening or to-morrow . . . all in whispers . . . outwardly, all was well.

We came down towards the Borkenna river, where I had landed once from an Ethiopian aeroplane. It was only fifteen miles to Dessye when we drove hard into the side of the hill and bent the steering tie-rod. Madros, who was a powerful man, hammered it out straight in an hour, without fire. We sat marvelling at his smithery, as he wielded his heavy mallet in the devil's glare before the headlights. In the open, we slept again.

Next morning the war struck us for the first time.

All morning, beside the Borkenna River, we had to shelter our lorry, while two, four, finally fifteen bombers droned overhead, scanning the mountains and the Imperial Road south of Dessye. White against the thin blue sky, they circled round the hills to our left. The fifteen, which had flown over Addis Ababa, drummed their celestial way back, three by three. The boys brought us *talla*, native beer, which we drank in the shade. In the hot springs by the river, under the pointed beanstalk shelters, naked women still splashed lazily with their children, their shammas dirty on the dry seamed earth.

Slowly we nosed our way through the mountain range of Kombolcha into Dessye. A mile outside we passed two lorries going back to Addis with the Ethiopian Red Cross . . . the Hungarian doctor whispered . . . "they're all going back." Two little boys, hand in hand, walked along the road. They said that they had been with their fathers in the Tembien: one of their fathers had been gassed . . . a plane passed overhead suddenly, from behind the shoulder of the hill . . . the little boys broke apart, and scattered into holes . . . like all Ethiopia.

Only across the valley to the west, over the caravan track which led from Dessye to Warra Hailu, curled slowly a long thin line of mules and men: an aeroplane which flew above them dived now and then to shoo them on, but they could go no faster. In a brown thread, like ants they trailed on until they could not be seen, lost in some fold of the Wollo mountains. We drove on until we came to the gates of Dessye.

The gates of Dessye are two poles stuck into the ground on either side of the road, with a third pole slung horizontally between them and dependent on two rusty nails in their sides.

Another plane flew above us. We hooted, for at this gate you must show your pass. No answer. The gate zabania had fled into the blue-gum copse below.

Our driver Madros was a strong man; but he had the Armenian's inborn dread of affronting authority, however weak. He would not go through without permission.

So Bentinck walked through to the caves of the Crown Prince's French-speaking secretary, Balambaras Mehata Selassie, where a huge crowd pressed against the rock and into the holes for cover.

While we waited the broken army, part of the ant-trail which we had seen upon the hills, streamed past the gate out of Dessye. I talked with them, as the planes dawdled along their column in vertical menace.

They were perfectly behaved, very friendly, rather tired . . . sick of the war. There were none of the signs of that starving, looting, indisciplined and hostile army that the terrified and the paid in Addis had prophesied before ever the war began.

Their wounded hobbled along . . . women in crude splints covering bomb wounds . . . immense suppurating swellings on the skin that they said was gas . . . others lay face forward upon their mules covered with a worn shamma.

Many carried Italian rifles and regimental scarves.

They said that the Italians fought all the time with aeroplanes, and that when they used gas you could do nothing . . . and then the Galla had attacked them . . . the Tigreans too were traitors . . . their chiefs were dogs. Then they joined the silent procession to Kambata, in the far south-west.

We entered Dessye at four o'clock, when Bentinck came back with a permit . . . the plane still overhead.

The crowd were now clamouring for passes outside the Balambaras' cave as we drove by. They turned their mules' heads into the cliff-side for the herded animals reared high at our rumbling lorry. We drove straight to the Seventh Day Adventist Mission, where the journalists had camped three months before . . . which the Italians had bombed in December.

But there were no people chatting round the gates of the Commercial Agency on Easter Monday. As we drove along, we saw them tearing down the red meat in the butchers' shops, packing up bundles of their household goods, saddling their mules, lighting fires for a last minute meal.

There was a chill of fear all over Dessye. The fires were there to warm and strengthen them also.

At the mission were Nystrom, the Swede, and his wife: Sister Margaret, a Norwegian nurse, and Baird, a small free-lance evangelist.

As we rolled in he was sitting on the veranda reading "The Count of Monte Cristo" . . . a very interesting book, he said.

The missionaries had been ordered three days ago by the Crown Prince to leave for Addis Ababa. But they had no lorry. That afternoon Major de Norman, last survivor of the Belgian Military Mission, had told them that they must go that night . . . the Crown Prince himself was going.

Six thousand of the terrible Galla were reported just beyond the mountains which close Dessye to the north. Still more at Lake Haik. The Italians were using them to clean the country ahead of them.

An exhausted Amhara, who had operated the government telephone somewhere south of Waldia, had run in that morning to report that the Italian cavalry had left Waldia on Easter Sunday, a day behind the Galla.

Dessye, they believed, would be sacked that night.

There was conspiracy within the town as well.

When Dedjazmatch Wodaju was wounded in February, at the battle of Shelikot-Antalo, his army fled down the southward track. They did not stop at Korem. In the middle of March they were back at Dessye.

They encamped on the hills above and refused to come into the town to meet the Crown Prince. Italian aeroplanes visited them and threw leaflets . . . the vicious little black fighting planes came, and buzzed about like tropical stinging flies.

From Korem, the Emperor wirelessed the Crown Prince

to arrest the ringleaders at once. Balambaras Mehata Selassie thought of a plan. . . .

A written declaration was sent up to the army on the hill. It promised the soldiers a free pardon. They could go back to their fields and need fight no more: if they wished to go to the war again, they would be given new rifles and ammunition. As for the leaders, they were invited to a great feast.

The soldiers, tired of the war, and liking the Crown Prince whose mother was of the Wollo family, scattered to their farms.

When the chiefs came to the feast, the three greatest of them were carried out drunk into a Ford V8, heavily chained, and driven off to the Borkenna aerodrome, where Weber and his Junker plane were waiting to take them to Addis Ababa. . . .

Dessye for a while had peace.

When the battle of Mai Chow was preparing, the planes came back to Dessye again, pursuing Holmes and the British Red Cross as they withdrew after their bombardment near Lake Ashangi.

Pamphlets were dropped again. *"People of Wollo, rise against the people of Shoa, who stole all your fine horses in the time of Lij Yasu . . ."* Coloured lights, green, white and red, were thrown from the sky, signifying Savoy to the pilots and nothing at all to the population below.

A few days before we arrived the planes swooped into the valley, four thousand feet lower than when they bombed Dessye in December, and lashed the eucalyptus with high-explosive. They almost touched the trees.

The Wollo chiefs received messages to capture the Crown Prince and keep him for the Italians. He now had only two hundred and fifty soldiers: it was easier than a month ago.

On Easter Monday the Crown Prince's secretary thought of another plan. He invited all the great Wollo chiefs to a *gebir*. Delighted that he had played into their hands, they said that they would come, and assembled their fighting men near the Gibbi hill to provide against a misadventure like the last . . . but they had no fears . . . he had no soldiers.

Towards sunset we left the mission to see the Crown Prince with our letters. He came down from his cave opposite his Secretary's, and we met him in the valley road. Ragged soldiers pressed against his bodyguard, shrieking "Abyet! Abyet!" showing their wounds, shouting for money and cartridges. The bodyguard fiercely beat them off: part of the crowd at the causeway side still cried "Li-li-li-li" in respect for the son of Lion of Judah as he passed, riding slowly on a mule, very young, very worried.

With a courtesy that amazed us, for they were dealing blows on either side, the guard made way for us up to the Prince's stirrup.

He smiled, stooped to greet us, offered us two riding horses. Even at this moment of rout the ruling house of Ethiopia was dignified, kind, and remembered little things.

The boy on whom the responsibility for Dessye fell was only eighteen. We rode up behind him to the caves of his secretary.

As he dismounted the broken soldiers shouted all the more loudly for food, arms, money, permits, anything worth shouting for. They tried to press into the cave. He looked terribly harassed as he spoke to the Balambaras, turned to us, told us that we must go back at once to Addis Ababa.

We asked if we could accompany him, but he refused. "You must go back *at once*," he said.

We rode back across the wide Dessye market-place, pitted with bomb-holes. A solitary figure in khaki, rather stout and red, came running out of a *tukul*. It was de Norman, last of the Belgians . . . he stopped us. . . . "Take me away this evening," he said in a low voice, "save my life!"

"Last night the Wollos fired into my house . . . the whole town will be sacked to-night . . . they have already killed people . . . *les coups de fusil, les cris hier soir . . . c'était terrible!*"

The people of Dessye, those who had property, were hurrying out to the south as we talked. Night fell, and the cup of the hills echoed with desultory rifle fire: one could see brief flickers of flame among the trees.

No one dared light a fire that night except in the Gibbi, which was ablaze at every window.

The Dutch Red Cross were stationed a little north of the town, and one of their number was stranded in the Adventist Mission. So while Bentinck collected necessities for our flight, Madros and I took the Hollander to his station. They were firing up the road and across it as we drove up. Alemayu and I lay on the top of the lorry cab with loaded rifles ready, but as we passed they respectfully stopped their battle. We only heard screams at the roadside.

The Dutch jettisoned all their equipment, drained their last bottle of Geneva with me, and pulled out at once. They left at ten-thirty.

At eleven the lights went out in the Crown Prince's Gibbi. The Wollo chiefs had assembled for the *gebir* at which they intended to capture the Crown Prince. And while they were pinned to the drink, he slipped out of the Gibbi, joined his soldiers below, and made off to Warra Hailu.

Shooting spread all over the town.

I had a quarrel with de Norman, who wanted to take not only his clothes but all his supplies of food. I threw them off the lorry.

The missionaries' servants burst out crying, so we gave them all the mule saddles and de Norman's food to cheer them up. They were to take the dangerous caravan track back to Addis: it was covered with *shiftas* now.

What remained of the Seventh Day Adventist and the Belgian Military Mission rolled through Dessye just before midnight, in the dark, between the trembling eucalyptus, with shooting on either side of the road. The Galla had come in from the countryside to rob.

As we stole slowly down the pass of Kombolcha, the Dutchmen's headlights beaconed to us far away at a mountain hairpin, and a few ineffective parting Fusil Gras pooped at us from the hillside.

With my rifle still loaded, and with the missionaries singing missionary spirituals behind—"*Over there, Over there, Over over over over there,*" I lay on the cab roof, jolting and slipping on my stomach, for that night and the next day, sometimes sleeping.

"*Over there, over there, over there, Over over over over . . .*" refers to heaven, but if I ever hear it again when I have a loaded rifle in my hand . . .

Bentinck and I were very tired. The last Ethiopian lorry to travel the Imperial Road did not stop until seven the next evening. . . . We made Addis two days later.

It is a wonderful sensation, running away.

The day after we left Dessye the Italians occupied it.

XVIII

Colonel Konovaloff, who is still in Addis Ababa, has written for me the story of the Emperor's last battle. He was, as I have explained, the only European who saw it on the Ethiopian side.

The Emperor went into the battle-fire at Mai Chow because his army was exhausted by the continual spraying with yperite, which burnt their shoulders and feet, blinded them, and burnt the mouths of their pack animals when they chewed infected grass.

The Shoans were saying that they wanted to go home . . . to look after their crops and houses . . . what was the object of sitting at Korem under the gas? . . . they had come out to beat the Italians and get their rifles and clothes, what profit was it sitting and doing nothing when the fields were ripening at home?

It was impossible, for reasons of honour alone, for the Emperor to retire without a battle. Retirement also would encourage general revolt among the Galla and as far south as Dessye.

He knew also that he could not attack in force, for his men would be annihilated by the machine-guns and the artillery of the enemy.

He decided therefore to attack the front posts of the enemy before the road from Amba Alagi had been completed and the Italians enabled to bring up their medium and heavy artillery. He hoped to score a small victory, gather some loot for his soldiers, and withdraw into the mountains.

His plan was ruined by the gross inefficiency and procrastination of his chiefs, who delayed eleven days before the battle could be fought. The Italians have told me that they were informed of the precise hour and direction of the Ethiopian attack and the strength of the attacking columns. Konovaloff, who was a member of the late Czar's last military mission to Great Britain, *begins his story with the arrival of the defeated Ras Kassa at Korem in the middle of March.*

On March 19 what remained of the armies of Ras Seyyum and Kassa, after the fatiguing retreat of three weeks, drew near to Korem. What were their numbers? That was difficult to tell: an Ethiopian army resembles so little any other army in the world.

Dressed each according to his taste, wearing no military insignia; followed by a welter of pack-animals, donkeys and mules, and by their women folk who acted as an Army Service Corps; by their children who carried their rifles and other lumber, and finally by their servants and slaves, this army looked more like the emigration of a whole people.

In theory, the armies of the great Ethiopian Ras were numbered at the beginning of the war in several hundreds of thousands. These were perhaps twenty—but who can tell? They had travelled without end for half a year living on their "sink," supplies of food brought from their own homes. But at this time they were buying their needs with what was left of their pay and their cartridges, which are their principal medium of exchange.

Long periods of inactivity, their own disorderly manœuvres, the continual menace of the aeroplane, checks in the field and finally the great retreat had demoralised these fighting men. They were far from thinking of battles or of victory. Our movement towards the south gave them hopes of reaching Shoa, where many of them were born, and where they could at last forget the weariness of the long forced marches, the horror of bombardment from the air, the mortal danger of the machine-guns; the lack of hospitality among their neighbours whom they often found actively hostile . . . where they could in a word renew their old everyday life. That the enemy was advancing more and more, occupying one district after another, and would eventually reach their own homes; such an idea never entered anybody's mind.

On March 20, from the mountain heights which encircle the valley of Korem to the south, we saw at last the town itself, a little burg of purely African type lying on bushy hills, and we sighted the blue surface of Lake Ashangi.

Towards midday, when we had crossed valley and hills, we struggled down a steep hill slope which led us to the caves where the Emperor and his staff lived.

The usual picture; all the elements that make up the retinue of a great Ethiopian chief. Mules, soldiers and servants, without number, wandering everywhere . . . the smoke of the camp kitchen fires.

Following a narrow path we came to the caves. There, upon little platforms of beaten earth were gathered nearly all the personnel of the Imperial household of Addis Ababa.

We, three Europeans who had come with Ras Kassa, were invited to enter a little pavilion tent where dinner was served to us; then we were led to the Emperor. He seemed thinner, but nevertheless determined as ever in his khaki uniform. He received us graciously.

He cross-examined me minutely upon the causes of our retreat, the difficulties of the march and so on. . . . "Are you convinced that Ras Kassa could not hold on to the Tembien any longer? Was he really forced to retire?" he asked me.

It was difficult to answer the question. I thought again of how Ras Kassa had retired; with an absence on his own part as on the part of his chiefs, of the slightest initiative or any display of forethought or decision. They knew nothing about modern warfare, nothing at all.

"We allowed every moment to escape when we could do anything to remedy the evil. And so the Italians by a neat manœuvre encircled us on all sides," I answered him.

I did not want to sadden the spirit of the Emperor with the revealing details . . . the total ineptitude of the chiefs, the complete disorganisation and demoralisation of their forces . . . to tell him how we, once tens of thousands against thousands of Italians, used to abandon our positions at the first caprice of the chiefs or their soldiers, to hide in our distant camps, in caves and huts scattered mile over mile, until our armies became a chaos beyond my power to paint.

"What do you think of the situation, sire?" I asked.

"It's all going normally. Up to now we have resisted as best we might and kept them back—I see nothing very dangerous in the situation." We were served with wine and apples. "I suppose it's a long time since you have eaten fruit?" he asked with his usual charming smile.

Noticing the shabby condition of our clothes—we had lost everything—he gave orders to bring each of us three Europeans a complete outfit of camping kit, blankets and boots. We took our leave, and were given a permit to go back to Addis Ababa with the British Red Cross Ambulance. After all those months of privation and fatigue, I was going home at last. . . .

As I was leaving next morning for the lorries, I was stopped. The Emperor wanted urgently to see me. He and his troops had already advanced beyond Lake Ashangi.

"I have decided to attack the Italians at their camp near Mai Chow," he told me, "before they have gathered in force. This is where they are"; and he opened a notebook with ornamented covers. "I am no engineer like you, and you'll probably think my draft plan a wretched one."

I saw on a leaf of the notebook the profile of the mountains, drawn in perspective.

"I want you," he continued, "to visit these mountains with three of our officers who were at St. Cyr, and make a complete plan of the region occupied by the enemy as well as a note of possible positions for us."

On the Emperor's orders I and three Ethiopians who had completed the course of St. Cyr entered the region called Aia, where from a high summit we enjoyed the view, challenging and magnificent.

In the background the lofy passage of Debara, by which goes the road from Amba Alagi to Korem; then, lower down, the second pass of Togule with an Italian camp disposed nearby. We could also see the hills of Mehoni, occupied by the Italians, with the light trenches and breastwork which they had constructed.

On a lonely mountain, very high, there were two observation posts with, so it seemed to me, a post of artillery.

One could see to the north-east, behind the first range of mountains and in front of the plain which develops into the Azebu waste, a second group of Italians who had arrived by the eastern pass of Alagi, longer but easier to traverse than the main pass. It is the way of the caravans.

Through our field-glasses the view of the tents in order, the movement of people and animals in the Italian camp, was quite clear.

I had already admired the same picture in the Tembien and near Makalle.

On the hills in front of us, I thought, there are a group, probably of two or three thousand Italians. They lie on enemy territory with a pass of great natural difficulties behind them, over nine thousand feet high.

These troops, more than two hundred kilometres away from their own frontier, lay there to provoke to battle what remained of the Ethiopian northern armies, the Emperor's own.

Its numbers? Beside the five thousand Kebur Zabania, "the soldiers of honour" of the Imperial Guard, there were the troops of Ras Kabada and Ras Getatchu, as well as those of the ex-Minister of War Fitorari Birru, of the Court Chamberlain Likaba Tasso and a long string of Dedjazmatches. Probably, they numbered altogether between forty and fifty thousand.

We had about two hundred machine-guns of every possible type, eight guns of 37 mm. calibre, one French 75 mm., six Brandt mortars and eight new Oerlikon anti-aircraft guns.

It was obvious that the Italians were preparing some astute manœuvre for us.

In front of the group at Enda Mehoni, which we saw behind the mountains to the north-east, lay an easy detour which allowed them to avoid the mountains in the neighbourhood of Lake Ashangi. They could make straight for the road behind us which was our line of communication with Korem.

We were also able to find that the Italians were advancing in the direction of Sokota to the west, on the left of our point of observation.

They were already carrying into the caves near our peak a large material of war: cartridges for every kind of rifle, clothes, locked boxes containing thalers, provisions, tinned food and drinks. Towards evening the Emperor and his General Staff were at Aia, accompanied by troops, who spread themselves everywhere.

A cave about forty feet long, which looked as if carved in rectangular form, was covered with soft carpets, while at its entrance employees of the Ministry of Public Works raised a wall of middling height with a door veiled by white silk stuff.

As soon as the Emperor had arrived a *gebir* or feast was offered in the cave. Everybody came, from important chiefs in their turn to the humblest soldier of the Imperial escort.

The Emperor, seated on an improvised throne, had on either side the two Ras, Kassa and Seyyum. To the side, but sitting lower, were the other chiefs before the "massobs" —the baskets with feet which are the tables of Ethiopia.

As I entered the banqueters were eating their favourite dish, raw meat, offered at each table by a young man who was a servant of the Imperial household. Others offered tej in little cups or zinc receptacles. After the meal the Emperor approved my proposals and made his comments on the draft.

He traced with his own hand the arrangements for the battle, ending by saying: "Don't destroy the enemy who come over to us, but make them prisoner and send them to the rear."

The decisiveness of the sovereign, his intention to meet the enemy, proved that our last throw would be made that very night.

After the convocation of a council of elderly chiefs, however, it was clear that the soldiers were not ready for the attack, that not all of them had reached Aia, and that lots of other things were missing.

Obviously the old chiefs wanted to postpone the day of attack. They wanted the Italians to take the initiative.

I saw that the Emperor was very displeased with the turn that affairs had taken. He insisted upon an immediate attack. But to no purpose. "Our troops are not here," they grumbled.

It was morning of March 23 before the cave had been put in order. Thirty priests made their entry, their missals in their hands, and began to mumble prayers in a half-tone. A little later the Emperor left his tent, pitched at the cave's side. While the mass was being celebrated the sight of a great three-motor plane flying almost level with the cave took us by surprise.

It circled, approached the cave, and started bombing. The roar of the engines, the explosion of the bombs and the rattle of machine-guns and musketry made a deafening noise. For one moment it seemed that the machine was flying straight into the cave.

Suddenly a shout of joy from all throats. Poking my head out of my refuge, I saw that the middle part of the fuselage was enveloped in dun-yellow smoke which left the plane in a long trail. And it, promptly dropping all its bombs, turned homeward.

"It's burning, it's burning!" they shouted everywhere. The Emperor broke off the mass and came outside.

At my side some Ethiopian nobles were saying that they were determined to give up their salaries for two years and even, if need be, a *gasha* (forty hectares) of land, in order to buy aeroplanes and crews complete to meet the air forces of the enemy, which were in their view the chief reason of their unsuccess. Everybody agreed with this proposition.

Next morning the Italian aviation displayed greater activity. There were many planes dropping bombs.

The Ethiopians took refuge in anything like a dugout that presented itself to them. In the ravines, behind piles of stones, between the roots of trees and in old holes. With remarkable promptitude they had prepared their refuges already and masked them with branches. Only the donkeys and mules which brayed in hundreds betrayed the presence of so many human beings doing their utmost to hide away from death.

The bombardment of that memorable day killed several and wounded many, who were brought at the dinner hour to the place in front of the Emperor's cave. Why, one might ask, there? Already there was a continual traffic along the narrow path. It was crowded with people.

They were taken to the cave because the Emperor is a centre towards which all Ethiopians unconsciously direct themselves. The wounded in their dirty clothes spattered with blood were laid almost in spite of themselves before the entrance of the cave, while an Ethiopian doctor rendered first aid.

March 25—new bombardment.

An aeroplane bearing the numbers 60-6 came down even lower than the planes before. The Ethiopians set two machines on fire. They were sure that they had seen them wrapped in smoke and burning. Probably the petrol tanks had been pierced.

Our offensive upon the positions on the pass of Togule and the hills in front of the little village of Mai Chow is always being put off. . . .

Details are discussed; there is an appearance of preparation. . . .

The commander of the Imperial Guard tells me that we are waiting for the arrival of the 75 mm. The Emperor did not wish to begin before the gun was there.

On March 26 a large machine again flew so low that we thought it would enter the cave. The brilliant Italian aviation is doing its work irreproachably and risking more than it ought to risk. The Emperor, at whose side I remained during the attack, turned to me and said: "They are really very brave."

A fine rain is falling and the air is misty, but that does not interrupt the methodical business of the Italian aviators. I see them again rising out of the fog, their wheels seeming sometimes just to skim the trees.

On March 27 and 28 the Emperor ordered observations to be made with large optical instruments, the attack being liable to begin one day or the next.

What really was preventing it?

As we learnt later, we were negotiating with the local population, the Tigrinised Azebu Galla—the same Azebu who had killed the Minister of War, Ras Mulugeta, his elder son and many of his soldiers during their retreat from Makalle. Their corpses, decomposing now, littered the road between Mai Chow and Lake Ashangi.

All the Azebu who were "on our side" were being summoned.

Libs were distributed among them: long striped silk

shirts and black satin capes, the complete outfit that is given to petty chiefs. Arms and money were also given to them. One party of them was armed with Italian Mannlicher and Alpini rifles.

For three or four days these people filled the Imperial cave and the place in front of it. They left the Emperor clutching in their fists the ten or fifteen thalers which he had just given them. In their striped shirts with their filthy cotton rags underneath they looked savages enough.

They had been given their instructions. They were to strike the enemy in the back on the morning of the offensive.

Our observers assured us that enemy reinforcements were coming up.

Once more the propitious moment seemed to have been missed. The Emperor meanwhile was more than ever determined to attack.

Continual business round the cave. . . . Each day brought some new obstacle to delay the offensive. It had almost been fixed for the 28th when Ras Getatchu and Likaba Tasso declared that they were not ready . . . the Azebu promised their help for Monday . . . more delay . . . the same day our camp was bombed heavily.

In Ethiopia Sunday is a day of rest, and so another day was lost.

The Emperor asked me how many Italians I thought were assembled at Mai Chow. I answered that for lack of any service of information it was difficult to tell. But I thought five to eight thousand.

"Not twelve to fifteen thousand?" he asked: and so the number of Ethiopians to be thrown into the attack was raised from fifteen to twenty-five thousand.

On Sunday evening the Emperor crossed the mountain covered with bush which faced the enemy hills. A plain three kilometres long separated us from the Italians. He climbed to the top and from there inspected our artillery positions.

"Wasn't there some protected place for me?" he asked. Dedjazmatch Wolde Emanuel had naturally taken all our workers to make one. "Hasn't he done anything?" I asked in my turn.

"No, the rock that they worked on was terribly hard and they haven't been able to do anything."

That was characteristic of the Ethiopians. Three days before this Dedjazmatch, formerly tutor of the Emperor, had said that he had found a place where he could make a dugout for the Emperor near the front line.

He had done nothing: and he had not even told us that he had done nothing.

I got down at once to the job with my men and cut a trench with defences—work which took the whole night.

A high full moon lit up the little platform with the Imperial tent, the southern slope of the mountain and that sad road where every step was covered with the frightful dead bodies of Ras Mulugeta's army. The Emperor was obviously at high tension. He ordered the position of his tent to be changed several times.

The great chiefs came again to beg the Emperor to put off the day of the offensive. Their forces were not all assembled, they said. Besides, they added, they had not properly studied the country by which they would have to attack.

A kind of military council was called by His Majesty, but it was almost impossible to speak and utterly impossible to hear. The soldiers, strung up by waiting so long for the offensive, kept on firing their guns into the air. Some of the nearer ones were arrested and beaten soundly, but that did not stop the row.

The military council postponed the offensive unti Tuesday. I climbed to the mountain crest again. In the moonlight, grey masses lay tumbled anywhere on the slope . . . Ethiopian warriors wrapped in their shammas and sleeping after a tiring day.

On Monday morning the Emperor, his suite and the different chiefs climbed to the hilltop. The Emperor spent a little while in the trench which I had prepared for him; then got out, and dropping the black cape from his shoulders, leaned against a tree. He fixed his eyes on the enemy positions in the distance.

I looked at him.

Slim, still young in appearance, very carefully dressed . . . he did not look like an Ethiopian at all. The way he stood, motionless and concentrated, betrayed a mind working hard.

What was he thinking about?

Perhaps the same as me. Without conscious effort, almost involuntarily, I saw again those twenty years of fruitful government over Ethiopia during which he had mastered every obstacle. The internal enemies who had never ceased to give him difficulty had been defeated. But here was a new enemy, more terrible and stronger, which had put itself in his way. He saw it from afar, three kilometres off, behind the light fortifications around which, glittering in the sun, lay pieces of broken glass to injure the naked feet of their enemy.

"The defeat of my army will be the end of all for me—we must act with all carefulness," he had told me one day. The Emperor maintained his pensive attitude.

On the day before, the advanced camp of the Italians near the pass of Togule had been almost completely withdrawn when the Ethiopians were imprudent enough to discharge several shells from the 75. Meanwhile one could see that the fortifications had been strengthened: only most of the tents had been removed.

Behind the camp and beyond the mountains which the enemy had fortified there was great activity; unbroken movement of transport . . . unloading of pack animals . . . arrival of new convoys. New Italian camps had been installed between the passes of Togule and Debara. Work as systematic as the revolutions of a machine went on over there. Each man knew his place and his job. Refuges masked with branches sheltered those who held in their hands the doubtful destinies of the Ethiopian people.

Alone against his tree the Emperor continued in silent contemplation. Two Italian guns threw shells over his head: we heard them burst on the fatal road behind.

For our attack, definitely fixed for the morrow, nothing had yet been prepared. None of the participants seemed to be sure of his rôle. At our back some tens of thousands of Ethiopian soldiers who were going into the attack tomorrow, lay sleeping in the ravines, in holes and under bushes.

By what miracle had we not yet been discovered by the Italian planes? One could see them flying over our old territory, now almost deserted, dropping bombs with a dogged persistence.

If they were to discover us we would undergo heavy losses and that would naturally have its influence on our offensive.

The moral effect of aviation in this war was enormous. If the land space was unconquered yet, the aerial already belonged to the Italians. From their heights they penetrated our life, turned it upside down. They could intervene on all our movements. They prevented us from eating and warming ourselves after a heavy march round our camp-fires, which we were afraid to light.

They turned us into moles who dashed into their burrows at the slightest alarm.

Insignificant though the losses which they inflicted upon us might be, each Ethiopian thought that he was the special target of the bomb released. All the day under the menace of an enemy who followed us step by step, with something near impunity, since he knew that he was master. . . .

The Ethiopian armies are not united either by an experienced command, or by a general discipline, or by Western ideals of patriotism and militant idealism. They had no arms to answer. It was not in the least surprising to me that the planes which every day roved abroad to discover and terrorise them had an enormous effect upon their morale.

At midday the Emperor, some ten of his chiefs and I went down to a cave where lunch was served, under the monotonous drone of the aeroplane motors and the whirr of the shells as they passed overhead, to fall upon the fatal road behind us.

The Emperor is disturbed. He is waiting for the concentration of all the troops. That evening they are to advance along the bushy ravines up to the front; then, after a short rest, they are to assemble at five o'clock for the attack. They are to be led in three columns, commanded by Ras Kassa, Seyyum and Getatchu.

Why by them, and not by others of greater energy and capacity? Because the sovereign had to reckon with his feudal seigneurs of the Empire although they had proved their ineptitude already and had lost the first part of the war. He had better men, but he could not use them.

His plan was to turn the Italian positions on the right between the conical mountain near the road and the hills covered with tuia and cactus: then to attack the positions in the rear which would be less well protected than those in the front line. In our glasses we could see the camps quite open. Standing alone, the property of the local hereditary chief Dedjazmatch Aberra Tadla, which had been burnt some days before, offered an excellent point of concentration in the rear. It stood on a hill and the double wall of stone which surrounded it could serve as fortification all ready for us. The Italians were taking no great precautions against the Ethiopian artillery: they were not afraid of it.

A small Ethiopian detachment had to turn the enemy's attention in the direction of his front.

Towards evening the Emperor summoned all his high chiefs and showed them from the mountain top where they had to go and, point after point, how they were to attack the rear enemy positions.

It was the first time since the war began that Ethiopian commanders knew what they had to do and saw the terrain over which they were going to attack. For lack of any service of information or of a regular system of pickets or advanced posts we still knew nothing about the numbers or the disposition of the enemy.

"You will find me with the reserves near that mountain covered with the cactus," the Emperor concluded, "I will send reinforcements wherever there is any difficulty."

The Emperor was very animated. He turned from side to side of the ring of chiefs, who listened to him in silence. Correct as ever in his European dress, his beard and moustaches neat and trim, what a contrast he presented to the mass around him . . . each dressed according to his fancy, most of them enveloped in their shammas and bernous, or with a muffler twisted round their necks.

There was a time when some of them had intrigued against the future Emperor, then Heir to the Throne. He had forgiven them. Others owed their career to him; they were chosen by him, educated and given high positions in spite of their obscure origin.

But most of them were illiterate, ignorant alike of foreign languages and of the Western method of warfare.

One could only count on the Imperial Guard and the detachment of Gerazmatch Aberra, all of whom had done their service under the Belgian Military Mission. About five thousand rifles, no more. The rest, some tens of thousands, were simple Ethiopian warriors who had been given no military education.

As we had decided on a sudden surprise, only a few dozen machine-guns were issued. The troops were not to be overloaded.

Towards midnight the Emperor gave the order of attack. I slept on the mountain awaiting daybreak.

At five-twenty in the morning, as at the stroke of a magic wand, the silent chain of mountains woke to a rattle of rifles and machine-guns.

Thousands of little blue lights burst at every moment from different points.

The Italian artillery shelled our lines, the Ethiopians answering at random.

From the blue lights which sparkled behind the Italians I could judge both the strength and the objective of the Ethiopian assault.

As the sun rose, the lights became invisible; but I had already noted the end of the fusillade on the Italian left flank in their two fortified camps. The Ethiopians had got in.

With their habitual thoughtlessness and boastfulness the men round me cried, "They've driven the Italians out!"

At about eight o'clock three large planes arrived and began to bomb our rear, while five small planes attacked our front line with machine-guns.

They flew over our heads with remarkable calm, almost grazing the ground and inundating us with bullets.

The Ethiopians had set fire to a little village lying to the rear on the left flank of the enemy. From far off it looked like a great torch of fire.

The Italian right kept up an intense fire against the Ethiopian troops that faced them . . . who were in fact only a few hundred men meant to divert them.

I saw them clearly in the daylight—motionless grey bundles in the ditches and behind the bushes. They held a position just between my mountain and the Italian lines.

That evening I returned to the Emperor. At every step there were bodies stretched out resting, or people aimlessly wandering. Groups of Ethiopians had gathered round the fires and were roasting on iron plates flat loaves of bread, their shammas round their heads.

Who would have said that in this picturesque land of cactus and tuia, against the rare silhouettes of Ethiopian huts and their enclosures, among the soft murmur of the streams and the heavy smell and the calm of the countryside, a bloody battle for life and death had opened that very day, in a row of cannon and machine-guns sowing terror and destruction.

Indifferent to results, the Ethiopian is incapable of an intense or prolonged effort. He lacks tenacity.

"The Ethiopian soldier, if his assault succeeds, does not go on—he withdraws. And if he loses a position, instead of trying to take another one he withdraws too."

These are words which I had heard uttered by many serious people in Ethiopia, including Ras Kassa, and I remembered them now.

What had happened that day?

Near Cactus Mountain, the three columns had met the Italian advanced posts. There the firsts shots were exchanged. The Italian advanced posts were forced to withdraw and the Ethiopians had occupied the mountain, which neighboured the left flank of the Italian front line.

At this moment the columns whose duty it was to turn the enemy front line and attack it from the rear passed on, between the mountain and the track leading to Mai Chow. Their progress was noted by the Italians, whose artillery began to bombard the positions which the Ethiopians had already made good and from which they were continuing their offensive.

Their shells burst behind Cactus Mountain, where the Emperor stood with his reserves.

The column commanded by Ras Seyyum, made of the relics of the Tigrean army and numbering three to four thousand men, advanced on our right and attacked the Italian camp in the rear which formed the left flank of their line, and had not even been fortified. According to the Ras the Italians, here rather few, made some resistance and then retired to the east upon their group at Enda Mehoni.

The troops of Ras Kassa, relics of his old army and mixed detachments, advanced slowly and took the little village which I had seen burning.

The column of Ras Getatchu, with the Imperial Guard and other detachments, advanced towards the more heavily fortified positions in the enemy's rear: including the high hill where used to stand the Gibbi of Dedjazmatch Aberra Tadla, a redoubtable point.

Because of the continual postponement of our offensive the rear positions had already been fortified. It was clear that our attack had not been unexpected. The Azebu Galla, after enjoying our hospitality to the full, had decided to venture on further profit from the Italians. They had been cross-examined by the enemy on the whereabouts of our troops, their number, the direction that they were taking . . . another fifteen thalers, and that clinched the matter for the Azebu Galla.

After taking a few less important positions the Ethiopians stopped before those which were fortified and powerfully held by the enemy, who here were Tripolitans and Eritreans. The Ethiopians at once took cover and flattened themselves out in folds of the ground and holes.

The bravest, some nine hundred men, struck at the redoubts. But the rest lacked the courage to advance and crown their efforts with the capture of the Italian works. Under cover, they preferred to blaze away until their cartridge belts were empty. Then they withdrew.

The Ethiopians say that at one place where they had to run some hundred yards to take a strong redoubt they were stopped halfway by small planes which machine-gunned them. Even the Italian aviation was ready for the land offensive.

Our gunners had no idea of the objectives which they were supposed to bombard. They shot at random and sometimes hit their own men. The Ethiopians also attacked fortified positions without proper artillery preparation. Giving the order to his artillery to fire, the Emperor had said, "Our men must hear their artillery shooting. It will give them courage and improve their morale."

The Italian works were generally stone walls, rather low

—some were only two feet high. Only in rare places were these walls formed into turrets to hold machine-guns. If anybody in the Ethiopian army beside the Emperor had known how to fire artillery they could have been shot to pieces.

It was clear that the offensive had failed. What remained of the northern forces, the Emperor's own army, would not beat the enemy. None of the three positions taken by the Ethiopians had been held properly by them. Shortly afterwards they abandoned them and returned to their old line.

All would begin again under far more unpleasant conditions after the losses which we had incurred.

One would have expected that these Ethiopian masses thrown into an offensive against the drastic fire developed by modern military technique would suffer severely, but their casualties as a matter of fact were relatively small.

The Ethiopians advance where the danger is not great. They have a great sense of cover. They do not like battles of long duration. They do not hold positions taken from the enemy.

There is a decisive moment when they face the enemy, forget everything, and hurl themselves on him like men possessed. In peace-time we saw that mad climax in their private quarrels. But the Italians at last found a remedy for it which they used in the third Tembien battle. A hand grenade is enough to check this fighting fury.

We turned back that same Tuesday evening under a fine rain from the side of our old mountain which faced the Italian front line. It was difficult to find a shelter. On Wednesday morning the Emperor mounted the crest. Everybody knew that a decision had to be taken—but what? Nobody cared to say.

The day passed in vague conversations and discussions. After lunch the Emperor said to me: "I feel that we ought to renew the offensive. I'm glad that we attacked the enemy. It was a question in which our honour was involved. But I never dreamed of driving out the Italians at one blow, or of advancing to take Debara and Amba Alagi...."

From our observation point we could see the same grey

forms, now much fewer, fixed in the same places, perfectly motionless. The offensive seemed to have failed in advance. I understood from the Emperor's tone that he was not certain that he could renew it. And besides, we could see the movement of the Italians coming down the Debara pass towards Mai Chow. Our own troops were withdrawing of their own accord.

"There is nothing for Your Majesty to do but retire," I answered, when the Emperor asked me for my views. The retreat was approved by his entourage and the same day we were at Aia near the caves recently occupied by the Emperor.

On the way the son of Ras Kassa said to me: "These Kabur Zabania! They're no better than our simple soldiers—and how much money they have cost us!"

In my view, too, the Imperial Guard had not justified the hopes reposed in it. Made of a collection of Addis Ababa townees, recruited without any selective principle and commanded by illiterate officers most of whom had risen from the ranks, from the moment that they had passed out of the care of their Belgian instructors they had lost the appearance of regular troops. Not once did I see them conform to any military discipline, or even in ordinary ranks.

That day we dined in the cave of Rass Kabada, and at nightfall we were at Aia. Footing it up the high mountain slope, for the caves were near the summit, we found the road hard to follow in the darkness and our weariness. But at last we were on the narrow strip of earth in front of the grottoes and the Emperor's cave.

Tired and preoccupied, he went on in front. The words of the French command broke through the night— *"Presentez armes . . . Reposez armes!"* Without looking at his guards posted at the cave mouth, the Emperor entered and glanced around him.

Nothing there seemed changed. All that was missing was that thing that we had left on the high hills facing Mai Chow, with their light fortifications and the debris of broken glass spread on the ground and glittering in the sun; and that was hope. The Emperor knew well that the whole force which he commanded in the north had only confronted the advanced posts of the enemy and had not beaten him. And that enemy had penetrated so deeply already into Ethiopia.

Next morning the same impression remained. Nothing had changed since our departure. It was only when we accompanied the Emperor to his observation post that we saw that the Italians had begun their counter-attack.

Chains of soldiers were moving from their old positions on the mountain side that we had occupied yesterday. A light train of artillery was halfway from the place, and a little plane performed acrobatic miracles as it showered bullets on our soldiers in retreat. They abandoned their cannon and Oerlikons.

I asked myself: "Why did the Emperor take the command of his army in hand when he only had the remnants, so easy to demoralise by propaganda and by the spectacle of other armies in retreat?" He could at least have postponed the disastrous finish: he would certainly have avoided the errors committed by his mediocre chiefs.

Would he not have done better to hand over the command of his armies to foreigners acting in the name of the Ras?

As far as the Emperor himself was concerned, his conduct during the offensive was irreproachable. He was always in the zone of artillery fire and continually exposed himself to danger. In the end he went down into the plain and machine-gunned the enemy himself with terrific effect. Low flying aircraft could not hit him.

But the Azebu Galla calculated the outcome of the battle well enough. They gave not the slightest help to the Ethiopians: they knew how slender were their chances. At the same time they had drawn double recompense for doing nothing, for they were paid by both sides. Thirty dollars can last an Azebu Galla for a lifetime.

I asked the Ethiopians about the behaviour of the Italian soldiers in these battles. They all had the same answer— "You can't do anything against them, they are *gobos*" (which means brave determined men).

And here are some other Ethiopian views:—

"The Italian soldier never forgets his duty. He knows what is expected of him and never loses a minute in battle.

Their machine-gunners follow attentively the way the battle goes, and change the direction of their fire wherever it is needed."

"The officers during battle often give their orders standing up. One of them in a white cap gave the direction of fire to his men with a riding crop. We blazed away at him with every species of rifle but we couldn't hit him."

The Ethiopians did not tell me, as they did at the beginning: "We will hack them with our swords like sheep." Their last words were: "There is nothing to be done, they are *gobos*."

Among the men of rank whom the Ethiopians lost in this battle were the Dedjazmatch Mangasha Ilma, Director of the War Ministry, and uncle of the Emperor; Dedjazmatch Aberra Tadla, ballabat or hereditary chief of Mai Chow; Dedjazmatch Wonderat, who forty years before received an Italian bullet in the chest (this second bullet at Mai Chow struck him mortally in the same place). The Minister of the Court was also killed during that sad day.

. . . To-day I had an interview with the Emperor. He seemed to understand that the war in the field had been lost and that other issues to the situation had to be sought. "I fail to understand the rôle of the League of Nations," he told me. "It seems quite impotent. And to think that on this battle we have already disbursed a million thalers," he said at the end of our conversation.

That evening the sovereign called many chiefs, great and small, and made a long speech to them, demanding of each one of them his views. He then delivered his own, and ended: "We should not lose courage. The Ethiopian army is at this moment in a very dangerous position. We ought to retire beyond Korem into the mountains, and there give the Italians a new battle."

Everybody was in agreement with this final point: the younger chiefs were eager even to attempt another attack from the spot on which we were.

Ras Seyyum with the remnant of the Tigrean army had to leave us and return to Seloa. There he was to try and break through into the Tigre to raise the countryside against the Italians in a new "guerrilla" war. The Ethiopians translate guerrilla with the word *shiftanet*, meaning brigandage. Poor Ras Seyyum, careless and credulous type of the Ethiopian *grand seigneur*, who never had the habit of thinking beyond the present. Possessing all to let him live in comfort and repose and now over fifty years of age, he became by force of circumstances a *shifta!*

I recall that in the telegram which he received at the beginning of hostilities the Emperor had advised him not to engage in open battles, which he described as useless, but to fight a guerrilla war.

Seyyum had replied: "I am too old and too tired to become a *shifta.*"

And in his turn the Emperor had telegraphed: "Stand firm and be patient. It is probable that we will soon have allies."

Of all the Ethiopians now, the Emperor who alone had worked to impose on Ethiopia the most elementary juridical forms, alone seemed to find himself deceived and utterly perplexed. He really believed that there existed over there, beyond the seas, that pure justice, just as he knew of the existence of a western culture with all its perfections. . . .

On Friday morning, at six-forty, a large aeroplane appeared. From our mountain height, icy cold, a marvellous view opened to our eyes. A sea of clouds white as milk lay at our feet lightly touched with pink by a rising sun. In the gaps fresh stretches of the earth green with grass and barleyfields were crowned in a deeper green with the superb tuias, so like our own pines and fir trees.

Above this sea of clouds and these green islands an Italian plane white as snow flew towards us. It had discovered the retreat of our troops.

I returned quickly to the Emperor's side. From the cave below came the melancholy chanting of some tens of priests and the continual ringing of a great bell, monotonously shaken.

A thin thread of incense escaped from behind the silken stuff which protected the cave mouth. The sad chants, the incense, the mournful faces, the Emperor with an expression of indifference upon a face of stone—all gave the impression of a funeral mass.

The plane was already dropping its bombs on us. Without

their old agitation the Ethiopians raised their heads from their shelters to look. A machine-gun without mountings was brought out of the cave and put in the place of our old Oerlikon. Alas, all our eight new Oerlikons had been abandoned in the lines. No one had thought of dismantling them or bringing them back.

The Emperor came out of his cave with his glasses in his hand, and leaning against the stone wall looked into the distance.

The clouds were already scattering. Across their light serrated borders one could see the high Debara and the mountain chain in front of Mai Chow where were the Italian lines which we had attacked.

The Emperor had just received information that the enemy had taken possession of the mountain where we had spent the night before the offensive, and that the Italians were advancing on the west also.

It was seven o'clock.

Ethiopian chiefs, mules, soldiers, the whole retreating army were climbing our slope. The narrow path was filling up with a mass of people pushing and shouting at each other. Men posted there tried to shove the crowd of soldiers back and keep them from coming near the Imperial cave, with blows of sticks to left and right.

The row was unbelievable.

"What disgraceful disorder!" said the Emperor, turning to me with a bitter look, "when we ought to be ready to stop the Italians from turning our right. Fitorari Tafere! Where is he? Bring him here!" and cries of "Fitorari Tafere!" resounded on all sides.

A squat Ethiopian chief with a big sword cut of long ago across his forehead presented himself to the Emperor.

"You see that mountain covered with bush," the Emperor pointed. "You must occupy it with your men and stop the *ferengi* from taking it."

The Fitorari seemed undecided. He only vaguely grasped the problem posed to him, since he knew neither where the enemy was coming from nor the size of the forces he had to face, nor probably the number of men which he had at his own command. "Go on!" said the Emperor, and the Fitorari departed.

The Emperor re-entered his cave where he held a council meeting with his chiefs.

Two hours afterwards I saw the Fitorari Tafere once more. Seated on a heap of stones, without a care in the world, he was chatting blithely with other Ethiopians.

It appeared that of all his soldiers he had only found fifty, whom he dispatched to the hill indicated by the Emperor: at whose side he preferred to remain.

The dinner-hour approached. Processions of women and boys came quickly for fear of the bombs, for the planes were always overhead: they carried on their heads baskets full of injura and pots of baked earth covered with scarlet cloth containing *wot*, the peppery dish of the Ethiopians. Behind them in the *gombos* was carried mead.

After all these meats had been lowered at the entrance to the cave everybody hurried off to find shelter: no one can enter the cave while the Emperor is holding a *koita* or secret council with his chiefs.

At this same hour something happened on the front which the Ethiopians had abandoned. The explosions of the enemy shells, though less frequent, sounded very near. Everybody knew how critically placed we were.

It was impossible to find a single man ready to obey an order or even in his proper place. Soldiers drifted about in every direction and in disorderly crowds: the mountain was full of them. The Emperor returned to his observation point after a late lunch, but there was a heavy mist and one could distinguish little. Before nightfall a new council. A little later they began to examine the objects which filled the cave to see what could be taken away; much opening of trunks and cases.

Near nightfall the Emperor began to distribute in person the things that he could not take with him: cartridges, oddments of clothing, liquor, preserved foods, supplies of all sorts. The cave filled up with soldiers who wished to profit from the occasion. When the Emperor wished to leave the cave he could only force a passage with the greatest difficulty. Beatings, shouts, gesticulations, and at last the mob left the place with their booty.

At nine-thirty we left Aia and took the road for Korem. Behind us they exploded all the artillery and rifle ammunition, the tins of petrol and drums of oil, which destroyed along with them all that remained of the piles of striped shirts and black satin capes with which we hoped to draw the Azebu Galla to our side.

The field radio station was abandoned with the rest.

The descent from our mountain was terrible, so dark was the night.

Every minute the road was jammed. When the Ethiopians march the main object of each man is to pass all the others. This mob of people trying to thread its way through donkeys, mules and hundreds of other Ethiopians created an incredible disorder.

We took the whole night to cover the ten kilometres or so which separated us from Lake Ashangi. I had lost sight of the Emperor and the sons of Ras Kassa with whom I had travelled before, and was marching now with a group of soldiers. It was only at dawn that two of the Emperor's pages joined me. They too had been separated in the crowd.

We hurried. At every moment the aeroplanes might appear.

These last days they had continually bombarded the shelterless borders of Lake Ashangi and the two passes to north and south of it, full of baggage trains and soldiers. After a moment's halt I decided to go on to Korem: my companions did not continue with me.

It was seven o'clock in the morning when the first aeroplane was seen. Bombs rained upon our troops in retreat. Other aeroplanes appeared. When I had crossed the pass and come down into the valley the bombardment was let loose in all ferocity.

Fourteen planes took turns to hurl their bombs upon the unbroken flood of humanity which surged towards Korem. I had to travel rather to the left of the crowd.

I shall never forget the picture that I saw.

The wide valley, which during the season of rains is inundated in part, lay level under the blazing African sun. To its side the blue surface of the lake was lightly ruffled by the breeze. Along the road the weary people dragged themselves, scattering for a moment in panic or massing together in groups. Four, six, eight bombs burst one after the other. They fell some distance from the road and hit nobody. . . .

The people quicken pace. Here is another aeroplane which seems to be choosing its victims as it flies just over their heads. One explosion . . . then another which raises a jet of earth clods, sand and stones.

People are hit this time. Everything round me disperses. I turn round and see someone dying on the ground. A form that slightly moves.

Fear pushes the survivors upon their road without attending to the wretch who cannot follow them, for he has lost his legs.

At the same moment our allies the Azebu Galla fire on us from the hill tops where their villages lie. When they see stragglers they kill them and strip the bleeding bodies of rifles, cartridges and clothes.

Before us there is a corner of hell which none of us can avoid. On one side of the road is the lake, on the other are the mountains. The pass is narrow, and the human flood finds it hard to press forward and through.

Everybody knows that in the bush and behind the rocks hide the treacherous Azebu, on the watch. A hail of bombs bursts all over the pass wounding animals and men.

Poor little Ethiopian donkeys! . . . how often have I seen them on the road, their jaws smashed to pieces, their eyes blown from their sockets, their stomachs opened by a bomb.

We crossed the dangerous pass. Blot after dark blot along our road. These were stains of blood dried quickly by the lively sun: they showed us the way.

We hurried on over bodies sprawled and tumbled. Once more I found myself in a wide open place where I tried to keep my distance from the crowd.

Behind a turn in the road a bomb has just burst. I see the Ethiopian in front of me bending over an extended body. "Ato Gabre Mariam?" he says. "What has happened?"

"Pomp, bakon madanit" ("bomb, please, medicine"), answers the wounded man, turning his eyes in supplication to me. *And I do not want to be left behind. See us, me and the Ethiopian following me, running on along the road.*

As I go, I see again a face now no more than a pulp of

bleeding flesh, over which a young boy hangs sobbing, trying his best to help the wounded. Others are falling around us . . . we run on and on . . . and at last we are near the caves of Korem which will shelter us from the Azebu bullets and the aeroplanes.

On a range of hills, covered with bush, there are *tukuls* and the characteristic small properties of the Ethiopians, surrounded by palisades. Farther off on a small mountain there is a larger property kept more tidily. It belongs to the local *shum*. I run down the hill and on towards the slope where the caves are dug.

At my feet, until lost to view, spreads the valley inhabited by the terrible Azebu Galla. It is time I reached my refuge—two planes are already flying over me. . . .

I found there Dedjazmatch Wodaju, who was wounded in the battle of Shelikot-Antalo and who was acting as governor of Korem now. Ras Getatchu was also there, he, too, slightly wounded.

It was three o'clock in the afternoon. I was offered food, after which I stretched myself out. My body felt as if it were broken in pieces.

I was woken by the noise of a quarrel.

At first I could not understand what it was all about, but quickly it all became clear.

The cave had filled up with soldiers who were taking everything that came to hand. A clumsy movement overturned the lamp which stood on one of the cases . . . an echo of broken glass.

The quarrelling, the blows, the theft of everything in this narrow place, illuminated by the sinister spread of the smoking petrol from the lamp. . . . These promised to end in something nasty. The soldiers shattered the locks of the cases and stuffed their pockets with cartridges.

Someone found a box of thalers. The whole mob dropped on it with a fearful scuffling and shouting.

Two Galla soldiers who had seen me, the only European there, threw themselves upon me and before I had time to move shoved their hands into my pockets shouting—
"Silver! Revolver!"

I gave them a little rough treatment. They fell and were lost in the confusion. I threw myself out of the cave.

"Where are the chiefs?" I asked the people on my way. "There are no chiefs," they answered.

"What has happened, then?"

"The story's got round that the Emperor has fled, and the Azebu Galla are going to attack the cave and take all there is in it. That is why our *zabanias* have decided to clear it for themselves."

"Where are the soldiers who have come back from the battle?"

"You will find them behind that hill. Hurry up if you don't want to be left behind."

I struggled on among the broken trunks of the Imperial train, the broken bottles, and the tangle of tents which stretched along the path. I climbed the summit.

People were flooding in on every side. I joined them and crossed a plain to the south of Lake Ashangi and southeast of Korem. From there we clambered up a tall mountain, near the church of Saint Michael, where lay the cave which once gave refuge to the British Red Cross. There were others, too, more spacious, which now held the Emperor and his great chiefs.

We noticed that many people were missing. As always in Ethiopia, nobody had been told the itinerary and therefore a considerable number had strayed. One part of the army had gone on in front, others stayed behind.

At about ten in the morning we could see from our high cave, one and a half hours' march away and to the north of Korem, an Italian camp. They were either following us step by step or they were a column which wanted to turn us.

We had learnt from a source of information which had not been checked that they numbered two thousand, Eritreans mostly. The Emperor decided to attack them, as he said that he would at Aia.

But now all the great chiefs declared themselves against the offensive.

Our troops, scattered over a huge country, were completely demoralised by a chaotic retreat, by their defeat, by the attack of the Galla, and above all by the Italian aviation.

"I hate the sight of these swine in tatters," said the private secretary of the Emperor, Wolde Giorghis, pointing for my benefit at a warlike crowd of soldiers who with no object whatsoever fired their rifles into the air. "Had I the power I would have the whole lot shot,"

"And the guard?" asked I. "The guard have gone mad, too," he said.

The Emperor was in a very sombre frame of mind. Believing that it was one of the most favourable moments to attack the enemy, before he had assembled large forces or fortified his position, he thought that we had some chances of a small victory which might stem the course of demoralisation.

"Is it impossible to collect one or two thousand soldiers ready for the attack?" he asked.

The Emperor was sitting at the back of a huge cave, called for some reason the *Faras-Biet* or Stable, behind a large curtain which was fixed by its two ends in front of his chair and separated him from the rest of the cave where his servants and courtiers were trooped together. Behind him I could see animals, the mules of the Emperor, his suite, and the great chiefs. Beyond them there was an improvised kitchen where our lunch was being prepared. All in the same vast cave.

The ill-humour of the sovereign was apparent. Since his chiefs would not move, he had to remain inactive too. Outside, the undisciplined soldiers kept up their infernal din and the bombs dropped by the aeroplanes burst. Far off a fusillade showed that the Amhara and the Azebu were still at it.

The Emperor felt oppressed by his own impotence. After lunch I asked him what he intended to do.

"I do not know," he answered. "My chiefs will do nothing. My brain no longer works."

After long talks and deliberations without end it was decided to withdraw as far as possible from the enemy and the planes that were pursuing us, and to reorganise.

Nobody defined the meaning of this word, but it was said that the hungry and weary soldiers of Ras Kassa must be sent back home, with those of other chiefs who had spent a long time at the front, that a new recruitment must be made, the provisionment of soldiers regularised and their methods of warfare entirely changed.

A serious and sweeping programme, which naturally did not find people of capacity enough to put it into practice. The Ethiopian chiefs, completely off their balance as they were, had never been prepared for a thing like that.

The idiotic fusillade still filled the air outside, growing louder.

At about five o'clock in the evening the Emperor gave the order of departure. Our direction was Lalibela in the south. The route to Cobbo had been rejected for fear of the districts peopled by the Azebu and the Raia Galla.

We only left at six o'clock. Many could not find their mules in the prevailing disorder.

We had scarcely left the cave before, from their hill tops, the Azebu Galla opened fire upon us once more. We made speed to another path more sheltered by the mountains. But we had lost some dead and wounded. . . .

Our soldiers answered with shots at random.

It was already full night, and we at last reached a valley where the furious fusillade ended.

We were marching now more or less free of all encumbrances. Most of our tents, baggage, cannon and cartridges had been left behind, or thrown away on the road.

We marched all night. In the morning we reached a place with several useful caves. A plane discovered us a little after sunrise, and dropped some bombs. We spent the day here, taking the road only at night-fall in order to conceal the direction in which we were moving. The Italians might think that we were taking the Cobbo-Dessye road or that we were going toward Sokota. . . .

On the way we asked the peasants if there were caves in this place or that. Once more we stopped for the day in a place where there was cover.

Aeroplanes flew overhead but did not seem to see us. Only one of them dropped bombs and injured several people: I do not think that it was aiming at anything in particular. Other planes were bombing the country-side some distance away. Occasionally they took peasants and cattle for our troops. Or perhaps they were trying to panic the population.

. . . A long night march in drizzling rain. . . . In the morning we reached the rocky bank of the Mihandir river which runs in a deep gorge. Our shelters were caves again, in the precipice side. The aeroplanes seemed to be looking for us but could not find us. Steep rocks concealed our much diminished army.

We heard that a number of troops under Kenyasmatch Tekla Markos had moved off towards Dessye, and that others commanded by Ras Getatchu and Likaba Rasso had passed through Cobbo making for Monja, where they had heavy engagements with the Raia Galla.

All these days no provisions were to be found, and we had to eat kosso and little balls of grilled barley flour, moistened with water before they were cooked. The Ethiopian soldier is fond of this frugal fare, the more so as it requires little care in the preparation. They take large supplies of it when on the march.

But to-day the people of the country came bringing cereals, honey and *talla*, a native beer made out of barley. As there are no small monetary units in this district, the soldiers paid with their oldest cartridges. Gras were willingly accepted as all the peasants here had old rifles. It was the last week of Lent and no meat or milk was to be found.

Before evening we left the mountain heights, nearly ten thousand feet up. They are uninhabited, inhospitable and cold, their only vegetation a wretched scrub. In spite of our fatigue we clambered down again looking for places richer in firewood. The Ethiopians love a fire and keep it ablaze all night.

A whole world of mountains stretched in range upon range as far as the eye could see. Lit up by the evening sun they took on fantastic shapes of castles, towers and gigantic stairways. In those great piles of water-washed stone there must be every geometrical shape imaginable by man. As the sun went down each had its own colour from dark green and the most transparent of greys and blues to the brightest red. At our feet in a broad sandy bed a river zigzagged between the bright green of the fields and irrigated plantations. We filed down an easy slope and crossed a canal of crystal-pure water. A bridge was thrown over the river at its narrowest point, and the natives used it during the rainy season to carry their loads over on their heads. In red pepper plantations women with curious headdresses were pulling up the weeds. Nearby the cotton bushes drooped pale yellow flowers. I stopped by the river bank and I do not know why, but all this exoticism about me awoke again the adolescent dreams which brought me to Ethiopia so many years ago. . . .

The troops are arriving . . . soldiers dressed in the Ethiopian fashion and troops in western uniforms, all marching past me. Here is the Emperor in a steel helmet and khaki mantle. Near the sovereign are his suite, some in uniform with embroidered collars and cuffs, and some wrapped up in their shammas. Ahead of the others, on a mule, is the Likamaquas. I observe his very unmartial attire: he is dressed in civilian clothes and a check overcoat.

A young boy stops beside me and bends down to drink from the river. In his left hand he is carrying a round shield of thick hippopotamus hide with beautiful gold encrustations; in his right an automatic rifle of the latest Belgian pattern. This was the whole of present-day Abyssinia. She still loves the useless but picturesque things that have seen their day. She is eager for the modern things which she cannot yet understand.

Already bands of soldiers had broken loose in the pepper plantations, pulling off the fine red fruit and stuffing it into their pockets; red pepper is the chief spice of native food. Shouting and calling to one another, some drawing water, others washing their feet, they scattered along the river bank. Others, a thin thread of brown forms in the distance, went marching on.

Where were all these men going?

At the time of our first withdrawal from the Tembien, Ras Seyyum and his chiefs always said to their soldiers: "Be patient, Ras Kassa will soon join us, his troops are well organised and well fed, all will change for the best." We had left Tembien again with the same Ras Kassa and all our hopes were then placed in the Emperor, who in Ethiopia symbolises power and safety, and in his army which was still intact and provided with food and ammunition. And now we were retreating with this same Emperor, with nothing more on which to rest our hopes, not even *Etiopia Amlak*, the God of Ethiopia, who until this day had never abandoned her. He seemed no longer to stand by her; everything had fallen away. . . .

The chiefs would ask me often now: "Do you think that Germany will come to our help? If she does, let her take all that she wishes"—"and England?—Some say that the English are on the road from the Sudan to Gondar." "We have heard that the aeroplanes which they are sending us have arrived at Zeyla. They say that the lives of the pilots have been insured." "What about Japan? It seemed that they were going to help us."

Every day the same questions rained upon me.

We left the hot tropical valley which our river followed and crossed a high range. A brisk north wind blew through and through us. The Ethiopians wrapped their heads in anything that they could find, shawls, scarves, blankets, even carpets. We were just dragging ourselves along.

We were in Ras Kassa's province. In the morning as I woke up I saw a procession of people carrying baskets and earthenware jars on their heads. They brought *dergo*, the food and drink collected from the peasants by the local official who offers them to his master returning from the wars.

After lunch I had a talk with the Emperor. He asked me what I thought the Italians were going to do. He no longer asked me whether they intended to take Addis Ababa. For the first time he made this confession to me: "It is beyond our power to hold them back."

We are now travelling south across the high plateau of Ethiopia. Each one dreams of his home or of Addis Ababa, which in the far distance seems a promised land.

The soldiers have begun to loot the population. In their turn the peasants kill isolated soldiers or small parties straggling in the rear. The aeroplanes too have made the peasants hate the war. The aeroplanes are breaking Ethiopia into her tribal parts. Every day one hears more rifle shots.

One wonders how the Ethiopians manage to feed themselves. By some miracle they always manage to find flour or corn. At every halt they light their fires and prepare their simple meal.

On Easter Sunday (April 11) we were once more on a mountain range, where we spent the cold night.

The Emperor and his suite went down to Bohaié, where they partook of the traditional meal which ends the Lenten fast. In accordance with custom bullocks and sheep had been slaughtered and all ate raw meat with relish. But this feast was not a gay one: the Emperor of Ethiopia and the highest lords of the land celebrated Easter in a small and filthy tukul; they did not even drink their traditional mead; and sadly they thought of the abundance and pomp at the great banquets in Addis Ababa.

On the first day after Easter we moved into the Gibbi of the Governor at Lasta, Fitorari Balai.

All the population came up with *dergo*. There were thousands of *injura* (cakes of barley flour), hundreds of sheep, dozens of oxen, and *gombos* containing *talla* which had been ordered by the chiefs. The Emperor gave orders to distribute the sheep and the *injura* to the chiefs and to give one thaler to each soldier.

We were in one of the richest and most thickly populated parts of Ethiopia. Everywhere there were villages and hamlets, conical thatched roofs, fenced compounds. The fields were full of cattle.

On the first day of Easter, when we crossed the Takkaze river to enter the house of the Governor of Lasta, the Emperor gave a great *gebir*. A hundred soldiers at a time were collected in an immense round tukul whose roof was supported by twelve pillars. The feast lasted from eleven in the morning until four in the afternoon. The Emperor suddenly decided to go to Lalibela, which was not on our original route, for we were making straight for Dessye. The Emperor left that evening with about a hundred soldiers. We arrived late at night.

Lalibela town is built round eleven churches carved out of the solid rock. We lost two days going to Lalibela. But although the visit was of æsthetic interest to me, to the Emperor it was something more mystical, more like a pilgrimage. Lalibela is a monument to Ethiopian glory. Perhaps the Emperor was seeking new moral strength in this contact with a holy place of Ethiopia. Perhaps he wished to commune with the spirit of the Emperor Lalibela the Great, who like him had brought the Mediterranean

world into Ethiopia and struggled to civilise his country
. . . who in the thirteenth century had cut these shrines
of the faith out of the pagan rock.

After his return from Lalibela the Emperor called his *koita* once more. The old Ethiopian chiefs had completely lost their heads with the catastrophes on all fronts. They could give no advice and would take no steps to prevent the breakup of the army, which continued daily. By this time the Ethiopian army was nothing more than a band of robbers: the soldiers were even robbing each other. About this time I too lost seven mules and all my belongings down to my blanket.

After lengthy deliberations the *koita* came to an end and the councillors came out of the Emperor's tent looking tired and disappointed. First Fitorari Birru and Ras Kassa, the first prince of the Empire: then young Ras Getatchu and several Dedjazmatches. Immediately after them the Emperor himself went into his sleeping tent for the night. I could see that he was very worn . . . his face was thinner, his forehead full of new lines.

On Wednesday, April 14, the servants and baggage of Ras Kassa and his sons arrived from Lalibela. They had left the Tembien before us and their caravan had been stopped and attacked by the natives near Lalibela. The caravan was rescued by the priests who took it under their protection on the land of the monastery, but the servants remained prisoners until the Emperor arrived and freed them. I was surprised by this episode, but it was explained to me by a member of Ras Kassa's following, who said: "There is much sin in Ethiopia, and it is in this way that God punishes us for our sins."

On Friday we crossed the Shita river. From our high tableland we could see in every direction dark silhouettes of mountains on the horizon.

Everybody was asking who we were. A few rifle-shots were fired at us, then a regular fusillade from all sides. The Emperor sent off some soldiers of the Guard to disperse our assailants. Under the threat of our machine-guns the villagers quickly dispersed and the soldiers came back bringing prisoners, who were given a good beating and released. We then continued our journey in greater peace and comfort, although a few shots were still audible in the rear.

The country through which we were passing was a high plateau cut deep by rivers and dry ravines. There was not a tree in sight. On all sides we saw fields of barley still green. In the distance there were flocks of the black sheep which are the wealth of this country. A sheep here only costs a few pence.

We had some respite from the aeroplanes. Sometimes we heard the distant drone of their engines and immediately hid. But as we never saw them near, we went on marching.

On Saturday we reached Dalanta and we came near to Wagaltash, the centre of that region. The altitude here is under eight thousand feet, and the country-side changed. The valley grew broader and flatter, the vegetation was greener and there were shallow rivers everywhere. In the west was a place where the various chains of mountains seemed to meet and further to the south was a bigger river, above which hung another broad tableland with sheer edges. These were the Gishene springs, and beyond them was Dessye, our destination.

Everything this time was very different. The villagers brought hardly anything and the Gibbi was half empty. Not a soul came out to meet the Emperor.

In the Gibbi were two brass cannon taken from the Egpytians by the Emperor John.

On Saturday at eleven o'clock several aeroplanes appeared and flew round us. The Emperor and his suite left for a cave in the hills, and we took shelter in a small house which had once been occupied by the British. It was on this very spot, at Wagaltash, that the Emperor Theodore learnt for the first time of the arrival of Napier's expedition: upon seeing their camp he asked, "To whom do those tents belong?"

We had lunch in the cave and it was then that the Emperor heard of his betrayal by the Wollo chiefs, Dedjazmatch Abaukau and Dedjazmatch Balai Kabada. He was much saddened at the news. At the same time, however, we learned that the people of Waldia, on the Imperial Road, had fled into the mountains when the Italians told them to lay down their arms.

We soon found that only a part of the population had turned outlaw.

After lunch the Emperor sent for his Guard, a few hundred soldiers, and read to them the following order:

> *Never forget what a soldier should be, especially at this present time. Up to now you have not all done your duty. Try to do it in the future.*

We took the road again at half-past three in the afternoon. Almost the whole way was along a green valley surrounded on either side by high escarpments, and on the slope of one of them we spent the night. Next day we went down towards the river Bashilo, a large watercourse which flows into the Blue Nile. Near its sandy banks we found plantations of cotton. After the desert of the high plateau it was good once more to see great shady trees and sweet-smelling bushes of jasmine.

We crossed the river and made our way up the dry bed of another. The river-bed was full of corpses, naked and decomposing. The whole of the road and the river-bed seemed to be full of them.

They were the bodies of soldiers who had started to loot and had been attacked by the villagers. We did not know it at the time: we only guessed it when heavy rifle fire was directed against us as we marched up the road. We retaliated with rifles and machine-guns and marched on towards the foot of Magdala.

Everywhere there were the traces of the passage of Ethiopian soldiers. Charcoal unburnt, and heaps of cinders . . . old discarded clothes . . . broken vessels of earthenware . . . grain. On both sides of the road villages which had been burnt by the soldiers who had marched ahead of us were still lazily smoking. Our men went off to villages further away and after burning the houses brought back grain, chickens and honey. Round about us everything was in flames. A detachment was sent off to bring in the villagers and lesser chiefs. Their deputations came very late in the evening and by way of apology brought two hundred and fifty flat loaves, three oxen and, to our surprise, new Mauser rifles and four automatics which they had looted from our soldiers.

"It is always like that with the Ethiopian," said Ras Kassa to me. "In the grip of his natural instincts he loots and even murders, but his Christian conscience always forces him to admit his guilt and offer himself for punishment. You have just seen a case in point."

To our left were the steep rocks of Magdala, in whose fortress the Emperor Theodore took refuge from the British. The low mountains and undulating hills from which the British bombarded the fort with their artillery lay in front of us. They were the first Europeans to enter Ethiopia under arms since the Portuguese came in the sixteenth century to help the Ethiopians against Islam. It was a sight which had never been seen before: the British columns with their artillery and cavalry in perfect order surrounded by the disorder of the Ethiopians.

I remembered the words of the Dedjazmatch Wolde Emanuel as we were hiding in the cave at Aia. "I was at the other battle of Adowa: I was wounded there. But what a difference! In those days there were only rifles and very little artillery. We could do anything we liked with the Italians then. But now . . ."

We left Magdala on Tuesday, earlier than we had expected: the Emperor had been informed that the people of the district were planning to surround and attack us. It may have been true. As we left, volleys of rifle fire opened on all sides.

From our shouting and disorderly column men fell dead and cruelly wounded. Some of the Emperor's servants were killed at his side. The Emperor sent his Guard up to Magdala where most of the firing was coming from. We continued our march, burning the houses and compounds of our enemies as we went.

Hundreds of houses were now burning round the great fortress mountain of Magdala and our road was covered by the bodies of the dead, the fresh dead and the dead long since. It was with difficulty, so terrible was the stench of decomposition, that I saved myself from being sick. These conditions continued for several kilometres and it was only after hours of trudging along that the passage to the south of Magdala was cleared and we could make again for the high plateau. The volleys of rifle fire died down. We were able to sleep in the great Gibbi of a local chief.

In the morning we continued our march. Although there were villages burning round about, there were still a lot of huts untouched ahead of us. Dedjazmatch Aberra, the son of Ras Kassa, the same who fought the Italians throughout the rainy season, went ahead of us as advance guard to clean up the road. This day the march was uneventful except on two or three occasions.

We now had to find out something about the movements of the Italians in order that we should not fall in with them, and to prevent our road to Addis Ababa from being cut. So when we were still forty kilometres north-north-east of Dessye we made straight for Warra Hailu. The Emperor had other reasons for choosing Warra Hailu. It was the centre of several telephone lines and he was anxious for news of Addis Ababa and the outside world. He knew that Dessye had been taken by the Italians, nothing more. For up to now he had been out of communication with his capital.

One of the most modernised chiefs was saying . . . "Nowadays war is three-quarters politics and one quarter fighting. What is the Emperor doing with troops that no longer obey him? He might easily be killed. He should attempt a political solution, negotiate with the League of Nations and with foreign governments. But perhaps some king would be willing to help us. England, for example, would be able to take Lake Tana."

I smiled involuntarily.

The great chiefs were losing little by little all their prestige. The Ras and the Seigneurs who usually travelled aloof from the crowd now mingled with the throng of soldiers.

The Emperor himself was losing a great part of his authority.

It was Death who followed us everywhere, and seemed to be stronger than the aristocratic power of the Emperor and his chiefs: he made us all equal, and it was he who drove us from the places where he was able to reign.

The soldiers continued at times to pillage and burn

occasional houses. The Emperor was forced to issue an order arresting marauders and punishing them with the lash. The culprits lay down quietly on the ground to receive a dozen strokes.

When we were thirty-five kilometres from Warra Hailu we learnt of its occupation by two hundred Italian cavalry followed by infantry. A fresh disappointment, a fresh secret council in the tukul occupied by the Emperor. He was for attacking Warra Hailu: the chiefs refused.

A decision was taken to go by Dabat (or Doba) to Jirra, whence a lorry-road leads to Addis Ababa. The commander of the garrison at Warra Hailu had fled with his soldiers at the approach of the Italians and had been attacked by the population.

Everywhere the people wanted, above everything, rifles and cartridges. The whole of the plateau was in chaos: they would kill anybody to get a weapon to defend themselves with. The structure of security was broken in pieces by the war.

We learnt that the Ethiopian troops moving in front of us had fought with the population at the crossing over the River Jamma at Haiafech, and at Doba. All the roads, we were told, were covered with corpses.

So we turned the head of our column once more and made for Fiche, whence Addis Ababa is reached by a hundred and twenty-five kilometres of lorry-road.

We had to leave the thickly populated province of Wallo which always produces good soldiers. When we asked one of the Wollo chiefs, "Where are your soldiers?" we received the reply, "What do you mean by soldiers? To-day there are no more soldiers: they are all brigands, for whom we no longer exist. Most of the chiefs have already taken to flight."

The disintegration of Ethiopia continued at a galloping speed. The population were pillaging shops, supplies, deposits of money. No authority was recognised. Wealth could only be built up on theft, for no other profit could be anticipated.

We passed through the provinces of Legambo and Logasheda and crossed a flooded river to emerge on the high table-land of Jameda. This region, populated by Galla and Amhara tribes, impressed us: everywhere the villagers had live-stock and lived in peace. The frontier between Jamma and Midi is fortified with large stones which remain from the time when those two provinces made war upon each other. . . .

In the morning we were noted by an aeroplane, which brought another. The two bombed us, killing four men near me.

All day our road led on over a wide green plateau. The contrast with the rocky ravines was pleasure to the eyes.

In the evening we reached the place for our night's rest.

Everything was peaceful, no breeze disturbed the air. Around us the plain seemed limitless. The slim eucalyptus planted near cone-shaped huts emphasised the branches of the acacias which spread like motionless kites on the grey-blue sky as it softened at sundown.

Everything gave the impression of an easy and abundant life.

The weary Ethiopian soldiers dragged themselves over the fields. They entered the houses, although they knew that the place where they had to sleep was not far.

I dreaded another fusillade.

It was strange to see the broken remnants of the army which in the month of December the Italian Air Force mentioned in the following terms . . . "Dense columns of Ethiopian troops making their way from Dessye towards Amba Alagi and Makalle." . . . Dense columns for two hundred kilometres.

To-day the Emperor received a telephone message brought from the line by a runner, to say that all was quiet in Addis and that the southern front was holding firm.

This news led to a fresh council. At the same time we heard that all Gojjam was in revolt.

The Emperor was in a hurry to reach Fiche. We went on . . . we arrived at Fiche on Thursday night. Five lorries and five cars were awaiting us there. After a disorderly *gebir*, for each soldier forced his way in after the day's fast, we took our places on a lorry, forcing our way in, too.

The Emperor, whom I had not seen this evening, for he remained by himself all the time, passed with a hurried step to his car. He was the first to leave on the Addis road I saw in the headlights his thin, tired face.

We waited until everyone had packed into the lorries. There were sinister rumours in the crowd . . . there was talk of plots and generally it was whispered that everything was going badly. . . .*

---

* End of Colonel Konovaloff's story.

XIX

I HAVE A PARTICULAR WEAKNESS for the Ogaden army. It was the only one that I ever travelled among, meeting and knowing its chiefs and men, seeing their equipment which though petty toy-military compared with that of their opponents was yet the best in Ethiopia, and inspecting their queer little camps from Jijiga down to the Webbe Shebeli. Thus, except for Wehib Pasha, I am the only white man living who visited the camp at Gorahai which was the key to the Ogaden, and which was defended with such dogged courage by Gerazmatch Afewerk until his painful death. The wide open thorn among occasional long low hills, the brightly feathered birds and herds of buck, the sun in the waterless stretches, the Ogaden mimosa in white flower made me love the place. The soldiers were tough and steady—six months of vicious bombardment from the air without a weapon to answer back must prove that their bravery was above the normal. Some of the chiefs, Afewerk and Malion in particular, possessed resolution, cleverness and sense of duty far in excess of their class. Then at Jijiga were the two Turkish *numéros*, Wehib Pasha and Farouk Bey, and the Sudanese Tarik from the Turkish General Staff, with his sweeping curved tribe-marks on either black cheek and his strenuous devotion to the principle of African liberty. Bar Konovaloff, the trio from Stamboul were the only foreign military who did an ounce of service for the Emperor. Grand men, all: hard work, fight and comedy, tied up in a parcel and dropped into the Ogaden.

In Addis after December, it was difficult to get news from Harrar and the south-east: after the bombardment of Harrar it became impossible.

Only when I took my last train from Addis and met old friends in Djibouti who had served in the Ogaden, was I able to discover what had really happened since my visit to Jijiga at the beginning of December. The Ethiopian after defeat is extremely frank: nor were Ethiopians my only informants. There were others, still waiting in French Somaliland for their arrears of pay. This is their story: the dates differ from the Italian.

It seemed incredible to them, and it still seems so to me, that General Graziani did not continue his drive against Harrar after the fall of Gorahai. The Ogaden at that time was practically empty. The best of the Ethiopian commanders had been killed and his army routed. Yet Graziani never took up the initiative again until Nasibu had plunged into a senseless offensive against Danan in the middle of April. Then at last the great General moved, with difficulty took Borkut and pursued sluggishly to Harrar. From December to April he has nothing to his credit except the side-show against Desta, which was quickly finished and of which he took not the slightest advantage—for it ought to have developed into a major operation. Perched with five hundred disgruntled soldiers upon the heights of Adola, still waiting for his Fitoraris, Adams and Tadama with their fifteen hundred men. wandering along the palm-stretches of the Ganale Dorya, Desta could only have maintained the most feeble resistance to a courageous assault—and the route to Erga Alem, to provincial revolt in the south-west and to Addis Ababa was open. Yet the conqueror of Libya dared not move against this incompetent Ras, and his only pastime from then until April was to send the bandas of Olol Dinle, Sultan of the Shiaveli, unsuccessfully twice against Bayenna Mared.

At this period the road to Harrar was blocked by nine thousand Ethiopians, no more, strung out, except for five hundred at Daggahmodo along the direct Gabridihari-Jijiga lorry-track, a wide dusty stretch running between infrequent water-holes. South of Daggahmodo there were only a hundred men at Sagik, a Somali market-place which had to be held in order to control the tribes, and north of Daggahmodo there were no soldiers until Harrar, then guarded by a hundred town *zabanias*. A motorable road ran from Gabridihari to Danan—which the Italians speedily occupied because it opened the flank of Gorahai: thence it went to Daggahbur, where there were then three thousand men. The Italians could either have attacked and destroyed Daggahbur as they had destroyed Gorahai, or maintaining a strong defensive position at Daggahmodo they could have afforded to neglect Daggahbur while they constructed a motor road through Babilli to Harrar, as the Ethiopians were able to do two months later. Harrar, one knew it all the time, was in Graziani's hand if he dared even to seem daring.

What were the resources which Nasibu could mobilise against him if he chose to move? At Jijiga eighteen hundred men, five hundred of them his own and thirteen hundred "regulars'" belonging or connected to the First Belgian battalion trained before the war at Harrar. At Daggahbur, a hundred and seventy-five kilometres south, five hundred men of Fitorari Shefara, and two thousand five hundred of Dedjaz Hapte Mikael, a rich army contractor who had made enough to tip his ceremonial spear with gold. He enjoyed less control over his troops than over their pay, and has since made a happy submission to the Italians in Addis. At Bulale eight hundred under a delightful old man with the manners of an angel and the heart of a lion and a Hotchkiss which would not go off: Fitorari Wodjáku. At Sasabaneh the sixteen hundred who had left Gorahai and taken the tanks at Anale, with another fifteen hundred under Fitorari Malion, the best of them all. About this time, too, five hundred men were sent to Awareh, to the east of Daggahbur, to guard against an encroachment of the Dubats from Ado through Harradigit, previously unoccupied by the Ethiopian because its *ballas*, wide circular mud depressions in the rock, were waterless.

The average number of rounds per man at this time was two hundred, with reserves for half a day's battle. About forty per cent. of the rifles were modern or looked it. Nasibu's army had less than a hundred automatic rifles, that is one to ninety men, and ten machine-guns, of which the Colt and Hotchkiss types failed to oblige: four more machine-guns were stripped from the tanks which arrived in Jijiga late in November, each with three hundred rounds. And the artillery, ah, the artillery! The finest pieces were four Oerlikon anti-aircraft or anti-tank guns, two of which were parked at Daggahbur and two at Sasabaneh, these moving later to Borkut: ammunition was limited, Four Maxim-Nordenfelds of nineteen hundred, sterile tubes, impressed the Somalis around Sasabaneh, but were exceeded in point of age and incapacity by eight guns captured at the first battle of Adowa, which were kept by Wehib Pasha as a last stand-by in what he called his *"dèuxiéme Verdun"* at Jijiga.

This was the sum total of the Ethiopian armament in the South, against air bombardment, tanks, gas, field artillery and machine-guns, and troops of usefulness varying from that of the Libyans to that of the Blackshirts attached to Legione two hundred and twenty-one, political chatter-boxes of no mean order.

The Ogaden army was directed by an Ethiopian and by two military missions, one consisting of two Belgians and the other of three Turks. Dedjaz Nasibu, though a first-class shot with an uncanny mastery over the clay pigeon, had never fought a war before. Neither had one of the Belgians.

As Farouk Bey said to me of the whole Belgian military mission: *"parmi les types là il y avait des avocats, il y avail des commercants, il y avait des comediens d'ailleurs."* The Turks were great fun. Wehib Pasha, an old man at sixty, sat unshaven in his blue artificial silk zip-fastener shirt and set into activity an imagination of unparalleled scope. Defence was his continual theme. Wehib had been defending the past since the Dardanelles. The secrets of his *"deuxième Verdun"* would, he promised Taylor, be revealed after the war was over, would revolutionise defensive theory and startle the General Staffs of Europe. And well they might. A few miles south of Jijiga the Tug Jerrer runs close to the Daggahbur road, and here lay Verdun *in extenso*. For twenty kilometres over the hills quarter-circling Jijiga on the south-eastern side, meandered two lines of trenches a kilometre apart. They had taken three Ethiopian months to dig, and were fitted with a parados behind instead of a parapet in front, thus shrewdly exposing the soldiers within them to the rifle-fire of the enemy. Firesteps were lacking, so were telephones, and so in most places was water. Fifty small rolls of barbed wire had been set aside in Addis for the peculiar use of the Ogaden: forty went to Sasabaneh and the rest stayed in Jijiga, but I doubt whether they ever found their way to the Verdun sector. Incidentally, it would have taken over thirty thousand men to fill the trenches, and Wehib in Jijiga disposed of the one thousand eight hundred mentioned above.

The other two Turks were both good soldiers of long experience, Tripoli, the Great War, Anatolia. Farouk Bey, an angular disciplinarian with frequent lapses into whimsy, organised for the Ogaden a satisfactory supply system, but his frankness dissatisfied Nasibu. Tarik Bey had imported his set of maps and his skilled Ethiops educated abroad, who later gave a fine account of themselves at Borkut where the defences as well as those at Sasabaneh were planned by Tarik—crude, for the lack of material, but serviceable in the proof. The pair elaborated an Ogaden strategy which if fully applied might have broken Somali and after that Italian morale east of the Webbe Shebeli; but Nasibu thought better, advanced and was defeated.

The land lay so at the beginning of December, when Graziani should have struck. During December reinforcements arrived: I saw their minute tents, camouflaged with ochre, in the glistening green khat plantations outside Harrar, and at that time two of them were flogged for shooting a peasant while trying to lift his sheep. They were inspected by the Italian planes which followed the Emperor up from Jijiga and glittered like summer dragonflies over the high white-washed tower of Ras Makonnen's palace where I stood surveying the rich fields of Harrar. Three thousand men of Dedjaz Amde Mikael, from the Arussi, three thousand of Dedjaz Abele, who brought also his three young lions from his wild province of Gofa, and finally Dedjaz Makonnen Endalkatchu with twelve thousand Wallegas. Amde was a nice elderly man, who once in a supreme moment of drunkenness had ordered a machine-gun for himself from Europe: his men displayed a middling armament, mostly Fusil Gras, a few automatic rifles. I consider Abebe, who is anyway quite the reverse of his brother, Ras Desta, a typical *good* Amhara officer, quick, resolute and courageous; but his province was wretchedly poor and he had scarcely a modern rifle, ten to twenty automatics. The lions were, I suppose, as useful as his artillery, two of the unavoidable Adowa bits. But the man who had really taken trouble and spent money—his own—on his army was Makonnen: his twelve thousand were armed as to eighty-five per cent.—extraordinary proportion for Ethiopia—with modern rifles, and he had silver over to buy fifty automatics besides. He had clothed his men well. To talk to he was much more wooden, less soldierly and less spirited, than Abebe, who lived in a lion atmosphere: both were conscientious, both patriots in their own way. Amde's machine-gun was, of course, the only one between them.

Much later, there arrived upon the Jijiga scene four German anti-tank guns of ultra-modern type, out of a clutch of thirty-six imported by the Emperor for the whole of Ethiopia. The Turks have described them to me as magnificent: they ran on tyres, their calibre was thirty-seven and they fired thirty sighted shots a minute. Forty-six Ethiopians were trained to serve the battery up to twenty-two sighted shots, and proved themselves quick learners. The guns eventually went to Daggahbur, where their variety would have fought their first war, if they had ever been used. They were left behind in the retreat, for lack of traction. To no Ethiopian advantage, they complete the list of Ethiopian effectives.

The Italians meanwhile had posted a regiment at Gorahai, according to Ethiopian information, with advanced battalion behind a spider-web of barbed-wire, machine-gun nests and light artillery at the hill fort of Gabridihari. The Dubats, later reinforced by whites, were at Danan and Harradigit was occupied at the end of December by between two hundred and three hundred mixed Italian soldiers, who threatened Bulale and Awareh from that junction of tracks through the thorn, and therefore were a continual eastern menace to Daggahbur. Gorahai was an advanced air-base, where there were nearly always planes.

But the Somali air-arm, so long as it did not use gas, did little hurt to Ethiopian morale and none to Ethiopian physique. At Daggahbur, the chief aerial target, trenches were dug and the dry riverside undercut in the Tug Jerrer, where there was shade. Here the soldiers and people of Daggahbur rested secure after the first alarm had been given, usually by the pie-dogs who slunk yellow and snappish out of the town half an hour before the planes arrived. The average casualties were one forgetful woman or one chicken injured for each bombardment. The planes never found the Tug shelter, where the telephone, too, was removed after the "exchange" tukul had been hit by an incendiary. The only real damage they did was to the church, a conspicuous square building with a cross atop whose arms were decorated finally by bulbous white ostrich eggs. The priests, who like other Ethiopians believed that an aeroplane actually aimed its bombs at the man or mouse which it wanted to hit, trusted in the visibility of their cloth and lingered in the sanctuary. They were struck twice by strays.

Arrangements for the movement of an Ethiopian army are not so easy as the movements of that army once collected and under way. Abebe Makonnen and Amde, who were descending into a country where there were no food resources beside the Somali herds and the fields of mashila near Jijiga, had first to organise not only transport for their men but supply from a base hitherto unknown to them, Harrar. Here they were ably assisted by the head of the granary for Harrar province, Blatta Hapte Mariam, who was murdered by Italian troops when they entered the town five months later. For transport there were one hundred and fifty lorries at the government garage in Jijiga, but these were serving the whole Ogaden as well at the time.

By the end of December, Nasibu, gratified as much by the inactivity of the enemy as by the arrival of new men, had pushed forces south of Sasabaneh to Anale —never more than a small post thirty-six kilometres on, and to Borkut, fifteen kilometres further. Malion and his fifteen hundred men took over this camp, where Tarik Bey dug trenches and bomb-shelters and placed his Ethiopian Foreign Legion with two Oerlikon guns. At Sasabaneh were left the 2nd Belgian battalion, six hundred and eighty strong, which had led the bolt from Gorahai.

Now the area between Webbe Shebeli and the Tug Fafan began to fill up. At the end of the year Abebe was moving down to Daggahmodo on foot through Babilli, and since transport of any kind was lacking, justifiably feeding his men on the country, Somali meat and camel's milk. He had to hurry because of the movement then threatened by Olol Dinle and his Shaveli bandas in the south, which culminated later in their defeat by Dedjaz Bayenna Mared at Karanle. Dedjaz Amde had arrived in Jijiga by the end of December also, raising the garrison to nearly five thousand though the sum total in the Ogaden had decreased in the interval: Dedjaz Hapte Mikael had been tipping his spear to such effect in Daggahbur that over seven hundred of his men had deserted.

January was not over before Makonnen and his twelve hundred men were encamped near Jijiga, and the motor road to Daggahmodo necessitated by Abebe's occupation of the town had been finished. Simultaneously Graziani pounced on Ras Desta between the rivers Dawa and Dorya west of Dolo, mangled him with tanks in easy country, and drove him back across cotton soil and open pampas to Sidamo.

The panic in Addis was great. Government departments like the customs were combed for reinforcements to Sidamo, and transport was commandeered. Abebe in faraway Daggahmodo heard of his brother's distress and sent orders to his province of Gofa for men to aid him. Fifty Gofas turned out and marched to Adola—this is typical, I think, of the Amharic feudal system as well as of the disorder reigning under Desta. Desta gave them no food: of fifty, there were twenty constantly travelling to and fro between Adola and Gofa to supply the remaining thirty; while the Ras enjoyed a five-course meal daily, with champagne for distinguished visitors.

Desta had enchained Fitoraris Adama and Tadama on their arrival at Adola: because, as he averred, they had not brought back all the automatic rifles which he had entrusted to them, and had retreated without orders. The soldiers of the Fitoraris, who knew that if they served under Desta directly they would get no food, and who liked their leaders—both good fighters—reminded Desta that he had himself retreated at breakneck speed when the Fitoraris were still making progress against the enemy, and advised him, with various unmistakable cut-throat gestures, to release

Adama and Tadama. They next extracted from the Ras a promise that he would feed his army regularly, once a week. That done they advanced and occupied Wadara, whence the Italian patrols had just withdrawn.

Thus the situation in Sidamo was most precarious; and it was only later that reinforcements totalling about ten thousand were stationed in Desta's rear and to the west of him, along the Addis Ababa-Mega motor road. Nasibu was informed by the Emperor, quite rightly, that a demonstration was needed in the Ogaden to cover these activities. He decided therefore to advance and occupy on a wide front, step by step, vaguely determining upon an ultimate objective, the plain of Gorahai.

First Shefara was sent with his five hundred men from Daggahbur to Jigo, a hilly position south of Daggahmodo, where he was positively of use at last. He massacred Somali *bandas* who were creeping in upon the left of Bayenna Mared. Dedjaz Makonnen left the neighbourhood of Jijiga in mid-February, went back along the Harrar road to Babilli, and made speed down to Daggahmodo by the new lorry road, then in far better condition than the old Ogaden roads to the east which were thick in skid-dust. Abebe abandoned Daggahmodo in front of him and advanced by the direct caravan route which leads through bush to Danan without passing Jigo: he occupied Malenko without resistance. The *bandas* had frequently squatted in it, but at the moment it was empty of them. At the very end of February, however, Abebe led a small party of his men down the Danan path to effect a smart surprise by night upon this Italian front screen, and killed a large number.

This action, like that at Jigo, followed a pattern long advised by the Turks Farouk and Tarik Bey at Jijiga. Since organised offensive and organised defence both depend upon fire power, in which the Ethiopians were pathetically inferior to their enemy, the Turks pressed upon Nasibu the following tactic: to form bands of anything from thirty to four hundred men, good shots under tried leaders, to establish these with independent camel transport, and to send them out upon night surprises. Their instructions were to attack, massacre, loot arms and food, but not to hold the position:

instead, to shift off quickly to their base, while another party attacked in a different, unexpected area.

About the same time as the affair south of Malenko, this tactic was played out in the east—once only. A small band of one hundred and fifty, led by Fitorari Abati Tafari, attacked Gurati (Harradigit) at midnight in the last week of February, killed straightway two hundred Somalis and whites who had negligently garrisoned the *balles* since December, captured a nice stock of rifles, ammunition and much needed food, and went home with hardly a loss. Information reaching the Ethiopian command that week showed that the garrisons at Wal Wal and Wardair had been seriously weakened, and that these wells were an easy prey to the night raid. But Nasibu never carried out another, though the series across the front was already beginning to alarm the Somalis who covered the Italian positions and formed their intelligence system and their shock troops. Jigo, Malenko, Gurati, satisfaction, finish.

Nasibu was thinking big. In the middle of February he moved his headquarters permanently to Daggahbur, followed shortly by Dedjaz Amde and his men: Hapte Mikael returned to Jijiga with his artificially depleted army. Nearer the war zone, Nasibu dreamed of a great offensive. What he had been cogitating since the beginning of February developed finally into designs of a mass attack upon Danan to culminate in the recapture of Gorahai. In the Ethiopian style, he decided; then called upon his foreign advisers for their views.

Their report written on March 8 which is in my possession, told His Excellency that such an advance would be fatal: on the other hand they argued for a renewal of the surprise offensive which had already proved successful, while the rest of the troops were to be withdrawn to the Harrar area, where alone they could organise a compact defensive system, free from those difficulties of provisionment which were beginning to tax the rutted tracks, the creaking camions and the minds of the simple commanders in the Ogaden. The advantages were, besides compactness and improvement of supply, that the Italians would be forced to operate over five hundred kilometres of territory already known to the Ethiopian, in which their small offensive commandos could always range without risk of lacking water. Wehib

Pasha of course still wished to defend his *"deuxième Verdun."* But as it was now clear that the *deuxième Verdun* was neither in itself defensible, being bare as a plate, nor defended any other part of Ethiopia, since Harrar was attainable through Babilli, the old man's advice did not sway his colleagues.

Nor of course did his colleagues sway Nasibu. Throughout March the preparation for the great stroke went forward: for such nimble individuals Ethiopians take a long time to concentrate, since they are not naturally amenable to discipline or order. Makonnen and Abebe were still calling in outlying groups at the beginning of April, by which time the Italians were fully informed from Somali sources of the move evidently prepared against them. On March 22, 23 and 24 they carried out the mass bombardments of Jijiga: from the end of March onwards, until mid-April, they steadily gassed Daggahbur, Bulale, Sasabaneh, Borkut and Daggahmodo.

The latter action had grave moral, some material effect. Jijiga on the other hand was taken completely by surprise on the first day, since the south telephone reported Italian planes approaching twenty minutes after twenty-seven of them had already arrived over the town. The bazaar was crowded, the destruction of life severe, and Jijiga never really recovered from the shock. During the three days that the Italians hovered over this defenceless market town, centre of the Ogaden transport system, they dropped between eighteen hundred and two thousand bombs, three hundred and fifty of which were heavy. They did not injure a single lorry, but they broke the morale of the workshops and garage, which removed hurriedly to the Karramarra pass and hardly operated afterwards. Food was in future carried only half by lorry, half by camel, and the troops who were to attack Danan were the first to run short. Abebe high-handedly commandeered five hundred animals which were part of the system and had been sent down to him: so the Somalis who hired the beasts out refused to supply more and took to the bush.

The Italian reinforcements at Belet Uen were moved nearer the front: the defences of Danan were strengthened.

On April 10 Makonnen and Abebe were ready with seven thousand men for the attack. Of the rest of their fifteen thousand, some—not many—had deserted, some were sick, some had inadequate arms, but most were garnering food. Makonnen had an average of one hundred rounds per man, Abebe much less since he had spent a lot of ammunition in skirmishes. Strange fire-power for a grand offensive. At dawn on April 16 the seven thousand descended on Danan, and the action lasted until late afternoon.

Both the chiefs went into battle with their machine-gun rifles, as brave Ethiopian commanders always do. They led the front skirmishing line and performed the usual circling movement round the camp, then rushed in, massed. Part of the defences were taken, as well as seven small tanks, a few lorries, and some machine-guns—as usual, at the point of the sweeping Ethiopian blade. They renewed the furious assault until one o'clock, when the ammunition of many had given out and Italian reinforcements appeared. But *they* had no reserves to call upon—of the Ethiopian armies only the Emperor's was so modern—and after three hours' resistance in the hot bush they broke and ran. Abebe and Makonne reached Daggahmodo with their suites next day and the *katama* was entered by the Italians on the 18th. Profiting from this failure of an Ethiopian offensive, which always had to fail, the General Graziani counter-attacked with troops amounting in the view of the enemy to a division (actually four).

In the Ogaden east of the Tug Fafan the average number of rounds per man had sunk to sixty: there had been no fighting, but food had been short for two months, even the daily *dourah* which would constipate an English chicken but which is relished by the Amhara soldier. He therefore exchanged cartridges against food with the local traders or Somalis. Malion, who cared better for his men had, despite his distance from the supply base as he sat in Borkut, preserved an average of about one hundred and twenty, with a certain reserve. His force was now a trifle over two thousand five hundred, with a small lookout post at short distance manned by Tarik Bey's specials. The 2nd Belgian battalion still lay behind, defended by barbed wire at Sasabaneh.

Borkut is in undulating bush country, slightly relieved by small trees not as wide open and sandy as Anale, but with nothing like the shelter of Sasabaneh, which was the only position of value between Jijiga and the Italians. Here wide dry brown mimosas and great rocks on a hill-side were proof against the air and even mechanised land attack.

On April 23, after an aerial bombardment, an Italian mechanised column attacked Borkut, which Malion defended with great tenacity throughout the grilling day. First the Somali troops, then the whites were thrown back from the crude little camp, whose narrow trenches were its only protection. Towards evening the Italians withdrew. Malion's casualties were not high, though ammunition was running short and the two Oerlikons had been shot out.

Next day the Italian reinforcement had come up to supplement the column from the south, and another Italian column was directed upon Borgut direct overland from Danan. Malion received instruction from Nasibu to quit: the Dedjazmatch had made up his mind at last to take the advice of his advisers, and defend Harrar. So Malion left Borkut to the triumphant and talkative Legione 221, Fascists raised abroad who were capable of describing their walkover in any language under the sun. When he reached Sasabaneh he found that it had already been abandoned by the 2nd Belgians: nor could he reform his troops there to stand and face the enemy. An Ethiopian army, retreating at high speed and in disorder, was beyond the powers even of Fitorari Malion to control. Express, next stop Daggahbur, was the order of retirement.

At Sasabaneh Malion and his own bodyguard stood and resisted for a time. Then they struggled on between the shelving stony hills, where the mock tributaries of the Tug Fafan seam the road with their thick sandfloors; until, from land that broadened out into a plateau, they could see the trim bush houses of Daggahbur across the Jerrer, now broken by bombs, and traversed meagre fields of guinea-corn and the thorn to reach the mysterious headquarters of Dedjazmatch Nasibu, which he changed as frequently as his mind.

Every day because he was afraid that Somali spies would report his whereabouts to the Italians, Nasibu fixed a new rendezvous with his advisers and the two secretaries who formed his staff, in the bush, generally from five to seven miles out of Daggahbur. Wehib Pasha, a much older man, followed wearily to advise—defence.

When Malion arrived all was ready, except the brand new German quick-firing artillery, for retirement. As there was nothing to pull them, and as the enemy already driven off once were expected again with reinforcements at any moment from Daggahmodo, they were abandoned. Another Italian column had meanwhile driven out the defenders of Bulale, riddled with dysentery beside the great wells, and Daggahbur was therefore to be attacked on three sides.

Strangely, the Italians never thought of sending anybody ahead from Daggahmodo to Babilli, where they could have occupied Harrar without a shot fired and cut off the whole of Nasibu's army. The Ethiopian troops between Daggahbur and the railway line were only Hapte Mariam's unhappy seventeen hundred. It seemed that Graziani remained so uncertain of himself that he still preferred to use superiority of numbers as well as superiority of equipment. No Italian victory was gained in the Italo-Ethiopian war except when the Italians enjoyed both advantages.

Daggahbur was not defended. On the morning of April 25 ten aeroplanes bombed the place, now fuller by three thousand men, but they caused few casualties and after they had gone Nasibu ordered the withdrawal. The majority of the troops went straight up the Fafan for the Karramarra pass and Harrar, avoiding Jijiga. One hears, though I have no eyewitness for this, that Nasibu behaved well in retreat, organising what transport remained in Daggahbur before he left. Though Nasibu was no commander, he was a civilised man of some administrative capacity, a good mayor of Addis and a reforming governor in Bale before he went to Harrar. The Harraris admit that he ruled justly, giving their local courts under the Muslim *cadis* great independence and a widening jurisdiction. They liked him. But modern war was beyond him, and he knew it; hence his hestitation. Above his hesitations, the habitual independence, half suspicion and half self-defence, of the Amhara governing class towards all foreign advice.

His intention, then, was to obey Farouk and Tarik Bey, and defend Harrar. Meanwhile behind them all marched the redoubtable Fitorari Malion, his control over his troops finally re-established, fighting a real rearguard action for the first time in Ethiopian history. Just north of Daggahbur he held up the over-hasty *bandas* for a time, and south of Ageresalem, the telephone post within kraaled thorn which lies half-way between Jijiga and Daggahbur, he turned a second time and drove back the enemy with loss. Evidently they must have been very tired, or Malion must have given them the impression that he was very strong; after this brush they abandoned the pursuit and he went on peacefully to Jijiga, where he arrived on the afternoon of April 28, his army intact.

One hundred new automatic rifles, with a moderate amount of ammunition, had arrived at Jijiga in the last days of the war. The ill-conditioned rabble of Hapte Mikael were pilfering them right and left when Malion entered, but he strode in with his guard and took armfuls of over fifty. He stayed in Jijiga some time waiting for the Italians to show their forces before he chose his line of retreat; like most sensible men he imagined that they must long ago have entered Babilli and Harrar. But they were in fact resting from their strenuous efforts, and wondering whether Nasibu, who had got away clean in front of them, would turn, close the passes and defend the Harrar-Gue, that mountainous, well-covered district round the second town of Ethiopia, against their exhausted troops.

The Emperor solved the difficulty for them. He passed Diredawa on the night of May 2, en route for Djibouti, with an entourage of all the greatest in Ethiopia. Nasibu heard of it in the Harrar-Gue, abandoned the defence of his province and fled with Wehib Pasha to Djibouti by the next train. The other Turks had to follow—the Belgians, by the way, had vanished after the first bombardment of Jijiga. Nasibu followed the Emperor early to Palestine, while Wehib, informed at the dark midnight by a sinister visitor that the French intended to extradite him to the Italians, took a taxi instantly from Djibouti to Zeila, and thence transhipped to Aden, where he is believed to have made a statement to the Press. Abebe Makonnen and Amde also entrained at Diredawa for the coast.

So the brave little Ogaden army, which had responded often to courageous leadership, was left without head, without food, clothing, ammunition or money. For all these it turned to Harrar, the richest city in all Ethiopia, whose fruit-groves stretch for miles from the sandstone city walls and the midden heaps where Harraris throw their unwanted children to the white-hooded ravens: whose wide-horned Zebu cattle supply beef and milk of a quality undreamed of by soldiers nine months away in the Ogaden. The valleys towards Diredawa and Jijiga were full of corn, and the money-lenders in the town were known to have done superbly while the fighting lasted. A biblical place, Harrar. The broken army entered it, and the British subjects, *banyans*, Greeks, Armenians, high Ethiopian officials and clergy took refuge in the British Consulate, where they were ably defended by Mr. Chapman-Andrews and his guard from the Somali Camel Corps.

The missions were able to protect themselves. Dr. Feron found that his lepers were keen as boy scouts to form a hospital guard. So he packed them off into the town to get arms and ammunition at the Gibbi, and knocked them into military shape when they returned. *Shiftas* have their own way of doing things. If they wish to loot a property, they blaze away into the air around it: and if the guardians blaze a lot into the air in answer, the *shiftas* generally do not attack it. And so it happened with Feron's Auxiliary Leper Corps, except that they fired straight at the *shiftas*.

Malion had taken his dispositions, and entered the town on, I think, the 7th of May. The Italians were still at Babilli. He replenished his troops with loot, and rested his body. On the 9th he heard that the Italians were on the road outside. He was drinking tea at the time, and the grandson of Theodore rose and switched on his khaki mantle, clipped at the high collar by two silver lions' heads. Malion is a tall man, with charming easy manners, spare and handsome, a wide forehead, frank amiable face. A step rather like an old world actor's, a way of explaining orders to his troops which they liked. He walked through Harrar followed by two servants carrying his own automatics, and collected his men, whom he had already acquainted with his determination to resist as long as he could. They acclaimed him and followed him out in a long stream south-west of Harrar, to the mountains of Garamulata where Lij Yasu was long imprisoned in golden chains. At a *gebir* or raw meat feast which he gave to his loyal soldiers, one party got up and named him a Dedjazmatch, at which far more called him Ras.

XX

On Thursday afternoon, April 30, there was a great stir in Addis Ababa. Old chiefs, their heads swathed in the bandages of dignity, rode evenly and fast through the town on their tripping mules, supported by a scurry of retainers. Patches of dirty white moving over the high rocks where the road descends Mount Entoto showed that the shammas were out to meet someone. A car came down the mountain with black carabineers on either running-board, their purer togas flying. The dry eucalyptus, scaling its bark and dangling flat leaves in the parched season before the rains, gave a new dusty harshness to the crowd's acclamation, the penetrating Li-li-li-li of bees in swarm. It was the Emperor with Ras Kassa, back from the wars: behind followed Ras Getatchu, fat as ever, and beaming through his golden pince-nez. No soldiers with them. The Emperor's only guard were the Addis Ababa police who in their blue coats lined the route. The cars drove straight to the Great Palace, where a council of Ministers was called.

Horror and alarm struck the people when the Emperor alighted. The face, always sensitive, was haunted now. Its essential trimness was gone: the eyes seemed to have lost their quiet resolution. . . . The step and carriage were no longer resilient.

Fatigue and spiritual misery had done their work. The one man in Ethiopia capable of always taking the right decision had lost his gift.

Lorenzo Taezaz, the volatile little secretary, presented to the Emperor the plans for removing himself and his capital to Gore. Acting still with instinctive wisdom, the Emperor approved though the project was new to him.

He was not yet in contact with the will-lessness at the centre of his government which was to fatten his own indecision.

He received the heads of foreign missions. Barton was shocked by his appearance: he had never seen the Emperor of Ethiopia so exhausted. The Emperor asked him if he could give assurances that his Government would support an extension of sanctions at Geneva, in view of the changed military situation. Barton (rightly, in the view of his Government, honestly in mine) said that he could not.

The British Government had entered upon sanctions simply as an experiment. They wanted to see "if they would work." Their approach to the problem was purely "scientific": it showed something of the vivisectionist's superiority to the material on which he labours. They never observed that the analogy with an experiment does not work when you are dealing with human entities: that they themselves were dealing with human wills, their own will in the lead. They never saw that the success of their efforts in the laboratory depended first of all on their determination to make the laboratory a success. Theirs was a new testing-room, a new experiment on new material. But they showed none of the vision or dogged persistence of the scientist who proudly perfects a new invention. They lacked faith.

History, the study of documents, memoirs false and true, will disclose the reasons for their feebleness of will. Clearly it was in part deliberate: certain elements in the Cabinet and leaders of our economic life did not want an international experiment to succeed. They actively wished to blow up the test-tubes and cut off the gas. Others thought that European Fascism should not be weakened for the coming struggle of all the rights against all the lefts. Others simply panicked: the principle had struck in them such shallow roots that the slightest shock threw it out. These had settled for sanctions as a means to keep future aggressors in order: meaning Germany. As soon as Germany occupied the Rhineland, their resolution changed. They got such a fright that they lost their reason. The very activity of their future aggressor drove out of their heads the programme for dealing with them. In alarm, they simply reacted: they ceased to think.

Unsteadfast minds, ignorant of their real objectives, vacillating between the Peace Ballot and the City, naturally they could not answer a simple question in thirty-six hours. And Friday is the beginning of the English week-end.

The French Minister also saw the Emperor, and did not leave without impressing upon him the unwisdom of defending his capital: not because many Ethiopians would be killed, but because valuable foreign lives and property, parasitic on the Ethiopian system, would be endangered by the Italian artillery. Many of these foreigners already lay huddled in the heavy Armenian atmosphere of an artificial cavern at the French Legation. Their absence from the town, their closed shops, the immense stores of liquor behind the shutters imported to soften the hearts of the victorious army: all had combined to aggravate the idea of panic in the town and exercised a natural fascination on the appetites of the poorer Abyssinian. I felt like looting them myself.

The cave life at the French Legation was responsible for the riots which were to follow. They manufactured the panic, coolly and deliberately: they suffer now.

The American Minister visited the Emperor on a less sinister mission: America's interests in Ethiopia are only a little larger than her responsibilities under the Covenant. All he wanted to do was to present his new credentials. He noted that the Emperor's hair had grown longer in retreat: it was not his function to be more profound.

The Emperor entered his Council. All were very quiet. Vermouth was served to the officers and chiefs with him. The great men of Shoa bowed and kissed his feet. Dark Kassa loomed behind him.

They conferred in hushed tones for hours. No decision was taken, but the feeling of the Council seemed to be for moving west.

It was only later that the Emperor was able to take full stock of the military situation, and to find how thoroughly he had been betrayed by the officials whom he had left in charge at Addis Ababa.

Betrayed? Perhaps. Or was it the nature of the Ethiopians that they obey a leader but not a committee; that they answer quickly to the orders of Janhoi and postpone or disregard those of his servants?

Ato Makonnen Hapte Wolde, Director of Commerce, had worked day and night at the Great Gibbi: he never went back to his house; when he had to sleep he curled himself up in the back seat of his car. But while he kept control over communications, regularly rang up the different telephone posts, ordered the dispatch of munitions and men and of the engineers who were to destroy Tarmaber, the other executives muddled time away.

At noon on the day before the Emperor's entry into Addis Ababa, part of the Italian column advancing on the capital had climbed Mount Tarmaber, where the Imperial Road rises on dizzy hairpin bends into the Gib Washa range. Its destruction had been ordered, but the rough metal might have been gnawed by mice. The armies of Shoa had been told to hold it with six thousand men: three hundred and fifty boys of the Emperor's Cadet School under Captain Tamm of the Swedish military mission manned the last defence of Addis Ababa. Captain Tamm had seen the Italians on Tuesday, coming down to the Robi River, far across the rolling plain: next day, through his glasses, he saw them nearer, advancing across Shola Mieda and approaching the shrine of Debra Sina at his feet. Captain Tamm went back for reinforcements.

The boys under his command withdrew a little later.

The British Red Cross and Taylor, the British Military Attaché, were camped over half-way to the mountain, near Debra Brehan. Tamm passed through fast: he was followed a little later by a few of the boys under Lij Nasibu.

Three hundred had manned the mountain, thirty the caravan route from Warba Hailu, whence two thousand Eritrean cavalry were advancing.

Herbert Masser, the young ex-*Reichswehrman* who at the beginning of the year had brought thirty-six German anti-tank guns to Abyssinia, was told to come up to Addis with his guns, take over the ammunition and accompany to the front the brigade of two thousand who had been training under him and the Swedes at Hulota, west of Addis.

He brought up the guns. But the Afa Negus, the Ethiopian Prime Minister, had already commandeered the lorries in which the shells were travelling in order to convey some of his own troops to the front.

Guns and ammunition cost the Emperor a million marks: not a shot was fired out of their barrels against the enemy. Nor did the troops of the Afa Negus ever leave Addis Ababa.

Certain of the volunteers who had enrolled at Jaumeda went out; but instead of attempting to bar the Italian mechanised column at Tarmaber, they straggled off on the other, the direct caravan track to Warra Hailu. Of the other reinforcements sent earlier to Tamm, only eighty got as far as Debra Brehan: the Military Governor of Addis Ababa had failed to supply them with the necessary food, although there was no shortage in the city and prices were low.

A Potez machine flew out that Wednesday evening along the Debra-Brehan-Tarmaber road to see what had happened to the troops sent out from Addis. The pilot's heart must have throbbed louder than his engine when he passed over Entoto in the sluggish little plane. With the Italians only a hundred miles away as the Caproni flies, he was taking a fearful risk. But there were still individual Ethiopians with guts in their bodies.

He saw nothing but the British Military Attaché's car and the grey Red Cross lorries coming back at a shaking pace over rough road on the North Shoan plain. The flapping tent covers over the Red Cross personnel must have flashed him the message of general retreat. Nothing else, but still the stragglers of the leaderless armies of Dedjaz Moshesha and the dead Bidwoded Makonnen, entered in twos and threes and fours, little specks, the eucalyptus belt round Addis Ababa.

It was leadership in the centre that had failed, not the Ethiopian fighting man. The institution could not carry on when its head, the Emperor, was removed. Tamm was not supported . . . reinforcements were unfed . . . stragglers waited for commands which none gave.

The Ethiopian brand of feudalism, weakened by the Imperial reforms; and the Imperial Civil Service, only half certain of its power, had played from one to the other the onus of decision. A society, developing peacefully from disorder to organisation round the centre, was too delicately poised to withstand external aggression as well.

When the Emperor came in, his capital was doomed. It was on that certain knowledge that he went to sleep.

I spent Thursday evening with Margarita, Lolita and Lee of the Legation. The coming chaos was quite hidden from me. We all imagined that the Emperor would go West, and that the Italians would enter, as they promised, on Saturday. We discussed whether I should go up to the Legation before they came in, for they were then the only risk which I thought I had to face. The Italian radio had already branded my reports as grotesque and ignoble. . . .

Eventually my curiosity got the better of my suspicions. I decided to stay in the town.

Occasional shots were echoing into the crisp clear sky of the African evening. The people of Shoa were welcoming their soldiers back from the war with joyful musketry. In the groups of tukuls they drank and pulled the triggers in fantasia as the young men straggled in. But no singing followed. The soldiers all spoke of defeat by the "aeroplan," of "pomp" and *"Muz"* (poison, meaning gas).

The Emperor, Kassa and Getatchu had marched back from the war to Fiche in two columns, with about ten thousand men. At Fiche there was much whispering: Konovaloff presented a report to the Emperor describing the demoralisation of his army, in the sombre terms of which only a White Russian is capable. The men from Addis Ababa were stealing back to their city every night for food, by twos and threes. Of the rest, those who were not directly under the hand of Dedjaz Aberra Kassa, Kassa's son, were splitting off under their captains of fifty and ten into *shifta* bands. The drone of the planes over their secret concentrations made them uneasy, irresponsive to orders, quick to scatter. The ordinary disciplines of their life had been quite shattered by the war.

The Emperor slept that night in the Little Palace with the Empress, who was to leave the country on Saturday. Preparations had been made to receive her and the children at Djibouti, and to embark them in *Enterprise*, Captain Morgan, R.N. The special train was ready at the station: Pasteau, the young French Rightist who was railway company diplomat, had kept it all very quiet.

The Empress had made up her mind that the Emperor should come with her, as a determined woman would. Backed by the mysticism of the Coptic priests who influenced her, abetted by the great comfort-loving eunuch who always stood at her side, she would take the Emperor to Jerusalem, the Sacred City, where the aid of heaven would be invoked before the aid of Geneva.

She saw that he was tired and that she was strong and fresh. All the influences that worked upon her were defeatist—the church, a static class who were always the first to yield to the invader; the palace women, terrified of planes and the use of gas; Kassa, her cousin, a Christian pacifist at heart who was sick of the war.

Behind it all, the fearful prophecies of the Wooha-Boha, weird pagan priest of the Abyssinian lower classes, and through them penetrating to the very head of the State. Horribly dirty, his crazy face and skinny neck adorned with amulets of leather and lion-claws, his ragged clothes hanging foul threads to which attached the awful physical attributes of birth and death, splinters of dried bone and specimens of afterbirth: the Wooha-Boha represented the chief criminal investigation department of Ethiopia.

All our servants honoured him. He smelt out thefts and petty misdemeanours. As non-Christian, he represented at the same time the underworld and the underdog; for most of their fathers were originally non-Christian and they themselves had only been Christianised through their servant status. For help in difficulty, they turned instinctively to the occultism of the filthy Wooha-Boha: his very loathsomeness attracted them, starting, as it seemed to them, out of their native earth. A rugged, dirty, shapeless man, as men first moulded cross-eyed divinities out of the crooked lines of rocks and trees.

The central government did not like the Wooha-Boha. Seriously attempting to civilise the country from Addis Ababa, they drove him out into the hills. He in his turn bore a grudge against authority, and now through the servant classes who frequented this oracular Scotland Yard, the crabbed *Nieblung* was preparing a sharp revenge. Day by day he prophesied failure: it crept through the servants and shivered their masters. The Coptic priesthood itself in some way respected the Wooha-Boha: casting his tendentious clairvoyance into a more religious form, they whispered into the Empress's ear.

The Emperor did not wake refreshed on Friday.

The Council of Ministers met to continue its deliberations. Organisation of the removal of the Government westward proceeded. Blatta Takale, the Director of the Municipality, a fine-looking, youngish Ethiopian with a good grip on any situation, a martial stance and a steady luminous eye, had told the Legations during the Emperor's absence that he would maintain order until the Italians were near; but he would not wait to submit to them, he would withdraw with his police and private fighting men along the Addis Alem road.

He got the lorries ready. Tasfai Tegan and Spencer, the young American adviser, were to leave next morning with them, the archives and an escort for the West. Tasfai, delightfully stout and blasé, the social success of the Emperor's Civil Service, was leisurely fitting on a pair of khaki jodhpurs, dexterously tailored to his waist and the large part of him which he carried behind. Spencer was quite schoolboyish about his first caravan: during the last few days he had been travelling round Addis in his new khaki helmet, and buying new shorts to tan the pale knees of international law. All the mules and the tents were ready; Spencer was looking forward to the backwood trail.

Kassa spoke in the Council, which consisted, of course, of Ethiopian grandees alone. Kassa was the most powerful Ras in Ethiopia: he had, until Lij Yasu's escape and recapture by Tafari, been the ex-Emperor's jailer and therefore the greatest baron of Ethiopia, for he could always reproclaim him. Even during the war, as I have shown, he had to be humoured.

In 1916 he was a claimant for the throne: he had taken the refusal of the chiefs, their choice of Tafari, with a good grace, though his pedigree was a little higher than his rival's. He had always been faithful: correspondingly, the Emperor had trusted his cousin. They worked well together throughout the war and the retreat.

This gave more weight to Kassa's words. He advised that the Emperor should not go to the West, where the Galla might attack his weakened and ill-fed army, but to Djibouti and Europe, to appeal to the Powers who were bound to aid Ethiopia under the Covenant. Ras Getatchu and Fitorari Birru, the ex-Minister of War, supported him.

It was believed then that the Italians would be in Addis the next morning: they were already reported near Debra Brehan, about a hundred miles of smooth running round the eastern ridge of Entoto and over the North Shoan plain. The Council had to decide that day: there could be no more postponement.

Three opposed Kassa—all three were men who had held posts in Addis during the war and had already made the preparations for the removal to Gore. They were Blattangeta Herrouy, the Foreign Minister, a devoted partisan of the Emperor; Dedjaz Igezu, the Military Governor of Addis, and another unknown to me. Igezu was a man of immense standing, except in the physical sense, for his legs were old and bandy. The lower part of his brown face and his neck were light pink, and his beard sandy, for Igezu suffered from a pigment disease (not, as Monfreid says, leprosy). He said Gore with great determination and, a heavy Menelikish figure in blue cloak and muslin-bandaged head, he stamped the floor of the council chamber with his black buttoned boots. To no good. In the afternoon of Friday, the Council at last decided to leave for Djibouti by twenty-one votes to three.

The vote was conveyed to the Emperor.

He was still tortured by indecision.

The Council, the Empress, Kassa and the priests were now all pressing him to go. Strange that they should have kept it from the people; for the people never thought that the war was over, they were certain that the Emperor was leaving for the West. The journalists, too, in the breakdown of the censorship which accompanied the preparations of all officials for the Westward journey, were busily writing interviews with Haile Selassie, in some of which he said that he would stand to defend Addis, in others that he would withdraw to Wallega, but in none that he was leaving next morning for Djibouti. None of the stories got over, for the transmitters at the radio station left early to secure rifles and ammunition: they were afraid of a fight in the dark on the way home with *shiftas* or disbanded soldiery.

The Emperor was now two instincts and two reasons.

Instinctively he wanted to fly the country—as instinctively every man defeated in battle and fighting with inferior weapons would wish to go. And instinctively he felt that flight was not brave and tactically unwise; for he had known throughout the dispute and the war that the only way to persuade Europe to carry out the smallest part of her promises was by an appearance of strength and equanimity.

His reason was divided equally for going and staying.

He did not accept the feeling of the other Amharas of his Council, that the Galla of Wallega would turn against him if he went west. Dedjaz Hapte Mariam, the Galla ruler of Lekempti, who paid him twenty thousand malers gold tribute yearly, was a loyalist. He flew the green-yellow-red of Ethiopia, his well-armed, well-organised Galla force had helped to suppress an Amhara revolt in Gojjam—the so-called subject race had fought for the Imperial authority against the ruling class . . . Hapte Mariam was rich, young, well-educated, orderly minded. He knew enough French to grasp the meaning of patriotism: he admired the Emperor's reforms. The Emperor's own army was ragged now and would have to live on the land, but the Emperor preferred Hapte Mariam and his Wallega Galla to many of purer blood.

Yet he longed to go to Europe. From the beginning of 1935 he had reasoned, rightly, that only the collective measures of the other Powers could save Ethiopia from her aggressor. For months now, since the mechanical advance of sanctions had been blocked by the Hoare-Laval plan, he had planned to go to Europe to demand the just help pledged to him: and if Barton could not assure him that Britain would go on, he must go himself to represent his people in a last appeal.

In the palace they heard the noise of an Italian aeroplane.

The muslin-bound women hid in horror; but the Emperor was weary of concealment. He went down to the stables to see his Arab horses . . . few had returned from Dessye . . . they were ill-groomed and hollow-flanked. The emptiness of the cast-iron barracks at his Palace gates, where he had given the Imperial Guard coffee before it left for Debra Markos, struck into his heart and found it, too, empty of sensation, numb as the tomb.

Forcing himself to a decision, he ordered the drums to be beaten at the Great Gibbi before the banquetting hall of Menelik.

On knotty eucalyptus poles the Imperial flags of Ethiopia, green-yellow-red, with the wild-haired lion in the centre, were raised for the last time. The drums beat for an hour and a half that afternoon: the whole town heard them, above the clacking of Armenian automobiles which, as hurriedly as their feeble frames would trundle, carried to their fuggy grotto what the Turks had not thought worth destroying, but the French thought worth preserving.

The Shoan chiefs sped again through the streets: armed men, stragglers of the war, made for the Palace. Before a crowd of one or two thousand, the Imperial Awaj was read, written in the Emperor's own hand, summarily rejecting the advice of his Council.

He ordered out the armies of three chiefs, Ras Getatchu, Dediaz Mangasha the Governor of Saio, and a certain Fitorari. They were to meet the enemy at once east of Addis and delay him. The Emperor still intended to move to the West: this was to be a covering force. I heard the Awaj at the Palace, saw the silk flags for the last time as the sun fused with the western horizon of Ethiopia; then drove over to the Little Palace, where all the great were assembled.

The most indefatigable people that I met in Ethiopia were the missionaries.

I drove up with Buxton and young Gurney of the Bible

Churchman's mission. A large benzine box in the backseat seemed to strike a familiar note. I turned it over, and I am afraid that I was blasphemous. "Goodness gracious," said I, "those are the Gospels brought back from Dessye because I thought they were benzine." "Yes," said Buxton doggedly, "you couldn't get them through to headquarters then, so I'm going to present them to the Emperor now." He added that he wanted to ask the Emperor's permission to do another Gospel into Amharic: Mark, I reckon it was, but I was too stupefied by Buxton's singleness of purpose in the crisis to make sure.

All the Ministers were beside the Empress's pavilion at the Little Palace. In heavy silence Igezu sat on a chair outside, in the portico. Little Sirak Herrouy, wearing an overcoat and a B.N.C. muffler against his asthma, leant against a pillar: George, his brother, of Trinity College, Cambridge, in riding breeches, against another. Both waiting silent. Dr. Martin's sons were there, in khaki, their motor bicycles parked in the yard outside. Mischa Babitcheif stood alongside, rather pale, with Ayenna Birru in a British warm: Ayenna Birru, the young Wallega mining engineer, trained at the Camborne School of Mines, who had constructed for the Emperor the road surveyed by Bietry. All the little boys who had camped with him to learn road-making, had been blown to bits by bombs, or died of exhaustion in the retreat. Spencer waited with Tasfai, who looked bored. All the young Ethiopians stood around, waiting, doing nothing, talking very little.

Suddenly everyone stiffened. One of the two doors in the pavilion opened. Palace servants, bare-footed and their shammas drawn over the sword-arm, ran out to clear the porch. The Emperor followed.

He was dressed in khaki as a general. His aspect froze my blood. Vigour had left the face, and as he walked forward he did not seem to know where he was putting his feet. His body was crumpled up, his shoulders drooped: the orders on his tunic concealed a hollow, not a chest.

I did not know it then, but later I learned that the chiefs whom he had ordered out, some of whose troops had cheered the very order, refused to go.

They pleaded inability to assemble their soldiers.

They appeared behind the Emperor now, completely satisfied with their excuses. Getatchu had even donned a new pair of grey trousers, with a military stripe down the side, immaculately creased. He smelt of fresh scent.

They did not realise, as the Emperor realised, that their reluctance had destroyed the last chance of organised military resistance in Ethiopia. They still believed themselves to be great leaders of men: Getatchu wore his khaki cloak and period pantaloons with the air of an African Albert the Good. No discredit attached to him. . . .

Gates of the courtyard opened. A small boy in shorts, the sixteen-year old son of Addis' Mayor or Kantiba, led in his household troops. A dozen buglers ahead blew a smart salute. Nine hundred men followed, armed with new Mausers, marching well, carrying gas masks. As they passed the saluting base they eyes-righted the Emperor.

He did not respond, scarcely raised his hand. He recognised no one. His eyes focussed neither on objects nor on space. After the shock of the final disobedience, the parade which he was now forced to attend meant nothing, and he bitterly paid it no attention.

He went back into the pavilion. Buxton drew near with his box of Bibles, but he could not speak to the Emperor: none of us could speak to him, not even the young adviser Spencer. It was gathering dusk and I quietly mounted the Pavilion steps. Both doors were a little open, the right and the left. Many dark figures waited still, leaning against the walls and pillars. Shooting was beginning in the town below.

I stood between the doors and looked in. The Emperor lay back in the corner of a deep sofa, utterly exhausted, his high black hair showing like a halo over a face without feeling. The Empress sat erect at the other end, with her finger raised. Occasionally the white net on her head shook as she emphasised a point. When he said wearily that he would fight on, she insisted that he should fly. The sixteen-year-old boy stood by for orders, but they never came: he marched his soldiers of a day back to their homes, to the latest bugles of Ethiopia.

For hours the Empress lectured the Emperor. In the next room Ras Getatchu and the Crown Prince sat in the far corner on the floor, where thick carpets were piled, drawing their khaki mantles round them, joking and laughing. Under the coverless glare of the electric light which burnt from the yellow ceiling, they showed in its naked, almost effete outline, the terrible irresponsibility in time of crisis to which the Emperor was one of the few exceptions among leading Ethiopians. Ras Kassa, noble head and talkative tongue, was called into the Emperor's sombre chamber. Selecting the easiest chair, he crossed his legs for a long sitting, and opened his Nestorian preamble. The young Ethiopians outside grumbled a little more, then melted away into the dark. "We shall never see the Emperor," they said, "now that Kassa has got in." They never did.

I said good-bye to Sirak, George, the Martins, Ayenna Birru, to some of them for the last time, I fancy. They were all young men educated abroad, and they did their duty. With a premonition of regret I looked out after them into the blackness of Addis Ababa thinly pierced with flame even now.

It must have been then that the Emperor at last decided to go. Reason, the appeal to the League, allied itself to the instinct of flight: reason in exhaustion found itself the weaker second to the partnership.

Ato Wolde Giorghis was sent up to the British Legation. Ras Kassa stopped talking. Imru, who had arrived in Debra Markos, was informed by telephone of his sovereign's decision.

XXI

THAT NIGHT I HAD TO GO back to Ras Mulugeta Bet, my house, in a taxi. There was a lot of shooting into the stars all over the town, and as Margarita, Lolita and I sat in the flat two or three bullets dropped lightly on the side of the house and ricochetted into the gutters. Ozanne, the elegant dark correspondent of Havas who usually lived next door, had gone two weeks before, because, he declared, Mme. Hardy's flimsy walls were penetrable by rifle or pistol-fire, and if they were attacked they would be caught in a trap. So Ozanne had been given a small farewell party by the girls, who twitted him upon his anxiety, and had spent the short remainder of his days in Addis with Sibelinsky, the French radio director. For solidarity, they slept in the same room. Ozanne soon left for Djibouti.

Mme. Reval also, another most attractive French correspondent, abandoned Mme. Hardy's that night, darkly hinting that one might be able to see the show better from the station. (By this time the Emperor had decided to go, Pasteau of the railway had been informed, and Pasteau had warned his friend, Mme. Reval). Mme. Reval hurriedly packed up all her pretty belongings and drove to the station.

On the homeward road I felt an ominous calm. The bars were shut, there was no shouting or fighting to be heard. Ido had closed down and gone to bed. Mme. Ido could be seen taking her last or her penultimate stiff whisky. The zabanias who usually lounged, covering their blue Belgian uniforms tightly with a warm shamma in the rusty corrugated iron refuges provided by the Police Commissariat, had disappeared. They used to ask me sleepily as I walked by, "*sint saat?*"—"What's the time?", and the answer which regularly satisfied them, "*sidist saat,*" midnight, as regularly reminded me that my last interpreter had stolen my watch. But that night there was no one to ask as we drove by. Only through the town, from the direction of the Upper and Lower Palaces, huge lorries with blazing headlights passed with a roar through the dark, an endless chain of noise and ponderousness as they took the boxes of silver thalers from the bank to the station, took the Princess's shammas and first western clothes to the station, took the Emperor's own modest baggage to the station, and every time returned ravenously for more.

Balcha was at the gate with his spear and I went straight to bed, tired with the long waiting outside the Imperial pavilion. While I slept, at about four o'clock in the morning, the Imperial family arrived at the station, the relatives, the notables, the palace servants, some of the ministers and directors of some of the ministries, and the Emperor's dogs. One got lost and was recovered later by a French station employee, who did not like men who were not white and treated the little dog badly because it had been the domestic pet of one of them. "A very dirty dog," he said, judicially, after the terrified animal had been shut up in the kitchen and rubbed itself against the stove for four days. The Emperor drove to Akaki station at four-twenty, boarded the train, and so left his capital. The fragile figure, thin features shadowed by the long hands, leaned back against the white cushions of the Imperial coach. Palace servants embraced his feet to salute and comfort him, while in the luminous grey before sun-rise he looked out on the dim Shoan plain, cold and sleeping still, and thought in bitter impassivity of this fearful finish. The exhaustion was too much: he hoped that he had not betrayed his people, he only knew that many had betrayed him.

The train slipped slowly away down curve after curve, leaving the Amharic plateau. . . .

I woke up at seven; there was shooting all round. Bayenna, the new interpreter, was called in to explain. He said that the two Gibbis were open and one could take what one wanted. The Emperor, he said, commanded that all his possessions should be distributed among his people.

We took out Harrison's Opel, and together went off to the Gibbis. Bayenna tried to stop us. "They will kill you," he said. "They are getting out the new rifles," but we were off. At the cross-roads, by the cracking Parliament House which had not been used since the Emperor's speech in July, 1935, Ethiopians were running along laughing from the Old to the New Gibbi, furnished by Waring and Gillow only two years before. Some had drawn new rifles, which they fired off into the air to see if the ammunition fitted: others had disarmed the Adowa veterans at the Imperial Gate. There was none of that bored lounging which one usually saw around the Palaces: the petitioners who sat in a row nasalising "Abiet!", the thin brown line had disappeared. No longer was a torpid curiosity evinced in the tank which, camouflaged in the Ethiopian national colours, had been run out of the Palace some weeks before on to a neighbouring hillock for fear that it would be bombed with the rest of the building. No sitting, no squatting, no Amharic slumber. Everyone was at a smart jog-trot to see what he could get. We turned up towards the Little Palace.

Waring and Gillow were coming out by instalments. A chair here, a carpet there, an electric bulb in one hand and a book from the Emperor's library in another. A woman passed staggering under a roll of tapestry. Another gainful woman kicked her behind, rolled the tapestries off her back, and ran off with the brightest one.

We turned off along the road which led by the prison to the caves where ammunition and rifles were kept. The stocks were not meagre. The arms embargo, withdrawn a little after the Italian aggression was launched, enabled what stocks of arms the Emperor could buy to reach Addis, (slowly, because the French would not allow their passage by the railway from Djibouti), some time after the Ethiopian armies had gone north. The mobilisation for Sidamo in January had provided an outlet for some of these weapons, but most were still lying in the caves untouched. By a crooked turn of fate, the embargo was going to work itself out on the people who imposed it.

Round the caves they were fighting for weapons. The

criminals had slipped out of jail and were using knives. Once a gun or a box of cartridges, Mauser 7.95, was actually cornered the owner's claim to it, at this period, was admitted: zero hour for ownership struck when the trial shot had been fired through the bluegum branches. Before that, fists or knives could be used to hit or hack the loot out of the other man's hands. Balambaras Abebe, chief of the town police, went through the crowd with a few tough blue-coated *zabanias*, trying to beat it into order and silence. But it took no notice, so he captured most of the machine-gun rifles and went away. Bayenna disappeared. He had dropped down into a gulley to take seven hundred and fifty rounds of Mauser. We caught hold of the chauffeur as he, too, was moving off, and drove down to the station for the nine-twenty departure for Djibouti. All the shops were shut and barred, but the centre of the town was quiet.

Lorenzo Taezaz, on the platform, said he was following the Emperor to Diredawa. Actually he had not been informed of his master's movements until the Imperial train had gone; when the nimble Eritrean packed up his luggage and followed, his revolver in his pocket in case he met the Italians on the line. Nethercote, the British repair-shops expert, was off too, to try for another job with the Imam of the Yemen—bending Ethiopian rifles straight and knocking their sights back into position no longer appealed to him. The Swedish military mission was also making for the coast. The Emperor's cars and my own accompanied them. The train left late. Last minute Greeks and Armenians, sniffing the atmosphere in the capital, provided an opportunity for gain which the company could not refuse. Ten o'clock, and the train was off.

It was between nine and ten that hell broke loose in the capital: a general sort of hell to begin with, with a superintendent devil who grinned at you as he swigged the bottle, and never intended serious bodily harm. The police had got out of hand. Apart from the few behind Abebe, none had yet been allowed to go and loot their share in the palaces: they had to remain on irksome point duty. Some daring spirit suggested that they should enter Ghanotakis, the Italian-Greek grocer's shop which had been sealed as Italian property in October and consigned to the French, who protected Italian interests within as well as outside Ethiopia. Ghanotakis, once the smartest grocer in Addis, was now reduced to sultry exile at Djibouti, where he and his family sat hopefully before the progressive Italian pins upon a map of Ethiopia. He was known to possess excellent *Veuve Clicquot*. The police broke the heavy doors which had been shut seven months, cleared the champagne and the other drinks, shattered the bottle-necks upon the stone pavements and drained the contents through the jags.

Townspeople, back from the distribution of jumble at the Gibbis, saw this attractive sight. The *zabanias*, reeling slightly, thought of new shops to conquer. For the last ten days the Armenians had rolled up their steel shutters. . . . the French Legation. . . . In the flash of an eye, shop-breaking and looting became general. The poorer pillaged the richer and shot if they resisted. The class war, without distinction of colour and spontaneous as an African thunderstorm, broke with a crackle of rifles all over Addis Ababa.

I went back to our office, opposite the Radio, decided to clear and quit the place. Already Ethiopians, a little tipsy, were running up from Fernandez, the Goanese tailor's shop, comically covered with the top hats of the Diplomatic Corps, left there for ironing. Others in tailcoats followed, and a blind-drunk woman in a bowler, with a knife in her hand, brought up the rear of the gay procession. Best to get indoors, where I collected camera, field-glasses and cash, destroyed a few carbons of messages which I did not want the Italians to see, and idiotically forgot seven bottles of champagne stored there against my nuptials. Downstairs again, I took the old closed Ford with the dirty Reuter flag upon it that had once belonged to Collins, and made for Margarita's flat.

The roads, so empty when I passed to the station, were now full again with the mobs back from the palaces, all tight and all with rifles. *Mon Ciné*, the elite Greek cinema-bar of the town, was smashed through windows and door; they were throwing or thrusting the smart new chairs through the gaps, gulping the liquor, playfully unrolling the films and pocketing the pictures of their favourite film stars as I passed. We had booked seats for *"Hell Below"* that night. It crunched as I drove over it.

Up the road another band was stealing spare parts for cars never in their possession from Paleologue, the Greek agent of Ford. In the Greek bookshop which had once hung out *The Times Weekly* poster of October, "Nations Follow Britain's Lead," they were taking free copies of *La Vie Parisienne*. And all the Greek wine-shops or hotels, Magdalinos, Trohalis, Coccholios, Ageropoulos, who had imported huge stocks for the Italians, were voided by the Ethiopians in a jiffy. Their owners, behind the gates of the French Legation, regretted a stroke of commercial anticipation which had not reckoned with one essential factor, the Ethiopian in distress.

Margarita's flat faced this overflow of Chianti and stood next door to Ido's. the French Bar. To get liquor off a Frenchman without paying for it tickled the more political Ethiopians. There was shooting within and ceaseless shooting in the streets.

I did not want to leave the car behind with the thalers in it, so I sent Harrison's interpreter up to look for the girls. I waited alone and unarmed in the car, more or less hiding under my *terai* and watching Junod, Swiss representative of the International Red Cross, as he laughed to see the looters shoot up Ido's from the safe position of his wooden balcony above the street.

Junod disappeared for three days. He was still laughing when they set fire to the hotel underneath him.

Selassie the interpreter came back. "They're not there," he said. For a moment I was distraught. Then I ran up the stairs, which were marked with fresh blood, and found one of Mme. Hardy's servants beating an intruder with his sword. They were looting the shop, but had not reached the flat. Another servant, armed, beckoned to me; then I understood. He did not want to show where they were to anybody he did not know. He pointed up to the roof. They had gone into the loft.

Weber, the Emperor's pilot, arrived at the same time with an armed party from the German Legation and we took the girls down the ladder. Lolita rather frightened . . . Margarita calm as ever, her surface only a little ruffled by amusement at the situation in which she found herself. Mme. Hardy followed, fairly giggling with worry and bursting her stocking as she clambered down. They collected a minimum of vital necessities, powder, toothbrushes and make-up, assembled their bags of silver, and made for the car.

The Ford, though a grand old car, was not made for riots in towns where all the population walked normally in the middle of the road.

In Addis the streets were only asphalted in the middle: there was a rough area on both sides for mules and beyond that, above a gutter, were the pavements for the pedestrians. But there was one flaw in this neat layout. The pavements had never been asphalted or even levelled smooth. So the pedestrians took the centre of the road, the cars were forced into the area reserved for mules, and the mules had to pick their way along the pavements.

The Ford was a poor car for such conditions. Its self-starter no longer responded to the foot, and when you applied the brakes it seemed to slide along faster. I drove to the Legation in terror of knocking someone over, getting caught in a crowd, in a quarrel, and prematurely in a coffin. I was scared stiff as we covered the four miles to the Legation. They fired haphazard across the bonnet, they hit out at the roof with swords and sticks, they made funny threatening faces and put me all of a twitter, but I drove the car through. They were attacking the offices of the Ethiopian Red Cross as we passed, and the streets were rolling with dollars, bandages and postage stamps. Half-way we were out of the trading districts and the crowds were less, but hungrier. Their eyes were turning the repulsive yellow-red, their faces wrinkling with the hard, cruel lines in which an Ethiopian encases himself when he is drunk. We thanked God when we saw the barbed wire and the fringed turbans of the Sikhs, entered the neat gateway and climbed the cool, empty drive of the British Legation, under the eucalyptus trees planted in Menelik's day. The girls went off to Lee's house to have a drink. Don had just come back from a hair-raising journey in a small open car to the French Legation. The Ethiopians, who reasonably detested the area, had shot across him on the hill.

He sat down, rather pale, in front of the wireless sets in his drawing-room, and tried to make contact with the other Legations and with Gardiner, the lawyer and correspondent of the *Daily Telegraph* who lived in the town. No good. Squeaks. Pink gins.

I went out again in the Ford, for the last time, alone. The atmosphere was even more alarming, drunkenness was deplorably on the increase, and the independability of the Ethiopian when drunk is extreme. Many of them were quite friendly, waving their rifles and shooting them off at me at the same moment. Others seeing me unaccompanied threatened to bar the Ford's passage: the only way to deal with these was acceleration aided by a hoot and a shout. I went on to my house; had the gates shut and manned. Servants came up to tell me cheerfully of the loot which they had already collected—Wodaju, the squat loathsome cook, who battered his way round the house in hobnailed sandals, had taken five hundred thalers from the Red Cross . . . Wolde Giorghis, the sayce who used to make beer out of the horses' barley, had stolen a splendid old gun . . . Bayenna had returned with his seven hundred and fifty government cartridges. I handed out my own sporting Mauser and dead Burgoyne's shotgun to Wolde the headboy, collected tent, beds, shirts, shorts and notebooks which I valued, and returned to the Legation. The house was full of stores, eatable and drinkable. In a moment of stark unenlightenment I offered a bottle of whisky to Wolde and vile Wodaju. They were to hold the house till I came back, aided by the arms which I had lent them and the bottle of whisky to repair their spirits under fire. Wodaju boastfully waved his own revolver, but even at this preliminary stage his eyes was more closely fixed upon the bottle. I realised, too late, what an ass I had been.

Bayenna asked to come with me to the Legation. I said yes, and thought him a coward—and during the next three days found how loyal he was. The Ford was loaded up behind, but not high enough for the bedding to appear above the windows and encourage loot. As we left, the Klaxon, which had been hanging by a thread, fell off in a definite manner, and a tyre, torn to pieces by the broken glass which now littered the roads, quietly flattened out. Nothing to do now but shriek the whole time and beat upon the tin of the front door next the driver's seat, while Bayenna did the same with a stick at my side. The Ethiopians in the street, long advised of our progress, thought the combination rather too funny, rather too worthless to attack, though speed on the enfeebled tyre was funeral slow. Our pauper vehicle arrived before lunch at the British Legation, a perfect embodiment of Masefield's British coaster, whose cargo was a patriotic cacophony of old tin trays.

Harrison was there. So were Miss Collier, sister of the Director of the Bank of Ethiopia, and Mrs. Gardiner, who had both motored up at speed. Mrs. Gardiner was worrying about her husband, of whom no news by note or wireless. Mrs. Martin, the divorced wife of the Ethiopian Minister in London, had come in with her two daughters —her sons, she said, had left for the west yesterday. The Abuna was there, resting as usual: the noise in the town had been too much for that idle monk. His church had been looted, so had other churches. Evidently the work in the shops was over and they were going for large buildings, beginning with their own churches.

We heard that Armenians were defending themselves in their church on the main road, near my house. The Martins' house was being looted. The gilt Imperial chairs which had been stored there against an air-raid were departing in the direction of Dessye, man-portered.

There were still in the town—Wright and Press of the Bank, De Clermont and Davidson of commerce, and the English Church chaplain, Matthew. Missionaries were also defending themselves at odd points. The Buxtons, at the Bible Churchman's, maintained a gentlemanly restraint, but comic notes would come in from others . . . "SOS, *please*, we are fighting for our lives." Old Hanner, the Swedish surgeon, had seen his hospital looted. When he entered the dispensary they were opening the medicines and smelling them. "That is gas," said Hanner gloomily, and the Ethiopians scattered. Gathering up his little stock of Swedish grey steel helmets and sharing them out among his Swedish nurses, Hanner put the party into his Swedish glass-covered motor ambulance and drove them to the British Legation. There was quite a cheer when the Medicine Militant arrived, looking clean, blonde and startled, at the ironwork gate. The Sikhs saluted, gravely asked for arms, let them pass.

Americans, Armenians, Greeks, Syrians, Swiss poured in. Cypriots and Jews, Portuguese and Sudanese, Egyptians and Somalis: it was like Pentecost, all of them praising the wonderful works of Barton. There were French and Germans who did not wish to go to their own Legations. There were Indians of every creed known to Abyssinia, Hindus, Sikhs, Muslims, Bohras, Parsees and Goan Christians. All the revisionist powers were represented, bar Italy. Here a Turk prowled, there a Jamaican. Latvia was not forgotten.

As each arrived, he was registered and given a coloured ticket, for the big paddock behind Patrick Roberts' bungalow had been divided into camping areas, separating those who might otherwise clash on account of colour, creed, diet or matrimonial prejudice. All their firearms were taken away, and as old Stordy, the Quartermaster, put it: "scrupulous care in searching everyone entering the grounds had to be exercised, for even beneath the voluminous skirts of the Greek clergy automatic pistols and pouches of ammunition were to be found."

The Sikhs lifted up the voluminous skirts at the gates to look.

We found a fair amount of good European dum-dum. The arms were stored with the Quarter Guard, and we used to loot them whenever we wanted to go into the town.

The British Red Cross, it was said, were doing wonders there. After lunch we sallied out in Melly's car.

It was on April 30 that the British Red Cross Unit, which had last been in action when it rescued the Dutch Red Cross beyond Tarmaber, decided that it would give up field work. The Abyssinian armies in the north were broken and footing it wearily for the capital. Some were coming in from Fiche, where the Emperor's men lay, but most were of the armies of Bidwoded Makonnen of Wallega and Dedjazmatch Moshesha of Kambata, and their line of retreat was along the caravan track from Warra Hailu. I had met them before at Dessye.

Quiet, orderly, tired as they struggled along, they became

like wild animals when they were offered food or clothing. They grabbed madly at anything given to them, and shrieked for more. Then they relapsed into that emotionless state which is the sole outward sign of Ethiopian demoralisation: that, and conversation in whispers as they trudged along. It was from thirst that they suffered most. They had only lacked food in the last few days. A quick survey by the Red Cross Unit showed that eighty per cent. of them were suffering from amoebic dysentery. No typhus, little fever, but in this overwhelming proportion the milder of the two forms of dysentery, which would knock over a white man but did not incapacitate these soldiers from marching four hundred miles without tents or cover.

For endurance, speed and resistance to disease the Ethiopians, and with them their brothers the Eritreans, are some of the best material in the world.

These men, however, needed treatment before they went to their homes. The British Red Cross took over the sorting post in the plantations near the British Legation gate, and were given permission to use the Empress' school behind the Little Gibbi, a well-made modern building, typical of the Emperor's educational reforms. Next day they moved their lorries and stores of food into the Legation and started shifting the school-books out and the beds into the new hospital. It opened to in-and out-patients on the afternoon of Friday, May 1, at the same time as the Ethiopian Council of Ministers was holding its last meeting. In two hours twenty-five sick and wounded from the north had been bedded in the class-rooms. I don't think any, even of them, realised that they would wake up next morning to the frenzied fusillade.

On Saturday their interpreters, unlike Bayenna, ratted at once, though some of them had been with their masters for years. Of the nine members of the Unit at this time only Bentinck could talk really cursive Amharic: the rest could say "knife" and "saddle" and "bring it" and "shut up" and the other sensible words. The Austrian Schuppler and the Welsh Vaughan-Jones, who were added to their number before the day was out, brought with them no local linguistic ability. However, they divided up the hospital and the relief work between them, collected lorries at the Legation, and went out into the town.

Theirs were the first lorries to circulate in convoy—the old Bedfords with the tattered canvas covers to the wagon, and the rusting Red Cross on top and sides. In the Legation the emblem had to be concealed: we did not want the Unit to be bombed again, and in diplomatic territory. But now the camouflage was removed and the lorries, creaking already from their long war-service on the Northern Road, heroes of more than one bombardment, rolled out to do their last duty in the field. Three or four *zabanias* with rifles were stuck behind under the tent, and the driver, white or black, usually carried a revolver: a white member of the Unit, perhaps armed, sat beside him.

Their work was double. The relief of Europeans who were or might be attacked. Care for any wounded found in the streets or houses. Slowly coasting along, almost smelling the streets for corpses, they at once attracted curiosity when they stopped to pick them up: and in those days in Addis it was a short step from curiosity to rifle fire.

One saw little or no signs of conscious xenophobia during the Addis riots. The beginning had been a good-humoured affair, a Black Hampstead Heath or Dusty Mafeking. Everybody joined in: it was understood that picking or stealing, in such times, was innocent and natural. When Bentinck arrived at the Red Cross Headquarters to see if the records of the Unit could be saved, he found that the place had been housebroken already. So he sent his servants in to reconnoitre . . . grand boys . . . absolutely trustworthy. He waited in the car outside, two minutes . . . five minutes . . . ten minutes . . . irritably he rose, pushed into the Committee Room and there were the best boys in Ethiopia on their hand and knees, scrambling with all the other ragamuffins for thalers. They were severely admonished. This was theft. The boys looked partly mystified, wholly hurt. Theft? Good God, call it *theft*?

Drink, as the day wore on and rifles originally vertical dropped lower and lower, brought out that basic mistrust of the foreigner which the behaviour of Europe in the Italo-Ethiopian dispute had so fully justified. In their fuddled condition, the old ideas cropped up . . . .

Empey, the second-in-command of the Red Cross Unit, was patrolling the streets for wounded that afternoon. He stopped in the centre of the town to pick up a man covered with blood in the gutter. As he bent over him, an Ethiopian standing by shoved a rifle into his side and fumbled with drunken fingers for the trigger, grunting *"ferengi!"* Friendly Ethiopians, both of the escort and the crowd, pulled him off before he had stumbled upon that part of the mechanism essential to the discharge of his antiquated gun—"You fool, you bastard," they shouted, "Ghai Maskal!" "Red Cross!"

Empey staggered back under his load and they beat it for the hospital.

By midday the whole of Armenian Piccadilly had been looted. In the early afternoon fire began to crackle in Magdalino's Hotel, in the very centre of the town.

On the south-west side, around the market, the streets were sprinkled with dead. An old bearded Armenian, who had resisted loot, lay in the roadway where he had been dragged from his shop by the feet, which were lashed together by a rope. A bullet in the head had finished him. We called him "Old Bluebeard," and he got bluer and bluer as we passed on our evening evacuations.

The market itself, and the rickety Greek, Armenian, Indian and Arab stalls which, at points, gave it a claim to be something more than indigenous, were emptied early. Under cover of what structures remained, bands of Ethiopians were picking about in the ruins for humbler loot. But the dead who streaked the cobbles south of the market had fallen to the guns of British subjects and those mistakenly called "protected persons"; for they proved thoroughly capable of looking after themselves.

Centre of the British resistance was the shop of Mohamedally; dealers in all kinds of cotton and tinware, sellers of Chevrolets and benzine, manufacturers of flour and high-powered soda-water. Also private bankers and licensed experts in the thaler market. A grand firm from Bombay, India, owned and kept in the Mohammedan family. "Hindus make good accountants, but they're no good as salesmen," said a juvenile Mohamedally to me. In the directors' room, between walls from which looked amiably down the heads, in gold-braided caps, of the Mohamedally major prophets who had established the concern, with here and there a faded photographic glimpse of Menelik moodily stumping round their earliest wood and iron stores, the minor prophets of 1936 concerted with Mr. Hope-Gill, British Consul, organisation of the defence of their town property: concerted to a mad tune played upon the rifles of their faithful *zabanias*. Able lieutenant to their strategy was the Persian engineer who on happier days blew the bubbles into their celebrated soda-water.

Hope-Gill spent the whole of Saturday with them. I got rather worried; he was meant to marry me off on Monday. But when I drove down after lunch with Taylor, the Military Attaché, Hope-Gill was still well, beaming from under his cavalier sombrero and above his romantic beard as he manned the iron gate leading to Mohamedally's great yard.

All the glass of the front windows of Mohamedally had been smashed by bullets in the morning's concerted attacks upon the store. Bags of bran and flour had been hauled up level with the gaps which the Mohamedally major prophets, prognosticating with the fabled aplomb of the East, had fitted with iron bars. Bran and flour packed up the gate, which was of the kind of iron that looks strong but finally bends, like Clark Gable.

They started to blaze away again while we stood at the entrance and discussed the future with Hope-Gill. I turned pale and ducked, Taylor irritatingly began to knock his pipe out. Little Selassie, Harrison's interpreter, pleasantly took advantage of my prostrated condition to report that they had just killed another European above the market.

Arabs and Hindus, all British, lived on either side of Mohamedally. From their balconies they kept up a continuous fire on the streets. They lacked arms: so they picked off likely-looking Ethiopians carrying modern weapons, then sallied forth to strip the dead.

When this relationship was seen to be unprofitable to both parties, a truce of the kind described by newspapers as "uneasy" was arranged and *shiftas* with a surplus of rifles or cartridges would come forward to sell them to Britain at a modest price. Basra's shop was bristling with light automatics when I saw it on Sunday.

All Hope-Gill feared was fire. We picked up the Padré from the English church, then went back.

Magdalinos was well aflame; Ghanotakis, a mess of tortured iron shutters and broken bottles and counters, had caught the hot infection. A wind was blowing the fire in thirsty tongues across the roadway. Beyond the triumphal arch of Haile Selassie, nailed together out of gorgeous plaster, somebody had been tampering with the benzine in Paleologue's garage. The orange god of arson was licking the lip-like windows of Paleologue in preparation for a feat, and looking up the hill to the wooden shops and Armenian shanties that surrounded Giorghis; whose roof still seemed as if it had been made of silver.

We stopped at Mme. Hardy's. All looted. All the doors broken. Two drunken Ethiopians, a man and a woman, sat with an appearance of immovable sottish gravity upon two rocking-chairs. When they saw me and my melodramatic gun they slowly rose and, in a dignified way, tumbled the whole flight downstairs.

Old Bevan and Mrs. Bevan of a Mission nearby were called upon by Taylor, who in a military manner asked them if they would care to be saved. He spent a hair-raising twenty minutes in the car in front of the house while they squared the matter with their consciences within and the Ethiopians with their rifles without.

It was two days before their place was looted. An ancient Abyssinian convert, on Bevan's instructions when he left, sat behind the counter and handed, with appropriate solemnity, a copy of the Gospels to any thief who staggered in.

The clergy were at it too. As I passed Bohnenberger's, once the leading photographic firm of Addis, a tipsy Ethiopian priest staggered out with a roll of film in his hand. I fancy he mistook it for a sporting cartridge.

The poorest Europeans, pathetically shabby and dirty, were still struggling out to the Legations. Near the Makonnen Bridge which marked the right turn of Addis's main street, a wretched Greek woman stumbled along crying her heart out, supported and protected on either side by two hollow-eyed, hollow-cheeked elderly Levantines. Her reddish hair was streaming away where an Ethiopian had grabbed her hat, for many were running past her this way and that; she still wore an old fur-collared coat, and under her bedraggled sleeve she carried what looked like three pictures, no other luggage. As we came near, she stopped in the way and shrieked hysterically. We took her into the car, and the men clung to the running-board.

As we pressed on to our refuge gates she showed the pictures. They were ikons, her household gods. Perhaps the fall of Troy was something like it: perhaps the founder of Rome escaped through the flames with only these. She shook as she feebly handled them, she was thin and mad with fear; all she could say was Smyrna: poor wretch! it was her second massacre. Cheaply philosophising, I thought of the naked filthiness of war. The Virgin in the picture looked at us, in beautiful robes, oval-faced, bland and still.

That afternoon Flick and two other horses were ridden by Wolde and the sayces up to the Legation. Bayenna arrived with his wife and a little tent. I went out once more, in a Greek lorry this time, with the Greek priest, a martial young man whose swart hair was tied up in a bun in which he stuck spare cartridges. Wolde, good servant, put his arm round my neck and covered me unnecessarily. The streets were filled with smoke, the flames were running from shop to shop, cars which had crashed or been abandoned at the roadside were burning, hot black refuse in our way could be seen through the level glare of the descending sun and the harsh, irritating breath of the furnace which started tears from our eyes. A few Ethiopians, in bands, hacked at the side of the lorry. In the waste setting of broken and flaming Addis Ababa, with the telephone wires in tangled black nets dangling across the roadway, to the tune of shattered glass under our lorry wheels, their faces and the lie of the straddled corpses looked too unbearably horrible.

Order here had been a flimsy thing, sustained by the superb will of a single individual. Its destruction, in a welter of fire, dirt, explosions, was suddenly visible in every sordid detail. The bodies were beginning to stink, the people were beginning to loot the richer private houses. The Greeks, who had come out to save, they said, Greek families trapped behind Magdalinos, talked excitably together, shook their revolvers at salient passages and decided to return home, when their leader had salvaged all his personal luggage from a point somewhere nearer safety.

They said that they were afraid the bottles would puncture the tyres: I said I was afraid of a lot more things.

Eaten by flame, the Haile Selassie triumphal arch fell with a hollow smack in the Post Office square. As the General Post Office crumbled before the onset of the general fire, its corrugated iron roofing decapitated a body on the flagged path below. Only the double triangles of Solomon which crowned a little monument in the centre of the square seemed in their sapient aloofness to be standing the test of civil war. A machine-gun opened a chaotic conversation from Kevorkoff's, once the tobacco monopoly of Ethiopia: but the prices were down, the whole city was smoking now.

The Greeks decided to go home to the British Legation. As night fell, a great pillar of fire stood up from the city. Rifle-fire was still incessant, the Sikhs were at their posts round the barbed wire. Lolita and Margarita curled themselves to sleep on the sofa in the Bartons' drawing-room. The Belgian Minister cocked up a pair of heels under the picture of King George and Queen Mary in the Durbar Hall.

I went to bed in Taylor's room in Patrick Roberts's bungalow. Taylor collects reptiles, and his mantelpiece gave pride of place to a row of jam bottles full of the new varieties which he had gathered from the Ogaden and stifled in spirits of wine. It was while I was goggling at his unhappy frogs, purple, green and brown like the tickets for the refugee camp and similarly stuffed together, that I fell asleep.

Harrison and Lowenthal snored between the carpets in the room next door. That night Galla came in from the countryside and evirated the corpses round the market, while the Arab automatics kept up a running commentary.

The show was to continue for three more days. The disorganised looting in the city was to become more and more organised, the bands bigger, more clever and better armed. Eventually they were going to attack the Legation quarter.

Sunday morning we got up very early. Trapman, the Vice-Gonsul, who usually played Fox in the Paperchase, had been out collecting nuns till midnight. Taylor rolled out his little Ford pick-up, himself took the steering-wheel, and others of the Plughole climbed behind. Bayenna joined the crew with a rifle.

He told me that my house had been attacked and completely looted during the night. They had taken all his savings, about two hundred dollars.

We drove out slowly to the German Legation, upon a narrow, devious cobble track.

Little Weber came running down to the Legation gate and asked me to take him and his three mechanics to Jan Meda, the small central airport on the racecourse owned by the Diplomatic Corps, where he had been making his new plane, the Beby Weber. Behind his huge moustaches Taylor gruffed approval.

As we drove fast to the racecourse, the citizens of Addis Ababa walked unconcernedly past us, taking huge bundles of loot into the country.

One of the Emperor's cars drove by at top-speed. Abreast an Ethiopian inside fired a rifle plumb between me and Trapman, breezing past my longish nose, which I hastily withdrew and concealed. Trapman and I looked at each other in complete surprise: he had been happily singing, I day-dreaming.

At the edge of the airport, under the trees, the Junker aeroplane in which Weber had made many adventurous flights stood intact. He climbed inside, found the maps and his flying-suit were gone from the open cockpit. His German friends swung the propeller, in a minute it was running and the wind had whisked off the disguise of leaves on the silver wings. Slowly he taxied on to the course. To our astonishment the Government *zabanias* ran up from cover nearby and said "Stop!" They had been on guard at the aerodrome ever since the Emperor left.

Little Weber stood up sturdily in his cockpit, pointed to the Red Richthofen cap which was all that remained of his kit, and said: "Open the gates, I am the Government."

We covered the *zabanias* with our machine-guns, rifles, revolvers and cigarette-lighters.

Charmingly, like all Ethiopians when making the best of a bad job, they bowed to the earth, sliding back the left leg in a motion more graceful than a curtsey, kissed the ground at the wheels of the plane, opened the barriers:

Weber took off in a barrage of fire from the houses round the airport.

He flew straight for Roseires on the roughest of rough calculations, without maps or knowledge of the route. He was forced down by lack of benzine only a few miles from his destination, his luggage, a box of thalers and his gold false teeth: his chart his wits.

In the town we found some of the female missionaries at Fulwuha particularly troublesome. Mrs. Stadin, an old friend of mine at Dessye, had just succumbed to a spent bullet which, slipping through the roof at five a.m., had penetrated her temple as she lay asleep in bed. The other women had immediately bolted for the bombproof shelter, a magnificent structure worthy of "Journey's End" — every stage property was there; rocking rafters, falling dust, hard-bitten guys (the male missionaries) and hystericals (some of the females).

It took a quarter of an hour to get the women out of the earth, half an hour to decide them to leave the mission, and another half-hour to pack their belongings. Bentinck and I had rescued some of them before from Dessye: I was terrified that they would break out again into missionary spirituals to encourage the rapine of the Ethiopian. We publicly drained bottles of beer, not because we liked it, but to shock them into silence.

The nasty part of the show was that it was so unpredictable. Llewellyn, the Tanganyika colonel who looked after the base work of the Red Cross Unit, was saying how plumb safe it was when a drunk in khaki stuck his revolver into Melly's ribs outside Ido's ruined bar, and shot him through the lung. A fearful wound. The blood poured through his jacket as he lay back in the driver's cab and Gatward accelerated for the hospital.

I liked Melly immensely. I have heard that when he was in Abyssinia before the war he sometimes sang hymns during dinner. But when he came out as chief of the British Ambulance Unit, his religion had discarded an earlier exhibitionism and found more exhilarating humane work to do.

If there had been no Melly there would have been no British unit. We would not have had the honour to be bombed by Signor Mussolini's son, and the Ethiopians whom we betrayed would never have seen visible evidence of our intention to aid them. We might never have assured ourselves against the earnest hopes of official doubt, that the Italians really were spraying gas on savages.

A few hundred blacks would never have been treated for their wounds, but would have died, like the vast mass of their fellows, on the worn caravan tracks of Tigre and the edge of the plateau, waterless, gangrened, sunstruck, ragged and eaten with worms.

Our contribution to end the Italo-Ethiopian war was this little patch, stuck on to one of the thousand small-pox holes that covered Bellona's once pretty face. That was all that could be wrung out of England, who had pledged so much: I honour Melly who could do it.

He died on Tuesday, conscious and in pain until the end. His last three days were spent in the Legation, but it was impossible to save him. A missionary on the noble scale, he had planned before the war to build a modern hospital at Harrar which would be the finest in Africa, had raised the money and won the Emperor's approval. He died on Tuesday as the Italians bussed in, his work finished: pleased perhaps that he was no longer needed, since the aggressors were bringing peace, civilisation and occasion for still more hospitals to backward Africa.

The benzine store near the station, which had been enlarged greatly during the last fortnight and would have solved an Italian problem when Badoglio entered, shot up to heaven in a roaring funnel of flame.

Around it, day and night, the Ethiopians coolly loaded camels with the goods from the railway go-downs, including bales of Italian flags which had mysteriously passed up from Djibouti in the last week. Long strings of the brown plateau camels, tied neck to tail and sleeping contemptuously on their flat feet, paid no heed while their owners piled cotton goods, coffee and clanking tinware on their dry leather pack-saddles.

The railway police and the French staff kept up a desultory fire, occasionally dropping the old beggars who, dazed and deafened with disease, still crawled about the main street and scratched for sustenance; but they wisely stuck to their station defences. In the stationmaster's office Gerbal, the stout director of the company, was telephoning fiercely down the line. Yes, *shiftas* had attacked Mojjo, the station where one stopped for lunch on the first day down. *Ca va—telephone O.K.*—you can still get Hawash, and Hawash is sending to Diredawa for a party of French troops by the first train up.

Indiscipline was the rule at the station. Whenever a *Zabania* felt like it he fired his rifle into the sky: the ticket collector, now mobilised into an officer of infantry, would rush at him and box his ears. Another *zabania* would break the rule, a third amused himself by sending a spare shot through the station clock. Shouting on all sides, threats to chain up the disobedient only added to the turbulence of the defending classes. How the French get along astonishes me. They fight in a crazy atmosphere of mutual abuse and mock revolution, but they always win through. Their mutinous *zabanias* remained faithful to the end, sallying wildly whenever ordered, and shooting up every living thing in sight.

On the last day I went again to the station. There were only other people's servants to go for now. Rohrbaugh, the American missionary who had done *Times* work when I was in the Ogaden, lived in a house near the station which he defended throughout. But his domestic staff were unwise enough to unlatch the gate. In a frantic volley the railway *zabanias* killed one and knocked another flat.

Much of our killing was like that. If you give an Ethiopian a rifle and a lead he will take no risks in your defence. Bayenna was just the same: he insisted on joining every expedition that I was on. Whenever we drove past a nasty bunch of looters he covered them and twitched on the trigger.

By Sunday evening the centre of the town was burnt out. The shops had been looted on Saturday, undefended private houses on Sunday; it was the turn of the hospitals and the Legation quarter next. The American Legation, separated by the cinders and blackened iron sheeting of the town from the other Legations, sent up a message for help. The Sikhs, who had hitherto left their barbed wire entanglements only to patrol the road to the Belgian, German and French Legations, were dispatched by the Minister to evacuate their women.

Three lorries made ready in the dark, an officer in each

of the front two and myself sitting at the back of the rear lorry with an automatic in either delighted hand. The young Sikh who crouched by my side said, in soft English: "We won't shoot first, but won't we just shoot second." In the dark, illuminated only by the headlights and spurts of flame from the eucalyptus belt on the side of the town, we rumbled out of the Legation gates. Three Red Cross lorries and the vehicle driven by young Gurney of the Buxton mission followed us. We had taken out the wailing Ethiopian womenfolk of the mission that afternoon: only half an hour before one of his men had been shot down and the body rifled just outside his gate, but Buxton still refused to leave. We were going to fetch him now, with the rest of his men.

De Halpert, once Adviser to the Emperor's Ministry of the Interior, was running the Red Cross party. De Halpert is tall and good-looking, his hair grey to nearly white, in trimness of figure and face a very fit Englishman past middle age. The only one, too, who has walked all over Ethiopia—Amhara, Lasta, Wollo, Kambata, Kafa, Maji.

As a self-confessed sportsman, he had written the Emperor's licensing laws which more or less prevented you from shooting anything except at terrific expense, and gave the animals a wonderful time. Only in the south the bad men of the Galla border still poached ivory.

De Halpert was, I think, the coolest of the Europeans who patrolled Addis, at frightening risk, trying to see whether the people lying in the street were dead, drunk, or *bona fide* wounded. He even saved stray dogs. Dressed precisely as a member of the I.R.A., with long grey overcoat, sinister grey Homburg over one hawkish eye, and a pilfered British rifle slung across his shoulder, he never had to take a bead on any *shifta*. He only looked at them in a hostile manner and the criminal intention evaporated.

(Bentinck's method was different. He danced spasmodically on either leg and spoke fluent Amharic. But the effect was the same. The Ethiopian always bows to phenomena.)

We drove through the town, and for the first time I noticed the awkward flitting silhouettes of hyenas at the ruined roadside. Only Paleologue's garage was still burning in the centre, the fire was radiating out. No people about: volleys of shots from nowhere at nothing. The whole of Addis a gaunt empty shell, tangled with steaming rubbish and stifled with hot hanging air. The smoke still put the stars out.

Heroically we advanced upon the American Legation. We were prepared for anything, except to find that there was nobody defending the gate because no one was attacking it. Inside the refugees were twanging over their soup and beef hash. I have never assisted at such a sell.

Yet at that very moment a band were pouring shot into Gurney's lorry from the huts outside the mission. Two women behind were killed outright and Buxton received two bullets in the calf. Till then lorries had been sacrosanct.

We joined convoys again and went home. At a forced stop I saw a little heap beside the wheel. As I jumped down I noticed that everything round was smelling of stale Chianti, rotten bodies, unswept offal, the sort of things to which one was getting accustomed but in an exaggerated and more loathsome form. Old dead lay on the pavement.

The heap was a young boy, dead from a shot in the forehead. About fourteen, of a pale brown complexion, beautiful, once lively features, short nose and big eyelids. In his hand he had a blue *zabania's* cap which he must have taken for fun. Already the bone before his brain had coloured his skin purple along the fractures. His thin limbs were sprawled sweetly but a little stiffly over the broken road. The blood and they were slowly drying.

A stray shot must have levelled him among the drunken looters who fought for possession of something not worth having near the Pont Makonnen. I recommend that mothers keep their children indoors when the next war ends. The Ethiopians are poor shots, and for everyone of these massacred you will have ten in European streets.

War waged against the civilian population ends in the break-up of the civilian population into warring elements.

The dead in Addis were of all classes. Whites, Levantines, Amharas of rank, police, officials, priests, meat-porters, message-boys, beggars. They were of all ages. I saw dead women in the streets.

When the Italians came in they numbered them at over seven hundred. I believe that this, like most of their figures when they were discussing the enemy, was an exaggeration.

But of the many that I saw dead or dying, there is not one of them whose blood does not lie on the head of Mussolini. He is the deliberate murderer of all of them.

Let us give him a loan and bring him back into the European circle.

Monday morning was stored with fun for all of us.
The Armenians were put in the wood as a punishment.
Mlle. Margarita de Herrero spoilt part of the Legation garden.
Colonel Stordy tried to make bread.
And I got married.
I forget. One of the youngest Legation refugees blew his little thumb off playing with dum-dum.

I woke up determined to make a day of it. I had lost my own champagne, but I collared some bottles in the refugee camp: I shaved and looked about for clean clothes. Taylor, who was stirring early, advised a Russian marriage.

"A short one?" said I. "No," said Taylor contemptuously, "dress up like a Commissar." Taylor, who was always a little irritated by my slowness, thrust into my hands a khaki shirt, khaki trousers and my old boots. "That's quite enough for your wedding," said Taylor, and with a hint of scientific romance behind the violent moustaches: "our forefathers were satisfied with less," he added, glancing at the bottled frogs.

At the Legation gate I noticed an Ethiopian wearing a peculiar cap. Nearer, it became the D.L.V. (*Deutsche Luft Verband*) cap that belonged to Weber: so I took it off the Ethiopian to wear at my wedding.

An Italian plane flew over to see if the coast was clear. Falsetto applause from the Greeks and Armenians in the paddock. The Armenian children, who had been practising, jumped on their toes with delight. As a punishment, Lady Barton sped down to the paddock with a short umbrella and put them all in the Legation wood.

Margarita took advantage of her absence to pull up many of her arum lilies and super-daisies for a bridal bouquet. Bullets were still dropping monotonously into the Legation grounds and when Jean, Mme. Mardy's little boy had his back turned one went slick through his pillow at the garden side. Mlle, de Herrero leapt a trifle, but we decided to stick to our plan of an *al fresco* ceremonial.

By now the refugees were becoming uppish. Most had slept out on Saturday night, and though canvas was supplied on Sunday, exposed objects such as the countless sewing-machines which they seemed to value most, began to rust up in the rain.

Rations were distributed to them by Colonel Stordy, head of the Silver Star Veterinary Unit which had come out to Ethiopia for the R.S.P.C.A. in the last months of the war. Stordy comes from Midlothian, had once trekked up to Addis before the railway was built to see Lij Yasu, and experimented in wool-breeding for Leguia, the old dictator of Peru. He was appointed Quartermaster of the refugee camp and was responsible in the first place for its neat economical lay out. Stordy is broad, careful, elderly and eloquent.

With a Scotsman's gift for making passable oats grow out of stones, he watered the Greeks and Armenians from the nosebags of his Veterinary Unit. He soon had one thousand five hundred and twenty people to look after, whom he nicely docketed and camped out as follows:—

Americans, 31	Hungarians, 4
Arabs, 253	Jamaicans, 1
Armenians, 174	Jews, 16
Austrians, 8	Latvians, 2
Belgians, 12	Moslems, Indians, 198
Bohras, 160	Poles, 1
Brit. Islanders, 33	Portuguese, 6
Cypriots, 8	Russian, 12
Egyptians, 12	Scandinavians, 14
French, 15	Somalis, 30
German, 11	Spanish, 1
Goanese, 7	Syrians, 2
Greeks, 319	Turks, 29
Hindus, 161	

These unfortunate refugees he supplied with flour, rice, dal, ghee, lentils, sugar and salt, carefully measured to prevent excess.

Stordy has written a superb report. His copious Edinburgh style, with its warm after-glow of morality, cannot be equalled here. *Dura nutrix virum*, Old Stordy explains: "the more fortunate of the refugees eked out these by a small addition of canned provisions," but "the majority had to rest content with the plain but wholesome fare provided."

Did they just. Colonel Wordy, as we affectionately called him, continues on a homely Lowland note:

"The womenfolk of the various sections very promptly had their culinary arrangements made, camp fires set agoing and with such improvised girdles as iron drum-ends and petrol tin plates, and walking sticks for rolling pins, were soon busily toasting chapatees and scones for their families."

This pretty picture was not enough for the Armenian Family Robinson, who demanded a bread ration, and with the usual extravagance of unlucky minorities began comparing conditions under the Turks and the English.

Old Stordy, cannily detecting the rising temper of his charges, had been building a camp oven.

On Monday the clay was still damp and the fuel, as Stordy describes it, "was too green to be of any calorific value"; in other words it wasn't fuel. But Stordy had decided to settle with the insurgents before it was too late. He began to bake bread.

The dough made a lazy attempt to rise, then relapsed into a heavy sleep. With an optimistic look in his eye, Stordy distributed what he calls "small bread" to the refugee camp. "It cannot be claimed that the bread was a shining example of the baker's art," he craftily writes.

Small bread settled the camp once and for all. With small bread in their stomachs they never rose again, not even for an Italian aeroplane. Stordy showed us how universal constipation can lay a revolution.

"All thanks," he concludes, "are due to the skilled bakers who willingly gave their services in an endeavour to provide the camp with a bread ration."

About this time a lead bullet whizzed through the doorway of the Legation hospital, skimmed the head of a nun who was praying there, and fixed in the floor. Stordy, who is a good Protestant, writes that she was "recumbent," but in my view she was only an Irish Catholic.

The crew of the pick-up went down the town to see if any more respectable wedding garments could be found in my house.

Bedlam must literally have been let loose here, for the front steps were strewn with hay. Inside, not a stitch of clothing remained, only the scattered parts of boot-trees. All the furniture had gone, including vaunted fixtures like the wall-divans. Not quite all. The heavy desk, emblem of the distasteful intellectual effort of the West, had been revengefully stripped and kicked about, and the dining-room table, cracked across the top and legs, lay in a floppy invertebrate condition, only just bearing up in table formation.

There were two bullet holes drilled through the glass to show that the house had been attacked. Eventually, I found, the servants had given in and combined to sack Ras Mulugeta Bet.

They had taken pretty nearly everything except my Saturday morning bath water. In this floated, unassailed and ineffective as the Mediterranean Fleet, my sponge and my loofah.

The *shiftas* had not stopped to read the latest unopened copies of *The Times* which littered the floor of the front salon.

In the garden and the garage they had left behind two brand new tyres for my burnt car, a pick-axe, a bucket and an oil-sump: and Taylor picked up the largest unexploded cartridge that he had ever seen. We labelled it elephant-hunter's pom-pom, wrenched away the Government telephone as a memento, and got back to the Legation late for the marriage ceremony.

They were all there. The bride in utilitarian woollies, (later she ordered a khaki going-away, or rather expulsion two-piece from the Libanese *couturier* at the station). The Padré's lone dog-collar was just pure enough for the occasion. Taylor took his place at the bride's side and first the Consul then the Padré expeditiously settled our future. There was a delicate titter in the congregation when all the worldly goods were endowed. . . . Intervals between prayers and in the signature of rambling documents were punctuated by shots on all sides of the British Legation.

We drank just as much as was good for us but less than the Abyssinians, and drove round the grounds of the Legation in the old pick-up, with Taylor, Roberts, the Padré, Lolita, and Don Lee performing on the hunting-horn used on Plughole days

Then we went back into the town again.

I do not remember much about that afternoon because, as I suppose, I was in a rather fuddled condition. We spent a long time at Mohamedally's, partly because we were stacking up the lorry with food for the refugees and the horses (and Mohamedally's was the only store of food still intact and defended in Addis). And partly because a mild attack was launched on the place when we were inside it.

I remember, vaguely, supporting myself with one hand on the iron bars of Mohamedally's front window and emptying a revolver at a lot of *shiftas* who were taking cover in the smoking market place across the road. My stark courage at this moment astounds me, but I am relieved to think that it was mostly Dutch. After all I had just been married, a white carnation was in my buttonhole, and my sense of responsibility was clouded by the usual liquid consequences of the event.

When I grew tired of standing, I shot from a chair. But, as I say, I do not remember much, and I do not know if I sat shooting at anything in particular.

As we drove back slowly through the crumbled town, where the bodies were now smelling rank indeed, we noticed that the *shiftas* were gathering in large parties on lorries, and that they seemed to be assembling machine-guns in strength. But they did not fire at us as we drove past, marking them.

That evening, they began their attacks on the Legation quarter in an organised band.

The French Legation and the Turks, it is true, had already been attacked, the first on Saturday and the second on Sunday. But the French had been specially singled out by the young Ethiopians for a political vengeance:

the French, in spite of last minute galas to aid the Ethiopian Red Cross, and in spite of the personal amiability of their representative, were detested in Ethiopia.

An ill-armed rabble had gone for the Turks on Sunday evening, when I was in the town. I am sorry that I missed this event. Two Sikh lorries and the Plughole pick-up turned out to save the Turks who were hard pressed . . . Patrick Roberts in his Foreign Office suit, his horn-rimmed spectacles, and his Mauser . . . Taylor, his forked moustaches almost lifting his hat off . . . Don Lee with a handkerchief round his neck. They drove right into the battle, and killed five before the rest fled. To the Diplomatic and associated services may be attributed at least one of the dead.

Again I am sorry that I missed this event. I found that I was enjoying the idea of killing people. It was interesting to note the growth in myself of one of the normal processes of colonial warfare. The smell of bodies, the burning of houses, the breakdown of every social restriction was a part of it. You can't get away from it. Destruction and its physical attributes, putrefaction, arson, pillage, a demeanour of menace are things that attract one when they are really let loose.

On Monday night the *shiftas* brought up machine-guns on lorries and attacked the Belgian Legation. Major Charter sent out young Pearson with a party of Sikhs. After a short battle they cleared the wood with a Vickers gun: they thought that the band was about thirty strong. The noise was terrific, for the Belgian Legation was next to the British.

Patrick Roberts was giving us a cocktail party that evening in his bungalow, which lay at the bottom of the compound near the Dessye road. Lolita and Margarita were already there. The shooting into the compound was increasing. Just as I entered the drawing-room a Vickers gun answered from beneath the window, and the girls slipped in a supple manner which did them credit on to the floor.

After that there was no more shooting from the road, but the attacks on the Belgians continued.

Monday night refugee volunteers manned posts round the Legation. The Turks were especially efficient. With true Kemalist spirit, the Minister, M. Ayashli, submitted himself to the orders of his chauffeur because he was of higher rank in the Turkish Reserve. All through the night they fired at every bush that stirred, every jackal that cocked an ear. They went through thousands of rounds. They rushed out in desperate sally after desperate sally. Giving way only to their national weakness, they drank up all the coffee that Lady Barton had prepared for all the other posts.

Armed missionaries guarded another section of the wire, including little Baird who had come back with us from Dessye. They challenged so ferociously that none of the Armenians dared to draw water throughout the night. "Perhaps they will kill us," they told me.

White flags were hung upon poles outside the Ethiopian houses in front of the British Legation. The Italian Askaris, who had left Dessye only a day before Badoglio's mechanised column, had arrived on Entoto on Sunday morning. They had walked all the way, and were now waiting for the lorries to catch up. The lorries were reported only twenty kilometres outside, near the caves of the Akaki River.

It was a dull day, Tuesday, May 5. We distributed more arms in the town, but everything seemed much quieter. The place was emptying towards the west. Planes flew over.

Outside the German Legation we found a *shifta* car at rest. Taylor, Trapman and myself disarmed two of them with the revolver. One was my old interpreter, Joseph: he carried Burgoyne's old shot-gun with which I had armed my servants on Saturday . . . an age ago. I took a machine-gun rifle off another.

It was about four o'clock, and we went back to the Legation.

All was very quiet. We stood about the Legation gates.

There was a small noise, far away towards Dessye.

It was now a little louder. It could be analysed now, two noises making an emotional whole, the distant roar of engines and grind of tracks, the more penetrating higher Ethiopian acclamation of conquest by these means.

We drew out the drooping folds of the Union Jack that hung above the Legation gate. We waited as the noise grew much louder, and I slung my machine-gun rifle across my shoulder.

The Ethiopians in front, across the road, grinned broadly and raised their hands in the Fascist salute. We folded our arms. The noise, both treble and bass, was overwhelming.

As we looked out into the road disguising our humiliation under an appearance of chilly interest, the army which had brought so much misery to an obscure corner of the world roared past the Legation gates, with geraniums in their caps.

XXI

THEY PASSED IN EXTRAORDINARY BATTLE ORDER.

Believe it or not, but the leader of the conquering column was Angelopoulos, the Greek lawyer, in an old Ford.

After him came Marshal Badoglio (who was going to expel his advance guard in ten days' time) and the associated journalists, pressing on hard behind a screen of tanks. Then the Eritrean Askaris, who had come quicker walking: they looked very stark and trim, and waved their sickle swords. Finally the Italians themselves, tired and dirty, but of good physique. They did not look, and they were not soldierly; but they had great gifts of solidity and endurance.

As they passed the Legation gate and the Union Jack flapping there, some smiled, some waved, a few put their tongues out. One could not grudge them that mild demonstration. It looked a rotten flag.

Sixteen hundred lorries rolled by, packed with troops. All that afternoon and all night the enormous procession thundered by the gates of the British Legation into Addis Ababa. It was the largest mechanised column thrown out in history, but because the world so feebly withstood it there will soon be much bigger ones.

At the Italian Legation, standing on the very spot where Vinci had once over-dramatised resistance, the Marshal Badoglio raised again the flag of Italy and saluted King and Duce.

A nice young Italian journalist said to me: "We think that Geneva's just a collection of old women—we all think so, and we always have thought so."

It is for that reason that I thought, even then, that the

Ethiopians ought to be kicked out of the Assembly as the price of Italy's return to sincere collaboration.

The Italians immediately instituted a death penalty for two crimes: the first was participation in the looting of Addis Ababa, and the second was the possession of arms within three days of their entry. On the first charge they could have executed the whole population of Shoa except the Abuna and Mrs. Martin; on the second they could have shot most of them a second time since it took more than three days for the news to reach its destination. So wide was the vacuum of terror which separated the conqueror from the armed Ethiopian.

Eighty-five Ethiopians, accused of looting, were tried and sent to death by a Summary Court. But the shootings on the spot by the Carabinieri were far greater: and they were done without even the pretence of trial. If things that looked as if they were not his own were found in a tukul, the owner was shot there and then by the search party. French official inquirers calculated that at least fifteen hundred were killed in this way.

Addis was not encouraged to refill, though Italian aeroplanes scattered pamphlets saying that it was now safe to return. The town preserved its gaunt, empty air. The debris was cleared off the streets, but it lay in grey heaps behind the shell-walls of its burnt centre. A black and crumbled fabric, it presented no life as one drove along the Rue Makonnen, and through the market, and to Giorghis: once crowded with people on wet days and on dry.

Everybody had gone to the hills.

There were no cigarettes nor wine for the Italian soldiers.

In these solemn circumstances a victory parade was held, and the Italian Empire of Ethiopia was proclaimed. Poor Tasfai and Kidane Mariam were herded with other Ethiopian exhibits near the saluting base and instructed to perform the Fascist salute every time a detachment passed. The American journalists who had come with the Italians were mightily amused: it was great fun, they said, seeing Tasfai and Kidane nearly splitting their sides with the Fascist salute.

After that Kidane was flown away in an aeroplane and

not seen again. He had organised the Young Ethiopian Movement. His friends say that he was dropped out of the aeroplane, but I cannot believe that of the Italian people, who as Lord Rennell said in the famous slow motion gas debate in the House of Lords, "are naturally humane and kindly, and it is inconceivable that..."

The Italians now sat down to write invitations to all the Humanitarian Societies which represented Great Britain in Addis Ababa, cordially proposing that they should leave. There was the British Red Cross, which represented British sympathy with Ethiopian wounded, and there were the R.S.P.C.A. and Animal Welfare Society, who respectively do and do not believe in vivisection. The Wild-Flower Protection Society and the Anti-Litter League had not yet sent out Units of poets and art-critics to clean up the battlefields. They were still disputing the right of precedence with the British Association for the performance of the Covenant, which had forgotten to broadcast an appeal for funds or to inform itself on the local situation in Ethiopia.

At this moment, indeed, it was revising its charter and its sub-title. It found suddenly that it was not the Royal Society for the Punishment, but for the Prevention of Cruelty to Abyssinians.

I attended my last meet of the Plughole.

The Plughole was a society which centred round the British Legation for the purpose of hunting the Acting Vice-Consul, Trapman.

This young man dressed up in a pink shirt twice a week and rode away into the unknown on a fast pony, scattering paper. After a few minutes he was followed by Don Lee, who was huntsman with a horn, Patrick Roberts and Firkin Taylor of the British and Waldheim of the German Legation, rough-riders of the various animal succour societies, Davidson of commerce, one or two of Buxton's mission, and me. We simulated hounds.

Trapman was a clever fox and the eucalyptus groves mixed with plain or mud walls round Addis made ideal country. After the hunt was over we drank specially imported beer and played a series of popular records. The

Plughole was called the Plughole because it sang a song referring to one. . . .

"My baby has gone down the plughole
It won't need a barf any more. . . ."

After the meet I sold Flick and the other horses. We had a very good run that day. It was the end of my happy life in Addis.

On May 13, a Wednesday, two officers of Carabinieri and a dirty Greek were seen hanging round the Legation gates in a fishy manner. I had been staying at the Legation since the sack of the town. Trapman, good fox, asked them what they wanted and they admitted that they wanted to see me. But they said they were unwilling to enter the gates of the Legation to do so. This coyness struck us as unnatural, and finally they were induced to explain that they wished to drive me to a certain destination for examination. After they had been left a long time in the sun, they were told that they could not do so.

Next morning I received an expulsion order from the office of the new Viceroy. I had to take the Djibouti train on Saturday, "with my family."

No grounds were given, but from the others who were expelled with me I gathered that I was listed as Public Enemy No One, and esteemed to be chief of the British intelligence service in Ethiopia, arms salesman (dum-dum?), dynamiter of roads and conveyer of gas-masks. I and my family had no difficulty in leaving Addis Ababa on Saturday. What the Ethiopians had left of our possessions packed without surplus or discomfort into a small sack and a benzine box, labelled England.

Later the Italians also took their rake-off. They handed me a permit to export silver in Addis Ababa and revoked it in Diredawa. . . . But they did not shoot themselves. . . .

Last moments in Addis were spent sitting upon the steps of the railway coach with a typewriter upon my knees, tapping out recommendations for the servants Bayenna and Igezu who had been faithful in the riots, and a statement that Bayenna could keep my remaining horse, saddle and servant's tent. Without it he would be arrested and probably shot for looting: simply the possession of things which an Ethiopian should not, under white rule, be wealthy enough to have would be sufficient evidence for that.

Bayenna and Igezu, who had been so steady and true, put out their right hands to say good-bye. "We are going back to our own countries," said Igezu, who lived in the Cold Field near Debra Brehan, "God will provide for us, He knows what is best for us." They had lost all their savings because they had been faithful. They held my hand and kissed it. I could have cried. The wife of the French Minister stepped neatly off the train, where she left Monsieur and Madame Robillard, expelled after twenty-five years' work in Ethiopia. Old Robillard looked out of the carriage window at the station clock, at the customs sheds, the little toy engines of the Franco-Ethiopian railway, the cadaverous Arab porters in dirty scarlet turbans, all the cheap familiar sights which he was forbidden to see again. Twenty-five years! An old, ill man, he was past tears; there he sat, crumpled and helpless in the corner of the carriage.

Margarita kept Madame Robillard in conversation, talking easily about other things as her good nature knew best to do. Madame Robillard needed help of that kind: she was determined not to express emotion, and sat erect in her black prim dress, her neck sustained by the white emphatic bone and network that correct elderly women in France like to wear. But her face looked thinner than usual and her eyes were red with recent reflection upon the past, when she had helped her husband to run the *Courrier d'Ethiopie*, watched the tennis at the French Legation, and left Addis station so often, just like now, to spend the weekend at Bishoftu near the placid crater-lake where the egrets gather in white sleet from the African plain. Adieu! Germaine, her daughter, would have seven days' grace to stay in Addis and either export the printing press or sell it at a loss to the Italians. Moskopoulos, the Emperor's chief of counter-espionage, smiled wearily to other Greek friends whom he had to leave, carefully settled his portable gramophone upon his knees and the train jerked off.

Margarita and I laughed as loud as our distinct characters permit. Good-bye to Addis, no regrets: great fun being expelled. The other journalists on the platform, who had come with the Italians from Asmara, laughed as well: great fun seeing the Robillards go. Lady Barton, Patrick Roberts, Taylor and Lee, Bayenna and Igezu, all became distant objects, and I was sadder when I thought that now there were less English in Addis. They too looked a little gloomy as their faces grew smaller, but Don waved the brown silk handkerchief which always dangled from his breast-pocket and the Military Attaché passed generous interim judgment on the new Imperial Guard. So the Plughole hunts were over, the horses were gone, Bayenna and Igezu were left behind, Ethiopia and my work were finished. I came young, I went away older. I promised myself that I could never forget and never forgive.

We creaked along the rusty metals past the Akaki radio station, gutted and fused by the Ethiopians before the Italians entered Addis. We passed the old Hotel du Lac at Bishoftu, where the whole main building, in which we had eaten and talked and Lolita had played the piano on rare holidays, was burnt to the ground. But the Ethiopians themselves were unchanged. They still sold sugar-cane to the hungry third-class traveller at the station. An Italian bought some and liked it. Rambling, I thought of the agricultural adviser, Colson's friend, who Colson had told me way back in January wanted to come to Ethiopia but had been advised by Colson not to do it at this present time. . . . Could he have bettered that sugar-cane? And how prophetic Colson had been as he looked from the concrete veranda into the setting sun. Yet at that moment the Ethiopians were enjoying their greatest success.

All around the Shoan country-side moved to its annual rhythm. Nothing was changed. Only less men worked the fields: many wore black-bordered shammas. But the crops were ready, and the short knives were there, and the oxen towed crude little ploughs over fallow. The plateau which dissolves only a particle away every year into the Nile and the Hawash seemed untouched by, uninformed of, magnificent new feats of arms.

I promised that my mind would be as changeless as its body.

Moskopoulos put on a comic record.

At Djibouti I met all the refugees.

I said good-bye to my friend Lij Andarge Masai. He

seemed doubtful of the future, but I reassured him. "After all," I said, "we may have been slow, but we English do keep our word. We have solemnly signed a Covenant which guarantees, *guarantees* to you your independence and territorial integrity. We have said many times that we stand by our signature, and that we will uphold the Covenant in its entirety."

Lij Andarge really believed what I said.

INDEX

This Index is in two parts. In Part One are given the names of those statesmen, leaders and advisers most closely concerned with the conduct of the War; in Part Two is given a *dossier* of the significant events of the War. Since the Emperor Haile Selassie and Signor Mussolini are mentioned so frequently throughout the book, I feel it unnecessary to include their names in Part One of the Index and as there are so many different spellings for Amharic words in English I apologise for any errors I may have made.

G. L. S.

INDEX—PART ONE

Abyssinia, Crown Prince of, 165, 218, 247, 287, 293, 368.
Afewerk, Gerazmatch, 17, 46, 60, 88, 104, 169, 184, 199, 339.
Ato Ali Nur, Balambaras (afterwards Kenyazmatch), 19, 57, 82, 85, 94, 172, 184, 187.
Ayelu, Dedjazmatch, 60, 141, 147, 226, 272.
Babitcheff, Mischa, 184, 367.
Badoglio, Marshal, 173, 197, 200, 231, 259, 399, 401.
Barton, Sir Sidney, 25, 64, 72, 207, 279, 357.
Bergamo, Duke of, 275.
Bidwoded Makonnen, 46, 159, 262, 379.
Blattangeta Herrouy, 208, 364.
Bodard, M., 207.
de Bono, General, 151, 200, 224, 232.
Ciano, Count, 138, 148, 223.
Colson, Everett, 13, 27, 33, 39, 72, 132, 139, 153, 207, 209, 251, 276, 282, 406.
Desta, Ras, 61, 64, 120, 196, 235, 255, 340.
Eden, Anthony, 20, 38.
Farouk Bey, 189, 339.
Gabre Mariam, Dedjazmatch, 15, 103, 247.
Getatchu, Ras, 63, 302, 356, 364, 368.
Graziani, General, 120, 159, 173, 177, 192, 196, 235, 340.
Haile Selassie Gucsa, Dedjazmatch, 62, 65, 123, 141, 144, 166, 197, 225, 250.

Harrar, Duke of, 82, 201.
Hoare, Sir Samuel, 135, 144, 207, 215, 284, 365.
Imru, Ras, 53, 60, 148, 226, 232, 248, 271, 369.
Kassa, Ras, 53, 130, 142, 151, 166, 202, 222, 229, 248, 253, 258, 299, 356, 363, 369.
Konovaloff, Colonel, 144, 151, 249, 270, 284, 298, 339, 361.
Laval, Pierre, 76, 144, 207, 284, 365.
Maletti, Colonel, 174.
Malion, Kenyazmatch, 60, 97, 193, 339, 345.
Mulugeta, Ras, 28, 44, 53, 55, 60, 123, 129, 143, 153, 159, 200, 218, 221, 233, 247, 258, 265, 290.
Mussolini, Vittorio, 279, 388.
Nasibu, Dedjazmatch, 55, 64, 100, 102, 185.
Olol Dinle, Sultan, 16, 235, 244, 340.
Seyyum, Ras, 53, 62, 130, 138, 141, 144, 197, 222, 229, 248, 255, 267, 299.
Shefara, Fitorari, 15, 91, 347.
Taezaz, Lorenzo, 73, 134, 356, 373.
Tarik Bey, 190, 339.
Vinci, Count, 47, 119, 131, 144, 153.
Wehib Pasha, 189, 339.
Wodaju, Dedjazmatch, 144, 261, 293, 323.

409

INDEX—PART TWO

After events mentioned in Introduction

Mustard Gas, use of, 8.
Danakil Expedition, 8.
Gondar Column, 8.
Harrar, Bombardment of, 8.
Addis Ababa (April 27th, 1936),8.
Addis Ababa, Sack of, 9.

Events in Chronological Order.

Ogaden, Clearing of, 15.
Italian Policy (1931), 15.
Walwal Incident, 19.
Italian Demand for Indemnity, 19.
Italo-Ethiopian Treaty of 1928, 19.
Stresa Conference, 20.
Zeyla Offer, 20.
Treaty of 1906, 38, 44.
Territorial Concessions, 39, 123.
Emperor's Attack on Italian Policy, 45.
Arms Embargo, 52, 154.
Emperor, Strategic Plan of, 63.
Rickett Concession, 72, 124.
Description of Ogaden, August, 1935, 75–119.
Munitions Loan, 126.
Emperor Signs General Mobilisation Order, 130.
Italian Entry into Ethiopian Territory, 130.
Adowa Bombardment, 135.
Abyssinia Declares War, 136.
Initial Movements of Ethiopian Armies, 141.
Fall of Makalle to Ethiopia, 143.
de Bono enters Adowa, 147.
Emperor Decides not to Defend Makalle, 149.
Difficulties of Italian Advance, 151
Gondar Levy, 151.
Army of the Centre (Ras Mulugeta's YAMAHAL SARAWIT), moves North, 153, 159, 161.
Departure of Italian Minister, Count Vinci, 155.
Emperor Reviews his Troops, 161.
Mobilisation of Wollo, 165.
Amba Alagi, Italian Bombing of, 166.
Army of Ras Kassa, 166.
Southern War in Ogaden, 169.
Italian taking of Tafere Katama, Shellabo and Gerlogubi, 171.
Bombing of Gorahai, Gerazmatch Afewerk wounded, 171, 172.
Ethiopian Capture of Motorised Column, 175.
End of Graziani's Offensive in Ogaden, 177.
The Emperor Goes to Jijiga, 184.
Ogaden Headquarters General Staff, 188.
The Emperor Goes to Dessye, 197.
Marshal Badoglio appointed Commander-in-Chief, 197.
Bombardment of Dessye and Gondar, 202.
Hoare-Laval Proposals, 207.
Emperor's Refusal of Hoare-Laval Proposals, 214, 215.
Ethiopian Strategy in the Tembien, 223.
Mulugeta Occupies Amba Aradam, 225.
Ayelu and Imru take Enda Selasi and Selaclaca, 227.
Hailu Kabada takes Abbi Adda, 229.
First Use of Poison Gas at Adi Quala, 233.
Strategy of Ras Desta, 235.
Italian Attack on Lama Shillindi, 238.
Italy Brings White Troops to Dolo, 241.
Bombing of Malka Didaka, 241.
Mutilation of Italian Airman, Minniti Tito, 243.
Italian taking of Semlei: Flight of Desta's Army, 245.
Taking of Negelli, 246.
Emperor Declares Total Mobilisation, 247.
Strategy of Marshal Badoglio in Makalle, 247.

INDEX—PART TWO

Only Night Raid by Ethiopians, 250.
Ethiopian Charge at Warieu, 253.
Second Battle of the Tembien, 254.
Bombing of Dessye and Korem, 257
Battle of Amba Aradam, 259.
Death of Ras Mulugeta, 265.
Third Battle of the Tembien, 267.
Battle of Shire, 272.
The Emperor at Korem, 278.
Use of Poison Gas, 279.
Committee of Thirteen Proposals, 280.
Journey to Headquarters with first Gas Masks, 286.
Evacuation of Dessye, 295.
Battle of Mai Chow (told by Colonel Konovaloff), 298–326.
Emperor's Retreat (told by Colonel Konovaloff), 326–338.
Description of Ogaden Warfare, 339–355.
The Emperor's Return to Addis Ababa, 356.
The Emperor Requests Increased Sanctions, 357.
General Retreat, 359.
Argument as to the Emperor's Destination, 362.
Troops' Refusal to Fight, 367.
The Emperor's Decision to Leave Abyssinia, 369.
The Emperor Leaves for Djibouti and Embarks in *Enterprise*, 371.
Sack of Addis Ababa, 371–399.
Entry of Marshal Badoglio into Addis Ababa, 400.
Italian Empire of Ethiopia Proclaimed, 402.
Author is Expelled from Abyssinia, 404.

Printed in Great Britain
by Amazon.co.uk, Ltd.,
Marston Gate.